A
History
of the
Christian
Movement

A History of the Christian Movement

The Development of Christian Institutions

A. Daniel Frankforter

Nelson-Hall
Chicago

Library of Congress Cataloging in Publication Data

Frankforter, A. Daniel
    A history of the christian movement

    Bibliography: p. 277
    Includes index.
    1. Church history. I. Title.
BR145.2.F69   270   77-8071
ISBN 0-88229-292-7 (cloth)
ISBN 0-88229-568-3 (paper)

Manufactured in the United States of America

Contents

Chapter Six: A New Environment

Preface

THE STUDY OF THE history of the Christian movement is an intimidating project. The movement's extent and complexity and the controversies that surround almost every aspect of its interpretation present students with innumerable difficulties. Those who seek a knowledge of the subject may be intimidated by the scope of the task to which they find themselves committed. Overwhelming numbers of monographs narrate the course of events, describe the careers of persons, or explain the development of doctrines that have contributed to the formation of a Christian tradition. There are encyclopedic works that attempt to survey everything, but whose size and detail obscure perception of the patterns of Christian history. There are specialized studies that assume a prior knowledge of the larger context in which their subject must be placed for its significance truly to be understood. It is difficult to find a place to begin.

This book attempts to say a little bit about a great deal in order to ease the problem of making a beginning. The work is a gesture offered for the assistance of those who seek a perspective on the vast subject of the history of Christianity. It attempts to identify key events and to indicate patterns within the course of the evolution of the Christian movement.

Even these modest goals may, however, lead the text to trespass rudely on the sensitivities of scholarly specialists and devoted believers. Faith is a subject that touches on deep personal commitments, and it is therefore difficult to discuss religion without inadvertently proselytizing for or against it. But the interpretations and judgments offered here have no such conscious intention. The function of the book is not to persuade its reader to adopt specific points of view, but to help him approach the complex task of understanding the Christian phenomenon.

Chapter One

---❖---

A New Covenant

THE CONTEXT OF THE REVELATION

THE REVELATION THAT WAS the message and person of Jesus of Nazareth was not, as early Greek and Hebrew Christians were eager to point out, an event entirely without context or preparation. To many it was certainly a surprise bordering on scandal that the long-awaited Savior of mankind should appear in the person of a carpenter from an obscure village in Galilee, but their shock was one more of taste than of substance. The mode of Jesus' appearance startled human expectation, but the possibility of his arrival was an idea for which his contemporaries had been prepared by generations of messianic speculation. The general terms in which he would be understood, the concepts by which he would be interpreted, had by the time of his appearance already been refined to a remarkable degree by prophets, rabbis, Hellenistic mystery cultists, and Greco-Roman philosophers. Jesus dealt with a world that had anticipated him. Frequently he sought to correct erroneous expectations, but he placed himself firmly and ultimately within the prophetic-rabbinic tradition of the ancient Jews.

Jesus' followers in later generations carried news of him to the gentile cultures and translated him into categories of meaning quite different from those he himself had suggested. But no matter how much the message developed and grew as a living word of his Spirit, orthodox Christians remained firm in their belief that a knowledge of the "old" covenant of the Jewish Scriptures was indispensable for a true understanding of the "new" covenant between God and man that they had experienced in Jesus as the Christ. Jesus was for them the fulfillment of an ancient expectation, not a completely new and original event.

Jesus of Nazareth was, despite the weight of religious meaning he came to bear, a real human being fixed in a period of time, not a symbol created in the eternal dimension of mythology. He was an event in history and a part of the Hebraic religious tradition which taught that God revealed himself primarily in human history, not in the repetitive, vacuous cycles of nature. The Jews held that God was not imprisoned in and revealed by the laws of nature, for he was the absolutely free Creator who had willed the universe into being out of nothingness. No preexistent matter had imposed its limitations on his creative work—as was the theory in the creation myths of many of the Eastern Gentiles. Nor had he built the cosmos out of his own substance—as Hellenic pantheists had suggested. God was not contained in his own creation, and he was, consequently, not subject to the laws he had established for nature and the mind of man. The natural order was something God had made, but it was not itself God. Therefore, no inference from man's knowledge of natural events could give him insight into the nature of God. The gulf between God's absolute reality and man's contingent one could not be crossed from the human side. God could be known only when God chose to reveal himself, and Hebraic tradition asserted that such revelation came in the dimension of human experience in which man became aware of his own power and freedom; in the study, not of the determining patterns of nature, but of the unique and unpredictable events of human history.

The Jews derived their knowledge of God, not from philosophical inference or poetic imagination, but from the prophetic interpretation of key events in their own history. They perceived themselves as a people called into being to reveal the will of God through their destiny as a nation. Before God gave them his name and his law at Sinai and invited them to stand in a special relationship with him, they had been a formless group of Hebrews (from *hapiru* or "foreigners") demoralized by generations of Egyptian slavery. Related to the Assyrians, Babylonians, Phoenicians, Arabs and other Semitic peoples of the Caucasian race, they had no distinguishing characteristics of their own until God gave them the power to win the land of Judea. In Judea, the Spirit of God working through judges, kings, and prophets welded the people into a nation whose sense of religious identity grew strong enough to survive the temporary loss of its land to the Babylonians (597–538 B.C.) and subsequent domination by the empires and alien cultures of the Persians (538–331 B.C.), the Greeks (331–63 B.C.) and the Romans (63 B.C.–A.D. 70). Even the final destruction of Jerusalem and the temple—the foci of international Jewry and the only places where the Jewish sacrificial cult could be celebrated—did not eradicate the Jews' conviction that they were still a people whose identity would endure and whose destiny would continue to reveal the will of God.

Because the followers of Jesus of Nazareth belonged to a tradition that looked for signs of the hand of God in historical phenomena, it was not at all absurd that they should have claimed to see in him, for all his limitations of time and place, a figure of ultimate and universal significance. The Jews had long believed that the infinite could be glimpsed only through the finite. They held that God revealed himself not vaguely and universally, but by becoming intensely real for particular persons at particular times and places. Jesus of Nazareth was revelatory of God for his disciples, not in spite of his historical particularity, but in part precisely because he was this man Jesus: a carpenter from Nazareth, a citizen of Galilee, a subject of the Roman Empire, and a Jew. His message was not a system of timeless philosophical concepts but took the form of address to particular local circumstances or of parables based on experiences and images common to his day. Since man's knowledge is derived from experience of events that happen in the mundane dimensions of time and space, the first Christians held that God accepted the limitations of men and made himself available to human knowledge by linking himself with the destiny of the Jews and by becoming in Jesus one of the events of human experience. Therefore, no real understanding of Jesus divorces him from his historical context or separates him from all the peculiar, transitory events that occupied him but seem alien or irrelevant to modern concerns. To remove Jesus from historical perspective is to reduce his humanity, to transmute him into a spokesman for one ideology or another, and to start him on the road toward becoming a creature of mythology.

The area where Jesus lived out the short span of his life was a small but turbulent backwater of the primary civilization of his day. His birth and career went unnoticed by contemporary historians, whose attention focused mainly on the exciting events that marked the emergence of the Roman world state. Palestine in Jesus' day, hardly larger than today's state of Vermont, lay on the vague eastern perimeter of the Roman Empire, far from the center of world affairs. Rome paid little attention to Palestine and, so long as the province remained quiet, preferred to leave it in the hands of cooperative native rulers. Jesus was probably born toward the end of the reign of the most famous of Rome's Palestinian client kings, Herod the Great (40–4 B.C.), and spent most of his life as a subject of Herod's son, Herod Antipas, tetrarch of Galilee. Another of Herod's heirs, Archelaus, ruled Judea and Jerusalem until A.D. 6, when the Romans deposed him for incompetence at the urging of the Jews themselves and made his territory part of the administrative responsibility of the Roman governor of the province of Syria. Jesus, most of whose time was spent in Galilee, remained distant from the notice of Rome and from the attention of the Jewish leaders in Jerusalem; for Galilee, an area north of Judea with a mixture of races and cultures, was separated from Jerusalem by the land of the Samaritans. The Samaritans were regarded by the Jews of Jerusalem and Galilee as mongrel remnants of the ancient Israelites and the gentile populations imported by their Assyrian conquerors in 721 B.C. The kingdom of Judea fell in its turn to Babylonian armies. But when the exiled Jews of the south were allowed to return to Judea in 538 B.C., they rejected the assistance of the Samaritans in rebuilding Jerusalem and its temple, and the two people split into mutually hostile camps. The Samaritans adopted their own form of the Hebrew Scriptures, focused their worship on an ancient shrine near Schechem, and formed an alien barrier between Jesus' Galilee and the center of Jewish culture in Jerusalem.

Small as the arena of Jewish affairs was, it was large enough to accommodate the struggles of numerous factions, and for most of his life Jesus had to deal with those who would identify him with the friends or enemies of one party or another. The official leadership of the Jewish cult was the inherited prerogative of the priestly families that claimed descent from Moses' brother Aaron. These families alone could care for the temple, offer the sacrifices decreed in the Scriptures, and perform other sacred rites. The ancient Jewish historian Josephus (*Against Apion* 2. 108) claims the priestly families had about twenty thousand members organized in twenty-four divisions. Each division served the temple for a week at a time on a rotating schedule. They were assisted in the temple by another hereditary class, the Levites, who served as guards, musicians, and caretakers. There were also men known as scribes, who had the privilege of copying and repairing the rolls of sacred writings, and who, because of their training and intellectual interests, became authorities in the teaching and interpretation of the law.

The definition of classes by birth or function tended to encourage the growth of religious-political parties that competed for influence in the Jewish state. The priests and Levites who governed the temple formed the party of the Sadducees, which the Romans considered the legitimate power with which to deal in Jerusalem. The Romans, who rarely cared to assume responsibility for the administration of the purely local institutions of their subject peoples, granted the Sanhedrin, a Sadducee-dominated council, jurisdiction over the religious life and law of the Jews—a power that may have extended even to the right to inflict capital punishment for crimes of blasphemy. As a Jew suspected of inciting public disturbances, Jesus was brought to the attention of the Roman state by this council which worked with Rome for the maintenance of local law and order. The Sadducees tended to be men who benefited from the status quo and who were thus the true conservatives of their day. They were wealthy, well educated along traditional lines, disposed to cooperate fully with the Romans in political affairs, and committed to a form of priestly Judaism that identified the requirements of their religion with the sacrificial rites and ritual obligations of the temple.

The scribes and the less aristocratic Jewish intellectuals gravitated toward the party of the Pharisees. The Pharisaic faction had roots that stretched as far back as the period of the Maccabean revolt (168 B.C.), a partially successful attempt on the part of the Jews to resist accommodation to the gentile culture of the Hellenistic empire of the Seleucids. However, the Pharisees probably did not emerge as an independent party until about 105 B.C., when they set themselves against the increasing tendency of the Sadducees to sacrifice aspects of Jewish custom for political convenience. The Pharisaic position was defined by a firm conviction that all aspects of life should be governed by the Mosaic law, but the Pharisees were, for all their veneration of the authority of the past, not true conservatives. In attempting to force an ancient system of law to apply to every situation in the life of a latter age, the Pharisees were compelled to develop elaborate interpretations of that law. Such interpretations often led, in effect, to the introduction of new ideas into Jewish tradition. The Sadducees regarded the Pharisees as innovators, for the Pharisees accepted as authoritative Scripture not only the Torah or the Pentateuch (the first five books of the Old Testament, attributed to Moses) but also the records of the prophets and a collection of various works known as the Writings (Psalms, Proverbs, Job, etc.). The Pharisees encouraged the development of such new religious festivals as Hanukkah and Purim and came to accept as orthodox Judaism many of the religious commonplaces of the ancient gentile world. They spoke of angels and demons and the resurrection of men. They indulged in the apocalyptic speculations that were popular in some of the pagan religions of their day, and they made great contributions to the emergence of the Jewish concept of a messianic deliverer. Their work was a sincere attempt to hold on to the living essence of ancient Judaism, but Pharisaic thinking was open to its own peculiar kind of temptation. In striving to govern every aspect of life by the law, the Pharisee could become obsessed with legalistic concerns and a subtlety of interpretation that exceeded the comprehension of his less intelligent or well educated fellows. Pharisees did occasionally express contempt for Jews who were unable to adopt the full burden of the law and sometimes cut themselves off from contact with those whom they held to be ritually impure because of incomplete compliance with the law. It was for this neglect of the charitable spirit of the law in the passionate pursuit of its letter, for this exaltation of technical piety over the needs of persons, that Jesus branded the Pharisees hypocrites (Matthew 23:13). But Jesus himself in his attempt to present Judaism as a relevant, living religion perhaps stood closer to the Pharisees than to any other party of his day, and the abuses of the Pharisaic spirit have remained a perpetual temptation to his church.

The Sadducees and Pharisees were the most prominent leaders of Judaism in Jesus' day, but there were other smaller and more extreme groups that had some effect on the environment in which he worked. Most dangerous to Jesus was the attempt to identify him with the party of the Zealots, who were calling for Jewish national independence and the violent overthrow of the Roman government. The Old Testament is witness to a long tradition of Jewish military actions, and there was always a Judean nationalistic spirit which needed only the right opportunity to generate a party of revolutionaries. The Hellenistic rulers of Syria had had great difficulty in attempting to integrate Jerusalem into their empire, and their Roman successors found things no easier. There were Palestinian guerrilla bands opposing Rome as early as A.D. 6, when Rome first took over the administration of Judea, and, within a generation of Jesus' death, popular support for the radicals was strong enough to precipitate a major rebellion that ultimately cost the Jews their land, their temple, and their political identity. The method by which Jesus was executed suggests that the Romans linked him with the Zealot party, but, if the teachings of Jesus reported in the Gospels are accurate, it is hard to imagine that he could have been a Zealot. Some of his followers were known as Zealots (Luke 6:15), and it is easy to see that, since the Zealots were the Jewish party that occasioned Rome most concern in Judea, the quickest way for Jesus' enemies to dispose of him would have been to accuse him of Zealotism.

Ever since the discovery in 1947 of the Dead Sea Scrolls, there have been renewed speculations that Jesus might have been linked with yet another ancient Palestinian party, the Essenes. The Essenes took a position, perhaps Pharisaic in its origin, that was almost diametrically opposed to the program of the Zealots. Instead of working for the violent overthrow of evil rulers and the establishment of a religiously perfect and politically independent Jewish nation, the Essenes withdrew from the distractions of society. They established themselves in quasi-monastic communities in the desert and led ascetic lives devoted to ritual purification and the study of the law. Their customs bore circumstantial resemblances to certain practices of the early Christian church: they endorsed communal property, employed baptism, celebrated a sacramental meal as the center of their worship, and nourished apocalyptic expectations. But there is no direct evidence that Jesus himself was ever a part of the Essene movement, and the public nature of his ministry and the lack of asceticism in his style of life and in his teaching suggest that the Essenes had little influence on him.

THE RECORD OF THE REVELATION

THE IMPACT OF JESUS of Nazareth on the course of Western history is all the more astounding when one realizes that he never committed any of his thoughts to writing and that no written account of him has survived directly from the hand of an eyewitness. No official governmental reports mention him, although the second century church father Justin Martyr (1 *Apology* 48) does allude to the possible existence at one time of records sent to Rome by Pontius Pilate concerning Jesus' trial. Not one of the historians of Jesus' generation discusses him. Josephus, writing about A.D. 90 (*Antiquities* 20. 9. 1), mentions Jesus in passing while reporting a postcrucifixion event involving his brother James in Jerusalem. The Talmud, an ancient collection of rabbinic commentaries on the Jewish law, accuses Jesus of illegitimate birth, idolatry, and the practice of magic, but the work presents no evidence in support of its invective. It is not until the second century that references to him and the Christian movement begin to appear in Roman documents. These references occasionally shed some light on the history of the early church, but they provide little information about Jesus himself. The Roman author Pliny the Younger, in a letter of ca. A.D. 111 to the Emperor Trajan, *(Letters* 10.96) described the worship of Christians and noted that they prayed to a certain Christ as if he were a god. At about the same time, the Roman historian Tacitus completed his account of the great fire that devastated districts of Rome during Nero's reign (*Annals* 15. 44). Tacitus explained that the Christians, on whom the emperor falsely placed the blame for the holocaust, took their name from a Christ who was executed by Pontius Pilate during the reign of the Emperor Tiberius. Also from the second century comes a confused report by the sensationalist Suetonius ("Claudius," 25) that the Emperor Claudius, Nero's predecessor, expelled the Jews from Rome because a man named "Chrestus" (*sic*) inspired them to disorderly conduct.

Apart from these brief references, everything the world knows about the career of Jesus of Nazareth comes from the Christian Scriptures, which seem to provide a great deal of relevant information, but which are notoriously difficult to interpret. Anyone who wishes to explore the history of Jesus must rely in particular on those portions of the New Testament known as the Gospels, or the "good news," of Matthew, Mark, Luke, and John; but the reader must be mindful of the fact that not a single one of the authors of these works considered himself to be writing a source for the objective study of history. By the time these accounts of the life of Jesus of Nazareth came to be written, the memory of Jesus' activities had been deeply affected by the conviction of the church that he was the Christ—the Messiah, who was a relatively well-defined figure in Jewish religious thought. The form the Gospels finally took was influenced by the difficulty the church had in explaining its faith in Jesus' messiahship. The identification of Jesus with the Messiah was neither immediate nor obvious to those who stood outside the faith. Jesus had not done the kinds of things most Jews expected the Messiah to do. Jesus had not been a king or an angel; he had not liberated Palestine from the Romans and had not built a Jewish empire; he had announced the coming of a new age, but the ordinary world of men went on after his death much as it always had. To counter such objections, the preaching of the early church related facts about Jesus that supported the proclamation of his messiahship. The preaching revealed the unique interpretation his life had given to the concept of the Messiah and proved that, indeed, the power of the new age of the kingdom of God had already begun to dawn through him in history. By the time the Gospel writers sat down to pull together their information, most of the material available to them had been filtered through Christian preaching. The only Jesus perceptible to them was the Christ who was, partially at least, a creation of the faith of the church. Many scholars believe the Gospels were composed by combining *pericopes*—stories of various lengths each designed to preserve one of Jesus' teachings or to describe one of his significant deeds. *Pericopes* would have grown up at random in the preaching and oral tradition of the church and would have circulated freely and independently. As a result, no one could always say for sure in just which order or in what context the events described had occurred in Jesus' life. The church's memory of Jesus was thus broken into numerous fragments which were combined and recombined according to the use Christian leaders wished to make of them.

If indeed this was the case, it would have occasioned little concern to the Gospel writers, for their interest was not objective history, but evangelism. John plainly states that his account of Jesus' life was designed not merely to provide information about him, but so "that you may believe that Jesus is the Christ, the Son of God, and that believing you may have life in his name" (JOHN 20:31). Since theological interests were uppermost, the Gospel writers freely organized their material according to need: they grouped *pericopes,* not in the order in which the events may have occurred, but according to the material's utility for illustrating certain theological themes. The Gospel of Mark, for instance, seems to be structured so as to explain the perplexing fact that Jesus had not been widely recognized as the Messiah before the event of faith in his resurrection. It seemed incredible that the Messiah should have come and gone and been perceived by so few. Mark suggests, therefore, that according to God's plan Jesus' entire life was a slow crescendo of revelation of his "secret" messianic identity. Jesus himself had a private confirmation of his messianic role at the time of his baptism (MARK 1:11); he was recognized as the Messiah by the demons he cast out of the possessed (MARK 1:24); his messianic vocation was revealed to Peter at Caesarea Philippi (MARK 8:29); it was hinted at by his triumphal entry into Jerusalem; and it was finally and unequivocably proclaimed before the high priest during Jesus' trial (MARK 14:62). The other Gospel writers, who adopt different organizational schemes, disagree with Mark on significant portions of his account of a "messianic secret." In John's Gospel, the revelation of Jesus' messianic destiny at the beginning of his public ministry was made not just to him, but to John the Baptist as well (JOHN 1:32–34). Matthew (3:17) agrees with the Gospel of John in this. In Mark (8:27–33), Peter's recognition of Jesus as the Messiah ends with a rebuke, but in Matthew (16:18) it earns Peter a significant promise as well. In Matthew (26:64) and Luke (22:67), Mark's assertion (14:62) that Jesus frankly admitted his messiahship to the high priest,

Caiaphas, becomes a noncommittal "you have said so" or "if I tell you, you will not believe." John reports no specific conversation on this topic between Jesus and Caiaphas (JOHN 18:12–28).

It is often the case that the attempt simply to accept what the Gospel writers say as objective history results in setting them futilely against one another and exposes a reader to the risk of distorting their message and misrepresenting the reality of Jesus. The Gospels were written as accounts of the life of Jesus by men who believed him to be the Christ. The accounts were intended for use in a church whose mission was to bring all people to see in Jesus the messianic Savior. Apart from the perspective of faith, the unadorned facts of the life of a man from Nazareth were not saving knowledge and were of little consequence. Thus, although the Gospels have frequently and uncritically been approached as biographies of Jesus, this was not the use for which they were intended. The focus of the Gospels is on the saving work of Jesus—his crucifixion and his resurrection—and on the words and deeds that put these events in messianic perspective. The first thirty years of Jesus' life, which contained no messianic activities, interested the Gospel writers very little; the itinerary of his travels was not crucial to their purposes; and the exact identification of persons, places, and dates was often unnecessary. The goal of the Gospels was not to present a bald account of the man Jesus, but to demonstrate how this man, through his death and resurrection, was the Messiah. In short, the Gospels' objective was not history, but theology.

Scholars have long debated different theories concerning the literary composition of the New Testament and the sources of the information found in it, but there is widespread support for the opinion that few if any of its accounts of the life of Jesus are the direct report of eyewitnesses describing events they themselves experienced. The Gospels and other elements of the New Testament were not consciously composed at one time to fit together as a unit. The Christian Scriptures were assembled by the church from many different kinds of material from many different sources. A document of the second century, the *Canon of Muratori*, indicates that by that time the four Gospels, the Acts of the Apostles, and thirteen of the Pauline Epistles were accepted as being of special authority in the Christian community, but it was not until the fourth century that the church finally agreed to limit the New Testament to the twenty-seven items that now compose the Christian Scriptures. The oldest documents in the New Testament are the letters of Paul (ca. 50–62), but they are not very helpful as sources of historical information about Jesus of Nazareth. Paul himself, who joined the Christians well after the crucifixion, never had an oppor-

tunity to meet Jesus and claims not to have been instructed in the faith
by any of the apostles who had been with Jesus (GALATIONS 1:11–20).
Paul's letters were written primarily to offer advice on the organizational problems of the infant church and to develop a theological explication of his faith in Jesus as the Messiah, not to provide an account
of Jesus' human career.

Paul never refers to the Gospels, and many commentators believe
these books were not compiled until after his death. It is not yet possible to date their composition exactly or to identify their authors with
certainty. It was a common and respected practice in the ancient
world to attribute one's own works to another person in order to give
the writings added authority or color. The names the evangelists used
may, therefore, not have been their own; but even if they were, the
names were not unusual for their day and the Gospels provide little or
no biographical data about their authors. By the second century, the
church fathers had already begun to debate the identity of the writers
of Matthew, Mark, Luke, and John. The Fathers reached certain conclusions, but their opinions have not been universally accepted by
modern students of the problem. The writings of Matthew, Mark, and
Luke, which are called the *synoptic* Gospels, utilized material in common and can be ranked among themselves in order of antiquity.
Mark's was the first Gospel to appear (perhaps ca. 70), for both Matthew and Luke (ca. 80–90) copy large portions of his text into their accounts. Matthew and Luke seem also to have shared another source
that has since disappeared, and each author had access to additional
materials that were uniquely his own. John's Gospel is textually independent of the three synoptics, and, although its advanced theology
suggests a relatively late composition date (ca. 100), the work may
contain materials as old as those found in the other evangelists' works
or even older. The dates suggested for the appearances of the Gospels
are inferences from elaborate, technical arguments, but it is easy to see
how all four works could be the product of the second-generation
church's attempt to preserve for its future an account of the witness of
the vanishing first generation of Jesus' companions.

None of the Gospels claims to be a complete or exhaustive account
of the deeds and words of Jesus, and much material is found in each
which is not shared by the others. There are often striking differences
between the traditions preserved in the synoptics and information
found in John. It is possible, therefore, that authentic bits of information about Jesus escaped the Gospel writers but entered into less respected bodies of literature. There are a number of ancient apocryphal
Christian texts that falsely purport to be apostolic documents, but that

might, despite their occasional flagrant absurdities, preserve authentic memories of Jesus. It is curious that the early Christian theologians Origen, Tertullian, and Clement of Alexandria occasionally quote words that they attribute to Jesus but that are not found in the New Testament as it now stands.

A reader of the New Testament should also keep in mind that, while its documents are all written in Greek—and most scholars are of the opinion that all four of the Gospels were originally composed in that language—Jesus, as a Jew preaching to the Jews of Galilee, would have spoken Aramaic. Aramaic was an ancient Semitic tongue used in common speech by many of the Eastern peoples of the Roman Empire who had resisted Hellenization. It is likely that Jesus was literate in Hebrew, for the Scriptures state that he occasionally read from and interpreted the Torah in the synagogue (LUKE 4:16), but there is no evidence that he knew any Greek. Even if he did know Greek, he would not have used it in addressing the Jewish masses or in offering private instruction to his Galilean disciples. Therefore, the words of Jesus in the Gospels are preserved in a language he probably did not speak and in a translation whose fidelity can rarely be authenticated.

The complexity of the tradition of the Gospels and the specialized nature of their literature make it impossible simply to collate parallel accounts in the Scriptures and recover a dependable history of the life of Jesus. It is senseless, however, to fault the Bible for not being what a historian might like it to be, for problems that thwart history may inspire theology. The fact that the Gospels and Epistles cannot be easily "harmonized" and reduced to the level of a simple story creates the permanent tensions within the texts that have made their accounts live and have stimulated people to find in them a perpetually new and relevant word of God. But an awareness of the limitations of the source materials does establish the essential boundaries for a discussion of the history of Jesus of Nazareth. An informed reader can avoid the simplistic acceptance as history of what was never expected to be taken historically or the equally uncritical postulation of imaginative inferences that the texts themselves never intended to suggest.

THE REVELATION

THE EARLY CHURCH'S CLAIM that Jesus was the Christ was based on belief in the saving power of his death and resurrection, not on a theory that accorded him a miraculous origin. The divine ratification of his mission was his triumph over death, not his incarnation. About a third of the text of the Gospels is given over to the description of Jesus' last days, and it appears likely that the heart of the early message of the church was the news of his passion and resurrection. Most of the other material in the Gospels was presented as background that came to focus and meaning in the last week of his life: the material formed a mosaic of prophetic word and deed that became clear only in light of belief in the resurrection. The early church, centering as it did on the story of the end of Jesus' life, seems to have given but brief attention to his origins. Two of the Gospels, Mark and John, ignore his first thirty years completely and begin their accounts with his baptism and the inauguration of his public ministry. Paul only mentions in passing that Jesus was the Son of God, born a human being (GALATIANS 4:4), and descended from David "according to the flesh" (ROMANS 1:3). Nowhere are we told that Jesus himself related stories about his birth or made acceptance of faith in a supernatural origin of the Savior a necessary precondition for belief in his power.

The major traditions concerning what have come to be known as "the lost years" of Jesus' life are contained in the opening chapters of the Gospels of Luke and Matthew, but the events reported there may not all have been intended to be read as simple assertions of facts of history. Both evangelists may have developed their materials on the assumption that, since Jesus' death and resurrection showed him to be the Messiah, all other events in his life must have conformed to Old Testament passages considered to be prophecies of the Messiah. Therefore, if Luke and Matthew had little reliable historical information on the Messiah's early years, they could develop likely theories about his birth and youth from prophetic hints in the Scriptures and use these theories to state at the outset their convictions concerning Jesus' identity.

Matthew and Luke share the opinion, which Mark suggests may not have been held by Jesus himself (MARK 12:35–37), that the Messiah was to be born of the family of David, the ancient royal dynasty of the Jews. The last Davidic monarch had been carried off by the Persians shortly after the Jews' return from the Exile (ca. 530 B.C.), and, although all record of the royal family's legal lines of descent had been lost, Matthew and Luke both present genealogies that purport to link Jesus with David (LUKE 3:23–38; MATTHEW 1:1–17). Their lists of Jesus' ancestors are not identical. In Luke, Jesus' descent is traced through David's son Nathan and in Matthew, through Nathan's half brother Solomon. There is another problem also in the fact that, although both evangelists connect Jesus with the house of David through his earthly father, they both claim on the basis of a prophecy in Isaiah 7:14 that he was born of a virgin mother and was not a true son of Joseph.

Some modern scholars have raised serious questions about Matthew's and Luke's exegeses of the Isaiah text and the evangelists' application of it as a Messianic prophecy. Isaiah uses a word that implies a birth from a young woman of marriageable age, not necessarily a virgin. The Greek translation of this word in the Septuagint version of the Old Testament, which the original texts of the Gospels quote, is also used in Genesis 34:3 in reference to a girl who is plainly no longer virgin. The theme of a miraculous conception also seems to mean something different to Luke than it does to Matthew. For Luke (1:26–38), the event exalts the position of Mary, who is described as receiving a special annunciation from a heavenly messenger concerning her son and his destiny. But Luke is not very consistent in his stories about Mary, for later on he reports that she is puzzled by the emerging indications of Jesus' messianic career (Luke 2:33; 49–50). Matthew (1:20–21) ignores Mary and notes only an annunciation given to Joseph to calm his fears about marrying a woman pregnant with someone else's child. The question of the virgin birth has occasioned considerable debate among the Christian communions and has assumed a meaning and importance it doubtless did not have in the early church. The Hebrew culture of Jesus' day did not prize lifelong virginity as the symbol for virtue it later became in the gentile world. Even though some have insisted on a belief in the virgin birth as a doctrine that protects faith in Jesus' divinity, such an idea may have been first developed in the church as a way of preserving Jesus' humanity against the influence of Gnostic heretics who would have deprived the flesh of any participation in his nature at all.

The perpetual virginity of Mary is an additional point of doctrine for some modern varieties of Christianity but does not seem to have been a part of the preaching of the earliest church. Luke (2:7) refers to Jesus as Mary's first-born son; Mark (6:3) lists the names of his brothers James, Joses, Judas, and Simon; Matthew (13:56) and Mark (6:3) both speak of his sisters. There is no textual support for or against the opinion that these siblings were in reality cousins of Jesus or children of Joseph by a woman other than Mary. There is, also, no reference in the Bible to Mary's own immaculate conception.

Jesus is referred to in all the Gospels as the Nazarene, and for most of his life he was associated with the small hill village of Nazareth in southern Galilee. Matthew (2:23) claims that his appearance in Nazareth was the fulfillment of prophecy, but there is no reference to the town of Nazareth in the Old Testament—as John (7:52) admits. Some scholars have suggested that Matthew may have stretched into a messianic prophecy a reference in JUDGES 13:5 to a "Nazirite" (i.e., a Jew who takes special religious vows) or that he may have been punning on the Hebrew word for "branch" in ISAIAH 11:1. At any rate, Jesus' contemporaries seemed to have considered Nazareth an unlikely place for the inauguration of the messianic mission (JOHN 1:46), and the famous Old Testament prophecies favored Bethlehem (MICAH 5:2), the village from which David's ancestors sprang (1 SAMUEL 16:1). The traditions about Jesus' birth in Bethlehem are not as well founded as they might be. Luke (2:4) suggests that Mary and Joseph were living in Nazareth and made the unusual decision to journey to Bethlehem toward the end of Mary's pregnancy in order to participate in a census conducted while Quirinius was governor of Syria. A serious question of chronology clouds the reliability of the report, for Judea did not become part of the administrative responsibility of the Roman governor of Syria until A.D. 6, when the novelty of levying what was apparently the first Roman tax census (ACTS 5:37) met with violent resistance (Josephus *Wars* 2. 8. 1). If Jesus' birth is placed this late, there are serious conflicts with other presumably well-founded dates in his life. Matthew seems to imply that Joseph and Mary were originally natives of Bethlehem who emigrated to Nazareth after a brief period as exiles in Egypt. John (7:41) may perhaps preserve a memory of a tradition that never associated Jesus with Bethlehem at all but saw him as a lifelong resident and native of Galilee.

The common assumption that the birth of Christ took place on the twenty-fifth day of December at the beginning of the first century of the modern era is a convention of the Christian church that appeared rather late and lacks scriptural support. The year A.D. 1 was determined in the sixth century by a miscalculation that passed into general usage. December 25, the date of the winter solstice in the Julian calendar and the festival of the rebirth of the solar deities, did not receive widespread acceptance as the birthdate of Christ until the fourth century. The Scriptures themselves give no hint as to the day and confusing suggestions as to the year. Matthew (2:1) and Luke (1:5) both state that Herod the Great, who died in 4 B.C., was still king of Judea when Jesus was born. Luke, however, goes on to claim that Jesus' birth coincided with the Roman census conducted by the governor, Quirinius. This census, as stated above, probably occurred in A.D. 6, when the Romans deposed Herod's son Archelaus and assumed direct control over and fiscal responsibility for Judea. If Luke is correct that Jesus was about thirty years of age (LUKE 3:23) when John the Baptist began his career (LUKE 3:1) in the fifteenth year of the reign of the emperor Tiberius (A.D. August 19, 28, to August 18, 29), the tradition that places Jesus' birth before the death of Herod seems to be the most trustworthy one. Some scholars have suggested that the arrival of Halley's comet in the Mediterranean sky in 12 B.C. might help date the appearance of the "star" that Matthew (2:2) alone associates with Jesus' nativity. But ancient peoples generally expected celestial phenomena to herald key events in human history, and Matthew's report may be a literary convention rather than a historical observation. Matthew (2:1-12) is also the only evangelist to report the visit of the wise men who followed the star. Legend has subsequently fixed their number at three, an inference drawn perhaps from three kinds of gifts they brought, and has supplied them with names and places of origin, but none of this is supported by the Scriptures themselves. Luke (2:8-20) alone mentions the shepherds who came to venerate the Christ child at the instigation, not of a star, but of an angelic messenger.

Most of the other incidents in Luke's nativity narratives are implications of the logical assumption that, since Jesus was born a Jew, all the normal obligations of the Jewish law were fulfilled in connection with his birth. He was circumcised at the age of eight days (LUKE 2:21) in accordance with the directive in LEVITICUS 12:3 and given the name Jesus. This name was assigned him by the angel of the annunciation but is a derivative of the relatively common Joshua, "the Lord is salvation." Luke reports also that the law was observed in Mary's purification and in the sacrifices marking Jesus' presentation in the temple as the firstborn son of his family. Luke has nothing more to report of Jesus' childhood save that he returned with his family to Nazareth and had an apparently normal life (LUKE 2:39-40).

Matthew (2:13-18), however, claims that there was a highly dangerous and unusual experience connected with Jesus' birth. The evangelist reports that, in response to the news of the wise men's quest for an infant born to be king of the Jews, Herod the Great had all the male children of Bethlehem murdered. Having received forewarning from God, Jesus' parents managed to save him by fleeing to Egypt. At the death of Herod, they feared to return to Judea to live under Herod's son Archelaus and chose instead to reside in Galilee under another of his sons, Herod Antipas. Apart from Matthew's report, there is no other ancient record of the "slaughter of the innocents." Matthew claims to see in the event the fulfillment of yet another prophecy (JEREMIAH 31:15); but the obvious parallelisms between the adventures of the baby Jesus, the experience of the infant Moses (EXODUS 1:22), and the exodus of the infant Jewish nation from Egypt, have caused some readers to interpret the text as Matthew's commentary on the divine significance of Jesus' life rather than a report of an actual historical occurrence.

Nothing more can be learned about Jesus' early youth from the Gospels. Mark (6:3) notes that Jesus was a carpenter, and Matthew (13:55) adds that he was the son of a carpenter. There is some debate about the authenticity of Mark's text as it now stands, but there would have been nothing at all unusual in a firstborn son of Jesus' day following his father's trade. Luke alone reports the only other incident that tradition has preserved concerning the first thirty years of Jesus' life. Luke claims that an event that gave another clue to Jesus' messianic destiny took place when Jesus reached the age of twelve, a turning point in the life of a male Jew when he receives religious recognition as a responsible adult. Jesus' family, as was their custom (LUKE 2:41), went to Jerusalem to celebrate the Passover. Mary and Joseph lost track of their adolescent son for three days and finally found him in the temple conversing with the religious authorities. Luke claims that Jesus identified the temple as his father's house and rebuked his parents' concern for him. If Luke intended to give a historical account of a real event in Jesus' youth, his description of the ignorance Mary and Joseph express concerning the meaning of Jesus' words is hard to reconcile with the promise that Luke says Mary received at the time of the annunciation that her child would "be called the Son of the Most High" (LUKE 1:32).

The narration of everything the church had to tell of the first three decades of Jesus' life required only two chapters in each of the two Gospels that undertook to preserve the material. But with the beginning of his thirtieth year and the appearance of John the Baptist, the portion of Jesus' life that was crucial for the faith of the early church began, and all four of the Gospels converge on the same event in different ways.

The figure of John the Baptist caused the early church such a problem of interpretation that there is little reason to doubt that he did play a real part in the life of Jesus of Nazareth. All the Gospels agree that Jesus emerged as a public figure only after his contact with John, and all but the fourth describe a baptism of Jesus at John's hands. Both of these facts raised hard questions for those in the early church who preached Jesus' messianic vocation: Why should the sin-less Messiah submit to a baptism for sin at the hands of an inferior? Did the fact that Jesus appeared after John imply that Jesus was John's disciple? The records of the Gospels are so filled with the inter-pretive perspective of the early church that it is now impossible to say for sure what the relationship between the two men really was. For the church, John became the forerunner who prepared the way of the Mes-siah. Matthew (11:14; 17:10-13) states that Jesus saw in John the prophet Elijah, whom Malachi (3:1; 4:5) predicted would herald the inauguration of the messianic age. John (1:21) rejects the Baptist's specific identification with Elijah, but clearly claims for him a role preparatory for the Christ. The importance of the Baptist in the tradi-tions about Jesus may perhaps be suggested by the fact that the only really precise date in the Gospels is the one marking John's emergence from the desert in the fifteenth year of the reign of the emperor Tiberi-us (LUKE 3:1). Luke (1:41) goes so far as to suggest a blood relation-ship between Jesus and the Baptist, but nothing is made of this claim save an opportunity to have the Baptist announce his inferiority to the Christ even from his mother's womb.

The brief descriptions in the Gospels of John's preaching (MAT-THEW 3:1-12; MARK 1:7-8; LUKE 3:7-14; JOHN 1:19-28) suggest that he spoke in the style of the prophets of the Old Testament. He called men to repent their sins in light of an imminent divine judgment and warned that mercy would come, not to those who trusted only in their birth as God's chosen people the Jews, but to those who practiced their relationship to God by treating their fellowmen justly. Like the prophets of the Old Testament, John had a very practical standard of justice. Those who had a surplus were to share with those in need; those who collected taxes were to collect only what was required; those who were soldiers were to be content with their pay and resist the opportunity that their strength gave them for dominating others. In an atmosphere as religiously and politically charged as first century Palestine, it was not long before words like these inspired the rumor that John might be the Messiah (LUKE 3:15). All the Gospels state that John clearly repudiated any such claim (MATTHEW 3:13; MARK 1:7; LUKE 3:16; JOHN 1:20), but this did not prevent him from building a band of followers who continued to have faith in him even after his execution. As late as the sixth decade of the century, Paul was still en-countering people as far from the Jordan valley as Ephesus who iden-tified themselves with John's baptism (ACTS 19:1-5).

Luke (3:23) states that Jesus was about thirty years old when he came to hear the Baptist. John (8:57) might suggest that Jesus was somewhat older, and, since thirty is an age associated with crucial events, in the careers of Joseph (GENESIS 41:46) and David (2 SAMUEL 5:4), it is difficult to know if Luke's figure is intended to be taken literally. The Gospels do not say where Jesus and John met. Matthew (3:1) speaks vaguely of the "wilderness of Judea," and John simply notes that the Baptist was active on other occasions at the Jordan near Bethany (1:28) and at Aenon near Salim (3:23). If the modern identifications of these sites are accurate, both places are considerable distances from Nazareth, and the Gospels say nothing about the events that caused Jesus to leave home and seek John out.

The Scriptures suggest that Jesus held John in very high regard. Matthew (11:11) and Luke (7:28) report that Jesus asserted that no man "born of woman"—and that would include Abraham and Moses —was greater than John. The first three Gospels note that Jesus submitted to John's baptism and show Jesus adopting a courteous, even cautious, attitude toward John (MATTHEW 11:6). The fourth Gospel omits any specific reference to a baptism but does make John a witness to the heavenly phenomena that the other evangelists associate with Jesus' baptism (JOHN 1:29-34). The Gospels differ significantly in their descriptions of what happened at the crucial meeting of John and Jesus. Mark (1:9-11) presents the baptism as a private affair. John and Jesus have no conversation, although John is reported in another context to have predicted the arrival of one "who is mightier than I" (MARK 1:7). Mark suggests that the descent of the Spirit on Jesus at the time of his baptism was Jesus' own internal experience. Luke (3:21-22), too, reports no public proclamation of Jesus' identity by the Baptist, and the voice from heaven confirming Jesus' mission is addressed to Jesus alone. But Matthew (3:14-17) claims that John openly acknowledged his unworthiness to baptize Jesus and that after the baptism the voice from heaven presented Jesus to those present as the beloved Son of God. Matthew's assertion that John knew who Jesus was at the time of the baptism contrasts oddly with his report that later John sent messengers to Jesus to ask, "Are you he who is to come, or shall we look for another?" (MATTHEW 11:3). The fourth Gospel (JOHN 1:29-34) states unequivocally that John preached his own subordination to Jesus and that he claimed to have seen the Spirit of God descend upon Jesus. The Gospel notes that this confession, as might be expected, cost the Baptist some of his disciples and that Jesus won his first followers, Andrew and his brother Simon Peter, from the company of John's companions (JOHN 1:37-42). Matthew (3:15) alone makes an attempt to explain the reason for the baptism. He describes it as a ceremony that Jesus submitted to in order to fulfill "all righteousness," not an act for the remission of Jesus' personal sins. Mark (10:18), however, states that Jesus repudiated a claim to a state of perfection that would have put him beyond the need of God's forgiveness and the benefits of baptism. Despite differences in description and interpretation in the Gospels, it seems clear that Jesus' contact with John was a turning point in Jesus' life, an experience that led him perhaps to accord John more respect than Jesus' own disciples felt was fitting.

The synoptics (MATTHEW 4:1–16; MARK 1:12–13; LUKE 4:1–13) report that immediately after Jesus' baptism, he retreated for a period of meditation to prepare himself for the mission he was about to undertake. The description of this period in his life, such as it is in the Scriptures, may have been filled out with images from his own preaching or from the messianic theories of the early church, for he had at that time no disciples who could have stood witness to his solitary wrestling with temptation.

Mark (1:14) implies that Jesus emerged as a public figure after the arrest of John and the termination of his activities but does not suggest that Jesus was in any way a successor to John's ministry. Jesus worked, as far as can be inferred from the synoptics, in Galilean territories with which John was not particularly associated, and the rite of baptism was not central to Jesus' personal mission. The fourth Gospel, however, speaks of Jesus almost as if he were in competition with John—preaching and baptizing in Judea while John was still active there (JOHN 3:22). Little survives of John's message by which to judge its relationship to Jesus' preaching, but some commentators have stressed a contrast between John's asceticism and pessimistic call to judgment and Jesus' more liberal life style and optimistic proclamation of God's mercy. But their differences may not have been all that visible to their contemporaries. Toward the end of Jesus' life, people were still speculating that he perhaps was a resurrected John the Baptist (MATTHEW 16:14), and the church lived for a long time in the shadow of their relationship.

At the beginning of his public ministry, Jesus followed a custom common to rabbis of his day: he selected a small band of intimates to receive private instruction. Since these men were personally taught by Jesus, they have come to be known in the traditions of the church as his disciples or, literally, "students." Since they later carried out his command to continue his work after his death, they are also called his apostles, which implies that they were men whom he sent out with a special commission of leadership in the Christian movement. The categories become a bit vague in the usage of the early church. Paul designates himself an apostle (GALATIANS 1:1) even though he did not have an opportunity to receive his authority from the historical Jesus. Tradition asserts that Jesus chose twelve men to be his special associates. The number twelve is clearly symbolic of his messianic mission to the Jews, who were customarily thought of as a nation of twelve tribes even though the tribes no longer numbered twelve. Luke (10:1–22) also speaks of Jesus' later selection of seventy followers for a task apparently intended to represent the church's ultimate mission to the "seventy nations" of the gentiles. The identity of the original disciples is not certain, for the four lists of their names preserved in the New Testament are not exactly the same (MARK 3:16–19; MATTHEW 10:2–4; LUKE 6:14–16; Acts 1:13), and specific information is given about very few of them. Jesus' invitations to discipleship are described only for the pairs of brothers Simon and Andrew (MARK 1:16–18) and James and John (MARK 1:19–20) and for the tax collector Matthew (MATTHEW 9:9), who is perhaps the Levi whose call is noted in MARK 2:14. In the lists of disciples, Simon Peter is always named first and Judas Iscariot last. It is not certain whether all of them traveled with Jesus at all times. Simon Peter, James, and John are the disciples most often specifically noted as being in his company. All the disciples, with the possible exception of Judas, were probably Galileans of relatively humble origin, and at least some of them, Simon Peter included, were married men (MARK 1:30; 1 CORINTHIANS 9:5).

No clear picture of the course of Jesus' travels with his disciples can be recovered from the Scriptures, for the synoptics and John all seem to suggest different itineraries. The fourth Gospel, which stresses Jesus' independence of John the Baptist, claims that Jesus and his disciples were preaching and baptizing in Judea while John himself was still working there (JOHN 3:22–23); that they traveled back and forth between Judea and Galilee, spending most of their time toward the end in Judea; and that Jesus' ministry lasted at least three years. John mentions three Passover seasons (2:13; 6:4; 12:1), two of which are clearly said to have been spent in Jerusalem. Mark's itinerary, which is expanded in the other synoptics, describes Jesus' ministry as beginning when John the Baptists' work ended and implies that Jesus confined his attention primarily to Galilee. He returned to Nazareth at least once but seemed to center his travels about the town of Capernaum farther to the north. It is suggested that he left Galilee on several occasions, perhaps to escape Herod's attention, and that he ranged as far north as Tyre, Sidon, and Caesarea Philippi. No mention is made of the length of his preaching ministry. All the incidents reported could have transpired in one year, and only one Passover and one visit to Jerusalem are noted. Luke adds to Mark's itinerary stories that supposedly derive from journeys Jesus made to Samaria, but these accounts contrast rather vividly with the order Jesus gives his disciples in MATTHEW 10:5 to avoid the Samaritans and with Jesus' conduct toward non-Jews in MARK 7:24–30 and MATTHEW 15:21–28. Some scholars have suggested that Luke, who may have written his Gospel with gentile readers in mind (LUKE 1:3), placed stories about Jesus in a Samaritan context in order to provide a precedent for the church's later mission to the gentiles and that Jesus himself did not actually preach in Samaria. It is possible that itineraries described for Jesus in the Gospels may relate more to the distribution of early Christian churches than to Jesus' actual travels.

Jesus' activities are described primarily as those of a teacher and a worker of wonders. The miracle stories are a witness of faith to the reality of his power and authority as perceived by the early church. Any attempt to rationalize the stories or reduce them to erroneously interpreted natural phenomena destroys their purpose and context. They were quite an important part of the message of the early church, and, although the traditions concerning them are not the best-attested in the New Testament (only one, "the feeding of the multitude," is recorded by all four evangelists: MATTHEW 14:13–21; MARK 6:30–44; LUKE 9:10–17; JOHN 6:1–14), the amount of space given them in the Gospels suggests the power they were felt to have as confirmations of Christian faith. The contrast between the natural and the supernatural was not perceived in the same way then as it is now, and the early Christians would have assumed it obvious that the Messiah sent by the Creator of nature had sovereign control over nature. Miracles were rather freely attributed to numerous kinds of people in Jesus' day (MATTHEW 12:27), and they are not presented in the Scriptures as the primary reason for belief in Jesus as the Messiah. To be the Messiah implied the ability to work miracles, but the ability to work miracles did not establish one as a messiah. It would probably surprise the Gospel writers to learn that their miracle stories have caused later generations, whose preconceptions differ greatly from those of the evangelists, to doubt the veracity of the Gospel witness to Jesus' messianic vocation.

The teachings of Jesus are no more amenable to easy explanation

than are the reports of the miracles with which they are closely associated. Jesus seems to have taught in two styles—offering private instruction to his disciples and addressing sermons to mass meetings.
But his message was the same in both modes. There was no secret doctrine taught only to the inner circle and hidden from the uninitiate. He
spoke simply and made extensive use of parables and commentary on
the Hebrew Scriptures, but his message is impossible to summarize.
For almost two thousand years, people have wrested from Jesus'
teachings ideas that are fresh and relevant to each succeeding generation. Even in his own day, his thought was never presented as a consistent philosophical position—a system of inferences from stated
premises—but appeared instead as a series of powerful stimuli to a
style of meditation that has lived on in the Christian church. Several
things might be said, however, about the historical context of Jesus'
preaching and the way in which it was perceived by the early church.

Jesus of Nazareth seems to have conducted himself very much like
many of the Jewish religious leaders who were his contemporaries.
People addressed him as "rabbi" or "teacher" (MATTHEW 22:24); on
occasion he taught in the synagogues (MATTHEW 4:23); and much of
his instruction took the form of commentary on the Jewish law. He
seems to have limited his contacts to Jews. Paul, the great champion of
the mission to the gentiles, admitted that in carrying the Christian
message to the gentiles he departed from Jesus' custom, for Jesus himself had preached only to the Jews (ROMANS 15:38). The Gospels of
Matthew (10:5) and Mark (7:24–30) also represent Jesus as having no
interest in work among non-Jews. It is true that Jesus often came into
conflict with the Pharisees and was upbraided for his liberal interpretation of the Sabbath laws (MATTHEW 12:1–8), but nothing in
his practice or that of his early disciples suggested an intention to depart from the traditional duties a Jew owed the temple, the synagogue,
and the law of Moses.

Jesus' message, like that of many of the religious visionaries of his
era, contained an apocalyptic element. Matthew characterized Jesus'
earliest sermons tersely as calls to "repent, for the kingdom of heaven
is at hand" (MATTHEW 4:17). Although it is stated that Jesus rejected
any attempt to predict just when history would reach its climax (LUKE
17:20), it is implied that he felt the end would fall within the span of
his own generation (MARK 9:1; MATTHEW 16:28) and that his mission
therefore was urgent. The fact that the eschaton did not arrive in the
years following his death presented the church with a problem of interpretation. For some, the apocalyptic theme in Jesus' preaching be-

came a messianic proclamation of the end of the old order of law and
the beginning of a new aeon of grace: the announcement of an event
that had already occurred in history with the incarnation of the Messiah. Some modern theologians have explained Jesus' apocalyptic
message as his claim that he himself was the end of time manifested in
time, the new order revealed within the old. But these metaphorical
interpretations of his words have never succeeded in completely replacing for all Christians the older, simpler expectation that the end of
the historical world and the second coming of Christ are imminent
events.

Jesus' call for repentence, his announcement of God's pending
judgment, and his proffer of grace and forgiveness doubtless caused
many of his contemporaries to see him as one who stood in the line of
the ancient Hebrew prophets. The Gospels report that on numerous
occasions his audiences expected him to manifest prophetic characteristics (MARK 14:65; MATTHEW 21:11; JOHN 7:52), and he himself may
have encouraged this expectation. In describing the rejection of Jesus'
message by the people of Nazareth, all four Gospels quote him as identifying himself as a prophet who received no credence in his homeland
(MARK 6:4; MATTHEW 13:57; LUKE 4:24; JOHN 4:44; note also LUKE
13:33).

Whatever it was that the historical Jesus taught, the church never
claimed that he was the Messiah merely because of his message. Salvation as the Christ brought it was not simply the acceptance of a new
series of ideas, a mental assent to propositions, or a new intellectual
comprehension of old values. The Messiah was not a philosopher. He
did not invent an ethic or a metaphysic. It was not the appeal of an
original system of ideas devised by Jesus that won him followers, but
the impression he made on his hearers of being a man who could speak
the old promises of Judaism with true authority. Much of what he
preached was not new to the Western religious tradition when he
taught it. He departed from accepted custom and changed emphases in
old rules to point up the spirit of God's law when he felt the law's observation had been obscured by a passion for its letter (MATTHEW
19:3-9). But, at heart, the message of Jesus seems to have been very
much the message of traditional Judaism. He himself spoke of his
work, not as the imposition of a new law, but as a fulfillment of the old
religious expectations of his people (LUKE 4:21). The early Christians
preached their faith in Jesus as the Messiah, not because his teachings
differed radically from the religion of their ancestors, but because He
taught the old verities with an authority approaching that of God

himself. The theme of the church's preaching about Christ was his power as manifested in word and deed, not simply the validity of his ethical precepts. For the church he was not someone who merely created a philosophical option for understanding the human condition; he was an event that changed man's possibilities for life.

The message of Jesus was felt by the church to be a message of salvation because of the identity of the man who spoke it, but his identity only became clear to the church in the culminating events of his life—his crucifixion and resurrection. The Gospels give the impression that, until these events took place, the disciples continued to hope that Jesus would show himself to be a Messiah who fulfilled their traditional expectations of triumph and power (LUKE 24:21). It was only after his death that they came to understand, in light of faith in the *IMP* resurrection, that the messianic victory was over sin and the grave, not over men and nations. The death and resurrection of Jesus of Nazareth thus became for the church the key events in his life and formed the center for the church's understanding of him. These events showed him to be God's Messiah, the "anointed one," or, in Greek, "the Christ." It is not surprising, therefore, to discover that the Gospels devote more attention to his death than to any event in his life. *Ill*

The Gospel accounts of the last week in the life of Jesus are more extensive, but no less varied, than their descriptions of earlier periods in his career. Even here, in events central to the church's preaching, it is impossible to establish exactly what happened. Jesus' decision to go to Jerusalem is depicted by the synoptics as an unusual and courageous act designed to bring his work to fruition. But John suggests that Jesus regularly traveled to Jerusalem for the Passover. All four Gospels describe his entry into Jerusalem as a triumphal procession that fulfilled a prophecy in ZECHARIAH 9:9: "Lo, your king comes to you; triumphant and victorious is he, humble and riding on an ass, on a colt the foal of an ass." Matthew (21:7) understands the prophecy to make reference to two animals, an ass and a colt, and has Jesus ride them both. For Matthew (21:12-13) and Luke (19:45-46), this Palm Sunday procession ends spectacularly in Jesus' assault on the businessmen in the temple. But Mark (11:11) claims that he simply entered Jerusalem, toured the temple, and then went quietly back to Bethany outside the city to spend the night. It was not until the next day that he returned to "cleanse" the temple (MARK 11:15-17). The synoptics suggest that it was this attack on the temple that precipitated the Sanhedrin's decision to have him killed. But John (2:13-16) places the attack on the temple at the beginning of Jesus' career and makes of it a characterization of the whole of his ministry, not an explanation of the crisis of his final week.

Jesus' teaching during this period is variously represented by the four Gospels. The synoptics put his discussions of the sources of his authority and the authority of the state in this context; John emphasizes his predictions of the difficult times that lay ahead for his followers. All the Gospels agree that the chief event in his private life that week was the final supper he ate with his disciples, the last opportunity he had to enjoy their company in peace and privacy. But John and the synoptics differ as to what kind of meal the Last Supper was. The synoptics, following Mark (14:12), specifically state that it was a Passover celebration. John (13:1) claims that, although Jesus made special arrangements to eat the meal in Jerusalem as required of a Passover pilgrim, the meal was held a day before Passover and Jesus was crucified on the day of preparation for Passover (JOHN 19:14). The Gospels are united in the opinion that Jesus died on a Friday sometime before the beginning of the Hebrew Sabbath at sundown, but they disagree as to whether that Friday was the day of or the day before the Passover meal. John's chronology may have been influenced by a desire symbolically to link the crucifixion of Jesus, "the Lamb of God" (JOHN 1:29, 36), with the slaughter of the Passover lambs. But Mark (14:2) indirectly supports John by noting that the priests and scribes plotted to take Jesus prior to the Passover feast so as to minimize the possibility of a public disturbance. Paul never describes the Last Supper as a Passover meal, but he does speak of Christ in John's fashion as a paschal lamb (1 CORINTHIANS 5:7). Christian communions that follow the synoptic tradition employ unleavened bread in their celebrations of the meal, but none of the other symbols from the Passover ritual have entered into the Christian liturgical tradition.

All the Gospels assert that, at the Last Supper, Jesus predicted that one of his intimates would betray him; but the accounts disagree on exactly what happened. In Mark's (14:18–21) and Luke's (22:22–23) accounts, Jesus merely predicts a betrayal. In Matthew (26:25), Judas responds to the announcement, asks if Jesus is referring to him, and receives a noncommittal answer. In John's Gospel (13:26), Jesus clearly accuses Judas. Mark (14:11) and Luke (22:5) claim that Judas received money for his treachery, but only Matthew (26:15) sets the price at thirty pieces of silver—a reference perhaps to the prophecy of Zechariah (11:12-13). Luke (ACTS 1:18) suggests that Judas died from a disastrous fall, but Matthew (27:5) claims that he hanged himself.

Following the supper, Jesus and an unstated number of his companions followed a custom that must have been common among the poorer Passover pilgrims. They camped for the night at Gethsemane, outside the crowded city. The Gospels have much to say about Jesus' private meditations on this occasion, but they give no indication of the source of their information. Since he is described as going apart from his disciples, who are rebuked for falling asleep and leaving him alone in his vigil, the disciples would not have witnessed what he did that evening, and they had no further opportunity to talk with him before his death. The prayer attributed to Jesus on this occasion bears a resemblance to what the church remembered as his general teaching on prayer (MATTHEW 6:10) and may have been reconstructed from the liturgies of the early Christians. The appearance of Judas and the men sent to capture Jesus seems to have led to a brief struggle or simply to a rout of the disciples. Mark (14:51–52) adds the curious detail that a young man present escaped a pursuer by wriggling out of his clothes. Some commentators have seen this colorful story as clear evidence that Mark's account derives from eyewitness testimony; others suggest that the anecdote is simply another reference to Old Testament prophecy (AMOS 2:16).

From Gethsemane, Jesus was taken to the Jewish authorities for examination. The sources of Gospel information on this episode are, again, difficult to identify. No disciple was present at the examination of Jesus, and, judging from Peter's reaction on that occasion when accused of being one of Jesus' followers (LUKE 22:56–60), none would have risked making inquiries until the event was long past. The synoptics' reports of the trial indicate departures from what might have been standard Hebrew judicial procedures. The trial was rushed through with illegal haste, and the stated charge against Jesus does not seem to have been substantiated. Mark (14:61–65) says that Jesus was convicted of blasphemy for confessing that he considered himself to be the Messiah, but the other Gospels suggest that Jesus never openly claimed a messianic identity. In any case, the Messiah was held by Jewish tradition to be a human figure or at least a being inferior to God himself; so a claim to be the Messiah, as long as it did not directly involve the name of God, was not necessarily a blasphemy. The Sanhedrin's procedure after examining Jesus has also suggested to some students that the body was unable to convict Jesus of a religious crime, for the Sanhedrin turned Jesus over to the Romans and did not undertake to execute him on its own authority. No one, however, is certain what the powers of the Sanhedrin were under the Roman procurators, and it is not clear whether or not the Sanhedrin could have executed Jesus under the mandate given it by Rome. Josephus (*Wars* 6. 2. 4; *Antiquities* 14. 9. 3) implies that the Sanhedrin had at one time carried out death sentences for Jews convicted of religious crimes. Acts (6:15–7:58) describes the death of the martyr Stephen at a slightly later period in terms of a trial before the Sanhedrin and a legal execution by the traditional Jewish method of stoning. But John's Gospel gives some support to those who believe that Jesus was never officially tried by the Sanhedrin at all. John makes no reference to a formal trial of Jesus by the Sanhedrin but suggests that Jesus was taken and examined by the high priest who then accused him in the Roman courts of the crime of treason.

The interpretation of Jesus' trial before Pilate is complicated by the possibility that ulterior motives may have shaped the Gospels' description of the event. At the time the Gospels were written, the Christians were being forced out of the synagogues (JOHN 16:2) and were attempting to establish themselves in gentile society. The church's future interests lay in a rapprochement with the Roman world, an objective that could be achieved more easily if some of the blame for the death of Jesus were shifted from the Roman government to the Jews, whose relations with the empire were at the time going from bad to worse. Luke (23:6–12) alone reports that Pilate tried to return jurisdiction over the case to the Jews by sending Jesus to his regional overlord, Herod Antipas, the Jewish tetrarch of Jesus' native district of Galilee. Matthew alone preserves the stories of Pilate's wife's dream (MATTHEW 27:19) and of Pilate's graphic disclaimer of any responsibility for Jesus' execution (MATTHEW 27:24–25). All the Gospels report Pilate's offer of amnesty which the Jews transferred from Jesus to Barabbas, and all the Gospels treat Pilate with surprising sympathy.

In the end, however, it was Pilate who condemned Jesus to death by a standard Roman method of execution, on what appears to have been a political charge of treason against the Roman state. Roman executions were public spectacles planned to deter the masses from a repetition of the condemned man's crime. Therefore, the Romans designed the punishment to reflect the nature of the crime. The style in which Jesus was mocked by his executioners suggests that they thought he had aspired to monarchy: he was draped in a red cape, given a comic scepter, and crowned like a Roman official—with a parody of a laurel wreath. At the place of his execution, a sign was posted reading "Jesus of Nazareth, King of the Jews." The royal title might be applied in messianic literature to a strictly religious figure, but for the Romans its political and revolutionary implications were an obvious danger.

While the fact of the crucifixion is undoubted, the exact nature of what transpired during the event is uncertain. The Scriptures do not clearly locate "a place called Golgotha" (MATTHEW 27:33), and it was not until the fourth century that tradition fixed the site of the shrine now designated by that name. The Scriptures are likewise vague in identifying their sources of information about what happened there. It was never claimed that Peter was an eyewitness of the crucifixion. Mark (15:40–41) mentions as present and watching "from afar" only certain women from Galilee, among whom were Mary Magdalene, Mary the mother of James, and a certain Salome. Luke speaks of a crowd, identified as "all his acquaintances and the women who had followed him from Galilee," which observed the proceedings from a distance (LUKE 23:49). John (19:25–27) alone specifically notes that a disciple, who is unnamed, was present and that he, Jesus' mother and aunt, and Mary Magdalene stood close enough to the cross to hear Jesus' words. The synoptics also refer to a certain Simon of Cyrene, whose sons Alexander and Rufus may have been personally known to the author of Mark's Gospel (15:21). Simon was forced to carry Jesus' cross for him and would therefore have been present at the execution. John (19:17), however, omits reference to Simon and clearly states that Jesus bore his own cross to Golgotha.

The words and the experiences that the Gospels attribute to Jesus at the cross can be closely correlated with Old Testament passages that the church held to be messianic prophecies: PROVERBS 31:6 (MARK 15:23); PSALMS 22:18 (MARK 15:24); PSALMS 22:7–8 (MARK 15:29–31); ISAIAH 53:12 (LUKE 23:32); PSALMS 22:1 (MARK 15:34); PSALMS 31:5 (LUKE 23:46); PSALMS 69:21 (MATTHEW 27:48); PSALMS 34:20 (JOHN 19:36); ZECHARIAH 12:10 (JOHN 19:37); etc. It is impossible, therefore, to be certain which of the events reported in the Gospels are historical and which are the church's later witness of faith to the meaning of what transpired at Golgotha.

Mark (15:25) puts Jesus' crucifixion at about nine in the morning; John (19:14) implies that it occurred somewhat later. John (19:33) notes that Jesus died much sooner than his executioners had expected. Death by crucifixion results from pain, shock, and exhaustion, not directly from injuries inflicted by fastening the body to the cross. Depending on his strength, a victim of crucifixion could suffer for quite a long time. John (20:25) speaks specifically of the nails of the crucifixion having been driven through Jesus' hands, but the more common practice must have been to fix the body firmly through the bones of the wrist rather than through the soft flesh of the palm.

The story of the deposition of Jesus' body is somewhat mysterious, at first glance. The Gospels all record that the corpse was claimed from the cross by a Joseph of Arimathea. Although John (19:38) identifies him as a secret disciple of Jesus, Joseph appears nowhere else in the Scriptures and is described in the synoptics simply as a "respected member of the council" (MARK 15:43), a body that Luke (23:50–51) clearly believes to have been the Sanhedrin. It is not necessary to credit him with Christian sympathies, for it was an honorable practice for wealthy Jews to assist indigent members of their society in the observance of religious duties. The disposal of the abandoned corpse of a crucified Jew on the eve of the Sabbath would have been the kind of act of charity and public service that was expected of a responsible Jewish leader.

The synoptics imply that, because of the approach of the Sabbath, Jesus was hastily, and perhaps temporarily, placed in Joseph's family tomb. They state that the women came to the tomb on the morning after the Sabbath to anoint the corpse with embalming elements. John (19:39) disagrees with the synoptic tradition in this and paints a very different picture. He states that Jesus' body was fully prepared for burial, being wrapped with linen and about a hundred pounds of myrrh and aloes, before it was sealed in the tomb. Only Matthew (27:62–66; 28:11–15) tells of the soldiers who were sent to guard the tomb and subsequently bribed by the chief priests to spread the rumor that Jesus' disciples had stolen his body from the grave and fabricated the resurrection.

There are numerous differences in the scriptural accounts of Jesus' passion, but none of the variations affects the central Christian witness to the reality of his crucifixion, and many can be understood as details later added to the story to interpret its meaning from the perspective of faith in the resurrection. The resurrection itself, however, cannot be approached as a simple historical event. It is a unique revelation of God's power in history, and, like key events in the Old Testament, it does not lie within the range of the critical tools that the historian uses to interpret mundane occurrences. It is a fact of faith based on, but not proven by, events in history. The early Christians preached faith in Jesus as the resurrected Christ, not because they had discovered his tomb empty and his body missing, but because somehow they had experienced his living presence in their midst. This living reality, variously attested, was the reason for the faith of the church in

Jesus' messianic identity. The resurrection provided the perspective that caused everything else to fall into place, but it was itself an experience of faith, not an inference from bald historical data. The Gospels suggest that it was as much a surprise to the mourning disciples as it would be to any modern person (JOHN 20:9).

The earliest scriptural report of the resurrection is Paul's account (1 CORINTHIANS 15:3–8) of what he had been taught after his conversion: that Jesus had been raised on the third day, that he had appeared first to Peter, then to the rest of the apostles, then to more than five hundred others, and finally to Jesus' brother James and to Paul himself. Luke (24:34) implies that the risen Christ was first witnessed by Peter or by the men on the Emmaus road. Mark (16:1–8) mentions no resurrection appearances, but describes the discovery of the empty tomb by Mary Magdalene, Mary the mother of James, and Salome. Although a "young man" at the tomb instructed the women to tell Jesus' disciples that he had risen, Mark (16:8) says that the women told no one. Some manuscripts of Mark's Gospel contain twelve additional verses that state that Jesus appeared first to Mary Magdalene, but most scholars see these verses as later additions to the original form of the Gospel. Matthew (28:6) agrees with Mark that the women —Mary Magdalene and the "other Mary"—found only an empty tomb and claims that an "angel" told them of Christ's resurrection. Matthew says also that, as they were returning from the gravesite, they encountered Jesus himself, who promised to meet the disciples on a certain mountain in Galilee. According to John's Gospel (20:1), Mary Magdalene alone discovered the empty tomb, and, after Peter and another disciple had investigated it and departed, Jesus appeared first to her. Subsequently, John says, Jesus showed himself to ten of the disciples gathered in Jerusalem (JOHN 20:19) and, eight days later, appeared to all eleven, giving special proof of his reality to Thomas, who had been absent on the first occasion (JOHN 20:27).

It is clear that many traditions about Jesus' resurrection appearances came to circulate in the early church and that the concept of a resurrected Messiah was a startling idea which was not easy to accept. Matthew (28:17) admits that even some of the disciples who witnessed Christ on the mountain in Galilee doubted. John (20:26–28) describes the callous scepticism of the apostle Thomas. Despite the intimations of Jesus' destiny scattered through John's Gospel, he claims that, before their experience of the resurrection, the disciples "did not know the Scripture [perhaps HOSEA 6:2], that he must rise from the dead" (JOHN 20:9). Luke (24:41) depicts some of the disciples as disbelieving "for joy" and agrees with John that only after the experience of the resurrection did the disciples come to understand that the Scriptures foretold the death and resurrection of the Messiah (LUKE 24:45-46).

The early church seems to have formed no clear consensus concerning the nature of the body of the resurrected Christ. Luke (24:41-43) stresses the body's normal physical attributes by reporting that Christ proved his reality to the disciples by eating a piece of boiled fish. John (20:27), too, emphasizes Christ's physical reality by claiming that Jesus offered himself to be touched by Thomas. Yet Paul's discussion of the resurrected body (1 CORINTHIANS 15:42-44; 50-54) centers on the body's spiritual features and its freedom from the attributes of corruptible flesh.

Disputes over the understanding of the resurrection and bizarre claims based on supposed experiences of the Christ could have become occasions for danger to the unity and integrity of the early church. But the church successfully resisted the temptation to make of the appearances of its resurrected Lord a source of mythology, authority, and secret teaching which would have cut Christian roots in the realities of history. Belief in the resurrection provided a new perspective on the life of Jesus of Nazareth, but the church continued to draw its doctrines more from its interpretation of the meaning of his historical existence than from theories concerning his translated heavenly being. The church taught (ACTS 1:1-11) that Christ ascended to heaven within forty days of his resurrection. People continued to report visions of him; Paul tells of one in GALATIAN 1:16. But individual claims to a unique experience of the resurrected Christ were gradually replaced by the common experience of the Holy Spirit in the community of the church. This experience was a confirmation of faith in the revelation of the Messiah through Jesus but not a source of radically new revelations which would depart from the authority of the tradition Jesus had left with his disciples. The church remained firm in the conviction, inherited from its Judaic past, that revelation comes through the interpretation of historical reality, not the imaginative proliferation of myths meditating on the supernatural.

THE REACTION TO THE REVELATION

IT IS NOT AT all clear from the Gospels what kind of community Jesus expected his disciples to form after his death. Both he and the first generation of Christians seemed to have assumed that, because the kingdom of God was imminent (MARK 9:1; MATTHEW 16:28), elaborate plans for the future were unnecessary. It does seem that neither Jesus nor his disciples envisioned any break with Judaism. Jesus went to his death still observing the requirements of his ancestral religion, and his followers seem not to have broken the routine of the religious law. The women who intended to prepare his body for burial did not approach the tomb until the Sabbath was over (MARK 16:1), and Peter and John frequented the temple at the prescribed hours for prayer while they remained in Jerusalem (ACTS 3:1). In their preaching they went only to the Jews, and the first Christians seem to have thought of themselves simply as Jews whose Messiah had come.

The transformation of the Twelve from their role as disciples of a human Jesus to a more independent position as apostles of a messianic Christ was accomplished by their common experience of faith in the resurrection, a faith that moved them from an extreme of doubt and despair to a posture of radical assurance. It is not possible to learn from the Gospels exactly what the historical Jesus thought about his own messianic identity, for the evangelists interpret him from the perspective of their own convictions that he was the Messiah. They differ radically on the question of whether he ever openly and plainly put forth a messianic claim. But all the Gospels do agree that the messianic hopes that focused on Jesus while he lived were erroneous and came to defeat at the cross. Ancient Hebrew messianic speculation took many forms: some people spoke of a messianic age ushered in by God without the mediation of a specific Messiah; some predicted the sudden appearance of a king descended from the old Davidic dynasty; some imagined that the Messiah would rise from the Maccabean family of the Levites; some claimed that the Messiah would come as a priest—or that the messianic age would be inaugurated by the dual labors of a priest and a king; some dreamed of a miraculous "Son of Man," a being created before the world began and destined to be its judge and its redeemer. Jesus' intimate associates seem to have thought of him most often as a potential military or political leader (MARK 11:10; LUKE 24:21; ACTS 1:6). All the traditional messianic expectations assumed that the Messiah would manifest invincible power and meet with success. All the traditional expectations were disappointed by a man whose defenseless weakness led to a cross and the grave. Despite the events and the teachings that the Gospel writers later came to interpret as predictions of Jesus' destiny, it is clear that his disciples were unprepared for his crucifixion and death. It was only after his resurrection that "he opened their minds to understand the Scripture" (LUKE 24:45) and they came to understand how wide of the mark traditional messianic expectations had been. The mission of the first church became the task of opening the minds of men and women by reinterpreting the concept of the Messiah and proclaiming Jesus as the fulfillment of the previously misunderstood prophecies of the Scriptures.

Jesus seems to have left very few specific directions for the guidance of the apostles in this task. Some scholars have even questioned whether Jesus intended to found a new and permanent religious institution such as the church became. The Greek word for church, *ekklesia,* appears only twice in the record of Jesus' teachings, and both appearances are in Matthew's Gospel. MATTHEW 18:17 seems to be a clear anachronism, for it talks of Jesus recommending the disciplinary use of an institution that did not yet exist. But MATTHEW 16:17–19 has elicited very careful exegetical examination, for here Matthew claims that, in response to Peter's confession of faith in Jesus as the Messiah, Jesus predicted the future establishment of the church and Peter's supreme authority over it. All the synoptics include the story of Peter's confession of faith in Jesus, but only Matthew adds the saying concerning the church. Elsewhere in the Gospels, authority over the church is promised to all the disciples (MATTHEW 18:18; JOHN 20:23). The interpretation of these passages is vastly complicated by the confessional stances of the various Christian communions. The Roman Catholics see in the passages a Scriptural basis for their belief in the unique authority of the pope, whom they hold to be the direct heir of the episcopal office that Christ here bestowed on Peter. Protestants, on the other hand, often interpret these verses in light of their rejection of papal claims. Two points can, however, be made with some assurance. First, Jesus could very possibly have spoken of an *ekklesia* in the sense in which the Septuagint uses the word—to indicate the people of Israel or the faithful remnant of the chosen people who would heed his word. Second, Jesus never devoted much time to discussing the form a religious movement in his name might take after his death, and there is no evidence to suggest that he anticipated his followers' radical departure from traditional Jewish laws, ceremonies, and institutions.

The inadequacy of the records makes it impossible to describe the stages by which the first fellowship of the church came into existence. Although the Gospels speak of Jesus' resurrection appearances in Galilee and although he spent most of his life in Galilee, his disciples made Jerusalem their center, and all indications are that Peter, whom Jesus had nicknamed "the Rock" (MATTHEW 16:17; MARK 3:16; JOHN 1:42), was instrumental in forming the group that gathered there.

Luke, the probable author of the Acts of the Apostles (the major source on this period in the church's history), places great emphasis on the solidarity of the band of disciples, for they were to him the witnesses and guarantors of the traditions about Jesus preserved in the church. Luke claims that one of the first items of business in the new church was the selection of Matthias to replace Judas as an apostle so that the symbolic number of twelve leaders might be maintained (ACTS 1:21-26). But there is no evidence suggesting that the twelve actually formed a board of governors for the church. Their offices were not perpetuated by elections to replace later vacancies, and the further activities of most of the Twelve are not recorded in Scripture. Peter and Zebedee's sons James and John are almost the only apostles whose activities are specifically described. Tradition has provided very imaginative destinies for the other apostles as missionaries of the church, but there is no Scriptural record at all of their contribution to the growth of the Christian institution. Of their group, only Peter figures as a major missionary in the stories preserved in Acts.

The Scriptures provide ample evidence of the church's memory of Peter's preeminence among the apostles and his leadership of the church in the immediate postresurrection period (ACTS 1:15; 2:14; 4:8; 5:1-10; 5:29; 8:14). But it is equally apparent that he did not long maintain his position of influence in Jerusalem. Shortly after James the brother of John was executed by the Jewish authorities, Peter was imprisoned, and, after staging a miraculous escape, he found it expedient to leave Jerusalem for "another place" (ACTS 12:17). Acts (15:7) notes that he returned to Jerusalem at least once for a church conference, and Paul's letter to the Galatians (2:7, 11) says Peter worked in Antioch with special responsibility for the mission to the Jews. Nothing more is recorded of his life in the New Testament. The closing passage of the letter known as 1 Peter speaks vaguely of his presence in "Babylon," which may testify symbolically to the ancient belief that he worked in Rome, but nothing specific is said about his presence there or the tradition that he died a martyr's death under the emperor Nero.

Peter's position as leader of the church in Jerusalem was taken over by a certain James, who had a natural claim to authority in the Christian movement in that he was Jesus' brother. James is never said to have traveled with the apostles while Jesus was alive. He seems only to have been converted to belief in Jesus as the Christ after the crucifixion by means of a special postresurrection vision mentioned by Paul (1 CORINTHIANS 15:17). James appeared quite early, however, as a member of the Jerusalem church, and Paul sees him as having been one of its leaders from the beginning. He is the only man besides Peter with whom Paul conferred on his first visit to Jerusalem after his conversion. Paul also seems to see James as the "chairman" of the meeting that was held several years later in Jerusalem to iron out difficulties in the relationship between Jewish and gentile factions in the church. Tradition claims that he was much respected even by the Jews for his strict piety and observation of the law, and he is, perhaps unfairly, associated with the conservative party in the church which opposed any departure from Judaism in the lives of new Christians. After his martyr's death in A.D. 62, his position of influence as head of the "mother church" in Jerusalem seems to have been passed on to other members of Jesus' family. He was succeeded by a Simon, a son of a kinsman of Jesus' named Clopas. Eusebius claims that, as late as the reign of the emperor Domitian (A.D. 81–96), two grandsons of Jesus' brother Judas were leaders of the church "since they were confessors and kinsmen of the Lord" (*Church History* 3. 19f). Some scholars have suggested that the derogatory references to Jesus' family that are found in all the Gospels may derive from traditions that opposed the tendency to make the leadership of the church a hereditary caliphate. Such a situation never became a serious possibility, however, for the authority of the Jerusalem establishment declined rapidly toward the end of the first century in the series of Jewish wars that led to the destruction of Jerusalem and the exclusion of Jews from Judea and the site of the holy city. The Jerusalem Christians may have moved east across the Jordan and there come under the influence of older Jewish sects. The fourth century still knew of the existence of groups of "Nazarenes" and "Ebionites" who used Hebrew texts derived from the Greek Christian Scriptures, but the doctrines of these groups were by then held to be plainly heretical. The real future for Christianity lay outside the confines of traditional Judaism in the much broader scope of the gentile world.

Peter himself, although specifically charged with a mission to the Jews and knowing that the idea was a departure from Jesus' own practice (Romans 15:38), was not adverse to extending membership in the Christian movement to Gentiles (Acts 10:1–48). But the nature of the Biblical records has led subsequent generations to accord primary credit for the success of the gentile mission to Paul, or Saul, of Tarsus. Thirteen of the twenty-seven items that compose the Christian Scriptures are ascribed to him, and, although scholars are relatively sure that five or six of the items are not his, enough remains to establish his reputation beyond doubt as the first major Christian theologian. His influence has been so great that some commentators have argued that Paul was literally the "second founder" of Christianity and that he bears primary responsibility for the church's transformation of its memory of the human Jesus into a tradition about the divine Christ. It is quite true that Paul shows almost no interest in the history of Jesus apart from his crucifixion and resurrection. But Paul's image of the resurrected Christ survived as Scripture for the church because it was the clarified experience of his fellow Christians, not the arbitrary creation of his own intellect. In his day, Paul was far from being able to impose his personal opinions on his fellow Christians and seems to have received little of the respect that has been almost universally accorded him by later generations.

Paul was a Jew of the diaspora. He claimed descent from the tribe of Benjamin (PHILIPPIANS 3:5), but he had been raised outside of Palestine at Tarsus (ACTS 21:39), enjoyed Roman citizenship (ACTS 22:28), and was fluent in the Greek language. He occasionally supported himself as a tentmaker (ACTS 18:3), but it is impossible to deduce his social standing from this fact, for training in manual skills was a recommended portion of the education even of Jews who would never have to do manual work. Acts (22:3) claims that he was an ardent Pharisee and a student of the day's most famous interpreter of the law, Gamaliel, but Paul may never have been the most orthodox or fully informed of Pharisees. His attitude toward marriage (1 CORINTHIANS 7) and his occasionally blunt and uncompromising presentation of the Jewish law set him apart from the most honored rabbinic traditions of the first century. He himself notes (GALATIANS 1:13) that he was originally an extreme opponent of the church and devoted considerable energy to harrassing it; the legends in Acts (7:58) make him a witness and a consenter to the death of Stephen, the first martyred Christian. The reasons for Paul's antipathy to the Christians are never given, but Acts (9:1–19) claims that he was on his way to Damascus to stir up trouble for them there when he was suddenly confronted with a vision of the risen Christ that led to his complete and radical conversion to the faith he had previously opposed. The intensity of his experience was such that he felt that the Christ had bestowed on him an authority and office equal to that of the apostles who had been the companions of the historical Jesus (GALATIANS 1:1). Paul is quite clear that, in his opinion, his message and his right to teach it do not derive from Peter or from any other man, but from the direct commission of Christ himself (GALATIANS 1:11–17).

Not much is known about the early years of Paul's service to the church. He may have remained in the vicinity of Damascus or Nabatea for about three years until his situation became difficult (2 Corinthians 11:32–33). He then made the acquaintance of Peter and James during a brief stay in Jerusalem (Galatians 1:18) and returned to his native district of Cilicia. For about fourteen years, he may have worked in and about Tarsus and Antioch. But the New Testament records do not provide much information about his activities before the convening of the Jerusalem, or Apostolic, Council (ca. A.D. 50) which met to consider the question of the church's mission to the Gentiles. Acts (22:21) claims that Paul had a special revelation from God charging him to work among the Gentiles, and Paul's letters (Galatians 1:16) suggest that he felt that this responsibility was the primary reason for the grace of conversion that God had so liberally bestowed on him. He so persistently and eloquently proclaimed himself the apostle to the Gentiles that he may have obscured somewhat the roles others played in extending the fellowship of the church to non-Jews.

The question of the relationship between Jewish law and Christian faith had a long history of debate within the church before Paul became involved in the controversy. Almost from the beginning, there had been conflict within the church between those who proposed to continue a strict observation of the Jewish law and those who wished to prune and streamline their Jewish obligations. This debate between the strict and the liberal Jews brought to the surface the same kinds of questions that were later raised by the proposal to admit Gentiles to the theretofore exclusively Jewish Christian company. At issue in the argument was the church's first attempt to come to some understanding of itself: was the church to be a sect within Judaism obligated to maintain the full burden of the old law; or was the church to be a new religion—the community of a universal messianic age, the new chosen people who were free of the old ritual requirements that governed the period of waiting for the One who had finally arrived?

The Scriptures say very little about the domestic life of the church in the years immediately following the resurrection. It does appear, though, that most of the apostles, who were Jews of a relatively unsophisticated nature, simply assumed that they would continue, as "Christians" (a name they were later to acquire in the gentile world), the traditional patterns of Jewish life they had always observed. They had a consciousness of completing the expectations of the old religion,

not of supplanting it with a new and radically different order. The
Sabbath and the dietary laws continued to be observed. The temple
was honored, and synagogues were frequented. The Christian life,
with its baptisms, its communal meals, and its "gifts of the Spirit," was
an addition to Jewish life and subtracted nothing from Judaism's
older ritual.

First century Judaism, however, had reached no consensus concerning the interpretation of the requirements of the law and had not
agreed upon acceptable standards of strictness in the law's observation. Various subgroups of the Sadducees and Pharisees each had their
own positions and, in general, the Palestinian Jews seem to have
looked down on the Jews of the diaspora, who had drifted into strange
practices as a result of their prolonged contact with gentile cultures.
The tensions in Jewish society at large were soon reflected in the Jewish community of the Jerusalem church. Many of the most active converts, listed in Acts as having responded to the preaching of the apostles, had names that suggest they belonged to the class of Hellenized
Jews who had returned to Jerusalem from the diaspora. There were
doubtless many potential points of conflict between the somewhat
tainted Judaism of these foreigners and the conservative rural practices of Jesus' old circle of Galilean friends. In fact, certain anecdotes
preserved in Acts may indicate that the native Jewish Christians
treated the new believers with some disdain. Acts notes that the "Hellenists murmured against the Hebrews because their widows were neglected in the daily distribution" (ACTS 6:1) and that, as a result, the
apostles vested some authority in a board of seven men, all of whom
appear to have had Greek names and Hellenistic backgrounds. Acts
claims that the slight against the Hellenists was merely the result of
inadequate church organization, which was corrected by designating
the seven men to handle the practical affairs of the community while
the apostles conducted its preaching. But there must have been more
to it than that. It is strange that only the Hellenists' charities should
have been slighted under the old system and that only Hellenists were
named in the reorganization of the administrative structures. It is also
quite clear that the Hellenists did not restrict themselves to the internal affairs of the church but may have been as active as the apostles in
public preaching. Stephen, the first Christian to be martyred for his
proclamation of the faith, came from the ranks of the Hellenists, and,
in the crackdown on the church that followed his death, the distinctions between the public behavior of the Hellenistic Jewish Christians

and that of the Hebraic Jewish Christians were so clear to the Jerusalem government that the former were forced to leave Jerusalem while the latter stayed on unmolested (ACTS 8:1).

The departure of the Hellenists from Jerusalem seems to have provided the first great stimulus to the mission of the church outside the city and to have brought the church closer to the necessity of defining its future relationship to Judaism. The Bible says nothing about the existence of Christian communities outside of Jerusalem—even in Jesus' home territory of Galilee—before the Hellenist Philip, whom ACTS 21:8 dubs "the evangelist," took refuge in Samaria. On what was apparently his own initiative, Philip converted and baptized a large number of Samaritans and thus presented the church with the problem of integrating them into its Jewish fellowship. ACTS 8:16 insists that, although the Samaritans were baptized in the name of the Lord Jesus, they did not receive the Holy Spirit until Peter and John came north to give their blessing to Philip's activities. There was evidently some concern in Jerusalem about Philip's proselytizing, but it was not long before persons of all descriptions were joining Philip's Samaritans and flooding into the church.

It is not possible to trace the expansion of Christianity in its early years with any precision, but it seems to have moved rapidly. Quite early, a group of Christians north of Galilee in Damascus became large enough to attract Paul's hostile attention (ACTS 9:2). Antioch provided a refuge for some of the Hellenists who fled Jerusalem (ACTS 11:19), and, by the mid-50's, Paul was encountering Christians from Rome (ACTS 18:2) and possibly even from Egypt (ACTS 18:24). Peter is the only original disciple clearly described as active in the mission field, but the records are full of the names of many new persons: Barnabas, Appollos, Silas, Titus, Timothy, Prisca, Aquila, and Mark. Many of these persons were culturally distant from the conservative establishment in Jerusalem, and at least one of them, Titus, was a Gentile.

By the early 50's, it had become necessary for the church to come to some kind of agreement about the relationship between its Jewish and gentile members and thus to take a position concerning its obligation to its Judaic heritage. A meeting was called in Jerusalem; the description of its deliberations (ACTS 15) is not entirely clear. Paul (GALATIANS 2:7-10) seems to indicate that the Council decided to divide the church into a Jewish mission and a gentile one and to place on the Gentiles no Jewish burdens other than a responsibility for contributing to charities in Jerusalem—a Christian form of the old

Hebrew temple tax which may have been intended as a symbolic expression of the unity of the church. Such a plan was not feasible, for many churches must already have consisted of both Jews and Gentiles, and, although Paul expresses shock at the idea, these congregations would have had to split so that the Jews could keep to themselves and maintain their ritual purity and dietary laws. Even Peter, who was certainly very much in favor of the mission to the Gentiles (ACTS 10), submitted to the pressure of the conservative Jewish Christians and departed from the table fellowship of the gentile Christians of Antioch (GALATIANS 2:11-14). Had this kind of program been seriously enforced, it could only have led to increased tensions and the fracturing of the church. There were many who disagreed with it for a variety of quite different reasons. For example, certain extremists insisted that the unity of the church could be preserved only if the Gentiles accepted circumcision and the full burden of the Jewish law before being baptized as Christians, while certain moderates took the position that the Gentiles needed only to adopt as much of the law as required to facilitate their relationship with the Jews (ACTS 15:28-29).

Paul maintained yet another position. In his series of famous letters to his mission churches, Paul opposed any compromise with the forms of traditional Jewish law. He insisted that an acceptance of the validity of any point of the law as a means of salvation was a misunderstanding of the work of Christ. In developing his argument, Paul in effect established a basis for Christianity as a religion that could stand on its own, independent of Judaism. Paul claimed that the law had been given to make men and women conscious of their moral impotency and their sin. The law was a means of revealing man to himself and thus preparing him to accept the further revelation of God contained in the advent of the Messiah. As the Messiah, Jesus brought grace and a new life free from the law and from the hopeless struggle for self-justification. A Jew might continue to observe the law if he wished, but he misunderstood the Christ if he thought that solicitude for the old strictures won merit in the eyes of God or that God limited his grace in Christ to those willing to assume the burdens of the law. The meaning of the messianic event was God's free and loving gift of salvation to men who did not deserve it.

Paul's struggle with the question of the relationship between Jew and Gentile in the fellowship of Christ led him to the clearest attempt in the early church to define Christianity and earned his letters places among the Scriptures. His surviving letters all seem to belong to the period after the Jerusalem conference and are, with a few exceptions, addressed to the churches he pioneered after the conference on the coast of the Aegean Sea. Nothing is known about the means by which the letters were preserved, brought together, and eventually given general circulation in the church. It is certainly clear from the letters themselves that Paul intended them for very particular audiences and was frequently concerned that his understanding of Christianity might fail to establish itself in competition with the interpretations of the faith put forth by other strong and occasionally hostile parties. He was quite obviously not alone in the gentile mission nor fully in control of its program.

The final period in Paul's life has left more traces in the records than his early or middle years. After the Jerusalem meeting, he headed north to Macedonia, where he visited Philippi and then Thessalonica, the provincial capital. Next, he traveled to Berea, to Athens, and finally to Corinth, where he stayed for perhaps a year and a half (Acts 18:11). His last major mission station was on the Asiatic side of the Aegean at Ephesus, one of the largest cities in the empire. From Ephesus he returned briefly to Jerusalem before undertaking a journey to Rome and the West. In Jerusalem, he fell afoul of certain "Jews from Asia" (Acts 21:28), who accused him of profaning the temple and instigated a riot that led to his arrest by the Roman authorities. He was held in custody in Caesarea Maritima for two years and then appealed jurisdiction over his case to Rome. Acts (28:30–31) claims that Paul was sent to Rome and remained active there for at least two years. In his letter to the Romans (15:24), he expressed an intention to work in Spain, and an early tradition of the church, preserved in the letter known as *I Clement,* suggests that he did visit Spain before returning to die a martyr in Rome.

By the time of Paul's death, the Christian church was a firmly established reality which was steadily declaring its independence of Judaism and beginning to make its own way in the world as an increasingly gentile religion. The wars with Rome that devastated Palestine toward the end of the first century significantly weakened the Jewish element in the church, and the non-Christian Jews of the empire clearly proclaimed their desire for a separation of Jew and Christian when in A.D. 85 their rabbis inserted into the synagogue liturgy the prayer "May the Nazarenes and the heretics be suddenly destroyed and removed from the Book of Life."

Chapter Two

The Search for Definition

ENTRANCE INTO THE PAGAN WORLD

A COMPLETE ACCOUNT OF the beginning of the Christian movement will probably never be written, for adequate historical records do not exist. The history of the early Christian church must be derived in large part from the Biblical records and is almost as obscure as the history of Jesus himself, for many similar reasons. The documents that came to compose the Christian Scriptures were not intended by their authors to be objective accounts of the life of Jesus of Nazareth and the activities of his early followers. The writings derived from the preaching of the church and from theological reflection on the messianic significance of Jesus' life and the divine destiny of the community of his disciples. The documents were designed, not simply as records, but as tools to assist the church in its definition of itself and the forwarding of its mission to the unconverted. The four evangelists worked with different traditions about Jesus in different stages of development. As a result, they produced four Gospels that represented the events in Jesus' life in radically different and often incompatible ways. The authors of the Acts of the Apostles, the Epistles, and the Revelation to John—major sources of information about the history of the early church—dealt with their material in the same way and created a similar situation.

The first generation of Christians did not attempt to write a history of their own activities. Its preoccupation was with spreading the word of the Messiah's arrival, and its conviction that his second coming was imminent minimized its sensitivity to a need for historical records and the formal organization of its community. It was felt that not much had to be done to prepare the church for the future, for the future was to be very short. The oldest materials extant from this period are the letters of Paul, and they sometimes give the impression that the church was simply trying to hang on and muddle through for a short time until its Lord returned (1 CORINTHIANS 7:26).

The Pauline Epistles were not written to be histories of the early church, and, although they are primary documents generated by Paul's work in nurturing his mission field, they may be misleading if one uncritically assumes that the situation they depict in a few gentile communities in Greece and Asia Minor was necessarily the universal experience of the church. They say very little about the oldest Jewish Christian congregations that founded the church and even less about the general expansion of Christianity, but they do provide a firsthand glimpse into the lives of some of the churches of the gentile mission—a mission destined to become the mainstream of the Christian movement.

The church in Paul's day seems to have been a relatively formless organization. Paul speaks of the Christian leaders in Jerusalem (James, Peter, and John) as the reputed "pillars" of the faith (GALATIANS 2:9), but the church had no hierarchy of authority that guided his work. He remained in communication with other Christian groups and assumed charitable responsibility for their well-being, but he dealt on his own with the innumerable questions that came up as his churches struggled to work out a policy for Christian life in the secular world. He did not refer questions concerning marriage and divorce or Christian relations with the state to some higher eccelesiastical official or council, but he decided them himself in ways consistent with his own theology and personal tastes. Occasionally, he admits (1 CORINTHIANS 7:25) that his advice is merely his own opinion and is, therefore, not necessarily binding on all Christians, but there appears to have been during Paul's lifetime no structure of authority in the Christian movement that could define a universal belief or practice within the church. Paul knows nothing of a council of twelve apostles serving as an executive board for the church, and, when the opinions of Peter and James and the Jerusalem church come into conflict with his own, he shows no reticence in reproving the older apostles (GALATIANS 2:11).

Paul rests his authority in the church on nothing more nor less than his personal relationship with the resurrected Christ (1 CORINTHIANS 7:40). It was Christ who touched him on the road to Damascus, Christ who entrusted him with his mission to the Gentiles, and Christ who gave him the ability to instruct and discipline converts in their new faith (ROMANS 15:18). Christ ruled the church directly through the persons whom he called to stand forth and assume responsibility for the things that had to be done to maintain a Christian community, and the churches of the Pauline period seem often by preference to have been gatherings of charismatic individuals rather than organizations with clearly defined offices of leadership. Persons simply felt themselves called or inspired to discharge certain functions within the church, and the passion of their commitment was often sufficient credential for the authenticity of their authority. In his letters, Paul does refer from time to time to what appear to have been offices within his church structure. He mentions apostles, prophets, evangelists, pastors, teachers (EPHESIANS 4:11), bishops, and deacons (PHILIPPIANS 1:1), but he never pauses to describe them or define their duties. He creates the impression that the offices were probably not always distinctly differentiated from one another in the organization of his congregations. The ecclesiastical titles in Paul's letters may indeed refer not so much to a clearly defined hierarchy of service in the church as to the spectrum of the kinds of Christian responsibilities or congregational functions generally found within a community. Apostles, prophets, evangelists, pastors, and teachers may simply have been names characterizing different aspects of the church's responsibility for proclamation and pastoral care, and it is conceivable that one person could have discharged more than one of these functions simultaneously or consecutively in the course of his experience as a Christian. The titles bishop and deacon, which mean "overseer" and "servant" respectively, may have been late additions to Paul's Christian vocabulary. Paul's use of these terms may indicate that late in his life the church began to evolve noncharismatic officers to whom were delegated the mundane responsibilities of maintaining order in the worship and charitable obligations of its community. Paul's bishops were not yet the lone monarchical figures of a later generation, who had absolute control over territorial districts, for it appears that there could be more than one bishop in a single congregation (PHILIPPIANS 1:1). Perhaps the bishops were more like a board of elders who were acknowledged natural leaders of their churches. The letter to the Romans (16:1) suggests that women were to be found at least at the level of the diaconate in the early church, and women may have had more authority than the texts show. Paul finds occasion to greet numerous women in the audiences for whom his letters were composed, and women are occasionally noted as owners of the houses in which the church met (ACTS 12:12; 16:40; 1 CORINTHIANS 16:19).

The worship of the Pauline churches may have been as Spirit-dominated and informal as their systems of administrative leadership. Christians who were Jews and remained in close association with the synagogue and temple of their ancestrial religion would not, perhaps, have sensed a strong need for the elaboration of a distinctively Christian ritual. But, as Christians began to find the synagogues closed to them and as more and more Gentiles sought the fellowship of the church, an independent Christian liturgical tradition would have begun to appear. Paul's Christians seem to have met for services of prayer, preaching, study, and hymnody much as the Jews did in the synagogues, but the Christians' experience also included a new element. The meetings of the early church seem to have been replete with manifestations of the "gifts of the Spirit." Prophetic utterance and glossolalia, or "speaking in tongues," were such common phenomena that Paul seems to have been concerned that they might subvert all order and discipline in some congregations (1 CORINTHIANS 14:6–19). Experience with the emotional excesses of inspired persons must have led to a gradual dawning of an awareness of a need for authorities to control and regulate worship services and must, therefore, have contributed to the emerging church's willingness to accept stronger administrative structures.

The characteristic ritual of the early Christian cult was the celebration of a common meal that both memorialized the life of the Christ and provided an experience of the indwelling spirit of the Christian community. The practice of eating a meal together as a religious act was doubtless established as a part of Christian tradition long before its interpretation and symbolism were worked out. It would have been quite natural for cells of early Christians, who seem to have worshiped in each other's houses and to have worked and lived in close association, to share meals in common and to find in these meals an experience of a spirit of fellowship that was of divine significance. In the warmth and security of their relationships with each other, they revived their memory of the Christ and kept alive their own enthusiasm for their mission in his name. Not every church in every place celebrated the meal in exactly the same way or agreed precisely on just which aspects of their faith they were commemorating in it. The earliest celebrations seem to have been normal, complete daily meals that were preceded, in the fashion of Jewish table celebrations, by the blessing and breaking of bread and the sharing of wine. The focus, if one may judge from the enthusiasm of the Corinthians, was on the experience of the joyful reality of the Christian community more than on the memory of the sacrifices of Christ. In fact, Paul finds it necessary to suggest to his churches possible symbolic elements in their practices that would increase the solemnity and meaning of their already established customs (1 CORINTHIANS 10:14–17).

The early church also practiced baptism, but it is not known how the custom arose or exactly what interpretation was generally put on it. The church had before it the example of Jesus' baptism by John the Baptist, but the church's baptism was distinguished from John's as a rite not just of repentance, but for the bestowal of the Spirit (ACTS 18:25; 19:4–6). Paul does not seem to have considered baptism a major part of his personal missionary concern (1 CORINTHIANS 1:17), and the ritual had in his day probably not yet taken on the significance of an initiation or induction into an organized cult. Baptism was probably celebrated by full immersion of the candidate, and the ceremony involved the invocation of the name of Jesus and the laying on of hands by a Christian who had the power to confer the Spirit. There is no Scriptural reference to the baptism of children, and the African theologian Tertullian (ca. 200) suggests that this practice was an innovation of his own generation.

Paul and his contemporaries may well have thought of themselves as the first and only Christian generation, but, as the first century drew toward its close, a sense of the church as a permanent, continuing institution must have begun to develop. As the circle of Jesus' companions began to die off, a younger generation rose to positions of responsibility within the Christian community. The new leaders would have had a sense of Christianity as a heritage—a religious movement with a history older than their own experiences. They would also have had an ardent desire to retain their contact with the memory of the events that had inaugurated the religion they now guided. As the first generation of Christians passed away and took with them the natural authority over the church that their personal association with Jesus had given them, their successors undertook to preserve the original witness to the meaning of the faith and establish a legitimate succession of qualified leaders who could hold the movement on its proper course. It was, therefore, the second generation that was first motivated to acquire documents and develop structures for the church. In fact, the more the expectation of the Parousia disappeared into the future, the more interest Christians showed in their history and their organization. The letters of Paul were collected and circulated; oral traditions testifying to the deeds and words of Jesus were committed to writing in the Gospels; and an attempt was made, in the Acts of the

Apostles, to compile a record of the activities of the first Christians.

Acts is a continuation of the Gospel according to Luke and both books apparently had the same author. Although Acts adopts some of the conventions of ancient historical writing, the book must be seen as a part of the presentation of the Gospel and not as an objective work of history. The book of Acts was, together with its Gospel, an attempt to construct a favorable image for the Christian movement in the gentile world. Acts and Luke presented the church's mission to the Gentiles as an event prefigured in the ministry of Jesus himself, and it aimed at showing how God's ancient relationship with the Jews had now expanded, in Christianity, into a hope for all mankind. In pursuing these polemical objectives, Luke developed a model for the interpretation of the Christian mission that oversimplified the story of the growth of the early church and left many crucial questions unanswered.

Even though Jesus worked most of his life in Galilee and Matthew, Mark, and John report his appearances there after the resurrection, Luke insists that the first Christian church was gathered in Jerusalem. He has nothing to say about resurrection appearances or the inauguration of a Christian movement in Jesus' home district. If Christianity did take its origin from one mother church in Jerusalem, it is not always possible to tell from Luke's account just how the Christian message spread from this center to the other places where he mentions it. Luke claims that, following the resurrection, the original band of Jesus' eleven disciples returned to Jerusalem, elected a fellow Christian to their ranks to bring their number back to the symbolically significant twelve, and then began a mission to the world. In reality, though, Luke only has information about some of the missionary activities of Peter and Paul. He omits mention of the further activities of most of the original apostles. The Jerusalem church, which is described as following the leadership of Jesus' brother James (who was not an apostle), did not take a strong lead in proselytizing outside the Jewish community. Luke implies that the Christian message did not begin to spread to the outside world until the execution of Stephen and the banishment from Jerusalem of the Hellenistic Jewish element in the apostolic church. The Hellenists, who were forced to leave the city for unstated reasons, seem immediately to have turned their exile into an opportunity for missionary work. Philip the Evangelist quickly assembled a group of converts in Samaria, and, by the time Paul received his vision of the risen Christ, there were already Christian communities of note in Damascus and Antioch. The Hellenistic Jews were less strict in their observance of traditional Judaism than Jesus and his Galilean circle, and it was in their churches that the first major attempts seem to have been made to extend the Christian fellowship to Gentiles. Antioch became a major center for the gentile mission, and, at the time of Paul's death, there were churches in many of the cities of Palestine, Syria, Asia Minor, the Aegean, Italy, and, possibly, Egypt. The movement showed its greatest strength in the Greek-speaking eastern portion of the empire and even in the Latin capital at Rome. If one may judge from the leaders' names that tradition has preserved, the church long remained a Greek institution. The early church seems also to have been an almost exclusively urban phenomenon. It was to take so many years for the Christian religion to spread from the cities to the countryside that the Latin word for the rural peasant, *paganus,* evolved into a root for the English word *pagan.*

Luke does not point it out, but one reason for the rapid spread of Christianity among the cities of the empire is to be found in the fact that Jewish communities had long been established in these urban areas. The Jews of the first century were by no means a forgotten people confined in isolation in Palestine. A series of wars and conflicts, which stretched back to 586 B.C. and the Biblical period of the Exile, had scattered the Jews across the Mediterranean world, and they had flourished beyond all expectation in their diaspora. Some scholars estimate that, at the beginning of the Christian period, the Jews may have constituted between 7 and 10 percent of the population of the West, and they were by no means a weak or backward minority. Their religion, deriving as it did from memories of their history as an independent nation, helped them maintain a sense of themselves as a unique people and avoid complete assimilation by gentile cultures. Synagogues appeared wherever there were Jews and provided centers in which the belief in a special Jewish destiny could be kept alive. The synagogues established contact with one another and, after the restoration of the temple in Jerusalem, with the temple leaders, for the support of whom all Jews paid an annual tax. By the time of the birth of Jesus, Judaism was an established religion in most parts of the known world.

The Jews of the diaspora were by no means unwilling to explain their faith to their gentile neighbors and to open their ranks to converts (MATTHEW 23:15). The gentile world, in turn, showed an encouraging degree of curiosity about Judaism. The popular pagan philosophies of the Stoics and Platonists created widespread sympathy for monotheistic religions, and the Greco-Roman of the Hellenistic period seems to have had a virtually inexhaustible enthusiasm for the exotic color of ancient Eastern cults. Learned Jewish apologists, like Philo of Alexandria, were quick to point out apparent parallels between Hebrew and gentile philosophies, and many a synagogue extended a welcome to groups of gentile "inquirers" who wished to associate with Jews in worship and study. The proselytizing efforts of the Jews were visible enough for both Horace (*Satires* I, 4. 142) and Juvenal (*Satires* 14. 96–106) to notice.

Since the early Christian missionaries were Jews, they would have found synagogues in most of the empire's cities prepared to welcome them and provide an audience partially prepared to understand their preaching. In time, as the distinctions between Judaism and Christianity became clearer, these pulpits became closed to Christians, but by then the Christians had established footholds for themselves in important gentile cities. Since many Christians were willing to follow Paul in minimizing the importance of the Jewish law, the gentile friends of the synagogue must often have seen Christianity as a Hebraic religion a bit more sympathetic to their condition than traditional Judaism. Christianity did not require circumcision or obedience to a complicated set of dietary or Sabbath laws, but the faith did offer one a place in the fellowship of the "new Israel." For practical reasons, it was a convenient halfway house between paganism and Judaism, and many a Gentile who had originally set out to become a Jew must have been siphoned off into the new Christian movement (ACTS 8:27–39).

In some places, there must have been intense competition and bad feeling between the synagogue and the church. The Gospels contain anti-Jewish sentiments (e.g., JOHN 19:12–16); the book of Acts records numerous examples of Jewish hostility to Christian missionaries (ACTS 13:50); and the Roman historian Suetonius ("Claudius" 25.4) claims that the emperor Claudius was moved on one occasion to expel the Jews from Rome because of disturbances generated among them by the name of Christ. By the end of the first century, however, the contest was clearly being decided in favor of the Christians. War broke out in Palestine, and, in A.D. 70, the Romans evicted the Jews from Jerusalem and put a permanent end to the temple and its priesthood. Conflict did not cease until the final Jewish struggles against Rome, the bar-Kochba revolts, were extinguished in A.D. 135. By the time peace returned to the Middle East, Judaism had lost its center and whatever sympathetic working relationship it had earlier enjoyed with the Roman state.

The destruction of Jerusalem made a notable impact on the

evolution of Christianity by undercutting the older Palestinian Christian communities, which had long attempted to keep the new religion close to its Jewish roots. The weakening of the Palestinian churches accelerated the development of Christianity as an independent gentile religion. It was not long before Gentiles dominated the leadership of the church, and the formulators of Christian doctrines and rituals began to draw from pagan sources. It was inevitable that the nature of the Christian movement should change somewhat in being translated into a new and partially alien context, but the church was acutely aware of the dangers that threatened it. In order to meet the needs of its new clientele, the church became, in its thinking and behavior, similar to some of the popular pagan cults of its day; but it must have been conscious of the problems involved in deciding when its accommodations to its environment became an abandonment of its basic principles.

The Hellenistic world was replete with strange sects and bizarre religious enthusiasms which mirrored the spiritual tensions and challenges of life in a society that seemed to many to be in imminent danger of slipping out of human control. During the classical periods of Greek and Roman history, when the horizons of nations were limited and the scale of life smaller, Western religions expressed people's confidence that human reason and mundane virtues could provide secure contexts for their lives. But, as the autocratic Hellenistic empires replaced the ancient city-states and as professional soldiers and bureaucrats took over the administration of public life, the individual citizen began to feel overwhelmed by the mammoth institutions to which he made inconsequential contributions. The abilities of human beings, even those of heroic stature, seemed less impressive in the context of the new cosmopolitan world states. Many people therefore began to look beyond the earthly sphere for new kinds of divine power that could offer them special assistance in coping with an increasingly demonic world. The ancient religions of the East provided images of strange and incomprehensible gods that were often more relevant to the needs of the age than the merely superhuman deities of Greco-Roman polytheism. For this reason, Judaism, Christianity, and dozens of other cults found a ready hearing in the Greek and Latin worlds. But there was a danger in the enthusiasm that greeted the new religions, for this emotion often encouraged a naive desire to combine or transcend them and led to a proliferation of odd sects. No tradition was immune from the threat of perversion. The Jews knew radical splinter groups with names like the Herodians, Merists, Hellenians,

Masbotheans, and Sabeans. The Gentiles were acquainted with numerous cults, such as *Magna Mater,* that promoted behavior at odds with classical moral values.

At a very early period, people with unusual religious convictions had shown an interest in Christianity (ACTS 8:4–24), and it must have been very difficult for the Christians to tell their friends from their enemies. The message of first century Christianity had not yet been clearly worked out, and misunderstandings frequently appeared in the attempts made to communicate it. Paul, Peter, and the Jerusalem Christians were a long time in coming to an understanding of the relationship between their Jewish heritage and their Christian faith. When Paul finally solved the problem for himself by proclaiming the end of the law and the sole sufficiency of grace for man's salvation, he was shocked to find that some drew antinomian conclusions from his words (ROMANS 3:8; 6:1–23). The situation became even worse when the church's missionaries attempted to translate their Hebraic Christian concepts into the vocabularies of the gentile religions.

The church was no sooner in existence than its involvement with other religions brought it face to face with compromised versions of its message—in other words, heresies—which distorted or destroyed the efficacy of the faith. Some heresies were so close to orthodox understandings or popular opinions that it was difficult to prevent a few heretical images and concepts from slipping into the vocabulary of the church and influencing the formulation of Christian doctrine. But the church of the early centuries faced up to and rejected at least two of the options that were possibilities for its future development: an excessive enthusiasm which was always a threat but which only emerged as a distinct heresy in the mid–second century in the Montanist sect; and a too easy rationalism that existed in the many varieties of Gnosticism.

Christians of the type who were eventually tempted into the Montanist movement wished to center the faith on the charismatic behavior that prevailed in the early church, and they conceived of the church as a community governed by total spontaneity of Spirit. They did not favor the human appointment of leaders for the church or the definition of rigid doctrines. Instead, they insisted that the church rely for its direction on the continuing revelations of inspired persons. The church had always had a strong charismatic element that had been difficult to control (1 CORINTHIANS 14:4–12; *I Clement*). But a movement that began in A.D. 156 in Phrygia in response to the claims of a certain Montanus forced the church to face up to the dangers inherent in this aspect of its behavior. Montanus may have been a priest of the highly emotional Phrygian cult of the Great Mother *(Magna Mater)* before becoming a Christian. He declared himself, on the basis of his charismatic gifts, the incarnation of the Holy Spirit and the final spokesman for the revelation of God begun in the Old Testament and continued in Christ. Montanus assumed the authority to add to the message of Christ and preached Christianity as an ascetic ethic of preparation for an imminent last judgment. His ideas surfaced an ancient and popular strain in the Christian tradition, and he earned the admiration of important intellectuals as well as the less sophisticated masses. But the church was aware that, if it abandoned itself entirely to the inspiration of the moment, it endangered its continuity with the past and risked a radical departure from the message and work of the historical Jesus. Confronted with that threat, the church came to believe that the revelation of God in the Christ had been total and complete, and it rejected the suggestion that it accept new inspired utterances that differed radically from the apostolic tradition of its elders. The Montanists were vigorous enough to survive as a heretical sect for about two hundred years. The guardians of the orthodox faith, however, were not to be the inspired charismatics, but the properly elected and intellectually indoctrinated clergy.

The Gnostics presented the church with a different kind of temptation which was perhaps not always recognized for what it was or sincerely resisted. Gnosticism derived its name from a Greek word for knowledge, and the movement was distinguished by its claim to provide its followers with secret information from a divine source which awakened them to man's true destiny. Gnosticism, which may have originated before the inauguration of the Christian era, had a long life and an extraordinary appeal for ancient man. It manifested itself in Jewish and pagan forms as well as in Christian heresies, but, until quite recently, little was known about it at first hand. Its scriptures disappeared during the Middle Ages, and, for a long time, scholars could study it only through the arguments advanced against it by its opponents in the Christian church. In 1945, however, in Nag Hammadi, Egypt, archaeologists discovered a cache of Coptic documents that included translations of some of the Gnostic works familiar to the early Christians. Work proceeding on these unique sources should soon disclose much new information on the variety and sophistication of the Gnostic systems.

Many of the Gnostic myths seem to have developed the theme of a supernatural savior who entered the human world in order to reveal to mankind truths about itself that could not have been discovered in any other way. The secret knowledge revealed by the savior concerned the metaphysical description of the universe as well as rites and rituals needed to extricate oneself from the human condition. The Gnostics taught a kind of dualism that sharply contrasted the realms of spirit and flesh and depicted man as a fragment of the divine essence which was alienated from its true sphere and trapped in a world of corrupt matter. The Gnostics saw the creation not as an act of God, but as a cosmic error in which a portion of the divine spirit had become involved in its material opposite. Blinded as the human soul was by its encapsulation in flesh, it remained in ignorance of its true nature and origin until the divine savior broke into the creation and awoke it to self-knowledge. He then gave the privileged circle of followers who had received his revelation a true description of the various levels of being and prescribed secret formulas and rituals that would enable the soul to liberate itself from the bondage of matter and return to the divine essence.

Part of the appeal of Gnosticism lay in the fact that, for all its occasionally outlandish mythology and imagery, it was fundamentally a rationalistic system that reconciled many of the paradoxes of the Judao-Christian heritage. There was no problem of evil in Gnosticism. The world was not created by a good god who then inexplicably allowed it to turn bad; the creation was simply an accident to be recovered from as quickly as possible. There was no mystery concerning the salvation of man. The human soul by right was a temporarily misplaced part of the divine being and simply sought to return to its natural home. On the surface, Gnosticism offered a much clearer and more rational, if less profound, model for the understanding of the human condition than did Judaism or Christianity. And certain aspects of Gnostic myths must have been very appealing to the generally world-rejecting mood that was dominant in the religiosity of the late Roman Empire. The image of the divine spirit of man struggling against the temptations of the wicked flesh seemed as true to the human experience of many Christians as it did to the Gnostics. Paul himself, in his contrast of the radical perversion and total hopelessness of sinful man with the miracle of grace, introduced into Christian thought an opposition between life in the Spirit and life in the flesh (Romans 8:12–17) that might have reminded some of his early readers of Gnostic themes. The church formally rejected Gnosticism and affirmed the Judaic concept of the goodness of the creation and the flesh. But the enthusiasm for extreme ascetic disciplines and for the denial

of the body that became so much a part of Christian practice in the ancient and medieval period seemed at times to give the lie to official orthodox doctrine.

The threat of heresy was both a great danger to the survival of the
church and a healthy stimulus to its development, for the early Christians soon realized that, if they were to survive the distortions of
heresy, they would have to take a firmer hold on their true traditions
and create a more disciplined ecclesiastical organization. These problems of establishing order in the church and defining the distinctions
between Christian and pagan practices tended to dominate the works
of the Apostolic Fathers, the earliest extant noncanonical Christian
documents. The Apostolic literature includes a letter and a sermon attributed to Clement of Rome, a letter by Barnabas, seven letters by
Ignatius of Antioch, a letter by Polycarp of Smyrna and an account of
his martyrdom, a letter by Hermas of Rome, and an early manual on
church discipline known as the *Didache* or the *Teachings of the
Twelve Apostles.* The period is represented also by fragments from the
work of the historian Papias, from the early Apologists, and from a
corpus of Christian poetry.

The *Didache,* which had early dropped from view and was only
rediscovered in 1883, seems to reflect a primitive post-Pauline period
in church organization during which charismatic leaders still wielded
more authority than the bishops and deacons congregations appointed
for themselves. But it shows an acute awareness of the fact that distinctions must be made between true and false "prophets," and it rec-
ommends basing these judgments on the behavior of the individuals
involved. If a prophet stays more than a few days in one place or seeks
monetary advantage from his gift, his message is to be regarded with
suspicion. If he teaches one thing and does another, he is to be driven
off. Or, if his teachings depart radically from the traditions of the past,
he is perhaps not to be trusted—although the *Didache* warns against
the dangers of blasphemy inherent in challenging what might be authentic manifestations of the Spirit.

The problem of order and charisma seems also to be uppermost in
what may be the oldest of the works of the Apostolic Fathers, the letter
of Clement of Rome to the church at Corinth *(I Clement).* The Corin-
thian church had apparently suffered a serious schism in which a
group of younger men had appealed to the authority of their own inspiration by the Holy Spirit and had thrown off the established leadership of their elders. Clement was disturbed by this and cautioned that
peace and order were essential to the life of the church. He distrusted

novelties uttered in the Spirit and advised that the best course for the church was to find its unity and order by maintaining allegiance to properly elected bishops who had received their instruction in the faith from the tradition of the first apostles.

The seven letters of Ignatius, which may come from about the same period, are even more insistent that the church solidify its ranks by increasing the power of its bishops. Ignatius, who was the bishop of Antioch, wrote his letters to the churches of Asia Minor and Rome while on his way to Rome to be martyred for his faith. Meditations on martyrdom as an avenue of salvation are understandably central to his thoughts, but he is also aware of the Gnostic heresy, the pressures of Judaizers, and other threats to the unity of the Christian movement. His great theme is the indisputable need for unity in the church, and he suggests that unity can best be obtained by accepting the leadership of orthodox bishops. Ignatius is willing to go so far as to compare the authority of the bishops to the authority of God himself and to suggest that God the Father might be thought of as a kind of universal bishop (*Magnesians* 3. 1–2). Ignatius of Antioch's vision of the church as a community united in obedience to a fellowship of duly elected bishops would not have been accepted by all of his contemporaries, but it was a vision of the future the church was actually to have. As the threats of heresy, persecution, and internal schism increased in the second century, the church found itself more and more willing to accept the leadership of monarchical bishops and adopt a somewhat legalistic codification of its beliefs and disciplines. The second century saw the emergence of an episcopal hierarchy, a canon of Christian Scripture, the first of the official creeds of the faith, and a customary liturgy.

The evolution of the office of the Christian bishop is extremely difficult to trace in the extant records. The Pauline epistle to the Philippians (1:1) makes a reference to "bishops and deacons" in the church at Philippi, but these people do not appear to have occupied rigidly defined offices. Paul does not make a distinction between clergy and laity, and these bishops, who are addressed in the plural, may simply have been the elders and, therefore, the natural leaders of the church. The book of Acts speaks of the elders of the church at Ephesus as having an episcopal function in that they had been made "guardians" of their community by the Holy Spirit (20:28). At a very early period, however, a distinction seems to have been made between the authority of charismatic leaders in the Spirit—the apostles and prophets—and the more mundane church officers—the bishops and deacons. The *Didache* (15) speaks of congregations appointing their own bishops and cautions against holding these leaders in low esteem because their authority was not of charismatic origin. By the end of the first century, the church had become wary of excesses of inspiration and, in certain congregations, bishops seem to have increased in significance. The New Testament pastoral Epistles, I and II Timothy and Titus, make an attempt at describing an ideal church order, in which each congregation seems to be governed by a bishop with the assistance of a group of elders. But no single system had yet prevailed throughout the church by the time of the Apostolic Fathers. Polycarp of Smyrna makes no reference to a bishop in his letter to the church of the Philippians. In addition, a preeminent episcopal leader may not yet have been established in Rome. Clement of Rome seems to use the terms bishop and elder synonymously; and Ignatius of Antioch, departing from his usual custom and in spite of his strong advocacy of the episcopacy, omits a salutation to a bishop in his letter to the Romans. The "Shepherd of Hermas" also seems to know nothing of a monarchical episcopal office in Rome. By the end of the second century, however, the administrative advantages of a strong episcopacy seem to have made the monarchical bishop almost universal in the church, although in Egypt and parts of the East a more collegiate form of shared authority among bishops and elders may have prevailed until quite late. An ecclesiastical structure of great strength resulted from the combination of the episcopacy with the theory of the apostolic succession, a belief that the teaching authority of the first apostles could be handed down from generation to generation in the church. By A.D. 185, Irenaeus of Lyons was already arguing that there was an apostolic tradition preserved in the teaching of certain bishops—particularly the bishop of Rome because of his reputed connection with both Peter and Paul—and Irenaeus believed the surest defense against heresy was the maintenance of communion with orthodox bishops trained by teachers who learned their faith from the apostles.

The fight against heresy also led the bishops of the second century to approach a consensus on the status to be accorded various popular Christian writings that had come into use in local congregations. For the first few generations, Christians relied primarily on Jewish literature for their Scriptures; but as more and more works of specifically Christian nature came into circulation, some of them began to acquire authoritative reputations. In A.D. 90, a council of rabbis met at Jamnia and defined the official content of the Hebrew canon. They were motivated by a desire to exclude modern documents of questionable orthodoxy and by the need to reorganize and strengthen their hold on their traditions in the wake of the destruction of Jerusalem and the discontinuation of the temple cultus. No comparable Christian council was ever held, but the bishops of the church were similarly faced with a rapidly growing corpus of apocryphal Christian "gospels" and "acts of apostles" which forced them to debate the problem of the definition of a Christian Scripture. The issue became crucial in Rome in the middle of the second century. About the year 140, a Christian by the name of Marcion moved from Asia Minor to Rome and began to take an active part in the life of its church. Tormented by the problem of evil and the difficulty of accounting for the perversion and imperfection he acutely sensed in the world around him, he devised an interpretation of Christ's revelation that totally rejected Christianity's Hebraic heritage. Marcion refused to accept allegorical interpretations of the Scriptures and insisted upon reading the Old Testament literally. He was horrified by the image of God he found there. The god of the Jews was proclaimed good and omnipotent, but he was responsible for a creation that contained sin, filth, and innumerable monstrosities. This god could occasionally be described as showing the moral imperfections of anger and repentance, and there was something of the bully in him in the way in which he pursued and punished human failings. Marcion accepted the Jewish claim that the god of the Old Testament was the god of the creation, but Marcion also asserted that the creator god was a lesser being than the true God of love and grace who had revealed himself in Christ. The god of the Jews, the creator of the natural order, was a weak and evil figure who was not to be confused with the Father of the Messiah. Jesus had come, not to complete the Jewish revelation, but to contradict it by revealing the existence of a merciful and previously unknown Deity who had taken no part in the creation of the corrupt and sinful realm of the flesh. Marcion was convinced that Paul, in his rejection of the law and the forms of Judaism, had truly understood what Christ had preached. Marcion denied the authority of all Christian writings save ten of the Pauline Epistles and the Gospel of Luke—from which he removed occasional "interpolations" by "Judaizers" and the first two chapters, which dealt with the incarnation. The church in Rome excommunicated him, but his interpretation of the faith lived on for centuries in the East and forced the orthodox clergy to take a position on the question of authentic and spurious Christian documents. By the end of the second century, there was widespread agreement on the four Gospels, thirteen letters ascribed to Paul, Acts, and the letters known as 1 Peter and 1 John. Hebrews, James, 2 Peter, 2 and 3 John, Jude, and Revelation remained in dispute somewhat longer, but, by the fourth century, agreement had been reached throughout the church on the twenty-seven items that now compose the New Testament.

With the concern for the definition of Scripture went a desire for the delineation of some elements of Christian doctrine, and the second century church's fight against heresy and its pursuit of unity led to the clarification of some questions and their notation in the first Christian creeds. The oldest of the extant creeds, the Apostles' Creed, was accredited somewhat fancifully by medieval tradition to the companions of Jesus himself. But in reality the kernel of the creed first appeared in Rome about the middle of the second century, and the text developed for about five centuries before it assumed its present form. Many Christians have noted that the Apostles' Creed omits reference to a variety of crucial Christian concerns and is by no means an exhaustive description of the faith. The study of the creed's development suggests that it evolved only as Christians became aware of the necessity of taking positions on specific issues, and it was not put forth at any time as a completed outline of the Christian religion. Creedlike statements can be found as far back in Christian tradition as the letters of Paul (ROMANS 1:1–5), but the oldest extant creed of the church seems to have taken its origin from the formal profession of belief in the Father, Son, and Spirit that a candidate made at the time of his baptism. The creed doubtless served as a summation of the chief points of doctrine he had studied during his catechetical instruction, and it is not too surprising, therefore, to find the creed expanding over the years in areas that came into debate with a succession of heretics. Not all of Christian doctrine could be defined immediately or at one time, so it may often have been the case that an official position was not taken on an issue until a heretic had raised an embarrassing question about it. As the church became aware of objectionable heretical opinions, it clarified its own thought and added phrases to the creed to identify the orthodox position. Thus, the church rejected the Marcionite opinion that the God revealed in Christ was not the god of the Old Testament by inserting into the creed a phrase describing God the Father as the "maker of heaven and earth." Gnosticism, with its dualistic opposition of spirit and matter, was identified as an error by the credal assertion of belief in the "resurrection of the flesh." The creed fluctuated in its form and content with the interests of the church until Christianity triumphed over all its foes in western Europe in the early Middle Ages and serious challenges to its doctrines tapered off.

The move toward a definition of doctrine in the second century was paralleled by an increasing elaboration and standardization of ritual and liturgy. Baptism was no longer informally conferred on recent converts, but periods of instruction and probation of up to three years might be required to qualify a pagan Gentile for admission to the full fellowship of the church. As an interest in the significance of symbols developed, it became customary to administer baptism only on the night before Easter so that the birth of the Christian into his new life might correspond to the resurrection of the Christ. By the end of the century, the rite had been made very impressive by the imposition of fasts, exorcisms, and formal prayers—requirements that may have owed a great deal to the examples set by popular pagan cults. The communion meal of the church was no longer a complete dinner, but had been reduced to a participation in symbolic morsels of bread and wine that had been consecrated in exactly prescribed manners. The eucharist seems to have been thought of as similar to the sacrifices offered in pagan religions, and, if one may judge from the references in Ignatius of Antioch and Justin Martyr, its symbols were quite literally interpreted. The substances offered to God at the altar were changed by him into new materials that literally fused the flesh of those who ate them with the body of Christ. In his letter to the church at Ephesus, Ignatius spoke of the consecrated eucharist as a "medicine of immortality" (20:2) that made the body of the person with which it joined literally a container of the Christ's immortal being, and he drew from that belief vigorous lessons on the necessity of preserving the moral purity of the flesh.

Bit by bit, a cycle of festivals composing a church year also came into existence during the second century. From the earliest times, Christians seem to have worshiped regularly on Sundays in honor of their conviction that Christ rose on the first day of the week. Many had also observed a weekly discipline of Wednesday and Friday fasts that commemorated the Passion and corresponded to similar customs in Jewish tradition. The most important annual festival was Easter, which divided the church year into periods of penitential preparation and joyful gratitude for the gifts of God in Christ. It was not until the fourth century that dates were established to mark the birth of Christ and other significant events in his life. A growing respect for saints and martyrs gradually prompted the addition to the Christian calendar of days memorializing their passions. The first such festival noted in the historical records was established in Smyrna in A.D. 156 in honor of Bishop Polycarp. The extant calendars of martyrs listing official days for remembering the deeds of the saints do not provide many names before the end of the second century and suggest, therefore, that an avid cult of martyrs did not develop much before the third century.

THE STRUGGLE FOR ACCEPTANCE IN THE PAGAN WORLD

BY THE END OF the second century, the church had evolved a powerful organization with regular procedures, acquired a Scriptural heritage preserving the memory of its sources in fixed form, and begun the philosophical explication of its faith. It is possible to argue that the freedom from law and the message of God's merciful gift of unmerited salvation that Paul had proclaimed as the heart of the Christian message had not turned out to be the dominant ideology of the movement. In many ways, the creeds and disciplines that now emerged in the church came to constitute a new law and a new system for earning God's favor. A strict disciplinary code was probably necessary, however, because the Christian religion was involved in struggles with the pagan state and its religions that were to determine the question of the church's survival.

Generations of Christian meditation on the deeds of the martyrs have generated legends that serve piety more than history and distort the record of the persecutions. Things may not have been as bad as has sometimes been assumed. In general, it appears that the official Roman policy on the Christian religion was neither very unusual for its day nor, except in a few instances, a source of universal and enforced persecution. The Roman world was imbued with such religious curiosity and cultic enthusiasm that it became a fertile field for the development of sects of every description, and the polytheistic Romans saw nothing inconsistent in a person professing loyalty to a number of different religions at the same time. Roman mythology filled the environment with spirits of all kinds. There were the *lares* and *penates* who were the guardian gods of hearth and family, the threatening *manes* of the dead, and the encouraging *genii* of the living. The emperor Augustus himself promoted festivals in the spirits' honor in his attempts to strengthen ancient Roman traditions, but, while most households seem as a matter of course to have maintained their shrines, these cults satisfied only the most naive and superstitious level of religious consciousness. Considerably more elaborate and impressive in its public ritual was the worship accorded the great gods of the Greco-Roman pantheon, Zeus-Jupiter and his family and associates. It was to these gods that most of the great temples were raised, and these were the deities who were most visible in Roman art and literature. But the worship of the gods of the pantheon was largely an affair of state-supported colleges of priests who performed their rites on behalf of the entire community, and it was generally felt that Zeus-Jupiter was too remote to heed the religious needs of individuals. For personal religious fulfillment, the Romans turned either to the philosophies of the Stoics, Epicureans, or Neoplatonists or, more commonly, to a great variety of cults known as "mysteries." Some mysteries, such as the Eleusinian rites of Athens, were indigenous to the West. But most of them were imported from the alien cultures of the East. Many derived from fertility cults and used the symbols of birth and regeneration as means for offering their practitioners a hope of immortality. The cults employed elaborate secret rituals which sometimes excited uncontrollable emotions and generated bizarre behavior, but they offered many a Roman a perspective on his life, an outlet for his anxieties, and a sense of his significance as an individual that were most gratifying.

The government of the Roman Empire was tolerant of religious behavior to a remarkable degree—more tolerant, perhaps, than most modern states. But there was a limit to what it would permit, and the Christians were not the first cultists to experience the heavy hand of state regulation. As early as 186 B.C., the Senate had become concerned about reports of antisocial behavior generated in the worship of Bacchus-Dionysos, a new fad that had recently swept into Italy from Greece. Laws were subsequently passed regulating and suppressing the bacchanals (Livy 39. 17. 6). The Egyptian cult of Isis and Osiris occasioned suspicion as a dangerous foreign influence in 58 B.C., and the Senate moved to keep its altars out of the sacred districts of Rome. Augustus took similar action against the popular Egyptian sect again in 30 B.C. Continued governmental anxiety about the weakening of public confidence and the disintegration of traditional ethical values led the Senate to ban philosophers from Rome in A.D. 93 on the charge that they too promoted attitudes of skepticism that constituted a danger to civilization and morality. In 297, the emperor Diocletian imposed penalties on the Manichean cult before moving against the Christians. The Jews were among those who practiced a religion that struck the Romans as unreasonable and potentially dangerous. Exclusive Jewish monotheism, which entailed the repudiation of all the other gods of the empire, seemed hostile to the very basis of the Roman way of life. Attempts were made to induce the Jews to accommodate to Hellenistic polytheism, but the effort proved to be more trouble than it was worth. A compromise was eventually reached in which the Jews were granted their freedom from participation in the state cults and their independence of civic and military responsibilities on the Sabbath in exchange for demonstrating their loyalty to the state by making a daily sacrifice in their temple on behalf of the emperor. But many Romans never developed a sympathy for Jewish customs. The emperor Hadrian outlawed circumcision on the ground that it was a barbaric practice, and the first century Roman historian Tacitus characterized the Jewish way of life as "perverse," "absurd," "squalid," and "disgusting" (*Histories* 5. 5).

When the Christian religion first appeared, the Romans seem simply to have treated it as a species of Judaism. When early Roman historians speak of the practitioners of "Jewish customs," one can never be sure whether they were able clearly to distinguish Christian from Jewish groups. The first persecution the Christians experienced was not from Rome, but at the hands of the Jews. The Jews had good reason to regard early Christianity as a potentially blasphemous heresy within their faith, and they moved quite early to curtail it. Stephen, the first Christian martyr, was stoned by a Jerusalem mob a few years after the crucifixion of Jesus, and the book of Acts claims that it was the threat of Jewish persecution that drove the first Christians from Jerusalem and into the gentile mission field. Tensions between Christians and Jews were not confined to Jerusalem itself: Paul met frequent Jewish opposition to his work in Asia Minor, and Suetonius recorded a disturbance among the Jews in Rome in A.D. 49 that was associated with the name of Christ.

It may have been the tensions within the Judao-Christian community that first forced Rome to distinguish Jew from Christian and adopt a distinctive policy for dealing with the church. At any rate, it was not long before Rome became aware of good reasons for wishing to curtail the expansion of Christianity. The Christians were associated with the Jews, and the Jews had never been the easiest or most loyal of the empire's subjects. Christians were suspect of hostility toward ancient Roman values and customs (ACTS 16:21). Their refusal to participate in the state cult opened them to charges of opposing the political authority of the emperor (ACTS 17:7). And, in some places, the Christians were even held responsible for the economic decline of the empire (Pliny *Letters* 10). Their eponymous founder had been condemned to death and crucified as an enemy of the state. Their millenialism and otherworldliness drew citizens away from the service of their communities. Even more alarmingly, at the very time when the empire felt it needed the unquestioned support of all its citizens, the

Christian church was becoming a worldwide, semisecret organization flourishing within the state and promoting values quite different from those of the state.

Despite these many provocations, it took a long while for Rome to formulate a "Christian policy," and many local actions against the church occurred in the absence of any clearly defined objectives on the part of the state. The first of the famous persecutions of the faith took place in A.D. 64 in Rome in the wake of a great fire that destroyed large portions of the city. The emperor Nero is said to have used the Christians as scapegoats on whom to vent the anger and frustration of the suffering masses. Tacitus (*Annales* 15. 44) reports that brutal spectacles were provided for the people in the emperor's gardens by dressing the Christians in the skins of animals and turning dogs on them, by crucifying them, and by using them as human torches to light evening entertainments. Ugly as the persecution was, it was limited to the city of Rome itself, it was over quite quickly, and it seems not to have led to the promulgation of a permanent anti-Christian policy by the state. One wonders, indeed, if the Christians, by their vivid apocalyptic imagery and their preaching of an imminent end of the world, might not have shown a degree of enthusiasm for holocausts that could have given the Romans some basis for their suspicions.

There are no further indications of moves on the part of emperors against the church until the reign of Domitian (81–96). Some scholars see references to persecutions in the later portions of the New Testament as indicators of conflicts during Domitian's lifetime, but there is no report that the emperor issued a general edict against the Christian movement or undertook any kind of consistent persecution of it. The ancient historians Suetonius and Dio Cassius speak of Domitian's execution of his cousin Titus Flavius and the banishment of his niece Domitilla in such a way as perhaps to suggest that they were punished for association with the Christian movement. But much of the violence of the time must have been the result of local initiatives against the church and not an empirewide policy.

The lack of any such policy can clearly be seen in the letters exchanged by Pliny, the Roman governor of Bithynia-Pontus, and the emperor Trajan between 111 and 113. Pliny was attempting to govern a province in which there were strong tensions between pagan and Christian residents and in which numerous charges of treason and subversion had been laid against Christians. Pliny knew that the emperor had passed general laws prohibiting the meetings of secret societies and he knew that Christians had been brought before the courts in the past, but he was unaware if the simple fact of professing Christianity merited punishment. He wrote to the emperor to ask if it was necessary in addition to prove a distinct crime against society by the Christian under examination and if mitigating circumstances of the age and condition of the offender should be taken into account. The procedure he had developed for himself was to give accused persons three opportunities to recant their faith and then to punish the obdurate on the principle that "they had merited some punishment by their stubbornness and inflexible obstinacy" (*Letters* 10. 96. 3). Pliny was convinced that his leniency had had the desired effect, for he reported that it was common knowledge that services in the pagan temples were again drawing crowds and sales of sacrificial animals were thriving. Trajan approved of Pliny's tactics and simply cautioned that he should neither accept anonymous accusations against Christians nor seek Christians out. If they did surface in the courts on clear charges, then they were to be punished, but the state was not prepared actively to undertake their pursuit.

The attitude of the state toward Christianity was sufficiently ambiguous to encourage a number of Christians to hope that they might be able to reason with the Roman establishment and present their faith in such a way as to win it a degree of intellectual respect and toleration. The early second century saw the inauguration of schools of Apologists, who were the first Christians to attempt to systematize their theology and relate it to the dominant philosophies of their day. Their work was often naive and employed a dangerously misleading vocabulary, but the Apologists were pioneers in the attempt to fuse the best in both the Greek and Hebrew traditions—and there was much that was admirable in their optimistic hope that human reason could obliterate the effects of distrust and superstition. The oldest of the extant Christian apologies is probably a fragment of the work of Quadratus (ca. A.D. 125) preserved as part of the *Epistle to Diognetus,* but the most famous of the Apologists is Justin Martyr, who addressed his arguments to the emperor Antoninus Pius in Rome ca. A.D. 153. Justin spent some time refuting the popular slanders and absurd rumors that circulated among the simpler enemies of Christianity, but his primary goal was to depict Christianity as the culmination of Hebrew prophecy and the completion of Greek philosophy. He developed the image of the Christ as the incarnation of the divine *logos* or "word" that had inspired the Hebrew prophets and the Greek philosophers, and he attempted to convince his readers that the noblest of pagan values were simply early approximations of the truths that had finally been fully revealed in Christianity. There is no evidence that the works of the Apologists were ever read in the circles to which they were addressed or that they had a significant effect on the development of Rome's policy towards Christians, but they are historically significant as indicators of the emergence of a confidence within the church that it could deal with the world in rational terms. The Apologists' assumption that faith and reason are not antagonistic was eventually to enable Christianity to become a vehicle for the preservation and continuation of Western civilization.

There were occasional violent outbursts of anti-Christian activities in scattered sections of the empire during the second and early third centuries. Lyons and Vienne were the scene of a famous persecution in 177, and medieval legends of saints in both the Greek and Latin traditions preserve memories of the deaths of many martyrs in many different times and places. But it is doubtful if much of this persecution was led or encouraged by the central government. The personal attitudes of the emperors toward Christianity seem to have vacillated, and, although the Christian faith may eventually have been legally proscribed (Tertullian *Apology* 4.3-5, 10-11), the government's enforcement of its own law was erratic. Marcus Aurelius (161–80) is remembered in Christian literature as having been harsh toward the church, and the reigns of his successors—Commodus, Septimius Severus, and Caracalla—were troubled with a few outbreaks of persecution. Elagabalus (218–22) was a devotee of Eastern cults, which may have inspired in him a certain sympathy for Christian practices, and Alexander Severus (222–35) was said to have contemplated a fusion of Christianity with other faiths and to have honored a statue of the Christ in his private worship. Some scholars have even interpreted the letters of the Christian theologian Origen to the emperor Philip the Arab (244–49) as evidence that Philip was a professed Christian (Eusebius *Ecclesiastical History* 6. 34. 36).

The private opinions of specific emperors seem, however, to be irrelevant, for, prior to the middle of the third century, the persecution of Christians seems to have been more an affair of sporadic local initiatives than a worldwide policy of the Roman government. It was not until 250 and the reign of the emperor Decius that Rome launched a serious, universal attempt to root out the Christian faith. The project was understandable in light of the political condition of the empire. The Roman armies were slipping out of the control of the government, and emperors were raised up and tossed down by their soldiers with alarming rapidity. The borders were under attack from without, and there were rebellions and defections in key provinces. Decius knew his empire to be in a state of emergency and was disinclined to give benefit of doubt to groups that were less than vocal in their patriotism. The government no longer had the option of tolerating values and attitudes that might detract from its stability, and the Christian church may have seemed to many to constitute a hostile movement lodged within the very heart of the empire. Decius demanded, therefore, that the Christians—together with all the residents of the empire—make a public declaration of their allegiance to the state by honoring the cult of the emperor. The focus of his concern was Christian political loyalty, not Christian theology, but the inability of the church to separate the two and make its patriotism clear without abandoning its monotheistic principles inevitably led to a serious confrontation with the state. Decius's persecution was the worst the church had experienced; under his successors, anti-Christian activities continued fitfully for almost ten years. There were a large number of martyrs who accepted death or torture for their faith and a large number of weaker Christians who broke under the threat of persecution or used devious means to avoid it. In the end, however, the church survived the attack unweakened. There were, by the third century, simply too many Christians with too long a tradition of peaceful association with the state for the movement to be legislated out of existence. The empire was to make one more major assault on the church under the emperor Diocletian in 303, but Decius's failure was a clear indication of the future of programs of eradication and a lesson that Diocletian's successor, Constantine, took very much to heart.

THE VICTORY OVER THE PAGAN WORLD

THE EMPERORS DIOCLETIAN AND Constantine inaugurated a program of reforms that drastically changed the nature of the Roman Empire but thereby enabled it to survive for another century. Diocletian was a career soldier who had risen through the ranks to become commander of the palace guard and who moved from that position to the throne in 284 as the last of the "barracks emperors." These emperors were so named because most of them were creations of the army which had, by the middle of the third century, become completely out of control and overwhelmed the civilian branches of the government. Between 235 and 284, twenty-one emperors were elevated and in most cases destroyed by the troops. Endemic chaos in the central government pushed the Roman economy to the brink of collapse and

encouraged local authorities in Gaul and the eastern provinces to re-
assert their independence. The emperor Aurelian managed to return
the rebels to obedience and restore the territorial integrity of the empire by 274, but the situation was still desperate a decade later when
Diocletian came to power.

It may in part have been the utter exhaustion of the state and the
desperation of its citizens that created a climate of receptivity for Diocletian's program of radical reforms, for Diocletian decreed a wide-
ranging reorganization of the empire that touched practically every
person in it and broke the cycle of rebellions and assassinations that
had rendered the reigns of his predecessors impotent. In order to stabilize the central government and head off struggles for power within
the army, Diocletian issued a new constitution for the empire which
set up machinery for the peaceful transfer of executive authority from
one leader to another and established a new system of civil administration and military command. In March, 293, Diocletian's empire officially became a dyarchy. Diocletian, who assumed the title of
augustus, ruled the eastern part of the empire from his capital at Nicomedia. He granted his associate Maximian the same title and the authority to rule the West from its new capital, Milan. Each augustus
was provided with a *caesar* who served as his second in command and
his designated successor. The caesar was not a son or another relative
of the augustus with a hereditary claim on the higher office. He was
given his title because of his obvious power in the army and his potential threat to the stability of the state. By sharing executive authority
and by enlisting the cooperation of the empire's most powerful men
and putting them on a ladder of succession to the highest offices, Diocletian managed to quiet the military and bring it under control. To
inhibit the emergence of new strongmen, he reorganized the administrative units of the empire to reduce the resources available to
potentially ambitious persons. The provinces of the empire were
broken up into smaller units and their military and civil commands
were divided. The armies were redistributed into small troops of resident border guards or into large mobile strike forces that served in personal attendance on the augusti and caesari. The reorganization reduced local power bases so that they no longer constituted a threat to
the stability of the government, but vastly increased the numbers of
nonproductive personnel who had to be supported by the already
weakened economy. The agricultural and industrial technologies of
the Romans were extremely primitive, and their economy was a minimally productive one that may have required the labor of as many as

six farmers to support one nonfarmer. Rome could really afford only the smallest of governmental bureaucracies and the most modest of armies, but the only method Diocletian could devise to halt the dissolution of the state was to increase the number of people in nonproductive, tax-supported agencies. The result was a financial crisis from which Rome was never really to recover and which was to accelerate the development of the manorial and feudal institutions associated with the approach of the Middle Ages. The ultimate effect of Diocletian's reforms was to preserve the outward form of the empire while distancing its people from the values and lifestyles of classical antiquity and bringing them closer to the radically different social systems that were to dominate Europe for the next thousand years. When Diocletian retired in 305, Mediterranean civilization needed only two more elements to move into its medieval phase: the influx of large numbers of Germanic barbarians and the substitution of a universal Christian religion for the ancient pagan cults. Neither was very far in the future.

It was Diocletian's plan to give the caesar a realistic hope of succession by limiting the office of the augustus to a term of twenty years, and, after two decades of service, he induced his co-augustus, Maximian, to join him in stepping down. The two caesari, Galerius in the East and Constantius in the West, succeeded to the honors of the augusti and appointed Maximinus and Severus their respective caesars. Diocletian's scheme for the transfer of power was rational and fair, but it was not sufficiently realistic to become a standard procedure in the empire. It did not take into account the long tradition of hereditary succession in the Roman government and the problem of the ambition of natural heirs. Diocletian had no son and obvious successor, but Maximian did—and, what was more immediately to the point, so did the new augustus of the West, Constantius. On July 25, 306, a year after his ascent to supreme command, Constantius died. Severus, his caesar, should have succeeded to his office, but Constantius had an ambitious son, Constantine, who shared his father's popularity with the soldiers. The armies in Gaul and England recognized Constantine as their emperor and set off a chain reaction that destroyed Diocletian's constitutional system. Maximian's son, Maxentius, decided that, if Constantine could inherit imperial powers from his father, then he too could put forward a claim to the title of augustus. He induced the soldiers stationed in Rome to support him. Maximian then decided that he had really not wanted to retire, and he attempted to resume the office over which the two younger men were now fighting. Severus, the only man with a legal claim to authority in the West, died in 307, and his Eastern colleague, Galerius, refused to recognize either Constantine, Maxentius, or Maximian as a legitimate successor. He appointed yet a fourth claimant, Licinius, as augustus for the West. For a decade and a half, Rome returned to the wars of succession that had become an all-too-well established part of her political tradition. By 312, Constantine had established control over Rome and the West, but it was not until 324 that he eliminated his last rival and ruled over a united world empire. His prolonged struggle for the succession provided a significant background for his proposals for radical changes in long-established Roman policies.

In dealing with the economy, the military, and the civil administration, Constantine adopted programs much the same as those of Diocletian. But, in one area, he radically reversed the strategies of his predecessor and embarked on an experiment that verged on revolution. Under Constantine, the state ceased to oppose the Christian religion and became its patron. The resulting alliance between the institutions of the ancient pagan world and the values of the Christian movement was of incalculable importance in the subsequent evolution of Western civilization.

Constantine's action was all the more striking in light of the fact that Diocletian had been responsible for the last serious universal persecution of the church. Diocletian's motives for reviving the state's antagonism to the Christian faith after almost forty years of peace are uncertain. It may be that his eager caesar, Galerius, was more responsible for the change in official attitude than he was, for, by the time the first moves were made against the Christians of Nicomedia on February 23, 303, Diocletian was an ailing man looking toward retirement and his wife and daughter may even have been catechumens of the church. Diocletian seems, however, to have had sympathy for the reactionary argument that Rome's future security lay in inducing her citizens to return to the values and religions that had guarded her in the past. He himself took a quite traditional part in the ancient cults and seems to have been somewhat irritated by the religious scruples of his Christian courtiers. His first decrees against the Christians simply excluded them from positions of responsibility in the government and the army, but the persecution quickly turned bloody and became a serious assault on the church. Diocletian retired in 305, and the struggle over the succession that erupted shortly thereafter took priority over persecution of Christians in the western half of the empire. In the East, the new augustus, Galerius, continued the war against the church until shortly before his death in 311, and his successor, Maximinus, maintained a consistent position of hostility toward Christianity.

The policy of the future was to be determined, however, not by the East, but by the West; and in the West the enigmatic Constantine contemplated a radical change. Even in the ancient world, there was no agreement among observers in their estimations of Constantine's motives. The official position of the church was that his conversion was a vindication of the faith and a demonstration of the power of God, but the behavior of some Christian leaders suggests that the effect—and perhaps the intent—of his endorsement of Christianity was to give the church a stake in the survival of the empire and seduce it from its true, otherworldly goals. Modern commentators have interpreted Constantine's policy toward Christianity as everything from an act of calculated self-interest to a manifestation of sincere piety. It may well have been both.

Constantine was not the first Roman emperor to realize that a monotheistic religion was the best and most consistent ideology for the support of an autocratic monarchy. The emperor Aurelian (270–75) had promoted the worship of *Sol Invictus,* the Roman sun god and the patron of Constantine's family, as a symbol for the divine essence that expressed itself in diverse forms in traditional polytheism. Constantine was not the first Roman emperor to flirt with the idea of finding a way to enlist the support of the Christians for the state. A number of members of the Severan dynasty seem to have considered adding the Christian deity to the pantheon of officially recognized gods. But Constantine may have been the first emperor to grasp the fact that it was impossible to legislate an artificially created religion into existence and difficult to blend Christian and pagan beliefs into a syncretistic phenomenon that would win the support of the masses. He may also have sensed that the values of the ancient religions, like those of the simple city-states that had devised them, were anachronistic in his world. The survival of civilization was everywhere requiring the creation of stronger and larger hierarchies of power, and the religion that corresponded to the realities of the day was not that of the chaotic family associations of Olympic deities. It was a religion that emphasized the omnipotent authority and supreme lordship of one godhead.

There does not seem to be much reason to doubt that Constantine was personally convinced of the truth of the Christian religion and considered himself sincere in his practice of it. Tradition has credited his conversion to a miraculous vision that promised him God's help on the eve of a crucial battle, but he may have been favorably disposed toward the church even before that. There seem to have been Christian influences in his home, and his father was remembered for his moderation during the period of Diocletian's persecutions. It is also true, however, that much in Constantine's behavior remained distinctly pagan throughout his life. In part, this may have been due to a certain intellectual vagueness about the requirements of the Christian religion and to a very acute and prudent memory of the fact that many of his subjects had not yet been induced to share his enthusiasm for the church.

One need not assume that there was hypocrisy or inconsistency in Constantine's realization that, in addition to his personal preferences, there might also be political advantages for the state in reversing its policy toward Christians. The persecutions had not worked; if anything, the publicity accorded the church by the witness of the martyrs seems only to have strengthened the Christian movement. There was, in general, nothing necessarily threatening about a strong, worldwide organization like the church flourishing inside the empire if the organization could be induced to lend the support of its unity to the maintenance of the state. Quite fortunately for Constantine, it was also the case that Christians were most numerous in the eastern half of the empire, where a policy of persecution had alienated them from his rivals and predisposed them to assist an invasion led by a potentially more congenial ruler.

Constantine never went so far as to outlaw paganism and establish the Christian church as the only official state religion, but he set precedents that eventually enabled his heirs to move in that direction. His first official pronouncement was the famous Edict of Toleration issued in Milan in 313. It simply granted to Christians equality with the other publicly recognized religions of the empire, freedom to conduct worship, and the return of their confiscated properties. It soon became clear, however, that the emperor wished not simply to tolerate, but to favor the Christian religion. Christian symbols were adopted as standards for the army; Sunday was mandated a day of rest throughout the empire; Christian clergy were granted the same freedom from taxation and community service government officials enjoyed; and legislation took on a Christian moral tone. Gladiatorial combats and bloody spectacles were forbidden by law if not always halted in practice, and new marriage regulations reflected Christian attitudes toward the family and celibacy, which were quite different from the attitudes of the Augustan first century. The emperor made major financial contributions toward the erection of new churches, and, in the year 330, he symbolically marked the refounding of the empire by transferring its capital to Constantinople, a new and thoroughly Christian city he had built on the site of ancient Byzantium.

Constantine's magnificent generosity to the church was not rewarded by quite as much cooperation from ecclesiastics as he might have hoped. There is reason to suspect that the church was not yet in a position to offer the state the unified support and encouragement Constantine wanted. For the first three hundred years of the church's existence, the threat of persecution and a general exclusion from official favor had motivated it to bury its internal squabbles in a common struggle for survival. The result was that, when casually regarded from the outside, the church must have looked a lot stronger and more united than it actually was. No sooner was the threat of persecution lifted and an atmosphere of security provided for the church than ecclesiastical factions, which had long been developing, surfaced and threatened to dismember it. Constantine may have hoped that a strongly united church would contribute an extra bond of unity to his far-flung, unwieldy empire. What he found instead was a religious movement that threatened to disintegrate and add to the potentially divisive tensions of the Mediterranean world. It was necessary, therefore, for him to apply the resources of the state to promote a degree of organization and cohesiveness in the church that went far beyond anything Christian authorities had yet been able to achieve by themselves.

Constantine's first experience with the realities of ecclesiastical politics derived from his involvement with the Donatist controversy. The ink on the Edict of Toleration was hardly dry before Constantine discovered to his surprise that two parties of North African Christians were in dispute over which of them was indeed the true and legitimate church. At issue were questions of standards of discipline to be enforced in the church, of the status of sinners, and of the nature of the sins that could and could not be forgiven. The roots of the quarrel went back at least to a famous confrontation in 251 between Cyprian, the bishop of Carthage, and a Roman theologian named Novatian. In Egypt, a similar dispute had already divided the Christian community in the Meletian schism.

The basic problem that occasioned these tensions in the church resulted from attempts to deal with the success of the Roman persecutions. Not all Christians were courageous martyrs. Some weakened under persecution and denied their faith, and many of these subsequently repented their apostasy and begged to be readmitted to the

Christian communion. The church was not at all sure what it should do about them. Some leaders advised their readmission after a series of more or less imaginative penances; others, who may have paid a very high price for their witness to the faith, were less generous. The Donatist controversy arose because the party of a Numidian bishop, Donatus, refused to accept the consecration of a certain Caecilian as bishop of Carthage. The Donatists claimed that Caecilian's office had been bestowed on him by Felix, bishop of Aptunga, a man who had once denied his faith and thereby forfeited his ecclesiastical credentials. By challenging Caecilian's legitimacy, Donatus raised a crucial point of doctrine that the church had yet to clarify. Donatus argued that an unworthy or sinful bishop forfeited his spiritual authority and could not perform a legitimate act in the name of the church. He charged that Caecilian had been consecrated by such a bishop and therefore had not received true sacramental authority. Only the Donatists had avoided apostasy and preserved the true succession of apostolic power. Only the Donatists now possessed valid sacraments; and the baptisms, ordinations, and consecrations of their opponents were meaningless acts that could not bestow true Christian grace.

Donatus's case seemed morally reasonable, but it contained a hidden implication of far-reaching importance. Donatus seemed to suggest that the efficacy of the sacraments depended in part upon the personal sanctity of the clergy performing them. Donatus claimed that the authority of the church worked through its agents only when they were worthy instruments whose personal faith and moral standards kept them in a state of grace. The church certainly did not want priests and bishops who presented an unwholesome image, but ultimately it refused to accept Donatus's arguments. If Donatus had had his way, the sacramental system of the church would have been severely weakened, for, short of being able to peer into a man's heart with the eyes of God, who could have been sure that the priest who served him was in a sufficient state of personal virtue to mediate a valid sacrament? The orthodox clergy concluded that a priest at the altar acted, not in his own name, but, worthily or unworthily, as an agent for Christ in the church. A priest might himself be a sinner, but, so long as he taught proper doctrine and performed correct rituals, the benefits of Christ entrusted to the church could be obtained through him.

The doctrinal points at issue may not have been of much immediate concern to Constantine, but the Donatist controversy was his first opportunity to experiment with the church-state relations his new policy made possible. It cannot be said that his initial foray into this area was much of a success, but the attempt must have taught him some very valuable lessons in planning his later strategy for dealing with the church. When the Donatists laid their complaint before Constantine, he rightly assumed that it should be handled as an internal affair of the church, and he directed the bishop of Rome to convene a board of impartial bishops from Gaul to resolve it. The board delivered its verdict very quickly, and the Donatists objected that their position had not been adequately considered. The case was heard again by a larger synod at Arles in 314, and, when the verdict again went against them, the Donatists ignored the pronouncements of the bishops and submitted their evidence against Caecilian to the court of the African proconsul. The whole affair put Constantine in a difficult position, for it involved the state more deeply in the strictly religious concerns of the church than was wise. The Donatist material incriminating Caecilian was found to be false. The secular court upheld the verdicts of the ecclesiastical ones and so made the verdicts a matter of state policy and forced Constantine to compel the Donatists to submit. The Donatists were no strangers to governmental pressures. They simply charged that the state was reverting to its old policy of persecution, and they expressed their already well-demonstrated willingness to endure martyrdom. When Constantine found that he could not break the resolve of the Donatists, he flirted with the idea of reversing his decision and enforcing unity in Africa on their terms, but the orthodox party was as adamant as the heretical one. Ultimately, Constantine acknowledged that he was stalemated, and he abandoned attempts to reconcile the two factions. He advised the orthodox leaders to put up with Donatist insults as a kind of moral discipline, an act of self-sacrifice that would be meritorious in the eyes of God; and the Donatist division in the church of Africa continued until the Islamic invasions of the seventh century swept the area into a new faith.

The Donatist controversy taught Constantine something about the limitations of the state in dealing with issues of religious conformity and prepared him to take a more sophisticated approach to the most significant theological dispute of his reign, the Arian heresy. The Arian heresy was technically only a disagreement between an Egyptian priest, Arius (ca. 250–336), and his bishop, Alexander (d. 328), over the interpretation of the relationship of Christ the Son to God the Father. Arius argued that the Father was logically prior to the Son and, even though the Son had been created before the origin of time and space to be the agent through whom the creation was realized, the Son was himself a creature of the Father. Bishop Alexander objected to the radical subordination of the Son to the Father as a serious demotion of the divinity revealed in Christ. Alexander argued that Father and Son were coeternal, for one could no more be a father without a child than one could be a child without a father.

The debate concerned underlying issues more important than those that appeared on the surface and provided an opportunity for the emergence of serious differences of opinion that had long been fermenting in the church. At the heart of the discussion lay different understandings of the fundamental Christian hope of redemption, for the church of the early fourth century had not yet come to an understanding of what salvation meant and how it was achieved. The categories of thought popular at the time suggested that the answer was to be found in understanding how the human condition was related through Christ to the Godhead. Opinions on this question ranged between two extremes. Some Christians assumed that the redemption of man was the result of a miraculous metaphysical deification of human nature that occurred when true humanity and full divinity fused in Christ's incarnation. Others, of a more philosophic or even Gnostic bent, understood redemption to be an enlightenment and a liberation of spirit from flesh that resulted from Christ's appearance in the human world. The first position was premised on the assumption that Christ was fully man and fully God—else there could be no true fusion of total human nature with a reality that could guarantee it immortality. The second position was less physical and more rationalistic in its imagery. It conceived of Christ as a kind of special messenger who brought saving knowledge from God or performed a saving act on his behalf. It was not necessary for the messenger to fuse with the material world so long as he was visible in it by some means, for salvation lay, not in the transformation of the flesh, but in escape from it. It was also easier to avoid compromising the monotheism of the Christian religion if Christ were represented as an agent of God and not as his equal.

The understanding of redemption as a miraculous union of full man and full God in Christ was philosophically difficult, but it was an attitude that might have emerged quite naturally from the sacramental life of the church. Many Christians seem to have believed that a union was achieved between God and a communicant by means of the consecrated elements of the eucharist. The coming together of God and man at the altar was simply an extension of their association in Christ. Because Christian experience was more influential than theological abstraction in the philosophically unsophisticated West, the theory of redemption that postulated an incomprehensible union of the human and the divine had its most vocal supporters there.

The first major theologian to work in the West was Irenaeus of Lyons (ca. 130–202), who had been trained in Smyrna in the school of the Apostolic Father Polycarp, but who had become bishop of Lyons in Gaul in 178. Irenaeus was deeply concerned about the popular Gnostic heresies of his day, and he authored a refutation of their teachings. In this work, he attempted a clarification of orthodox faith. Irenaeus believed that God's intent in his act of creation was that man should mirror God by being perfect and thus share in the immortality that was a part of God's "image." Unfortunately, human pride had inspired a misuse of free will, and this abuse had deprived man of a true relationship to himself and to God. Hence, it was necessary for God to remake the creation. In Christ, God became a second "Adam" who did for man what man had failed to do for himself: he lived a perfect life that achieved the goal of creation and the deification of the human. The resurrection was a seal set on Christ's life to clearly demonstrate that his human nature had become immortal, but the real locus of the act of redemption was the incarnation. In this event, the created world fused with the divine and began its return to God. Irenaeus boldly proclaimed that God had become man so that man might become God through participation in the reality of Christ in the sacraments and fellowship of the church. Irenaeus and his followers could not accept any theory that suggested that Christ was not fully God, for then there could have been no union in him of the human and the divine, no deification of man, and no redemption.

Irenaeus's understanding of orthodoxy was consistent within its own presuppositions, but it failed to handle some philosophical difficulties. It simply posited the meeting of the radically different natures of God and man in Christ without explanation of how this could be possible without the obliteration of the human, and it equated the Father and the Son to such an extent that one could ask if there was any meaningful distinction between them. The West does not seem to have been seriously disturbed by philosophical problems, for Tertullian (ca. 145–220), the major Latin spokesman after Irenaeus, was quite content to admit that incomprehensible paradoxes lay at the basis of the Christian faith and that philosophy was helpless to explain the higher truths of theology. Tertullian was a pioneer in the creation of a technical vocabulary for Latin theology, and he delighted in the formulation of definitions that sharply pointed out the paradoxical meanings of theological concepts.

In the East, where the Greek philosophical heritage was stronger, fewer Christians were content with a position of pious ignorance, and more sought a rational explanation of the Christ. The Arian heresy was preceded by a long tradition of debate and disagreement over understandings of the mechanism of salvation and explanations of ways in which faith in Christ's divinity could be reconciled with the logic of monotheism. Serious problems were often raised by attempts to understand the doctrine of incarnation. Some felt that, literally interpreted, it was an absurd idea, for it suggested a confusion of the totally different realities of Creator and creation and produced an intolerable paradox by representing Jesus, a historical person limited by time and space, as the omnipotent, infinite Other. The Adoptionists solved the problem for themselves by teaching that Christ was simply a historical being who had been taken over by God to be an agent of his revelation. There was no "ingredient" of the divine combined with his humanity. The Docetists approached a solution from the other side by asserting that Christ only appeared to be a historical being and that he was always and only fully God. His humanity had been an illusion that facilitated communication with mortal men, but it was not essential to his being. The Modalistic Monarchians, who were also known as Sabellians or "Patripassians," held that there literally was no difference between the Father and the Son and that the names given them simply applied to the actions of one God in different contexts.

Arius's dispute with Bishop Alexander brought all these issues to a head and involved in open debate many of the hostile factions that had long been forming within the church. Their arguments were not the result of inconsequential hairsplitting, for the resolution of the conflicts required nothing less than reaching agreement on the understanding of the Christ, an agreement that would literally define Christianity and determine the adequacy of the religion the church would sponsor. Before Constantine, there had been leisure to conduct the debate slowly and to wait for a consensus to emerge from the results of numerous local discussions. But Constantine's endorsement of the Christian faith elevated Christianity to the status of the favored state religion and put it in a different context. The church was no longer a loosely integrated charitable fellowship of the faithful that survived precariously on the edges of society. The church was now called to be the Church, an integrated institution paralleling the state, wielding wealth and influence, and promoting one true religion for the good of the empire. If Christianity were to fulfill the proffered role of the religion of Western civilization, a decision had to be made about what Christianity was.

The church was probably not as well prepared to make that decision as Constantine had at first assumed. He realized, however, that if the church were to make its contribution to the unification and preservation of the empire, there was no question about the necessity of resolving its internal disputes as quickly as possible. The Donatist controversy had shown how difficult it was for the state or for local synods to deal with ecclesiastical factionalism; so when the Arian problem was called to Constantine's attention in 324, he developed a new strategy. The difficulty was that the church had no pope or other figure having authority corresponding to Constantine's position in the state and with whom Constantine, could cooperate in policing ecclesiastical order. Therefore, after a few unsuccessful attempts to deal with the Arian conflict as a local affair, Constantine issued an order designed to create a whole new structure of authority in the church. The recognized leaders of the church were the bishops, who in the past had disciplined the church and determined its policies by meeting in synods and expressing a common opinion that was weighted with the respect due their offices. The Donatist controversy had taught Constantine that local synods composed only of the bishops of a limited region did not always inspire sufficient awe to compel the obedience of dissident factions. Therefore, he proposed a universal synod, the first of the general councils of the universal church, to debate and resolve the Arian conflict. If the council represented all the bishops, there could be no appeal from its verdict to another body, and if it made a determination in the Arian case, the state could enforce religious conformity on the basis that it was acting as an agent of the church and not as an alien persecutor.

Constantine's theory worked better than his practice. In May of the year 325, some 250 bishops invited by the emperor met at Nicaea near Constantinople to share in determining the will of the church. The Council of Nicaea claimed to represent the entire church, but few bishops attended from the western districts of the empire. The bishop of Rome was not present, but he was represented by delegates. Eusebius of Nicomedia led the Arian party, and he quickly discovered that the majority of his colleagues were not in favor of Arius's assertion of an absolute distinction between God the Creator and Christ, his "son" by a special act of creation. But it was equally true that most of the bishops had some sympathy for Arius's charge that his opponents' position equated the Son with the Father and smacked of the heresy of the Sabellians, which denied all meaningful distinctions between the two.

The theological context for the discussion at Nicaea had been established almost a century earlier by the work of the most influential teacher in the Eastern church. Most of the bishops at the conference were in one way or another students of the thought of Origen and were committed to his theological vocabulary. Origen (ca. 184–254) had been a native of Alexandria whose precocious intellect had won him official recognition as an instructor of catechumens by the time he was eighteen years old. His relations with the bishop of Alexandria became strained, and in about 230 he moved to Caesarea, where he taught until his death during the Decian persecution. Origen stood in the tradition of Clement of Alexandria (ca. 150–215), the earliest known theologian of the Alexandrine school. Clement had taught that pagan philosophy, like Hebrew prophecy, was a lower level revelation of God that served to prepare man for the reception of Christ. He believed that philosophy could be quite appropriately fused with Scripture to obtain a fuller understanding of God. Origen employed an allegorical interpretation of the Bible in order to bring Christian images into line with the Neoplatonism that was the dominant philosophy of his day. He seems to have thought of Christ as a kind of Neoplatonic "emanation" from the absolute essence of God. To Origen, Christ was the "idea" containing all the individual particular concepts realized in the creation. Christ also represented the first of several levels of being that descended from God to the level of the human soul and ultimately to that of the inanimate material world itself. The distinctions between what was God and what was not God were not clear in Origen's fundamentally pantheistic system; so it was not surprising that he seemed sometimes to equate the three hypostases, or "subsistences," of the Godhead and at other times to subordinate the "emanated" Son to the Father.

The Eastern theological tradition consequently had no vocabulary that could make the distinctions that seemed to be called for by the Arian debate. Thus, while the council had little trouble in agreeing on the rejection of Arian extremism, there was great uncertainty as to how far the majority would be willing to go in defining an orthodox position. The determination they finally made and the creed they issued from the council probably owed more to pressures applied by the emperor than to clearly perceived theological convictions. Constantine was not a bishop. He had not even been baptized, for he followed a popular custom of his day and delayed reception of the church's most powerful cleansing sacrament until he was on his deathbed and beyond the likelihood of additional opportunities for sin. Constantine technically had no right to engage in the council's deliberations, but he was its host and he was the emperor. Few seem to have raised an objection, therefore, when he proposed that the council add the term *homoousia* to its creed and assert thereby that the Son was "of one substance" with the Father. A term equivalent to *homoousia* had long been in use in the Latin portion of the church, and Constantine's Western advisors may have suggested the wording as a step toward harmonizing Greek and Latin views. The emperor's suggestion seems to have taken the council by surprise or intimidated it, and, since the word had no clear technical definition, it was difficult for anyone to raise specific objections to it. Each delegate seems to have decided to interpret the word in a fashion congruent with his personal opinions and to leave it at that. Constantine was gratified by the bishops' willingness to cooperate, and the council adjourned with only two bishops dissenting from a creed that rejected the Arians by asserting that the Son was "begotten," but not "made" as were creatures, and that identified as orthodox the opinion that the Father and the Son were "of one substance."

The consensus reached at the council of Nicaea was more apparent than real, and the remainder of Constantine's reign was spent in a perpetual struggle to make the council's platform work as a basis for unity in the church. The emperor's primary interest was not theology, but peace; so it was not difficult to convince him, on the basis of a cleverly worded statement of faith, that Arius and his friends ought to be forgiven and returned to communion. Constantine seems to have been unaware of any deviousness in the Arians, and he found their conciliatory attitude more congenial than the hard line taken by their Nicaean opponents. The result was that the Arians steadily rose in influence with the court, and the orthodox party led by Athanasius, Bishop Alexander's successor, found itself in increasing disfavor. The government exiled Athanasius from his diocese in Alexandria five times during his career (328–73). Arius, however, remained in Constantinople until his death in 336. A year later, when Constantine lay dying, the emperor finally accepted baptism—at the hands of Eusebius of Nicomedia, Arius's champion at Nicaea.

In the years following Constantine's death, it became clear that the Nicaean Council had failed to find a position that satisfied the whole church. Constantine's three sons divided his empire into thirds, but the death of the eldest in 340 restored the older dyarchical system. Constantius, who ruled the East, continued the pro-Arian policies he had inherited from his father. His brother Constans in the West followed his subjects in their ardent support for the Nicaean formula. The Arian cause was greatly encouraged in 350 when Constans died and the whole empire was reunited once again under Constantius. New synods met and advocated abandoning Nicaea and all discussion of the "substance" of the Father and the Son. New creeds were advanced that simply asserted that the Son was "like" the Father. They had little success, for the Eastern clergy were generally not Arians. They disliked the Nicaean term *homoousia,* which they felt obscured the distinction between Father and Son, but they had no desire to follow the Arians in a radical subordination of the Son to the Father. Consequently, sympathy developed for a middle ground that used the word *homoiousia* to suggest that the Son was of "like substance" or "equal substance" with the Father. This position avoided the implication of identifying one with the other, and it made it easier also to account for the place of the Holy Spirit in its relation to both the Father and the Son—a question that was destined in its turn to push Christian factions into opposing camps.

Constantius died in 361 and was succeeded by his cousin Julian, whose reign was both short (361–63) and anachronistic. Julian's youthful experiences had left him with a low opinion of Christians. His Christian relatives had murdered one another in cold blood in their maneuvers for control of the empire, and the conduct of the Arian and Nicaean factions had suggested that no very high standard of honor was to be found among the leaders of the church. On assuming the throne, Julian announced that Constantine had made a mistake in supporting the Christian movement, and he resolved to abandon Christianity and replace it with a revived, purified paganism. His artificial religion failed to capture the popular imagination, however, and he died of battle wounds in 363 without having seriously weakened the position of the church.

His successor, Jovian, ruled for only one year, but he had time to restore the relationship between the empire and the Christian religion. He was followed by Valentinian I (364–75), who divided the empire with his brother Valens (364–78). Valens was sympathetic toward the Arians, but their star was now clearly descending, and the emperor's support seems simply to have solidified the ranks of their opponents. Valentinian's son Gratian succeeded to the whole empire at Valen's death in 378, and he appointed an experienced general, Theodosius (379–95), to rule the East. At Gratian's death in 383, Theodosius became the last man to wield effective rule over the whole empire. He was a Spaniard by birth and a westerner in his religious orientation. In 380, he completed the Constantinian revolution by establishing Christianity as the only legal religion in the empire and by defining it as it was defined by the Nicaean party and the Roman west. By 392, the shoe was completely on the other foot, and the government had begun the active persecution of obdurate pagans.

Arianism was still not entirely eliminated. It declined within the empire but had a vigorous existence for another century in the territories of the German barbarians. The Arian form of the Christian religion had been mediated across the Danube frontier as a part of the dominant Roman culture of the fourth century. An Arian named Ulfila (ca. 310–83) translated the Scriptures into the Gothic tongue, and missionaries carried the faith with great success to the Visigoths, Ostrogoths, Vandals, Burgundians, and Lombards. The result was that, with the major exception of the Franks and Saxons, most of the barbarian groups that broke into the empire in the fifth century were already Christians—although of heretical persuasion. Once settled in the empire, they were outnumbered by the orthodox Christians of the West and either assimilated or converted. By the seventh century, Arianism was largely a thing of the past.

The triumph of the Nicaean formula in either its moderate or extreme form set a certain perimeter for future discussions of the Trinity, but it failed to provide a basis for ecclesiastical unity. Old debates simply shifted their ground and continued to divide the church on new questions. Now the problem of salvation was discussed, not in terms of the relation of the Savior Son to God the Father, but in the context of understanding the redemptive relationship of the human to the divine in Christ himself. By the fifth century, the West was in serious decline and had little leisure for philosophical debate. But the eastern half of the Empire retained its balance well into the seventh century, and there great Christological controversies continued to divide the church and disrupt the state. The most popular heresy of the East was that of the Monophysites. They argued that, while Christ might be conceived as taking his origin from the two different natures of the human and divine, as one being he could exist only as one "nature." That one "nature" seemed to the opponents of the Monophysites to be too intensely divine to take into account the reality of the human in Christ, and they advanced different theories. The Nestorians, for example, seem to have taught that the two natures of Christ were metaphysically independent but worked together in perfect harmony. The Apollinarians maintained that Christ's human nature was not complete but was a kind of outer body vivified, not by a human soul, but by the word of God. The Monothelites theorized that the divine and human in Christ were linked by one common divine will. At times the distinctions and modifications must have seemed infinite in their variety. The disagreements had to be taken seriously, however, for theological positions were often fused with nationalistic loyalties and political ambitions. Parties in the church became a basis for revolutions in the state, and the eastern empire struggled for years to enforce order or find a middle path between orthodox and heretical positions. A famous general council met at Chalcedon near Constantinople in 451 to discuss the Christological problem, and it ended by endorsing as orthodox faith the traditional western opinion that had been spelled out by Pope Leo I (440–61) in his *Tome,* or letter, of June, 449. Its creed ignored the philosophical questions raised in the East and simply asserted that Christ was one person with two distinct natures that were neither confused, diminished, nor distorted by their association in him.

The work of the councils and the compromisers failed to unite the church, but ultimately outside influences created in the Christian movement a degree of homogeneity it had not been able to acquire for itself. In 638, Jerusalem and Antioch fell to Arab invaders; Egypt was taken in 641; and, by 711, Africa was no longer Christian territory and Spain was under attack. The portions of the Christian world that were most disrupted by the heresies fell prey to the expansion of the new Moslem faith, and, while the cost to the church was tremendous, the rise of the Moslem empire cut off the worst of the Christian dissidents and guaranteed that the future of the Christian movement would lie in the hands of the orthodox parties in Rome and Constantinople. The struggle against heresy was not over, and it was not totally to be deplored. The church of the early medieval period had still not worked out all the implications of its faith, but the prodding and exploration of the heresies had brought it to set important limits to its speculations. These limits helped preserve and protect essential mysteries of the faith.

Chapter Three

The Great Synthesis

SURVIVAL

IN 395, THE EMPEROR Theodosius was succeeded by his two sons: Honorius, who assumed control of Rome and the West, and Arcadius, who ruled the East from Constantinople. During the reigns of these two brothers, the defenses of the empire finally gave way, and the barbarian peoples who were destined to dominate the future of Europe won the lands that their descendents still control. There had been breaches of the imperial frontiers and territorial retrenchments before the generation of Honorius and Arcadius. As early as 270, the emperor Aurelian had abandoned a province north of the Danube, and it had long been a policy to admit barbarian tribes to the empire as allies in its defense. But in the fifth century, mismanagement by the government produced the collapse of the precariously balanced systems that had maintained the empire's security.

Some of the causes of the empire's difficulties lay far beyond the control of the Romans themselves. The stabilization of the frontiers of China in the fourth century diverted the attacks of the Huns westward and increased pressures on the Germanic barbarians who were Rome's neighbors. About 372, the Huns overwhelmed the Ostrogothic tribes of the Crimean area and occasioned panic among the Visigoths, who were their next logical target. The Visigoths fled westward toward the Danube frontier of Rome and, in 376, received permission from the emperor Valens to cross into the empire as its allies. Valens may have had good motives for acceding to the request of the Visigoths for sanctuary. It would have required a major military effort to keep them out, and, with the Huns on the horizon, it was wiser to seek friends than to generate unnecessary enemies. The admission of the Visigoths to the

empire proved, however, to be a serious mistake. Valens herded them
into refugee camps, but, when his government was unable to provide
them with the necessities of life, they became resentful and suspicious
of the intent of the Romans. In 378, they broke in desperation from
Roman control and went on a rampage. Valens attempted to stop
them near Adrianople and lost his life in the struggle. His successor,
Theodosius, managed to restore peaceful relations with the victorious
tribe—at the cost of recognizing their continued existence in the empire as an independent nation and allowing them a relatively free
hand in the crucial Balkan territories which bridged the East and the
West.

Theodosius's sons Honorius and Arcadius mismanaged the Visigothic situation and greatly increased the vulnerability of the empire
to barbarian invasion. Shortly after Theodosius' death in 395, the
Visigoths, under the leadership of a vigorous young king named
Alaric, began to put pressure on Constantinople. Arcadius responded
by adopting the easy, but shortsighted, policy of encouraging the Visigoths to migrate westward and seize a place for themselves in the
lands of his brother Honorius. Alaric invaded Italy, and, although he
was promptly repelled by Honorius's general, Stilicho, the openness of
Italy to Visigothic attack panicked Honorius. He withdrew to the obscure Adriatic coastal city of Ravenna, which had protective swamps
and easy access to escape by sea, and made it the last capital of the
western empire. The need for a stronger army in Italy to counter the
Visigothic threat caused Stilicho to pull troops away from the Rhine
frontier, and, during their absence in 406, large groups of Vandals,
Sueves, and Alans crossed into Gaul with little difficulty.

In 408, Arcadius died, and Honorius, fearing Stilicho's ambitions
in the east, had his general assassinated. The West was temporarily
left without a strong military leader, and Alaric pressed his advantage
by again invading Italy. Honorius did nothing for the defense of the
peninsula, and, in 410, the Visigoths made good an often repeated
threat to sack the city of Rome. The damage to Rome was not extensive. The Visigoths subjected the city to three days of looting—in
which they as Arians seem to have respected Christian sites—and then
moved on from Italy into Gaul and Spain. Emotionally, however, the
sack of Rome, the symbolic center of an empire that had been held to
be invincible, was a shock felt by every civilized person in the ancient
world. It was becoming more and more apparent that a new age had
dawned and that new powers were beginning to dominate history.

In the East, the empire went on without serious disruption. The

West bore the brunt of the barbarian incursions, and it declined much more rapidly than the East in the level of its civilization. The ghost of a legitimate Roman government lingered in Italy until 476, when the puppet emperor Romulus "Augustulus" was deposed and the title allowed to lapse. The barbarians who came to power in the West were not inimical to ancient Roman culture, and some of them made significant attempts to preserve it. Theodoric the Ostrogoth, who dominated Italy from 493 to 526, was the patron of the scholars Boethius (ca. 480–524) and Cassiodorus (d. 575), whose Latin translations served Western scholars of the Dark Ages as their major access to the treasures of Greek philosophy. In general, however, the barbarians simply were not equipped to continue sophisticated Roman administrative systems, and, although significant pockets of learning and high culture survived in a few places, the general level of society sank to a new and much lower common denominator.

By the year 500, the only surviving Roman emperor, the ruler of Constantinople, had lost contact with fully two thirds of the lands that had once been subject to his office. It took a long time for the Eastern government to reconcile itself to the fact that the West was gone. The emperor Justinian (527–65) devoted his reign to an effort to reconquer Italy, Africa, and Spain. He had some temporary success, but the long-range effect of his policy was to exhaust the resources of the East and visit such devastation on Italy that it fell easy prey to the incursions of the barbarian Lombards in 568. Constantinople maintained a foothold in Italy in the exarchate of Ravenna until the middle of the eighth century, but by that time most westerners had come to believe that the Christian church, not the empire, was the protector of European civilization.

Politically, the West succumbed to a degree of fragmentation from which it never fully recovered, and the only ancient institution that survived with any claim to imperial universality was the church. But the church, too, was exposed to the pressures that had dismembered the empire, and it succeeded only partially in achieving the unity Constantine had envisaged for it. The political division of the world between barbarian conquerors and the Byzantine emperor created a situation, that was quite difficult for the church, for its members were thenceforth to be drawn from vastly different and frequently antagonistic cultures. The moral leadership of the West slowly devolved on the bishop of Rome, whose see profited from the prestige of its control of the capital of the ancient empire. The Roman bishop maintained his ties with the past and continued for a long time to think of himself as a part of the Roman tradition represented by the court in Constantinople. But the unity of the church was ultimately lost under the strain of the cultural and political differences that separated the East from the West.

The early medieval Christians of Constantinople were spared the necessity of adjusting to a radically new world of barbarian customs and probably thought of themselves as simply carrying on the unchanging ancient traditions of the church. But in reality, by the fifth century the Christian religion of the East had already become a phenomenon clearly distinguishable from the faith and practice of the West. As contacts with the West diminished in the wake of the barbarian invasions and as the Byzantines sensed the cultural decline and intellectual inferiority of their western neighbors, the differentiation of Eastern from Western religious traditions accelerated. As might be expected, the two branches of Christianity achieved a de facto independence long before their leaders formally admitted that the unity of the church had been broken.

Because the cultural evolution of Constantinople went on without radical interruption, its Christian theology continued to center on the questions and concerns raised in the Trinitarian and Christological controversies. But Constantinople's separation from the West caused its religion to become more and more strongly influenced by ancient Eastern attitudes. Eastern Christianity became at one and the same time a highly sophisticated philosophical system, a radically ascetic repudiation of the world, and a lavish liturgical drama that used all the wealth and splendor of the material realm in the worship of a radically "other" God. Generally speaking, the East tended to stress the divinity of Christ at the expense of his humanity and thus to minimize the importance of the historical world. The religious heroes of the East were the ascetic saints who aimed at living a life that was "inhuman" in its material supports. The lavish churches of the East were designed to depict an environment not of this earth. And the Eastern clergy in their meditations dealt with problems and distinctions that concerned a world of other than human experience.

Byzantium produced a version of the Christian faith that was intensely mystical and philosophically subtle, but that tended to be less involved with the practical conduct of daily life than was the less sophisticated faith of the Western church. In Constantinople, the church became a department of the state with delegated responsibility for supernatural affairs. It was an extremely important and powerful branch of the government, but it was subsumed under the control of the emperor and integrated into his policies. It had little independence from its cultural and political milieu and seems often to have served more to implement imperial programs than to originate them. No figure comparable to the Roman pope emerged in the East. The patriarch of Constantinople claimed the title "ecumenical," or "universal," bishop and gradually acquired administrative authority over the Eastern clergy, but he lacked the political independence of the Western papacy and was forced to share some of his sacred charisma with the emperor. Following Constantine's example, the emperor assumed that his imperial office was divinely established, and he claimed ecclesiastical responsibility that often superceded that of the patriarch. This situation prevented the East from developing the polarity of church and state that proved in the long run to be so invigorating for the West.

The decline of the imperial government in the West was a serious inconvenience to Western Christians and a threat to their security, but in the long run it provided their church an opportunity to develop a strength and independence impossible in the East. In areas of the West, the church declined drastically or even disappeared. The Anglo-Saxon invaders seem to have rooted it out of England; it weakened along the Rhine and Danube frontiers; and Arian barbarians challenged orthodoxy in Africa, Italy, Spain, and Gaul. But many bishops managed to strike up livable relationships with the barbarian leaders who dominated their dioceses and eventually to bring them into the church. By the end of the sixth century, the Suevi and Visigoths of Spain and the Franks and Burgundians of Gaul were converts by choice or conquest to the Catholic faith, and, although centers of pagan and Arian resistance held out, it was clear that the West would share one common orthodox Christian faith.

The cultural and political confusion of the West did much to enable the Latin church to escape the caesaropapism of the East. Many Western bishops were temporarily assimilated into the power structures of their secular lords. But the West had no one supreme leader who could make this system permanent and universal, and there was in the bishop of Rome a figure who created a unique option for the organization of Western Christianity. Constantinople had always resisted recognizing the "primacy" of Rome in any but the vaguest and most honorific of terms, but the West had early accepted papal leadership. During the crucial period of the barbarian incursions, the popes managed to establish their independence of the new secular lords of the West and to profit from the fact that the Eastern emperor was too distant to do more than occasionally intervene in papal affairs. The papacy moved in the direction of becoming an independent Italian nation with a claim to universal spiritual authority, and the support it was able to give the scattered European bishops was enough to enable them to retain a memory of their loyalty to a church that was more than the religious dimension of their new states.

Primacy in the Western church was not a right the Roman bishop had always enjoyed from the foundation of the see. Rome had to acquire the prerogative slowly and arduously over a period of many generations. As early as the end of the first century, Pope Clement established a useful precedent by taking it on himself to write to the church at Corinth and advise it on the conduct of its internal affairs; but his letter was more an act of fraternal admonition than an edict of a governing authority. Other bishops in other sees did much the same thing. The relatively small and simple primitive church seems to have governed itself adequately by the informal gestures of aid and admonition that local congregations were willing to make in pursuit of the common good. As the church grew and as the threat of heresy became apparent, the Christian movement developed a need for more sophisticated means to achieve unity and preserve discipline. Bishops began to conduct the affairs of the church by gathering together in formal meetings known as synods or councils. The earliest of these convocations may have taken place in Asia Minor in the second century in connection with the Montanist heresy. The first major council in the West met at Arles in 314, and the great convention at Nicaea in 325 was the first universal gathering of Christian bishops.

The struggle against Arianism tended in the long run to diminish the authority of councils, for it occasioned the convening of too many of them—and all too frequently they adopted frankly partisan positions. Consequently, the fifth century was motivated to explore more centralized systems of government and showed an increasing interest in the development of hierarchical (a word that may have been coined by an anonymous fifth century author known as Pseudo-Dionysios) administrative structures for the church. There was no problem in establishing precedence in a hierarchy for the West, for, in addition to the prestige of residence in the ancient capital of the empire, the Roman bishop was the only Western leader who could claim apostolic foundation for his see. As early as the second century, Irenaeus of Lyons (ca. 177) had expressed the opinion that all churches had of necessity to agree with the faith as it was taught in Rome, for Rome's links with the origins of the Christian movement were stronger than those of any other church in the West. Gradually the idea took hold that the Roman bishop had no equal with whom he had to consult in determining doctrine, and, by the middle of the fifth century, Pope Leo I (440-61) was fully prepared to assert the papacy's independence of the decrees and deliberations of all church councils. The East was not as easily convinced of the validity of papal claims as the West. The Council of Chalcedon (451) identified five "patriarchal" sees of comparable authority: Jerusalem had been the scene of Christ's sacrifice; Antioch had been founded by Peter before his work in Rome; Alexandria claimed Mark, the companion of Paul; and Constantinople had irresistible eminence as the seat of the empire. Persistent heresies and the rise of the Moslem Empire gradually reduced the effective patriarchies to two, Rome and Constantinople, and the real struggle for supremacy was between them.

The theoretical underpinnings of the case for the Roman bishop were worked out by the end of the fourth century. The case rested on the establishment of a link between a particular theory of apostolic succession and a favorable exegesis of a crucial passage in the Gospel of Matthew (16:18-19). The idea of the apostolic succession was an ancient one that may have had its roots in Jewish traditions of hereditary priesthoods, but it is not clear exactly how the early church thought that it worked. There may have been tendencies in some places to think of apostolic authority as a heritage passed down in certain families whose ancestors had been associated with the foundation of their churches. Some communities may have seen apostolic authority as a corporate possession of the colleges of priests and elders that perpetuated themselves as the leaders of congregations by acts of election and appointment. This may have been the case in Rome until the third century, when the opinion began to be voiced that apostolic power was the possession, not of the elders, but only of the properly elected bishop, who received it as an inheritance from his predecessor. There were unfortunate early periods of disruption and controversy in the history of the papal succession—most notably the schisms occasioned by the competing claims of Cornelius and Novatian (ca. 260), Damasus and Ursinus (366), Boniface I and Eulalius (418), and Symmachus and Laurentius (498)—but the line of legitimate heirs was always held to be clear. This was of great significance, for at least as early as the reign of Damasus I (366-84) the claim was being advanced that the popes were the only legal successors to the absolute spiritual powers that the Gospel of Matthew reports that Christ bestowed on Peter. According to Matthew, Christ singled out Peter and said, "And I tell you, you are Peter, and on this rock I will build my church, and the powers of death shall not prevail against it. I will give you the keys of the kingdom of heaven, and whatever you bind on earth shall be bound in heaven, and whatever you loose on earth shall be loosed in heaven" (MATTHEW 16:18-19). The Roman bishops insisted that these powers were not intended for Peter alone but were an endowment for the church and passed down as a legacy to Peter's legitimate episcopal successors in Rome.

Papal claims to authority were often far in advance of papal ability to wield it, but a few of the early popes managed to set valuable precedents from which their medieval successors were able to profit greatly. Pope Victor (189-99) issued a ruling fixing the date of Easter and presumed to excommunicate whole regions where traditions of which he did not approve were perpetuated. His successors encouraged dissident Christians to appeal to Rome when they were dissatisfied with the decisions of local synods. Pope Leo I (440-61) boldly instructed the Council of Chalcedon in the correct Christological doctrine to endorse for the church, and he refused to be a party to any discussion of the matter. Pope Gelasius (492-96), during a temporary schism between the Eastern and Western branches of the church, asserted that papal authority was the spiritual equivalent of imperial power and that the pope and emperor were independent officers created by God to care for the separate sacred and secular concerns of human society. The inherent superiority of eternal, sacred goals to transitory, secular ones left little doubt, however, as to whose councils should prevail in the dyarchy of pope and emperor.

The effective exercise of papal authority often depended more on the fortuitous assistance of uncontrolled circumstances than it did on a hard core of real power, and, when it came to open conflict between pope and emperor, the pope was often humiliated. When Pope Silverius refused to accept certain compromises that the government in Constantinople wished to make with the Monophysite movement, the emperor Justinian deposed him (537) and replaced him with a more compliant figure. In 653, a disagreement over the theory of "the one will" in Christ's two natures inspired the emperor to have Pope Martin I arrested and carted off to prison in the East, and Gregory II was threatened with the same fate in the early eighth century when he refused to heed Emperor Leo III's edict against the veneration of images in Christian worship.

Ultimately it was the evaporation of the imperial government from the west which enabled popes to move the church into positions of independence and self-determination. But even the strongest popes of the medieval period fell far short of achieving the kind of raw political and military power that could challenge a monarch on his own ground. The most effective popes were those who were able by diplomatic maneuvers to influence delicately balanced situations and exploit the occasional vulnerabilities of secular leaders.

It was during the reign of Pope Gregory I (590–604) that the papacy first distinguished itself in providing leadership for Western society. Gregory was a member of the Roman aristocracy who had had a career in the service of the state before liquidating his family property and retiring to a monastic retreat. By 579, he had been induced to leave the monastery and assume the responsibilities of a papal legate in Constantinople. Eleven years later, he was elected pope by spontaneous popular acclamation. The situation he faced in Italy was desperate. The Byzantine attempt to regain control of the West had failed, and the last vestige of effective imperial government in Rome had faded. Chaos in the administration of the city threatened, and no army stood between it and the marauding Lombard tribes. As pope, Gregory was master of what may have been the largest single landed estate in Western Europe, and this resource enabled him to charge the administrative machinery of the church with responsibility for the maintenance of the functions of Roman civil government. He organized the defense of Rome and dealt as head of state with the Lombards. He fed and policed the populace, and he laid the groundwork for the independent nation that the Middle Ages would know as the "papal state." Gregory was well aware, however, that he was more than simply the protector of Rome: he was the ruler of the church. He successfully represented papal claims in Constantinople, and, during the period of greatest confusion and decline in Western Europe, he kept the bishops mindful of their connection through him with the universal church. He was extremely active in correspondence, giving whatever advice and assistance he could to the scattered Christian leaders who were coping with the task of adjusting to new and barbarous conditions. His sermons, essays, and letters spoke so directly to the concerns of the Dark Ages that they became classics of Western Christian literature.

In a way, Gregory's papacy looked backward as well as forward. Gregory conducted himself as an independent ruler with responsibility for both sacred and secular affairs, but he continued to think of himself as a member of the Roman Empire with ties to Constantinople. The division of the East and the West was not yet complete, and Rome was not yet prepared to commit itself exclusively to the Germanic peoples and nations that were to emerge from the ruin of the Latin West. An alliance of the papacy with the barbarian governments had to wait on the outcome of a massive missionary effort designed to Christianize the new Europe and inspire in it a respect and enthusiasm for the orthodox leadership of the Roman bishop. Gregory himself took a lead in the proselytizing of the barbarians in 597 by dispatching a team of Roman clergy to convert the pagan Anglo-Saxons and return the Christian religion to England—one of the few provinces of the old empire in which the barbarian invasions seem to have almost completely wiped out the church. In the long run, however, it was not the papacy that rebuilt European Christianity. The popes gave valuable encouragement, provided some resources, and attempted to coordinate efforts, but much of the work of preserving and extending the Christian movement was performed by monks acting on their own initiatives.

The early medieval period has been dubbed the age of monasticism, and the monastery was, in addition to the papacy, one of the most significant institutions to survive the collapse of ancient civilization and provide a basis for the revival of European Christian culture. The monastic movement had its origin in an impulse to flee the world in pursuit of spiritual goals—a desire that has surfaced as an expression of sincere religious conviction in many different faiths. The Greeks knew hermits devoted to the service of various gods; the Jews produced isolated religious communes like the famous groups of Essenes at Qumran; and Paul's letters suggest that Christianity from the very beginning included ascetic elements that favored monastic disciplines. Ignatius and Justin Martyr report the existence of groups of Christians within the church of the second century who formally renounced their sexuality, but most of these people seem to have been enthusiasts who freely elected to practice extra disciplines while remaining within their parishes and family homes. It was not until the fourth century, when Constantine had halted the persecution of the church and made the world nominally Christian, that a major monastic flight from society took place. In part, it was fueled by devoted Christians who wished to use a lengthy ascetic martyrdom of their flesh as a witness against a world that no longer provided the option of a sudden and bloody gesture in the arena. In part, it was encouraged by the progressive collapse of a society and a culture that to many must have seemed bankrupt and beyond reclamation.

Tradition credits the origin of the Christian monastic movement to fourth century Egypt and associates the movement with a wave of enthusiasm for the hermetic life generated by a certain Anthony of

Coma (d. 356). Anthony's biography was written in the 360's by Athanasius, the bishop of Alexandria who was deeply involved in the post-Nicaean controversies, and it circulated widely as a kind of model for other ascetics to emulate. Anthony was a simple, probably illiterate, man who chose a life of total isolation and spiritual concentration. His heroic acts of self-denial won him the respect of others and a reputation as a worthy spiritual advisor. He spoke out on occasion against the Arians, but his real contest was a private struggle with the impulses of his own flesh. He provided an ideal that appealed to his age, and, by the end of the fourth century, his type was not uncommon in the East.

A famous hermit occasionally found his life impeded by its own success, for his reputation attracted others who wished to live near him and study his example. The result would, of course, be an impairment of his isolation and the appearance of a need for some social organization and group discipline. The transformation of the monk (the word *monk* literally means "solitary") from a hermit into a member of a specialized religious community was effected by Anthony's contemporary, Pachomius of Tabennisi. Pachomius (286–346) was a military man who converted to Christianity and retired to the desert in pursuit of total isolation. After several years, he found himself the leader of a group of disciples, and his responsibilities inspired him to improvise a communal life that would assist them toward their spiritual goals. By the time of his death, he had founded nine similar communities for men and two for women, and he had pioneered a form of religious life that was destined to sweep the Christian world.

There were many reasons for the popularity of communal monasticism. The monastery provided a stable environment in which concentration on spiritual objectives was facilitated by a group effort. Communal organization enabled ascetics to provide themselves with the services of priests and the sacraments of the Christian life, which were not easily available to the isolated hermits of the desert. It provided a style of life that, although rigorous, had much to recommend it when compared with the disastrous conditions prevailing among the lower classes of the secular order. And monasticism was a vocation actively promoted by the church, which early discovered that the cloister had advantageous uses. The lone "saints" of the desert were often unlettered men of doubtful orthodoxy whose spiritual feats gave them great influence over the people and who were difficult to police, train, or hold within the bounds of sound doctrine. Once they were brought into a monastery, however, they could be kept under observation by trustworthy clergy and properly educated. In addition, their religious enthusiasm could gain an outlet that would not threaten the stability of the church. Throughout the Middle Ages, the church used monasteries as safety valves: religious communities were places in which reformers and charismatics could exercise extraordinary religious impulses without endangering the unity or peace of Christian society.

The monastic movement in the East began to have an influence on the West during the last half of the fourth century. Athanasius, whose see was in Alexandria, spent several years in exile in the West at Rome and Trier, and he did much to publicize the exploits of the Egyptian ascetics. Jerome (340–420), the translator of the Latin, or Vulgate, version of the Scriptures, was an ardent Western advocate of monasticism who was particularly noteworthy for his successful conversion of wealthy Roman women to ascetic disciplines. Ambrose (340–97), the powerful bishop of Milan, actively promoted monastic values and may have had some influence on Augustine of Hippo's decision to live in a monastic context. Augustine, who came to his Christian faith while a member of Ambrose's circle, was the most important of the Western church fathers and the theologian whose thought dominated much of the medieval period. His responsibilities as bishop of the African diocese of Hippo prevented him from living a life of total monastic isolation, but he organized his episcopal household in a semimonastic style that had great influence on the subsequent ordering of the lives of the European parish and cathedral clergy.

The first true monastery founded in the West may have been that of Martin of Tours (316–97). Martin was a Roman soldier who gave up his military career in order to live as a Christian hermit. About the year 360, he established in Gaul a monastery that gained great fame. It was followed, in about 400, by a house at Lerins and another at Marseille. The model for monastic life in these communities was Eastern. In fact, John Cassian, founder of St. Victor's in Marseille, authored a series of descriptions of the activities of Eastern ascetics, and these writings became the major literary source of inspiration for the development of European monastic life.

The West did not begin to find its own unique expression of the monastic impulse until the sixth century, when Benedict of Nursia appeared. Benedict (480–574) abandoned his life as a student in Rome in order to become a hermit in a cave at Subiaco in the valley of the Anio River south of Rome. His success as a spiritual mentor attracted followers and led him eventually to organize a community at Monte Cassino near Naples. For the government of his house, Benedict produced a "rule" or constitution which, although it was not entirely original and relied heavily on earlier sources, contained a simple, usable description of a monastic life superbly adjusted to Western sensibilities. The Benedictine rule may not have had much influence outside Monte Cassino for at least a hundred years after Benedict's death, but, by the ninth century, it had caught on and become the standard monastic model in use throughout Europe. The goal of the Benedictine life was not the practice of the extreme ascetic renunciations that were the hallmark of Eastern monasticism. The monastic disciplines favored by the East produced ascetic athletes who vied with one another in devising bizarre specialties. Some claimed to subsist for a year on a handful of figs; some spent decades standing alone on the top of tall pillars; others exhausted themselves in the repetition of formalized acts of prayer and physical prostration. The Benedictine monk, however, lived a strict but balanced life that had its harsh restraints but sustained his human strength so that he could use it in acts of prayer and intercession. The monastery was a community devoted, not to the extreme repudiation of the flesh, but to the maintenance of a perpetual round of services of divine worship. During a day that lasted from 2:00 A.M. until sundown, the monks met seven times in their chapel to repeat their prayers and hymns, and the purpose of their existence was simply the service of God in worship and the betterment of their society through acts of intercession and charity. The monastery was in concept a refuge from the world, not a social service agency or a settlement house. But it dealt as generously as it could with the needy who came within its reach, and it soon took on functions that were of incalculable worth in the effort to maintain civilized Christian life in Europe.

In order to insure its independence from the world and its freedom from secular concerns, the monastery had to become a self-sufficient community. If it could produce within its own walls everything it needed, it would be spared the dangers and distractions of dealing with a society that focused on other than spiritual objectives. Benedict decreed, therefore, that his monks should spend time each day in physical labor for their own support. He also realized that a degree of literacy was required for the conduct of the full service of God and that it would be necessary for his followers to provide themselves with schools, libraries, and time for education. The Western monastery thus became a self-perpetuating oasis of economic and intellectual order in the midst of the collapse of the secular institutions of the Roman Empire. The members of its community were almost alone in enjoying the leisure and resources needed for the perpetuation of the skills and materials basic to civilization. In the exercise of their religious duties, the monks thus unself-consciously made themselves into bridges between the culture of the old Roman world and the new medieval one.

There was some fault to be found with the monk as a transmitter of culture, for his interests were often too narrowly religious to allow him adequately to appreciate the worth of the ancient secular literary heritage that lay in his keeping. Much material failed to recommend itself to him and ceased to be recopied and preserved. The literature that survived was perpetuated primarily for the contributions it could make to the study of Christian doctrine or toward the acquisition of the literary skills needed for Christian scholarship. But the achievement of the monk in clinging to the treasures of the past was nonetheless impressive. Western institutions other than the church completely lost their hold on the tools of civilization, and, when Europe finally stabilized and reorganized itself for the next phase in its development, its literature and its schools had become predominantly ecclesiastical. For centuries, literacy remained a defining characteristic of the clergy, and European civilization and the Christian movement flowed in one common channel.

New Beginnings

NOT ALL EARLY MEDIEVAL literature was simply a repetition or reiteration of the opinions of the past. In the midst of the panic and confusion of the early fifth century, the Christian movement was able to inspire one of its most fertile and original commentators. Augustine of Hippo, whose life (354–430) spanned the period of the major barbarian incursions into the empire, became the most famous of the Western church fathers, and his opinions carried an almost Scriptural authority in the medieval schools. Augustine had been born in a Roman Africa that was basking in the afterglow of a brilliant pagan tradition. His mother was a Christian, but, as a youth, he identified himself with the philosophies taught in the schools where he prepared himself for a career as a rhetorician. His progress toward the Christian faith was a slow and painful one which he mapped meticulously in a unique autobiographical study known as his *Confessions*. In the *Confessions,* Augustine described how he enthusiastically embraced in turn each of the popular pagan ideologies of his day until, after careful study, he discovered their internal contradictions or their inability to answer crucial questions. For a while, he was very strongly attracted to the dualistic cosmology of the Manichaeans, and, even after his conversion to the Christian faith, the emanational metaphysics of the Neoplatonists had a strong influence on him. His writings—including the monumental *City of God*—were frequently called forth by a need to respond to specific questions or challenges, and, since his thoughts changed and developed during the course of his battles, he is not an easy thinker to reduce to a simple, consistent system.

Augustine attempted to develop an understanding of the Christian faith that would closely follow the Scriptures and be true to his own personal experience of God's grace. For him, the Christian religion was not simply a philosophy or a collection of propositions to which one gave intellectual consent; it was saving knowledge—a deep form of understanding and acceptance that worked a more than intellectual transformation of one's life. Many of Augustine's opinions on the nature of Christian salvation came to light in his disputes with various spokesmen for the Pelagian heresy. Pelagius (d. ca. 420) was a Briton whose attention was primarily given to moral philosophy. He strongly supported the monastic movement, and he devised a theory of grace and salvation that he thought provided an adequate basis for the strenuous Christian moral endeavors of the monks. Pelagius seems to have felt that moral precepts and admonitions and the vigorous disciplines of the monastic life made no sense unless they earned the person who performed them some credit in God's judgment. Such acts would be unworthy of praise, however, unless they were the result of real moral options that lay open to all men. Pelagius suggested, therefore, that sin was a completely voluntary action, not an inherited characteristic, for no moral responsibility could be imputed to an agent who did not have true freedom to assent to his own actions. Every person at every moment, Pelagius thought, had the chance to choose the good; those who did so were rewarded with salvation, and those who did not were damned. Augustine was wary of Pelagius's ideas, for, while they provided a rational basis for moral behavior, they also reduced divine grace to God's automatic response to and reward of human virtue. They represented Christianity as nothing more than a new form of the Jewish law—a new system for earning salvation. That seemed to Augustine to be a denial of the Scriptures and of his own Christian experience, for the events surrounding his conversion had convinced him that salvation was impossible without grace and that grace was a totally free gift from God. No one could deserve or earn it by acts of moral discipline; no one was good enough to be beyond the need for it and for the intercession of Christ. Augustine himself had spent many years in the active pursuit of virtue and faith, and his endeavors had convinced him only of man's inability to achieve moral worth. Virtue was more than the external actions that lay under human control; faith was more than a voluntary intellectual assent to certain theological principles. Only when Augustine had come to the end of his own striving and acknowledged his complete impotence did he receive a revelation that assured him he had been freely reconciled by grace with God in spite of his own unworthiness. Only then did he accept baptism and feel confident in counting himself among the Christians.

Pelagius did not have a very extensive dialogue with Augustine, but he had students and followers with whom the bishop of Hippo carried on a long debate. Augustine may occasionally have overstated his case in his eagerness to make his points, for numerous church leaders were as wary of his position as they were of Pelagius's. Augustine represented the human lot in such extreme terms of depravity, original sin, and moral helplessness that some Christians feared he might undercut all motive for human moral striving. Why should anyone labor to be good if man were totally lost, totally perverted by inherited sin, and saved only by an unmerited gift of God's grace that was bestowed, not according to degrees of human worth, but as an expression of the mysteries of an incomprehensible divine predestination? If all human actions were perverse and none led to salvation, why would anyone struggle and sacrifice to achieve a useless illusion of moral worth?

Augustine's radical predestinarianism troubled many of his contemporaries, and attempts were made to define more moderate, "semi-Pelagian," positions. But ultimately, the church decided that Augustine, like Paul, had come close to describing one of the essential mysteries of the orthodox faith. Somehow Christians had to make room in their thought for both the freedom of God and the freedom of man, for salvation by grace and for the pursuit of the redemption of the creation through responsible human labor. The simultaneous assertion of divine and human freedoms might lead to a paradox, but it was a paradox that accurately characterized one of the central convictions of the Christian faith. The tension between God's grace and human responsibility was irresolvable in simple rational terms, but it was a tension that worked creatively in human history.

The centuries that followed Augustine's death produced no thinkers who could rival his originality and profundity. The noted scholars of the period were compilers and translators like Boethius (d. 524),

Cassiodorus (d. 580), and Isidore of Seville (d. 636). They pulled together collections of ancient literature that served as the basic textbooks of Western Europe until the twelfth century, but the achievement of these scholars was more often one of preservation than one of original creation. That fact does not suggest, however, that the Christian community was moribund during the period of the early Dark Ages. In places, the church must have been even more active than it had been during its period of relative security in the late empire. But now its interests were focused, not on heresies and intellectual pursuits, but on the conquest of a staggering new mission field. The Arian and pagan tribes that inundated Europe were clearly to dominate its future, and the church could survive as a part of that future only if the Germanic barbarians were brought to accept the orthodox Christian faith.

Historical records do not preserve a complete account of the process by which Europe was reconverted in the early Middle Ages. The massive proselytizing effort of the Dark Ages seems randomly to have combined the conscious policies of the papacy, the personal spiritual quests of certain monks, and the vast informal influence of the native Romano-Christian populations. The leaders of the vital mission to the barbarians came from some very surprising corners of Europe.

Ireland, one of the last areas to receive the Christian faith before the final collapse of the empire, early became one of the most important bases for the mission movement. The chronicle of Prosper of Aquitain suggests that there was some papal interest in the conversion of Ireland in the early fifth century, but credit for the success of the mission seems to belong almost completely to the initiative of one man, Patrick of Armagh (ca. 389–461). Patrick was born in England of a Christian family but, at the age of sixteen, was kidnaped and carried off by a group of Irish raiders. He remained in Ireland for about seven years before escaping to the Continent and coming under the influence of the Eastern ideals of the Gaulic monasteries. He returned to Ireland in the 420's as a missionary bishop and had tremendous success in spreading the Christian faith. The Irish were a tribal, not an urban, people, and they tended to organize their church around rural monasteries, not city cathedrals. The abbot emerged as the dominant leader of the Irish church; many bishops were subservient members of cloisters and had responsibility only for liturgical and sacramental functions. The Irish monasteries received their Christian literature and their instruction from Continental monks who stood in the Eastern tradition. Therefore, Irish monasticism was distinguished by a certain ascetic harshness, and Irish learning preserved a memory of the Greek language long after it had disappeared from the Continent.

By the sixth century, the Anglo-Saxon invasion of Britain had pushed the remnants of Celtic Christianity into the mountains of Wales, and the Irish conceived an interest in a mission to their new pagan neighbors. In 563, a monk named Columba established a cloister at Iona on the western coast of Scotland and began to work among the Picts. In 635, one of the Iona monks received an invitation from the English king of Northumbria to found an Irish cloister at Lindisfarne, and Irish Christian influences began to be felt in the heartland of Britain.

The sixth century was not a healthy one for the Christian churches of the Continent. Christianity had survived and Arianism had been overcome, but the level of Christian learning and moral discipline had declined distressingly under the pressure of strong barbarian influences. The dominant political power on the Continent was the Merovingian dynasty of the Salian Franks. Under their king Clovis (d. 511), they had begun to pull together a state that reunited the Gaulic districts the barbarian invasions had torn apart. Clovis, a pagan by birth, married an orthodox Christian of the Burgundian tribe and accepted baptism himself in 496; but Christian influences were not very strong at the Merovingian court. The educational institutions of the church weakened, the literacy of the clergy diminished, and there was a considerable barbarization of Christian society. A turning point was reached, however, about the year 575, when an Irish monk named Columban crossed the English Channel and undertook to revive the Gaulic Christian community. He attempted to inspire a stricter monastic discipline and authored a rule that reflected the uncompromising authoritarianism of the Irish cloisters. He attacked the morals of the Merovingian court in an effort to reform society from the top down, and his invectives eventually led to his expulsion from Gaul. He ended his life in northern Italy after having inspired the foundation of as many as forty new mission monasteries.

The influence of the Irish monks was in part augmented and in part opposed by the missionary activity of the papacy. In the year 597, Gregory I sent a team of monastic missionaries to England. They managed to establish themselves in the southern district of Kent, and their leader, a certain Augustine, became the first archbishop of Canterbury—the capital city of the kingdom of Kent. The papacy poured considerable resources into the English mission and succeeded in giving the English church intellectual traditions and educational systems that ranked among the strongest in Europe. The Roman and Irish versions of Christianity soon came into conflict in England, for long years of isolation from Rome had allowed the Irish to evolve liturgical practices and organizational customs different from those favored by the papacy. The differences were considered significant at the time, but they proved not to be fatal to Christian unity. At the synod of Whitby in 664, the Irish agreed to abandon England to the Roman mission, and, by the end of the seventh century, northern Ireland had accepted papal jurisdiction.

The Anglo-Irish-papal Christian institution was the strongest in Europe, and, for several generations, it provided the educated people required to extend and elevate the practice of the Christian faith on the Continent. During the late seventh century, it was sufficiently vigorous to support serious attempts to extend the Christian religion beyond the frontiers of the old empire into districts where it had never been. About the year 690, Willibrod, a monk of the English monastery of Ripon who had also had some training in Ireland, located at Utrecht and began a mission to the Lowlands. He received papal support for the establishment of a series of dioceses in the territories he opened up, but the natives of the area seem to have identified him with the imperialistic objectives of the Frankish monarchy and to have accorded him only a very limited success. Much more impressive was the achievement of Willibrod's young associate, Boniface, a product of the English monastery of Nursling. Boniface (ca. 680–754) spent a brief period assisting Willibrod in Frisia, but the bulk of his life was spent working in the German territories east of the Rhine. The popes Gregory II and Zacharias and the kings Charles Martel and Pepin the Short backed his efforts, and, in 732, he became an archbishop with authorization to organize sees from Utrecht to Bavaria. He attempted also to reform the Frankish church, and he played a significant part in the political negotiations of the papacy with the Frankish monarchy. By the time of his martyrdom in Frisia in 754, he had established a chain of powerful monasteries throughout Germany, and the Saxon tribes of the north were the only Germanic peoples who remained temporarily outside the influence of these institutions. It required decades of warfare for the Frankish kings to bring the Saxons under control and begin their Christianization, but by the early ninth century, northern Germany was sufficiently pacified to serve as a base for a Scandinavian mission. Harold of Denmark was baptized in 826, and Hamburg became the seat of an archbishop for Scandinavia in 831. Paganism remained strong in the north, however, until the twelfth century.

The Slavic territories east of Germany were subject to Christian influences from both Rome and Constantinople. The expansion of the great German empires of the ninth and tenth centuries spread the Christian religion into Slavic lands, and the economic dominance of Constantinople served similarly to pull the area into the realm of Christian culture. The Eastern and Western branches of the Christian mission came into close contact in the Balkan territories. The Balkans had been overrun by pagan Slavs during the seventh and eighth centuries, but, by the ninth century, the Balkans had settled down sufficiently for the new citizens to be attracted to the superior civilizations of their neighbors. During the last half of that century, the Greek missionaries Cyril and Methodius were sent out from Constantinople to work in the Balkans, and they had noteworthy success. They invented a script for Slavic languages and developed vernacular liturgies that received at least temporary approval from the Roman church. The papacy joined in sponsoring the Balkan mission, and, in the tenth century, the kingdom of Hungary was organized under a Christian leader who accepted the jurisdiction of the Latin church. The Byzantine rite meanwhile spread north along the trade routes from Constantinople, and, by the end of the tenth century, Kiev had a Christian bishop, and the Russian king had allied himself by marriage to the Byzantine imperial family.

All of this vigorous missionary activity led to a significant reorientation of the axes of Christendom. Ancient Christian territories in Palestine, Syria, Egypt, Africa, and Spain fell to the new Moslem empire, and with them went the importance of the Mediterranean as the center of Christian interests. The church compensated for its losses in part by expanding northward toward the limits of the European continent, and this extension of Christian frontiers helped pull Rome and Constantinople farther apart. They each began to develop interests unique to their separate cultures, and they came to have less and less in common. Communication was difficult, misunderstandings occurred, and tensions between the pope and the emperor repeatedly led to a formal severance of communion between the Greek and Latin churches. The Eastern empire's attempts to compromise with the Monophysite heresy created a schism between Rome and Constantinople in 482, and there were similarly strained relations involving a variety of issues in 543, 588, 646, 692, and 726. In each case, however, problems were resolved and the nominal unity of the church restored, for the Roman popes continued to think of themselves as having stronger ties with the old empire than they did with the new barbarian peoples. In the middle of the eighth century events precipitated a drastic change in papal attitudes.

In 726, Emperor Leo III outlawed the veneration of images in Christian worship and inaugurated a conflict that disrupted the Greek church for over a century. In part, his program was motivated by a common ancient Eastern antipathy to physical representations of spiritual realities—a feeling shared by both the Jews and the Moslems. In part, his intent may have been to lessen the power that certain monastic factions wielded over the people through manipulation of superstitions regarding holy objects. There was much popular resistance to the emperor's decree in the East, and the Iconoclastic controversy troubled Constantinople until 843. In pursuit of support against the emperor, the icon venerators of the East appealed to the pope for approval of their practices. The emperor attempted to counter their maneuver by ordering the pope to implement the edict in the West. Pope Gregory II refused the imperial order, and, although attempts to take him prisoner were thwarted, the government in Constantinople was able to confiscate important papal estates and diminish the jurisdiction of Rome in the Balkans. By this time, however, the pope no longer stood completely alone in the West. The barbarians had settled down, a degree of stability had begun to return to Europe, and the activities of the monastic missionaries had inspired the Germans with a reverent respect for the spiritual authority of the papacy—an attitude in vivid contrast with that of the Eastern emperors. As early as the 740's, Pope Gregory III had made overtures to the Frankish king, Charles Martel, for aid against the Lombards. Charles had interests elsewhere and no desire to quarrel with the Lombards; so nothing came of the papal initiative. A decade later, it was a very different story.

In 751, the Lombards took Ravenna and Constantinople lost its major foothold in the West. The departure of the exarch of Ravenna removed the last Byzantine official to whom the pope could have appealed for aid against the Lombards and left him without a military ally in Italy. Fortunately for the papacy, this crisis occurred at about the same time that a delicate problem confronted the Frankish government. The Franks were still nominally ruled by the Merovingian dynasty. The Merovingians traced their ancestry back to the very dawn of the history of the Salian tribes, and there had never been another family that had shared their natural right to the crown. However, the pressures of feudalism had reduced the Merovingians to such poverty that they could not give real leadership to their nation. For years, they had served as figureheads for governments actually led by such families as the Carolingians—descendents of men who had got their start as palace officials. The situation was unwieldy but difficult to tamper with. The Carolingian Pepin the Short (741–68), who acquired control over all of the Frankish lands, decided finally to attempt to depose his Merovingian overlord and assume a royal title commensurate with the power he exercised. There was a problem, however, in that no one among the Franks enjoyed an authority greater than the natural charisma of the ancient Merovingian line, and so no Frank could legitimate the deposition of the Merovingians and establish a new dynasty. Pepin had the perceptiveness to realize that the Franks were no longer restricted to the horizons of their pagan ancestors. They were now orthodox Christians who harbored a great respect for the church, and Pepin believed that papal approval of the termination of the Merovingian succession and the inauguration of a new Carolingian royal line would do much to give his usurpation an appearance of legality. He explored the issue with the papacy, and, in 752, the pope empowered Boniface, the leader of the German mission, to anoint Pepin king of the Franks and approve the confinement of the last Merovingian in a monastery. Two years later, Pope Stephen II crossed the Alps to reconsecrate Pepin, and Pepin reciprocated by marching into Italy to halt the Lombard threat to Rome.

The alliance between Rome and the German king proved to be the beginning of a new period in the evolution of European Christianity. It was a symbol of the fact that the papacy had at last accepted the disappearance of the ancient world and thrown in its lot with the new peoples of the West. The West offered an environment for the development of the church quite different from that of the East, and, in the long run, Christianity found its most promising future in the West. Constantinople was culturally much more advanced than the Germanic lands in the eighth century, but its society drew upon ever diminishing resources and faded as the medieval period advanced.

Pope Stephen's alliance with Pepin contributed almost immediately to a strengthening of the papacy. Pepin recovered the exarchate of Ravenna from the Lombards, but he did not add it to his own Frankish kingdom. He had not obliterated the Lombard nation in northern Italy, and the territories of Ravenna would have been difficult for him to hold from the far side of the Alps. But the papacy, as the only surviving ancient imperial institution in Italy, had something of a claim to the recovered lands. Therefore, the Franks ratified an agreement known as the Donation of Pepin, which recognized the former Byzantine exarchate as a part of the papal patrimony and strengthened earlier precedents for the establishment of an independent papal state. It would be many years before the popes would exercise effective control over their lands, and their military resources would never be adequate to enable them to intimidate the secular leaders of Europe. But Pepin's act clearly recognized the pope's right to an independent existence and did much to guarantee that, in the West, the church and the state would attempt to maintain separate establishments. Their pursuit of an acceptable definition of their respective jurisdictions became one of the major themes of medieval ecclesiastical history.

Constantinople was in no position to do much about the new alliances that were shaping up in the West—save to ridicule the pretensions of the barbarians and to register empty objections to the usurpation of its former lands and honors. Papal support of the German monarchy was a serious new commitment that involved a radical break with Rome's past. Even with title to its new lands, the papacy was unable to defend itself against the Lombards without some sort of military assistance, and, in the absence of Byzantine aid, it was driven to rely on the Franks for continued support. In 774, Pepin's son and heir, Charles the Great (768–814), heeded a papal plea for help, crossed the Alps, and obliterated the Lombard kingdom. He reconfirmed his father's donation to the church, but the eventual unification of most of Europe under his control left the popes very little room in which to enjoy freedom or independence. Charles himself was a thoroughly serious Christian with a strong taste for theological discussions, and he felt as much responsibility for overseeing his kingdom's religious affairs as for protecting it from secular disorder. He presided over synods of bishops, made rulings on questions of doctrine and liturgical practice, and freely admonished the pope when he disagreed with Rome's opinions. In practice, he exercised an authority over the church quite similar to that of the Eastern emperor, but, in theory, the church and the state remained separate.

The increasingly ambiguous relations among the papacy, the Franks, and the Byzantines came to a symbolic head on Christmas Day of the year 800. Charles was in Rome in answer to an appeal from Pope Leo III, and, during the celebration of the Christmas festival, he received a crown from the pope and accepted acclamation as "emperor of the Romans." The meaning of these events for their participants is not certain. Charles was now master of most of the peoples of Europe and had a right to think of himself as something grander than a Frankish tribal king. The Byzantine throne was at the time under the control of a woman, the unscrupulous Empress Irene, and some Franks might have argued that females could not be emperors and that, therefore, the imperial title had lapsed in the East and could be claimed in the West. Pope Leo certainly wished to create the impression that Charles received his elevation to imperial status from the church and thus to suggest that the church had a certain superiority to the state. Papal arguments from the period made much of a peculiar document known as the Donation of Constantine. With complete disregard of the facts of history, the document claimed that the emperor Constantine, in gratitude for his cure of leprosy by Pope Sylvester I, had withdrawn from Rome to Constantinople and resigned title to the western half of the empire. On the basis of this totally fictitious legend, the popes did not presume to claim the authority of emperors, but they did assert an exclusive right to award the imperial title in the West. Some of the medieval sources suggest that Charles was not pleased by his coronation, but his specific objections are unknown. He may have been attempting to mitigate the precedent established by receiving the crown from the pope when he later bestowed the title of emperor on his son and heir, Louis, without the assistance of the church.

The coronation of Charles the Great was a clear proclamation of the West's new independence from the ghost of Byzantine authority. Constantinople no longer had any hope of a political revival in the Latin territories of the old Roman Empire, and, in 813, it acquiesced to the extent of according Charles recognition as *an* emperor. Another two centuries were required for the division in the political realm to find its parallel within ecclesiastical structures. The Roman popes attempted to keep alive their claim to jurisdiction over a universal church by intervening from time to time in the internal affairs of the Greek hierarchy, but East and West seem slowly to have lost interest in each other. A lasting formal separation of the Latin and Byzantine branches of Christianity finally occurred in 1054. The legates of Pope Leo IX and the patriarch Michael Cerularius met to settle a dispute over boundaries between the jurisdictions of Rome and Constantinople, and their negotiations broke down in a round of mutual excommunications. Their disagreement had no crucial or fundamental issue incapable of resolution, but neither side cared enough to work toward reconciliation. Reunion with the East on papal terms remained a part of declared Roman policy throughout the medieval period, but, although this goal was often discussed, it was never achieved. The armies of the Fourth Crusade occupied Byzantium in 1204, and Latin emperors ruled the East for over half a century. But the Latin church failed to establish lasting control over the East, and Roman influence there evaporated when a native Greek dynasty returned to power in Constantinople. In 1452, when Constantinople faced imminent destruction by the Turks, the emperor sought support from the West by decreeing a submission of the Greek church to Rome; but the gesture came too late. The West had no help to give, the Turks overwhelmed the city, and Eastern Christianity was left alone to work out its future under the aegis of a Moslem culture. A quite different destiny was enjoyed by the Latin church of the West.

LATIN CHRISTENDOM:
A SEARCH FOR IDENTITY AS CHURCH AND STATE

UNDER CHARLES THE GREAT, the West enjoyed a period of political reunification and stability in which the work of recovering from the destructive effects of the barbarian migrations could go forward. Charles himself took a personal interest in literature and education, and his generous patronage created a justly famous Carolingian Renaissance. Charles gathered about him a cabinet of noted scholars who represented the strongest surviving intellectual traditions of Italy, Spain, England, and Ireland; these men assisted him in an ambitious program of educational reforms. Charles's primary motive in the pursuit of higher intellectual standards for his society seems to have been religious. He was deeply convinced of the truth of the Christian faith and vividly conscious of a sense of personal responsibility for the spiritual well-being of his empire. It may have seemed to many that the West was losing its grip on the Christian religion. The mass and sacraments were often erratically or improperly administered by illiterate and ill-disciplined clergy. Sacred books were riddled with textual corruptions and handled with such neglect that they were in danger of disappearing completely. Peculiar local customs and ancient pagan beliefs had crept into Christian practice in many places, and there was little standardization of discipline or worship in the European church.

The faults of the church resulted more from ignorance than from perversity, and Charles sought to rectify them by rebuilding educational institutions and improving the training of the clergy. In the ancient world, when the secular institutions of the family and the school still functioned, the church had recruited its leaders from people who came to it already literate and prepared to carry on its traditions. The collapse and disappearance of the institutions of the ancient empire robbed the West of its schools and of the social classes that had previously assumed responsibility for the preservation and transmission of the skills of literacy. Groups of Christian clergy in monasteries and cathedrals had to some degree informally stepped into the vacuum and attempted to maintain tools for their own educations. But it was not until Charles's reign that the state found itself in a position to offer them significant assistance. Charles employed the best scholars he could find in Europe to collect the literature that survived, purify its texts, reproduce it in legible and multiple copies, and devise methods to teach the techniques of its study and preservation. He then ordered the monasteries and cathedrals of Europe to sponsor schools using the new literary equipment and to admit, not only oblates, but also sons of the aristocracy and others who might be destined for worldly vocations.

The improvement of educational institutions made possible the practice of a more sophisticated form of the Christian religion. During the course of his reign, Charles convened no fewer than thirty-three church councils which legislated numerous reforms for the Latin church. He endorsed the liturgy of Rome, which had reached completion about the year 600, for use throughout the empire; and the so-called "Gregorian" chant, which was primarily an achievement of the eighth century, acquired universal popularity through his efforts. The publication of standardized text of the Apostles' Creed halted the statement's further evolution. The Vulgate was cleansed of scribal errors and officially issued as the authorized version of the Scriptures. Improvements in the morality and discipline of the clergy were demanded; and the church, reversing the papal policy of the fifth century, required all clerics to wear distinctive clothing so that their vocations would be immediately apparent to all and their temptations to join unworthy companions in questionable places lessened. Monasteries were strengthened by reorganization and new endowments. Charles's son and successor, Louis the Pious imposed the Benedictine rule on all cloisters, and the customs of the Benedictines, or "black monks," soon came to dominate the practice of Western monasticism. Chrodegang of Metz (d. 766) even drew up a plan aimed at bringing the behavior of the parish and cathedral clergy into line with the values of their cloistered colleagues.

The Carolingian reforms occasioned a considerable improvement in the practice of the Christian life in Europe, and they proved to be a solid base on which the future could build. But in many places, their effect was a long time in being felt, and the political system on which they depended for support did not long survive Charles himself. Charles had restored to Europe some of the benefits of the unity it had enjoyed during antiquity as the western Roman Empire; but the strong regional loyalties of the new medieval peoples, the distinctive barbarian languages and cultures, and the decline of ancient world-wide institutions and avenues of communication made it difficult for Europe to continue as one nation under one government. Louis the Pious spent most of his reign (814–40) in a losing battle with a succession of rebels. His sons, Charles the Bald, Louis the German, and Lothair, ended a generation of warfare in 843 by agreeing to divide Europe into territorial units which eventually became the nations of France, Germany, and Italy. The title of emperor was to survive and be revived from time to time in the West, but there was to be no empire composed of the united peoples of Europe. Only the church, and in particular the papacy, survived as a symbol of the common universal culture of Europe, and, during the remainder of the Middle Ages, conflicting political impulses toward nationalism and internationalism found expression most often in the religious context of the struggles between popes and kings.

Apart from a general strengthening of the church, the Carolingian epoch did little to encourage the development of the papacy. Charles himself ruled the church as directly as he ruled the state, and he seems to have had little use for the bishops of Rome. His successors did not, however, enjoy his claim to universal dominion over Europe, and thus the position of the pope as the head of a church larger than their separate kingdoms came once again to attract attention. But it was to be several centuries before the popes would be able to attempt to exercise anything like the authority they claimed over Christendom.

The ninth century experienced an uncomfortable reaction to the rapid advances of Charles's reign. The empire proved politically unstable and dissolved in civil war. Even more unfortunately, Charles's conquests were revealed to have destroyed valuable pagan buffer states on the Avar and Saxon frontiers and to have exposed Europe to a new wave of barbarian invasion. The Saracens revived their attacks from the south, looted Rome, and lodged themselves in the Alpine passes. The Magyars raged across German and Frankish territories from the east, and the Vikings, striking from the north, forced their way up the major river systems of the Continent. Among the more lamentable casualties of the new invasions were the monasteries of Europe, which Charles had labored to make the bastions of religion and civilization. In England, the great tradition of the Anglo-Saxon monks, which had done so much to preserve Western culture during the worst years of the Dark Ages, was all but obliterated. The West Saxon king, Alfred the Great (871–900), applied his limited resources to the promotion of an "Anglo-Saxon Renaissance," but its achievements were modest. On the Continent, the monks suffered greatly also, but the new wave of invaders did not succeed in completely wiping out the advances that had been made.

The recovery of Europe was temporarily retarded, but not halted. While the kings and nobles were occupied with the new barbarians, the papacy was generally left to fend for itself. Under Nicholas I (858–67), it showed considerable initiative. Nicholas strengthened his control over the Western clergy by imposing his will on Hincmar, the powerful archbishop of Rheims, in a dispute over the appointment of a suffragan bishop. The pope demonstrated the church's independence of the state by forcing the emperor Lothair to take back the wife he wished to repudiate. And he kept alive the papacy's claim to supremacy in the church by intervening powerfully in the respective deposition and appointment of the Byzantine patriarchs Ignatius and Photius. Nicholas also gave a new legal basis to the claims of the papacy by endorsing a curious collection of church canons, or decrees of councils, which was probably drawn up in the diocese of Tours about 850. The Pseudo-Isidorian Decretals, as they are now known, were at the time falsely attributed to Isidore of Seville (d. 636), one of the most prestigious of early medieval scholars, and their purpose seems to have been to strengthen the position of the clergy against the laity by attributing vast powers to the pope. The pope was the bishops' most logical protector in quarrels with the secular lords who dominated their dioceses, and the more rights tradition accorded the pope, the fewer were the privileges that the laity could appropriate. The pope was an appealing master because he was less effective in exercising his prerogatives than the count who resided in the diocese, and the early medieval clergy may occasionally have hoped to promote their own freedom from the state by strengthening their ties to the church. The Decretals represented the church as an independent papal monarchy and were more accurate as a program for the church's future than they were as an account of its past. They were, however, quickly accepted as authentic ancient texts, and they remained in use in the church even after the humanistic scholars of the Renaissance proved them to be medieval forgeries.

Nicholas's successors in Rome were considerably less effective than he in the promotion of papal authority. During the late ninth and early tenth centuries, the papacy became so completely absorbed in the internal politics of the city of Rome that it ceased to have much influence on the international scene. The local Roman nobility fought over the papal throne incessantly and kept the see in perpetual chaos. Since there was no king in Europe strong enough to intervene and stabilize the situation, popes rose and fell with the rapidly shifting fortunes of their petty factions. Men of poor personal qualifications achieved the papacy with depressing regularity, and there was little improvement in the situation until the reign of John XII (955–64).

By the middle of the tenth century, Europe had begun to recover from the worst of the new wave of barbarian attacks. England was partitioned into Viking and Anglo-Saxon halves by Alfred the Great (d. 900). The Viking Normans received official recognition of their settlement in "Normandy" in northern France. Byzantine assistance helped push the Saracens out of southern Italy. Otto I set the German monarchy back on its feet again and ended the Magyar threat at the battle of Lechfeld (955).

The reappearance of a strong government in Germany quickly had an effect on the papacy, for the Carolingian tradition of the empire had established a special relationship between the popes and the German kings they crowned. In 951, Otto, whose family lands lay in Saxony in northern Germany, crossed the Alps and put an end to the possible ambitions of his southern dukes by claiming the Lombard crown for himself. He seems to have investigated at that time the possibility of receiving consecration as emperor from the pope, but it was not until 962 that the ceremony was performed and the empire officially revived. Pope John XII and Otto soon discovered that they had different understandings of their respective areas of authority, and John moved to limit Otto's caesaropapism by stirring up rebellion. Otto retaliated by forcing John to flee Rome and replacing him with Leo VIII, a pope appointed from the German court. John briefly regained his position in 964, but, when he died shortly thereafter in the course of a morally suspicious escapade, Otto restored Leo to power and forbade the people of Rome to proceed with a papal election without consulting the emperor.

Otto II (973–83) was not often available to attend to affairs in Rome, and, during his absences, the Crescenti family dominated the papacy. In 996, Otto III (983–1002) attempted to quiet the city by appointing one of his own cousins, Gregory V, to the papal throne. Gregory was followed by Otto's highly qualified tutor, Sylvester II, but the political difficulties that attended Otto's somewhat romantic and ineffectual reign eventually enabled the Roman nobility to regain control of the church. Rome was again a chaos of popes and antipopes when Otto III died at the age of twenty-two and his crown passed to his cousin Henry II (1002-24). Henry's piety was noteworthy enough to earn him canonization twenty-two years after his death. In his relationship with the papacy, he was imbued with a sincere desire for the good of the church. In 1022, a council met at Pavia and drew up a program of reform for the clergy, but the program had little opportunity to take hold. The Saxon dynasty came to an end two years later when Henry died, and the early members of the succeeding Salian royal line had to establish their position in Germany before they could attend to Rome. In the interim, Roman factionalism again disrupted the papacy, and it was not until the reign of Pope Benedict IX (1033-48) that the German kings again made their influence felt in Italy. Benedict had become pope at about the age of twelve, and his conduct had been shocking even to a society that had learned to expect little from its pontiffs. In 1046, the Salian king Henry III marched into Italy and appointed the bishop of Bamberg, Clement II, to replace Benedict and the two other "popes" who were contesting the papal office with him. Before his death in 1056, Henry had the opportunity to advance three other worthy men to the papacy, and his protégés succeeded in laying the groundwork for an extensive reform of the papal office.

The reform that began to reshape the papacy in the eleventh century was part of a larger movement for the improvement of the whole church, which owed its popularity to the influence of the monastery of Cluny. The Benedictine house at Cluny had been founded in 910 by Duke William of Aquitaine, and it was unusual in having successfully broken with the proprietary arrangements that accompanied most medieval gifts to the church. The church lived from its endowments, and it was a generally accepted custom in the early Middle Ages for the donor of a major gift to an ecclesiastical institution to retain some control over the organization. The clergy who served rural parishes owed their appointments to the local noble families who had established their churches; monasteries and even episcopal sees also functioned with a perpetual debt of obligation to lay lords. By the tenth century, many perceptive ecclesiastics were suggesting that the system of the proprietary church was the root of the corruption and incompetence that had infected many Christian institutions. Laymen most often exercised their control over clerical benefices in the interest of their families and personal retainers and not to the advantage of the church. Appointments to parish livings, abbeys, and episcopacies were made in order to provide for members of noble families or to retain the endowments of these institutions within family control. Staff chosen on the basis of political interests rather than considerations of spiritual or intellectual aptitude were all too frequently ill equipped to lead the church or to inspire adequate standards of clerical conduct. By the time Cluny was established, many a monastery had fallen into disorder and disrepute for these reasons, and the monks of Cluny convinced their patron that the discipline of their new house could be ensured only if they were free from the ill-advised meddling of outside secular influences.

Cluny recognized no master save the pope, and it proved by the quality of its discipline that an independent cloister could achieve an admirable degree of spirituality. Reform-minded monks from other houses came to Cluny to learn its procedures and ways of adapting them to situations elsewhere. Some cloisters placed themselves directly under Cluny's control and became dependent priories which shared the motherhouses's exemptions from control by lay lords and local bishops. The fame of the purified monastic vocation developed by Cluny attracted some of the most talented and committed Christians in Europe to a Cluniac movement, which promoted the principles of the famous monastery. The German-appointed popes of the eleventh century were strongly influenced by the Cluniac conviction that the church could be reformed only if it could be made independent of the laity.

An essential step toward the liberation of the church from secular influences was the establishment of the papacy as a self-perpetuating office in which qualified clergy were freed from political pressures and encouraged to pick the best possible spiritual leader for the church. The popes had traditionally obtained their offices by acclamation of the clergy and people of Rome, but this system subjected the papacy to the political whims of the city and formed an open invitation to factionalism. German kings had often usurped the right to appoint popes, but, if this custom had become permanently established, the church would have been subordinated to the state, and the papacy would have become a German institution without a claim to international authority. When King Henry III died in 1056, the papal counselors were, therefore, eager to test a new plan that they hoped would remove the influence of the German monarchy and the Roman nobility from the selection of a pope and adequately safeguard the independence of the church. Henry III's heir was a six-year-old child, and the weakness of the state during the long regency of his mother Agnes gave the papacy an opportunity to establish precedents for new electoral procedures. When Pope Victor died in 1057, the Roman clergy proceeded at once to elect his successor and simply informed the German government of their choice after the fact. There was no reaction from the empire to this initiative by the church; so after Nicholas II had been elevated to the papacy by a similar procedure in 1058, he promulgated a new papal electoral law (1059). Thereafter, the pope was to be chosen by the cardinal or primary bishops, who were his chief assistants in the government of the church and who were associated with him in Rome as kinds of special papal suffragans. The emperor was to be informed of the outcome, but he was to be given no voice in the decision. And, in order to increase the papacy's independence from the German state, Nicholas II struck up an alliance with the Normans of the Hauteville family, who had begun in 1036 to establish a power base in the old Byzantine lands of southern Italy and in Moslem Sicily. There was little response from Germany until Henry IV came of age, and, by the time he was ready to attempt to exercise the ecclesiastical prerogatives formally held by his ancestors, the new program of the reformed papacy was in effect and in direct opposition to his plans.

The great Investiture Controversy, which dominated the reigns of Henry IV (1056-1106) and Pope Gregory VII (1073-85), did not spring directly from the issue of papal electoral procedures but resulted from the related and much more serious question of the Cluniac party's intent to transform the church into an international papal monarchy. One reason for reforming the procedure for the selection of the pope was to help ensure that the church would always enjoy the inspiration of a worthy spiritual leader. But it was obvious that the church would profit little from even the best of leaders unless he truly had power over its clergy. The reformers in Rome were convinced that only if all appointments to positions in the church were made by churchmen without lay interference could the church successfully enforce its decrees against clerical marriage, immorality, and simony and assure an adequate level of education and commitment among the clergy. The system of the proprietary church had, therefore, to be discontinued and the clergy freed to function as members of an international ecclesiastical state under the government of an independent papacy.

It was impossible for the state to accept this new papal policy in its most radical version, for, by the eleventh century, the church had evolved into something more than a religious institution. The church's monopoly of educational systems meant that the governments of kings had to recruit their trained officials from the clergy, and a huge number of Europe's bishops combined the service of the church and the state inextricably in their careers. In Germany in particular, the kings had found it wise to grant lands to the church as a kind of counterweight to the influence of the feudal aristocracy. The lay nobles inevitably turned their royal endowments into hereditary family property and took them out of the king's control, but a bishop or abbot had no natural heir. When he died, his office and his lands returned to the king for regranting to a loyal dependent. By controlling appointments to church offices, a king made sure that sympathetic, capable men occupied key positions in his government, and, since the church may have laid claim to as much as a third of Europe's land, its declaration of independence was a blow at the root of royal power which could not go unchallenged.

The church and the state were not and could not be as distinct and independent in their respective spheres as the reformed papacy desired. The church could not give up its endowments without losing the resources that gave it a hope for survival as a free agent; the state could not afford to relinquish control over the lands it had managed through the church without seriously diminishing its strength. A compromise was needed, but, before it was achieved, each side attempted to test the resolution of its opponent. In 1075, Pope Gregory forbade King Henry to continue the ancient royal practice of investing clergy with the symbols of their offices. Henry ignored the papal directive and appointed a new archbishop for the city of Milan. Relations between Henry and Gregory then deteriorated rapidly. Early in 1076, Henry and his bishops declared the pope improperly elected and deposed him. Gregory then excommunicated Henry and released his subjects from their oaths of loyalty to the king. At first, conditions seemed to favor the pope. The German nobility were desirous of an excuse to weaken their king, and they invited Gregory to come to Augsburg and preside over a meeting that, under the threat of mass rebellion, would dictate terms to the king. Henry, however, did not allow himself to be forced into this trap. While Gregory waited at the castle of Canossa in Tuscany for an opportunity to cross the Alps, Henry seized the initiative and broke through the mountains in midwinter to meet the pope before he joined his allies in Germany. Henry did penance in the snow before Canossa for three days with such an obvious show of repentance that Gregory had little choice but to forgive him and lift the ban of excommunication. Gregory's German sympathizers immediately assumed that they had been betrayed, and the coalition between pope and nobles collapsed. Civil war broke out in Germany anyway, but Henry was able to survive it. By 1084, he was in a position to invade Italy and force Gregory, who died shortly thereafter, to flee into exile.

It remained for the next generation of church and civil leaders to adopt more moderate attitudes and at Bec in 1107 and Worms in 1122 to approve workable compromises for church-state relations in the Norman lands of France and England and in the German Empire. According to the terms of the concordats, the kings gave up the custom of investing ecclesiastical appointees with the symbols of their spiritual offices and guaranteed the right of the church to conduct free elections. In actual practice, however, elections were to be held in the presence of the king or his representative, and, although the monarch had no formal vote, his opinion strongly influenced the outcome. The civil government was able to continue to control crucial clerical appointments, but the church won a major theoretical concession. It won nominal recognition of its status as an independent, self-perpetuating international organization solely under the authority of the Roman pope.

It now remained for the medieval papacy to put into effect the rights and privileges it had successfully claimed. There were many conflicts and apparent setbacks, but from the eleventh to the thirteenth century the strength of the papal organization grew steadily. The papacy developed diplomatic ties with the emerging nations of Europe; it intervened among them with advice and offers of mediation whenever possible; and it developed a judicial system and powers of taxation that provided powerful new organs for the exercise of papal authority. The papacy's strongest opponent remained the German emperor, for he had a claim to Italian lands that were vital to papal interests and, on the basis of his imperial title, asserted a right to a God-given universal authority rivaling that of the pope. The kings of Europe and the cities of Italy were, however, suspicious of the ambitions of the emperors. They often supported the church against the empire, as during the long conflict between Frederick Barbarossa (1152–90) and Pope Alexander III (1159–81). Ultimately, the church won—but at great cost to itself and to its opponent. The powerful Hohenstaufen dynasty, which almost succeeded in combining Germany and Italy into a viable empire, was eradicated, and, by the end of the Middle Ages, Germany had been fragmented by its conflict with the church into numerous mutually suspicious petty principalities which no longer constituted much of a threat to the liberty of the papacy.

THE FLOWERING
OF THE LATIN CHRISTIAN CULTURE

THE STRUGGLE BETWEEN CHURCH and state in medieval Europe had a significance that transcended politics: it was both a symptom of and a stimulus for the emergence of a vital, independent Christian culture in the Latin West. The debate between popes and kings inspired their advisors to develop critical skills and to search for more adequate philosophical bases for the institutions they were called upon to defend. The intellectual climate of the eleventh century rapidly differentiated itself from that of the early medieval period.

The scholars of the Dark Ages had given most of their attention to the need to preserve the heritage of the past. Their sense of Europe as a society that was sliding away from civilization was strong; so it was logical for them to have conceived their task as one of preservation rather than innovation. In their schools, the modest goal of education was simply to master the work of the great authorities of the past. There was little expectation that the achievements of the ancient giants could be excelled, and little value was accorded the kind of thought that later generations would praise as original or innovative. Arguments and debates were conducted by citing passages from the Bible and the church fathers in support or criticism of the opinions under examination, and the truth was held to lie with the view that could muster the strongest backing from tradition. Most leaders and thinkers seem to have assumed that the contours of the future were of necessity to be defined by the customs and attitudes of the past.

During the eleventh and twelfth centuries, the church was brought by its struggle with the state to challenge the conservative intellectual attitudes it had earlier defended. In the struggle between lord and cleric, medieval tradition was plainly on the side of the layman who claimed a right to control appointments to ecclesiastical offices. The proprietary church had gone unchallenged in Europe for generations. But the reform-minded papacy had come to glimpse an ideal goal for Christian ecclesiastical leadership in Europe far surpassing the limited achievements of the past, and so the papacy began to argue that the dead hand of tradition could be challenged in the name of truth. Customs that had long prevailed still had tremendous authority, but people slowly began to develop a new tolerance for the opinion that a rational man had the right and obligation to correct his heritage from the past.

In part, the new rationalism of the Scholastics (who gained their name from their association with the influential universities that began to spring up in the late twelfth century) was a natural outgrowth of certain problems faced by the scholars of the Dark Ages. The leaders of the older monastic tradition had been editors and encyclopedists who had attempted to summarize and pull together huge quantities of ancient learning. Their goal was a kind of synthesis of human knowledge that would, as it approached completeness, delineate once and for all the dimensions of absolute truth. As the monks became more sophisticated in the handling of their material, they began to discover, somewhat to their discomfort, that not all of the ancient authorities on whom they relied for guidance were in agreement on all issues. When conflicts between respected sources appeared, it was impossible to escape the question of establishing a basis on which to judge the authority of the authorities. This fact was bluntly driven home in the early twelfth century by the Parisian scholar Peter Abelard (1079–1142). He authored a book, appropriately titled *Yes and No*, that catalogued the apparent disagreements among the ancients on vital points of Christian doctrine. The objective of the book was, not to discredit the early fathers of the faith, but to encourage the church and the schools to accept a powerful new critical tool that came to be known as the dialectical method. Dialectic was simply a process of rational analysis and careful inference which could be used to probe deeply into conflicts of opinion to see if they were real or only apparent. Reasonable as the method seemed on the surface, it had revolutionary implications, for it was based on the assumption that the fathers of the church were trustworthy authorities, not because of superior spiritual gifts, but because they taught ideas that could be justified by human rational inquiry. Therefore, the use of dialectic inevitably brought the church to confront the problem of the relationship between faith and reason and to seek out a basis on which to defend its own claim to spiritual and moral dominion over human society.

The roots of the Scholastic tradition went very deep. As early as the ninth century, some monastic scholars were raising questions that revealed assumptions of rationalistic or even empiricistic standards of meaning. In 831, Paschasius Radbertus, a monk of Corbie, wrote an essay on the Sacrament of the Mass in which he expressed the popular and widespread conviction that the act of priestly consecration caused the Elements of bread and wine to literally become the Flesh and Blood of Christ. Radbertus's attitude corresponded to the doctrine of transubstantiation that was to be endorsed centuries later at the Fourth Lateran Council (1215) and defined as Roman Catholic dogma at the Council of Trent (1545–63). But, in the ninth century, the belief was far from receiving immediate or uncritical approval. Another monk at Corbie, Ratramnus, attempted to deal with the problems raised by Radbertus's formulation, which posited an incomprehensible disruption of the normal laws of nature in seeming contradiction of the fact that no change in the sacred Elements could be perceived by the senses. Ratramnus suggested a difficult distinction between the function of the consecrated Elements as "figures" or symbols and the activity of the divine reality they mediated. But his technical theological vocabulary was inadequate to the complexity of his explanation, and it is difficult now to know exactly where he stood. The debate continued into the eleventh century and occasioned a famous exchange of arguments between Berengar of Tours and Lanfranc of Bec. Berengar took the position that, if no substantial change in the Elements of the Mass could be perceived, then there was no reason to postulate that one took place. Lanfranc opposed him with an argument that drew on Christian authorities and Scholastic reason. Lanfranc asserted that the tradition of the church did teach that there was a transformation of the substance of the consecrated Elements, and he further claimed that philosophy could rationally explain how such a change might take place. He argued that, if it could be shown that there was no necessary conflict between faith and reason, then there was no need to question the accepted opinion of the church. In his argument, Lanfranc drew on a distinction between *substance* and *attribute* that was a commonplace of Greek philosophy. He defined substance as the empirically imperceptible defining characteristic of a thing, and he defined attributes as characteristics that could be perceived by the senses. The persisting sameness of substance explained why a human perceiver could recognize an individual object as a member of a certain class of objects even though the specimens in the class differed in one or more attributes. In normal human experience, Lanfranc suggested, all objects present themselves as unchanging substances bearing changeable attributes; but in the miracle of the Mass, God could have decreed an exception that reversed the natural order: the Elements of the Mass might change their substances but not their attributes.

Lanfranc's argument is of symbolic importance as an indication of a new and adventuresome attitude in the Christian consciousness of the high Middle Ages. The argument suggests that Christian intellectuals were beginning to trust their abilities to rethink the dogmas of the past and to establish doctrine on a basis acceptable to human reason. Lanfranc's pupil Anselm of Bec and Canterbury (1033–1109) confidently expressed the belief that it was no sacrilege for a man of faith to seek as much rational understanding and explication of dogma as he could find, and he set about demonstrating the necessity of the most fundamental Christian concepts. In his *Monologium and Proslogium,* he approached the question of God's existence and concluded that the divine reality could be logically demonstrated in several ways—not the least interesting of which was an ontological argument that still attracts the attention of philosophers. Anselm claimed that the word *God* in Christian speech serves as a symbol for a concept of something greater than anything a human being can conceive. If the concept of God were, however, conceived as lacking the attribute of existence, it would not be a concept greater than anything one could conceive. It could still be augmented by the addition of the attribute of existence, but if it were not, it would of necessity be less than the Christian concept of God. Anselm concluded, therefore, that the definition of the word *God* implies the necessity of God's existence. In the tract *Cur Deus Homo,* Anselm conducted a similar inquiry into the rational necessity for Christ's death on the cross. He argued that human sin was an offense to God which placed man infinitely in God's debt. God was able freely to forgive the guilt of the act, but, since he was a God of justice as well as mercy, reparation was needed to restore the moral balance of the universe. Because the offense was man's, only man could make restitution. But, since man was God's creature, everything he had was God's already, and he had no surplus of merit adequate to repair the effects of his rebellion. Consequently, although man owed the debt to God, only God had the resources to repay it. Therefore, if God wished to satisfy the demands of his own justice and achieve the intended ends of his creation, it was necessary that he become man in Christ and, by means of a perfect human life of obedience and self-sacrifice, pay man's debt to God and do for man what man could not do for himself.

Not all early medieval thinkers were as successful as Anselm in coordinating their reason and their commitment to traditional Christian concepts. The philosophical basis of early Scholasticism was quite slight, and it exposed the pioneer Scholastic to the dangers of naive and erroneous inferences. Apart from Boethius's translations of a few logical treatises, nothing was known of the work of Aristotle, and Plato's thought survived primarily as filtered through the lenses of Augustine and the Neoplatonists. During the twelfth century, more and more of the work of the ancient Greeks became available for study in the West, but the material frequently came in the form of Arabic or Hebrew commentaries. This format increased the difficulty of reconciling Greek thought and the Christian worldview. It is understandable, therefore, that many early practitioners of dialectic fell into error and that the church was not always sympathetic toward their vocation.

Anselm had asserted that reason ought to accept the guidance and the limits of faith in its explorations, but some of his contemporaries in their enthusiasm found this advice difficult to follow. Peter Abelard (d. 1142), who had been an occasional pupil of Anselm's student William of Champeaux, boldly reversed Anselm's dictum and preached that nothing should be believed that could not be logically demonstrated to be true. The problem with Abelard's rationalism, however, was that there was no consensus among the schoolmen concerning the identity of the truths they thought they could demonstrate. Abelard himself attempted to bridge the gap between the camp of the realists—who followed Plato in teaching that general concepts referred to entities that really existed—and the nominalists—who claimed that class names were simply arbitrary conventions of human speech. A too-consistent realist found himself pushed into pantheism, and a rigorous nominalist found himself dividing the Trinity into three gods. Abelard himself was unable to effect a compromise that pleased the church and found his work condemned at the Council of Sens in 1141. Distrust of the potentially misleading nature of certain philosophies even led a synod at Paris in 1210 to forbid the reading of the new Aristotelian materials that were beginning to be imported from the East.

In general, however, the medieval church managed to hold to a position that avoided the temptations of antiintellectual obscurantism as well as the option of substituting a rationalistic philosophy for the Christian faith. The scientific curiosity of the schoolmen was nurtured, and twelfth century Europe benefited from numerous attempts to observe, gather, and synthesize data for basic scholarly disciplines. The *Sentences* of Peter Lombard (d. 1160) went beyond Abelard's bald opposition of conflicting opinions in *Yes and No* and produced a dialectical juxtaposition of primary sources that served for centuries as the fundamental text for the study of theology in European schools. About 1148, a monk named Gratian produced a *Concordance of Discordant Canons* which established a basis for a scientific interpretation and elaboration of ecclesiastical law. This publication stimulated the state to encourage the study of ancient Roman law as codified in the sixth century by the Byzantine emperor Justinian. The development of these two schools of legal opinion raised the debate between church and state to a new level of sophistication. Canon law held that the state had been created for the negative purpose of dealing with the disruptive effects of sin in human society. The state owed its existence to human imperfection and man's need for restraint. Its function was worldly and its authority derivative from the higher mission of the church—an institution it was charged to protect. The codification of

Roman law had been developed for use by the caesaropapist government of Constantinople, where a clear division of church and state
never developed. This law assumed that the state was the primary
organ of human society and that the church served as a specialized department of the state. The argument between the medieval theoreticians of the church and the state was of greater consequence than they
could have known, for their mutual attacks and counterattacks stimulated the growth of political philosophies and governmental institutions that have, through the influence of Europe, come to dominate the
modern world.

During the twelfth century, the people of Europe reached a pitch
of general enthusiasm for the Christian religion that has perhaps
never been exceeded. For a few generations, Western society enjoyed
the excitement of a faith that had no serious rival and the confidence
of holding a belief whose truth was universally recognized and considered virtually self-evident. The population and the economy of Europe
were both on the rise. A middle class was beginning to appear, and it
introduced an invigorating flexibility into the old patterns of feudal
society. New career options and lifestyles became possible. New lands
opened to cultivation, and the West began to turn from the defensive
posture it had maintained ever since the days of the late Roman Empire. People found a new self-confidence in the possession of a civilization that appeared to them to be more than adequate to cope with the
challenges of their future, and there was no doubt in their minds that
the strength of their society derived from the validity of their religion.
The church had brought Europe through its darkest days, and the
growing prosperity and vigor of Western society must have seemed to
many to be an obvious confirmation of the validity of their Christian
faith. Suddenly, there was a superfluity of energy and resources for all
kinds of projects and movements. Even the most radical of the Christian institutions of the past were insufficient to contain the religious
impulses that sought release at every level of society. Traditional
forms of Christian life were restructured and revivified, and bold new
outlets were sought for the expression of faith.

In the past, the monastic vocation had always recommended itself
to the most committed and highly motivated members of the Christian
community, but the old cloistered orders found it impossible to control
the new religious enthusiasms of the twelfth century. The Cluniac
houses had in the tenth century been the home of the most radical
movements of their day, and the successful revitalization of the leadership of the church owed much to the inspiration of Cluny. But, by the

late eleventh century, monasticism in the Cluniac form no longer served to mirror the popular religious ideals of the day. Cluny's critics argued that it had lost the balance of the original Benedictine life. In its enthusiasm for developing the canonical offices and the service of God in acts of formal worship, Cluny had created the most elaborate liturgy in Europe and built its cloister into a palatial setting for prayer. Under the abbot Hugh the Great (1049–1109), the monks erected the largest church in the West and enriched it with outstanding examples of Romanesque sculpture and ornamentation. The service of the choir was so demanding that no time remained for manual labor, and the monks came to live serious, but privileged and elegant, lives.

The vibrant intellectualism of the twelfth century may have caused some reformers to favor a religion less focused on material symbols than Cluniac worship, for support began to build for new monastic movements that favored harsher environments. Peter Damian (1006–72), a vocal advocate of the reformed papacy and one of the leading publicists of his day, did much to revive interest in the ascetic ideals of the ancient Eastern monks. His work seems to have heralded the emergence of a new mood among his contemporaries. Twelve years after Damian's death, Bruno of Cologne, a famous teacher at the cathedral school of Rheims, turned his back on his academic career and took up the life of a hermit. His example met with a powerful response, and a new community soon gathered around him at Grande Chartreuse. This community proved to be the beginning of one of the most severe of the medieval monastic orders. The Carthusians, who were named for the location of their motherhouse, strove to lead the lives of ascetic hermits in the context of the Benedictine cloister. They maintained separate cells and gardens and met together only when necessary for the conduct of the worship and business of their house. Their standards of discipline were so strict that, over the years, they earned the unique reputation of never needing reform or reinspiration.

More influential than the Carthusian movement was the Cistercian order, which took its name from the house that Robert of Molême established at Citeaux near Dijon in 1098. Robert had been abbot of a Burgundian cloister, but he withdrew from it to a house of his own foundation in order to be free to practice a literal observance of the Benedictine rule. His monks defined themselves somewhat in opposition to Cluny. They revived the custom of hard physical labor; they located themselves in wastelands where they would be free from the temptations of the world and from the feudal political obligations that came with the acceptance of gifts of developed land; and they adopted a "puritanical" outlook that rejected symbol and ornament in their places of worship. All the Cistercian communities were subject to visitation and correction by the abbot of the motherhouse, and he was kept faithful to the ideals of the order by the admonitions of his colleagues at annual chapter meetings. A popular subservient order of lay brothers was created for illiterate peasants who were attracted to the monastic life but unable to acquire the Latin needed for full participation in the divine service. The brothers provided a valuable pool of labor, and Cistercian houses had tremendous economic success in opening new frontiers and bringing marginal lands into production. By the end of the Middle Ages, well past the crest of the movement in the early thirteenth century, there may still have been as many as 1,600 Cistercian cloisters in Europe.

Enthusiasm for the monastic life was a hallmark of the intense spirituality of the high Middle Ages, and people of the day seem frequently to have assumed that the monk lived a form of the Christian life more pleasing to God than any other human calling. There was a tendency throughout society to emulate, insofar as possible in the various stations of life, a kind of monastic discipline, and many kings wore monastic habits in their graves. There were particularly strong pressures on the secular clergy, who served the world outside the walls of cloisters, to modify their behavior in accordance with the monastic ideal. Renewed efforts were made by synods and bishops to define and enforce higher standards of morality for parish clergy; and vigorous, if only partially successful, attempts were made to enforce the obligation of clerical celibacy. Clergy who had the benefit of association with colleagues in cathedral chapters and collegiate churches, drew up rules to help define a kind of uncloistered monastic existence. In the 1120's, Norbert of Xanten, a friend of the leader of the Cistercian movement, Bernard of Clairvaux, drew on the example of Augustine of Hippo to create a particularly influential rule for the secular clergy at Prémontré; and the proliferation of similar rules eventually led the papacy to recognize an order of Augustinian canons. The extension of monastic lifestyles to uncloistered persons led to a multiplication of specialized religious organizations that often departed drastically from the traditional image of the monk. For example, certain military orders reversed the usual ethics of the clergy and armed the monk as a man of war. Mendicant groups spurned all possessions and found the expression of their religious ideals, not in hermetic self-sufficiency, but in the pursuit of charity in populous urban centers. The number and originality of the new monastic experiments were so great that, early in the thirteenth century, the papacy moved to restrain a potentially chaotic situation by refusing to recognize any new orders. New groups continued to appear, but attempts were made to adapt them to already established models.

The massive monastic movements of the twelfth century were only one manifestation of the vigorous religious energies of the period. In addition to the thousands who sought permanent careers officially connected with the church, thousands more were inspired to serve their faith by lesser, if frequently sacrificial, commitments of time and wealth to a wide range of popular religious movements. A restless, confident, striving spirit seemed to energize European society and to set masses of people in motion on pilgrimages, on crusades, and in the service of the construction of supreme religious edifices.

Pilgrimage fervor mounted in Europe from the tenth century on, but the pilgrimage itself was not an invention of the high Middle Ages. Sites associated with Jesus, the apostles, or the saints had begun to attract visitors at least as early as the third century. Christianity was a religion rooted in historical events and the careers of real people, and the pilgrimage was an obvious expression of a believer's natural desire to draw close to the roots of revelation. The increasing stabilization of society and the growing prosperity of the masses in the twelfth century enabled ever larger numbers of people to indulge a desire for adventure and to satisfy a need for a special and flamboyant expression of their commitment to their faith. The diffusion of saints' relics throughout the West created literally thousands of potential goals for pilgrims, and every year huge crowds of eager Christians donned the symbolic dress of religious voyagers and voluntarily submitted themselves to the rigors and dangers of the medieval road. Popular opinion accorded special merit to the shrine of St. James, the son of Zebedee, at Compostella; to the numerous altars of Rome, the spiritual capital of Christendom; and above all to the sacred sites of the Holy Lands. Half a million people annually streamed into Compostella, and the crowds at Rome sometimes ranged up to two million in a single year. The need to accommodate religious travelers generated a whole new industry of guides, carriers, and hostelers which invites comparison with the modern phenomenon of recreational tourism. Part of the motive of the pilgrim was doubtless a worldly desire for novelty and excitement, but his objectives were religious and their accomplishment difficult. A trip to the Holy Lands might require three or more years of arduous travel under dangerous and exorbitantly expensive circum-

stances, and so the spiritual merit such a journey earned was purchased at a significant price.

The intense desires of the pilgrims made a major contribution to
the series of spectacular assaults on the Moslem world that Europe inaugurated in 1095. The medieval crusades were ambiguous ventures
that sprang from many causes—not all of which were either spiritual
or noble. In part, they were a sign that Europe had stabilized as a civilization and recovered to the point where it could indulge a desire for
imperialistic expansion. In addition, there is no denying that the crusades offered certain individuals opportunities for personal enrich-
ment. But it is a significant indication of the mood of the period that
the crusaders chose to think of their activities as expressions of their
Christian faith, and it is doubtful that any but a religious motivation
could have mobilized the masses of divided Europe quite so effectively
for a common objective.

The crusading impulse first became apparent in Spain at the beginning of the eleventh century, when the tiny Christian principalities
of northern Spain began to recruit armies for the reconquest of the
Iberian peninsula—a project that required over four hundred years to
bring to completion. By the middle of the same century, the Italian
cities were fighting the Moslems for control of the Mediterranean is-
lands. The balance of power in the Mediterranean shifted significantly
in 1090, when the Christians recovered Sicily. The more famous series
of crusades, which pursued the conquest and defense of the Holy
Lands, resulted from this rising tide of European self-confidence and
from the congruence of Byzantine and papal interests. In 1071, the
Turks dealt Constantinople a defeat that cost the Eastern empire the
province of Asia Minor—from which Constantinople recruited most of
its soldiers. The city itself survived with its wealth from trade undi-
minished, and, in the 1090's, the emperor Alexius Comnenus still had
enough resources to contemplate a counteroffensive. To raise an army,
he resorted to established precedent and advertised for mercenaries
from the West. His request for assistance in a great campaign against
the Moslems reached Pope Urban II at a fortunate time. Urban
(1088–99), who was the second heir to Gregory VII's quarrel with the
German Empire, was busily engaged in defending his position in the
church against the antipopes supported by the German kings, and he
saw in Alexius's appeal an opportunity to develop a useful image for
the papacy. By putting himself at the head of a great crusading movement, the pope could give a form of true international leadership to
Europe and perhaps increase the security of the church by giving the

military classes a safe and distant outlet for their energies. Urban preached the First Crusade at Clermont in 1095 and received an overwhelming response. No kings in Europe at the time were in a position to lead the armies, but their vassals turned out in droves. Crusading fervor even permeated the ranks of the peasantry and sparked migrations of thousands of unarmed men, women, and children, who blindly charged into the East confident in the expectation that God would reward their irrational gesture with a miraculous victory over the infidel. Their efforts failed, but the professional soldiers who followed them had better luck. The First Crusade descended upon Asia Minor and Palestine at a time when the Moslems were divided and warring among themselves, and the Westerners were able to achieve their goal of establishing a Latin feudal state with its capital at Jerusalem. Their first victories were their greatest ones, for, within a generation, the crusaders were forced onto the defensive and began to lose ground. News of Christian defeats occasioned periodic rebirths of crusading enthusiasm in Europe, and major armies headed east in 1145, 1188, 1204, 1218, and 1250. Although they helped open Latin civilization to exciting new horizons and to the stimulus of alien cultures, the armies met with little military success. The Moslems soon recovered control of the Holy Lands and ultimately went on to conquer Constantinople (1453) and to threaten the eastern frontiers of Europe. The church continued to define as crusades the wars it favored, but the authentic commitment of the true holy war faded with the confident religious enthusiasm of the twelfth and early thirteenth centuries.

Within Europe itself, a crusade of a different nature began an architectural renaissance. Centers of pilgrimage and the practice of religion itself were adorned with monuments that have long been acclaimed the greatest and most characteristic aesthetic and technical achievements of the Middle Ages. The strength, confidence, and extreme religious devotion that fueled the Cluniac reform, the Investiture Controversy, the universities, the wars against the infidels, and the exertions of pilgrimage led also in the eleventh century to the pioneering of striking new forms of ecclesiastical architecture. The relatively small, dark, and primitive structures of the early medieval period were unable to serve the increasing flood of pilgrims or to mirror the passionate religious emotions of the new age, and everywhere they were torn down to be replaced by buildings in a grandiose Romanesque style. In a remarkably short period of time, techniques of masonry were revived and complex engineering problems solved; ancient Roman models were studied and imitated; and a distinct new aesthetic language of massive arches and vaults was mastered as an original medium for the expression of Christian visions. The lavishly adorned sanctuary of the monks of Cluny—with a nave 100 yards long and a vault that rose to a height of ninety-eight feet—was the crowning glory of a style that spread to every corner of Europe.

By the mid-twelfth century and the completion of Cluny (ca. 1130), experiments with techniques for achieving higher vaults and brighter lighting had created the possibilities of the more daring and conceptually complex Gothic architectural forms. Some of the earliest traces of the Gothic are to be found in the monastic buildings created by Suger, the abbot of St. Denis (ca. 1144), but, unlike the Romanesque, the Gothic seems to have found its most vigorous patrons, not in the monasteries, but among the clergy of the urban cathedrals. Enthusiasm for the new style was so great that relatively modern buildings were torn down and rebuilt, and projects were undertaken on a scale that must have carried their sponsors to the brink of bankruptcy. The ten thousand or so residents of Amiens commissioned a cathedral large enough to contain their entire community at one service. Smaller cities, such as Norwich and Lincoln, augmented the facilities of some fifty parish churches with a major cathedral. Everywhere the passion for building was so great that, by the time the movement began to decline in the late thirteenth century, Europe may have achieved an average of one church edifice for each two hundred of its people.

The great period of excitement and innovation in Gothic architecture lasted only about a century (ca. 1150–1250), but this was time enough to begin most of the major monuments and to explore the limits of characteristic structural techniques. Dozens of major buildings were begun, and some of them advanced toward completion with surprising rapidity. The cathedral at Chartres, which has long been recognized as a superb model of the best in Gothic style, took shape in about sixty-five years; the great church at Amiens went up in half a century; and its predecessor at Laon was completed in a mere forty-seven years. The architects of Romanesque Cluny had achieved a vault almost 100 feet high, but Chartres rose to 131 feet, and Beauvais surpassed the limits of safety with a plan aimed at 157 feet. Towers soared 269 feet at Rheims, 300 feet at Chartre, and ultimately a proposed 525 feet at Ulm. Buildings on this scale presented problems of conception and execution that called for extraordinary efforts, but every corner of Europe was able to produce people in abundance who were equal to the challenge and eager for the work. Chroniclers speak of masses of men and women from every station of life who singly and in groups made huge financial contributions and occasionally threw themselves into the labor of hauling stone and physically assisting the professional artisans.

The cathedrals they raised were for them at one and the same time a labor of sacrificial love, an expression of human pride, and a bold proclamation of a supremely confident faith. The buildings exist today as the most eloquent of all the indicators of the mood of a period when the West found such unity and purpose through its religious traditions that all its potencies combined in an apparently invincible synthesis of faith, knowledge, and will.

Chapter Four

———◆◆◆———

An Age of Crises

THE POTENTIAL OF A UNIVERSAL CHURCH

BY THE THIRTEENTH CENTURY, Europe had reached the zenith of the medieval phase in its civilization, and its institutions were again providing a secure and meaningful context for human life. Between 1000 and 1300, the population of the West doubled. Commerce revived, urban life reappeared, and a strong middle class began to make its influence felt on traditional political and social structures. The divisive tendencies of feudalism were reversed, and strong kings strove to pull together centralized states with clearly defined frontiers and sophisticated mechanisms for internal administration. National cultures and awareness of national identity emerged in conjunction with a cosmopolitan outlook derived from frequent contacts with foreign cultures. The universities began the recovery and assimilation of the intellectual heritage of the Greeks and Romans, and major advances were made in law, science, and philosophy. Eloquent and uniquely European styles in the arts began to appear, and works worthy of comparison with the best of any age were accomplished. There were indications on all sides that Europe had fully recovered from the upheavals occasioned by the collapse of the ancient Roman world and that the old civilization of the West was clearly flourishing in the hands of new peoples.

Although there were still outposts of paganism on the perimeters of Europe and thinly veiled vestiges of heathen customs in even the most devout and orthodox communities, the Christian religion had triumphed. It was virtually unchallenged as the ideology of the West. Christian theology shaped the assumptions and preconceptions of European thought; it dictated the frame of meaning that structured all interpretations of human experience; it set the goals for human life. Significant differences of opinion might emerge from time to time, but it was generally assumed that participation in European civilization inevitably involved an affirmation of one common Christian faith and a declaration of loyalty to one universal Christian church.

The existence of a universal church and a consensus of faith provided the thirteenth century with the option of working toward the unification of all of its social and political institutions. Europe had begun its civilized history as a part of the Roman world state, and, under Charlemagne, the memory of the old unity had been nurtured. But, generally speaking, the tribal and regional loyalties of the Europeans had proved stronger than the forces that had attempted to unify the West and give political reality to the cultural concepts *Europe* and *Christendom*. By the thirteenth century, nations under the leadership of strong, independent monarchs had established themselves throughout the West, but the struggle between the forces of nationalism and internationalism was far from over. It was still possible for visionaries to entertain a realistic hope of achieving a united Europe, and many of them saw the machinery and ideology of the church as the most obvious vehicle for the creation of a new world order.

It was indisputable that the church was compiling an excellent record in the administration of its own affairs. A network of parishes covered Europe and brought the practice of the Christian faith within the reach of virtually everyone. The level of education and discipline of the "lower" clergy who served these parishes left much to be desired, but a hierarchy of "higher" clergy had been evolving and was acquiring ways and means to police the professional conduct of the people's priests. The agreements that ended the Investiture Controversy recognized the pope's right to supervise the appointment of bishops and metropolitans, and the universities provided him with a continuous stream of excellently qualified candidates for ecclesiastical offices. Bishops developed large staffs of specialists who helped them run their dioceses with an efficiency that was the envy of many a royal official, and the church frequently provided the models and the manpower for the improvement of the governmental machinery of the state. Episcopal agents toured parishes and visited monasteries and thus gave bishops the means to exercise authority over the clergy. The church developed its own court system that claimed jurisdiction over the moral and confessional conduct of the laity and over all the affairs of the clergy, and ecclesiastical authorities vigorously fought to establish the independence of men in holy orders from the judiciaries of the state. The papacy evolved complex bureaucratic structures, sophisticated means of communication, and a system of appellate courts that enabled it to make its influence felt in the lives of all Christians. It invented successful tax structures to support its staff, and it pioneered methods of administration that accelerated the development of modern techniques of government. In principle, the church sought recognition as an autonomous, self-governing papal monarchy that functioned freely within the territories of the various European nations.

By the beginning of the thirteenth century, the ubiquitous parish churches could be seen as the ends of lines of authority that were being gathered with increasing efficiency into the hands of an effective, centralized international government. The possibility of a world-state was, therefore, not simply a vision, but a partially achieved reality in the lives of medieval people. There were theoreticians who preferred that universal government find its ultimate realization through the expansion of the secular machinery of the Holy Roman Empire of the German monarchs. But, since the development of the government of the church at first outstripped that of the state, it was more reasonable to expect that a way would be found to use the administrative competence of the clergy to order the chaotic affairs of the emerging nations of Europe.

Innocent III (1198–1216), the pope whose reign has often been viewed as the pinnacle of the power and prestige of the medieval papacy, made a sustained and partially successful attempt to develop the church as a means for the achievement of European unity. His successes were, however, often more indicative of the weaknesses of the lay rulers with whom he dealt than of the raw political power of the church. Innocent was fortunate in coming to the papacy at a time when the kings of Europe were still somewhat insecure in the control of their nations. The delicacy of monarchs' situations often gave them an opportunity to intervene decisively in their affairs and develop a reputation for strong international leadership. Innocent, who became pope at the unusually young age of thirty-seven, was a remarkable man well equipped to handle the opportunities that came his way. He was a member of the aristocratic Conti family which counted Pope Clement III and several cardinals among its ranks. He was intellectually gifted and profited from opportunities to study theology at the University of Paris and law at Bologna. While still in his twenties, he was admitted to the college of cardinals and given valuable experience in ecclesiastical politics. He shared the enthusiasm of his age for monastic values and found leisure to write books on the sacraments and ascetic disciplines.

Innocent believed the role of the pope to be that of the vicar of

Christ who, as the unique representative of the King of kings, took precedence over all heads of earthly states, and he came closer than any pontiff ever had to exercising the universal dominion that had long been claimed for the papacy. His was, in theory at least, the highest authority in the world, and, by cleverly exploiting the blunders of other leaders, he was frequently able to wield a degree of influence that gave a new reality to papal claims. It was Innocent's hope to use the practical powers and spiritual prestige of his office to mediate among nations and to promote the unity of Christendom, and he had many notable successes. The kings of England, Aragon, Castile, Portugal, Poland, Hungary, Serbia, and Bulgaria made themselves vassals of the papacy, and few nations were able completely to avoid the influence of Rome's diplomatic maneuvers. In most cases, however, Innocent's triumphs were due to his personal skill in exploiting the blunders of his opponents and not to any irresistible power possessed by the church. His reign demonstrated the kind of visionary international leadership the papacy might hope to provide for Europe but adroitly concealed the fact that the church had little real political power.

The fortunate circumstance that set the context for Innocent's reign was the sudden collapse of the Hohenstaufen dynasty. A year before Innocent's election, the Hohenstaufens seemed on the verge of overwhelming the papacy. Frederick Barbarossa, who had restored the Holy Roman Empire and strongly asserted the divine rights of emperors in opposition to those of popes, had been succeeded in 1190 by a strong and capable son, Henry VI. In short order, Henry established his authority over Germany and the cities of northern Italy, intimidated Constantinople, and arranged a marriage with the heiress of Sicily. The marriage joined southern Italy to the empire and enabled him to surround the papal states. The situation was quite grave for the papacy until 1197, when Henry suddenly died at the age of thirty-two and left an infant heir, the future Frederick II. A few months later, Innocent became pope. For the remainder of his life, he enjoyed the advantage of dealing with a German Empire that existed primarily on paper. The young Frederick was designated a ward of the papacy and relegated to Sicily while his uncle, Philip of Swabia, sought recognition as emperor in Germany. Philip's claims were contested by the Duke of Saxony, Otto of Brunswick, who ultimately succeeded to the imperial title when Philip was assassinated in 1208. When Otto adopted policies in Italy that displeased the church, Innocent championed the rights of the young Frederick, and the empire was reduced to a state of internal disorder from which it did not fully recover until after Innocent's death. The immobilization of the empire by the exploitation of its weaknesses gave Innocent personal security and an opportunity to establish control over the lands the papacy claimed in Italy. Innocent earned the reputation of being the second founder of the papal states, and possession of a strong territorial domain provided him with resources that were useful in improving the organization of the church and in dealing with the governments of Europe.

Innocent's greatest apparent success in influencing the policies of a major nation came in his dealings with John, king of England. The contest between the king and the pope began in 1205 as a result of a disputed election to the see of Canterbury. A party of Canterbury monks backed one candidate for the archiepiscopate, John insisted upon another, and Innocent attempted a compromise by suggesting a famous English cardinal, Stephen Langton, for the position. John refused to accept papal mediation and precipitated a head-on confrontation between church and state in England. Innocent could do little of a military nature to advance the claims of papal authority against a king, but he had several spiritual weapons at his disposal. In 1208, the pope placed England under an interdict that closed the churches and cut off access to the sacraments, and a year later he declared John personally excommunicated and banned from the company of Christians. These moves failed to have the desired effect. John ignored the papal decrees, terrorized the clergy, and confiscated the properties of the church. He remained obdurate for four years until Innocent played his last card. The pope announced that an excommunicate could not hold legitimate authority over a Christian nation, and he declared John deposed. The pope could do little to implement his decree, but John was well aware that his English nobles were weakening in their loyalty to him and that the French might be prepared to use the papal pronouncement as an excuse to launch an invasion of England. With dramatic suddenness, John reversed his policy and capitulated to Innocent—giving the pope more than he had asked. John accepted Stephen Langton as archbishop of Canterbury, publicly apologized for his behavior toward the church, and demonstrated his future good faith by declaring himself a vassal of the papacy. Innocent's spectacular triumph proved, however, to be a Pyrrhic victory, for John was not without skill in the wiles of diplomacy. As John's nominal overlord, Innocent found himself in the unfortunate position of having to side with the king in his quarrels with the English people. Innocent soon tarnished the image of the papacy in England by absolving John from the

oath he had taken to honor the principles set forth in the Magna Car-
ta. Rome received little profit from its feudal suzerainty over England,
and papal attempts to meddle in the affairs of the nation contributed to
the estrangement of England from Rome in the Reformation of the sixteenth century.

Innocent achieved another apparent victory for international
papal diplomacy in his dealings with France, but here too his triumph
did little to increase the effective power of the church. In 1193, King
Philip Augustus of France married Princess Ingeborg, sister of the
king of Denmark. The marriage was not a success—the day after the
wedding, Philip repudiated his wife. Ingeborg refused to submit to his
insult and appealed to the pope for vindication of her marital rights.
Philip ignored the attempts of the papacy to mediate, and, in 1196, he
went through another marriage ceremony with Agnes of Meran, the
daughter of one of his vassals. The legitimacy of the children born of
this union was open to question, and Philip was justifiably concerned
to guarantee their right to inherit his throne. Nevertheless, he with-
stood Innocent's displeasure for fifteen years. After Agnes's death, he
finally gave in to papal pressures and agreed to a reunion with Ingeborg—but only after the pope acknowledged the legitimacy of Agnes's
children and only after it became apparent that Ingeborg's brother
might be willing to offer valuable naval assistance for a contemplated
invasion of England. Technically, Innocent won his struggle with
Philip and maintained his claim to be the guardian of the morals of
Europe. But his victory was primarily due to his concessions to Philip
and to changes in Philip's own diplomatic strategies.

Innocent did not limit himself simply to working through heads of
state in his attempts to influence the destiny of Europe. On several occasions, he undertook direct appeals to the people for support of projects that he represented as promoting the best interests of Europe as a
whole. In 1187, the Moslems had regained control of Jerusalem, and,
by the time of Innocent's election in 1198, the Latin presence in the
Holy Lands had all but disappeared. Innocent therefore lost no time
in declaring the Fourth Crusade and in recruiting its soldiers. No
kings took the cross, and a papal legate proved to be an inadequate
commander for the polyglot assortment of military men who declared
themselves a part of the venture. Many of the soldiers, who gathered at
Venice to await transportation to the Holy Lands, were poorly disciplined, poorly led fortune hunters, and their crusade soon disgraced
the pope who had inaugurated it. The Venetian government succeeded
in deflecting the troops from their sanctioned goals in the Holy Lands

in order to use them against Venice's commercial rivals in Christian lands. Key sites on the Adriatic were brought under Venetian control, and, in 1204, the great Christian city of Constantinople fell to the Latin crusaders—who never did achieve anything of significance in the fight against the Moslems. Innocent repudiated his crusade, but he was not entirely displeased. A Latin hierarchy was established in the territory of the old Greek Empire, and the papacy enjoyed the illusion of authority over the Byzantine church until the Latin government in Constantinople fell in 1261. The cost was clearly excessive. Latin troops wantonly destroyed much of the unique art and literature that Constantinople had cherished and preserved since the last days of the ancient Greco-Roman world. In addition, the Byzantine state was so severely weakened that its effectiveness as a buffer between the frontiers of eastern Europe and the Moslem Empire was dealt a mortal blow.

Innocent was responsible for another crusade of an equally ambiguous nature. Five years after the fall of Constantinople, Innocent declared war on the Cathari, who were also named the Albigensians for one of their principal centers. The Albigensians were not Moslems from the Holy Lands, but heretics who had long been resident in southern France. Church councils in 1179 and 1184 had called for action against them, but they had flourished in the fertile religious atmosphere of the twelfth century.

The origin of the Albigensian movement and the details of its theology are uncertain, but Albigensian thought seems to have been related to ancient philosophies that had long flourished in the East and that combined dualist metaphysics with a belief in reincarnation. The Albigensians apparently taught that there were two opposing forces in the universe, a principle of evil that manifested itself in matter, and a principle of good that ruled the realm of the spirit. The human soul belonged by right to the domain of spirit, but, in this life, it found itself trapped in a material body that was part of the kingdom of evil. In order to liberate the soul, the Albigensians prescribed severe ascetic disciplines, the renunciation of all pleasures of the flesh, and the utilization of holy rites that were believed to strengthen the spirit in its struggle with the material world. Salvation could be earned only by those capable of heroic deeds of self-denial; but for those who were not yet ready to attempt the most strenuous disciplines, there was another kind of hope. They were destined to experience, through reincarnation, a continued association with the flesh which was no improvement on their present lot, but which would give them a future chance for total liberation. An easy moral standard was an adequate guide for the present lives of those who were content with this destiny.

The Albigensians presented the church with a unique challenge. Since they believed matter to be evil, they rejected the Christian understanding of the creation and denied the full humanity of Christ, the reality of his crucifixion, and the use of material substances in the sacraments. Their theology was thus clearly heretical, and their moral standards were perhaps inferior to those the church attempted to enforce among its people. But their doctrines were rational and congruent with human experience, and their leaders, who were required to maintain the most extreme ascetic disciplines, were occasionally more impressive individuals than the somewhat worldly clergy who were all too visible in the orthodox church.

At the beginning of his reign, Innocent cherished the hope that a program of intensive missionary work might be adequate to eradicate the Albigensian heresy. The bishops of infected dioceses were exhorted to great efforts in defense of orthodoxy; the Cistercian order of monks was enlisted to assist them; and a Castilian scholar, Dominic de Guzman (1170–1221), won papal recognition for a special order of uncloistered Dominican friars, or brothers, who took as their primary mission preaching and the refutation of heresies. But, by 1209, Innocent had apparently come to believe that these peaceful efforts had failed to make sufficient headway against the enemy, and he endorsed a violent alternative. A crusade was proclaimed against the Albigensians (1209–29). Philip Augustus, the king whose domain was directly involved, refused to have anything to do with the project. The crusade appealed primarily to the lesser nobility, who saw in it an excuse to loot the rich provinces of the south of France. The campaign sputtered fitfully into the middle of the thirteenth century and had a devastating effect on the once-brilliant culture and flourishing economy of the region of Provence. The heresy was rooted out, and the French monarchy profited significantly from the weakening of the formerly independent nobility of the south. But atrocities had been common, and Innocent's policies contributed to the discredit of the crusading movement and to an eventual diminution of the reputation of the church.

The Albigensian crusade left one particular legacy that was to be of some significance in the history of the Christian movement. The church's lengthy attempt to combat heresy in France led to the evolution of an ecclesiastical court of inquisition which specialized in ferreting out and prosecuting persons accused of unorthodox thought or behavior. The Inquisition had its origin somewhat casually in episcopal searches for heretics, which the papacy began ordering in the late twelfth century. As the struggle against heresy became more and more serious, the conduct of inquisitions became the responsibility of specially appointed papal officers, who established a formal organization to assist them in their duties. In 1229, a synod in Toulouse endorsed a list of procedures for the conduct of heresy trials. These procedures so abused the rights of the accused that even people accustomed to the rough-and-ready principles of medieval justice should have been scandalized. By 1252, the papacy had authorized the use of torture in pursuit of evidence against heretics. But the worst horrors of the Inquisition were reserved for the sixteenth century and the uses to which the Spanish government put the courts of the church in its ruthless attempts to achieve national unity. Inquisition leaders justified the use of violence in defense of the faith on the theory that heresy was a kind of disease of the soul that placed one in danger of eternal damnation. Human communities had an obvious right to resort to compulsion to avoid infection from individuals who carried physical illnesses. Society was therefore equally entitled to use similarly drastic means to protect itself from persons who were a threat to the much more important health of the soul. Once established as part of Christian practice, the Inquisition had great success in perpetuating itself from generation to generation. The Protestant revolution of the sixteenth century gave it a new lease on life, and it was not officially discontinued by the Roman Catholic Church until 1834.

Innocent's attempts to strengthen the authority of the papacy within the church proved in the long run to be more constructive than his endeavors to use the church as a power in international politics. Under Innocent's direction, the centralization of church government was encouraged, and the pope exercised something of the same kind of authority over the church that contemporary kings were striving to develop over the nations of Europe. Innocent gained extensive control of appointments to all kinds of ecclesiastical benefices. He inaugurated a useful procedure for the direct taxation of the clergy. And, toward the end of his reign, he assumed the right to dictate a program for a detailed, universal reform of the Christian religion which touched the life of everyone in the Western world.

The edicts of the famous Fourth Lateran Council, which Innocent convened on November 11, 1215, summed up his program for the church and served as the crowning achievement of his reign. The council marked the first time an ecclesiastical meeting in the medieval West could lay claim to recognition as a convocation of the universal church. Five hundred bishops and eight hundred monastic leaders attended, and legations from the heads of state of the European nations made the meeting an event of international political importance. Despite its size, the council concluded its business with great speed and little discord, for it seems primarily to have affirmed and publicized the dictates of the pope. It defined and condemned heresies. It called for new crusades and the final submission of the Greek branch of the church to papal authority. It set high standards for clerical morality and ordered bishops to adopt programs of regular visitation of their clergy in order to enforce discipline. It pressed for more education for the parish clergy and called for the establishment of additional schools and for assistance to clergy who wished to attend them. It attacked simony, the charging of fees for administration of the sacraments, the financial exploitation of the people's faith in relics, the unwarranted granting of indulgences, and other crass abuses of spiritual authority. It endorsed the doctrine of transubstantiation, and it laid on all Christians the obligation to confess and commune annually. It accelerated improvements in judicial procedures by halting clerical participation in trials by ordeal. It forbade unseemly use of churches for theatrical performances. And, in a move that reveals the extent of the spiritual authority the papacy claimed over the whole of Europe, the council even legislated for those outside the church by ordering Jews to wear clothing that would distinguish them from Christians. Seldom in history has a Christian leader been able realistically to aspire to the degree of authority over the universal church that Innocent sought to exercise.

The final session of the Council was held on November 30, 1215. Innocent, still a relatively young pope, died a few months later on July 16, 1216. He was as fortunate in the timing of his death as he had been in the correlation of many of the events in his diplomatic program. The power of the medieval church had reached its peak by the early thirteenth century, and Innocent's vision of a Europe united under the spiritual direction of the papacy was soon to prove its impracticality. Innocent left the papacy looking much stronger than it actually was, and his successors were to learn from bitter experience that the true centers of political and economic power in Europe were those that were developing at the courts of kings. Ultimately, it was to be the church that succumbed to the divisions of the nations, not the nations that fused into the unity of the church.

Innocent lived long enough to become aware that the people of Europe were developing a new aggressiveness and independence in their apprehension of the Christian faith. They were becoming more difficult to lead and more confident of their abilities to make their own moral and religious judgments. In part, the new mood was due to a rise in general levels of education and to the middle class's increasing experience of effectiveness in self-government. The new confidence of the laity and the growing desire of the common man for greater powers of self-determination were testimonies to the success of medieval institutions in restoring a thriving civilization to Europe. But the civilization that was returning to Europe was equipping its people to examine and evaluate the very institutions that were its vehicles, and, as the Middle Ages wore on, the church and the state came under increasing scrutiny and bold criticism.

Innocent was sensitive to the fact that his attempt to use the spiritual authority of the church as a basis for international political power could lay the church open to the charge of worldliness. It was difficult for a churchman to deal as a politician with politicians while maintaining a stance of moral superiority to the harsh realities of political power. The more effective the papacy attempted to become as a political force, the more vulnerable it made itself to the charge that it was nothing more than a political institution. Its gains in worldly power often entailed sacrifices of reputation and spiritual authority. Innocent was alert to this danger and to the uncomfortable truths that lay at the root of the charges of materialism hurled at the orthodox clergy by heretics like the Albigensians. He therefore encouraged Dominic, the missionary to the heretics of Provence, to establish his credibility in the eyes of the Albigensians, to whom he intended to preach, by stripping himself of all signs of wealth and power. In 1210, Innocent also recognized a new order of friars, formed by followers of Francis of Assisi, that had the distinguishing feature of total poverty. The Franciscans were intended by their founder to be a society of religious men who accepted no property, established no cloisters, and simply wandered about witnessing to the love of God and living on what God provided through the charity of others. Implicit in their example was a criticism of the wealth and security of the more traditional clergy, and the Franciscan point of view won an enthusiastic response from the people. During the thirteenth century, the great bishops, abbots, and popes who enjoyed the use of symbols of power were far less popular than the humble Dominican and Franciscan friars. Their simple style of life seemed more congruent with the example of Christ and the apostles than did the aristocratic existences of the higher clergy, and the friars' ministries attracted more confidence than those of ordinary priests. The Dominicans and Franciscans found places for themselves as special preachers, confessors, and social workers in every corner of Europe, and, for a few generations, their ideals fueled a rebirth of enthusiasm for the monastic vocation. Innocent may have been wiser than he knew in endorsing the option for Christian life that they represented, for the sight of the mendicant in pursuit of his single-minded objective of selfless commitment to others did much to maintain the credibility of the church and to lessen the unfortunate impressions all too often made by the more traditional clergy.

THE PROFESSIONALIZATION OF THE CHURCH

THE POLICIES OF INNOCENT III and the pronouncements of the Fourth Lateran Council are indications of the fact that, by the early thirteenth century, the medieval church was coming to its maturity. It was developing a clear understanding of itself as an international papal monarchy. It was devising organizational structures that enabled it effectively to discharge the functions it claimed for itself in European society. And it was articulating systems of theology and law that prepared it to defend the hope it held for the evolution of European civilization and the place it claimed for a universal religion in the future of the West.

The church's plan for the future was, of course, conditioned by its experience of the past. For almost a thousand years, the church had labored in the West for the preservation of the values and skills of civilized life. For much of that time, the church had been the only institution in Europe equipped to oppose barbarism and guard the treasures of the Western intellectual tradition. During the strenuous period of transition from the ancient to the medieval phases in European history, it had been possible to educate only the small number of persons who served society as clergy. Since they alone were capable of retaining contact with the documents that were the repositories of Christian tradition and authority, only they were in a position to understand the Christian faith in its most sophisticated and profound forms. In the absence of the benefits conferred by a system of popular education, it was impossible for them to communicate complexities of doctrine and philosophical subtleties to the ignorant masses who formed the laity of the church. It was all too easy for the clergy to assume that this unfortunate, but enduring, situation was to be accepted as a permanent condition of life.

The fact that the clergy functioned on a higher level of Christian understanding than did the laity led to the conclusion that the clergy had a unique duty to care for the laity and to live Christian lives of special intensity so as to help compensate for the inadequacies of those who followed lesser, secular callings. The church came to be seen as an institution charged with the responsibility of mediating between God and mankind. People believed it was the profession of the clergy to engineer the salvation of those who were ill equipped to assume spiritual responsibility for themselves. Large endowments were therefore established for the support of communities of monks and nuns whose lives were spent in a constant round of prayers and deeds of ascetic self-sacrifice. Their labors were devoted not simply to achieving salvation for themselves as individuals, but also to interceding with God on behalf of the patrons of their cloisters and society at large. The secular clergy who served parishes and administered dioceses provided laymen with access to the church's fund of saving grace. As a result, the laity came to think of the church as a professional organization that cared for them and did for them things of spiritual significance that they could not always or adequately do for themselves. It was not absolutely necessary for laymen to understand the full meaning of the words and deeds the clergy prescribed in the practice of the faith; it was essential only that the laity submit to the guidance of those who were professionally trained and divinely equipped to assist in the pursuit of salvation.

The source of the grace that reconciled God and humankind was the work of mediation performed by the Christ. It was he and he alone who had made salvation possible, and, although no new sacrifices would ever be required for the continued satisfaction of God's justice, it was necessary constantly to renew the application of Christ's merits to the events of history. The medieval church saw itself literally as the heir of Christ, the sole agent empowered to act in his name for the salvation of his people. It believed itself to be the only link established between the human and the divine, and it labored to articulate its channels of grace as clearly as possible. It taught that all authority derived from God the Creator, but that he delegated absolute powers through his son to the apostle Peter, the first head of the church. These divine privileges were then passed on from generation to generation through the unbroken line of Peter's successors, the Roman popes. The Christ-ordained office of the papacy, in turn, established the legitimacy of the church's hierarchy of clerical specialists. The clergy existed for the purpose of continuing Christ's work in history by representing men to God and God to men.

In practice, the work of the clergy consisted primarily of acts of ritual intercession and of attempts to enforce obedience to moral codes. The leaders of the church regularly urged their clerical subordinates to preach and teach an understanding of the faith to the people, but the inadequate educations of the lower clergy and the laity defeated attempts to develop the intellectual aspects of the Christian life. Unlettered people found it difficult to deal directly with concepts, but responded instead to the dramatic symbols contained in the rituals of worship. The illiterate masses could not comprehend a profound explication of Christian theology, but they had no trouble understanding the Christian faith as a system of compliance with specific moral and religious duties imposed by a divinely ordained authority. Most people experienced secular life as an existence characterized by the need to submit to unchallengeable feudal powers. It was natural for them to assume that the life of the spirit was governed in an analogous fashion by clergy, and that laymen need not always understand clerical activities in order to benefit from them.

The primary professional tools of the medieval clergy were not words, but sacraments—liturgical acts that were believed to focus the effects of God's grace on specific human needs. By the early thirteenth century, the sacramental system of the church had been fully developed, and there were rites designed for the nurture of human life from birth to death. Since a sacrament was a human act that mediated divine grace, almost anything the church did could be interpreted as having a sacramental dimension. It was a long time, therefore, before theologians reached agreement on the number and identity of the distinct acts that Christian tradition vested with major sacramental potential. Some of the early church fathers seem to have regarded baptism and the Eucharist, or "Lord's Supper," as the only essential rites of the church, but their medieval successors disagreed. Peter Damian (1006–72) identified at least twelve, and the famous mystic Hugh of St. Victor (1096–1141) believed he could distinguish about thirty. The popularity of Peter Lombard's *Sentences* as a theological textbook in the universities led eventually to a general acceptance of his list of seven, and, in 1439, the church officially confirmed the popular consensus by defining the sacraments as the rites of baptism, confirmation, penance, Eucharist, extreme unction, marriage, and ordination.

The medieval church held baptism to be absolutely essential for salvation, for this sacrament was defined as the act that overcame the effects of the lethal heritage of original sin, which placed every human child in danger of hell from the moment of its birth. Because the guilt of sin was imputed to infants, it was essential that they be baptized as soon as possible after birth, and, if it appeared that a newborn was in imminent danger of death, it was considered legitimate for a layperson to improvise the rite. Important as the sacrament was, however, the circumstances of its administration may often have left adults in doubt as to whether or not they had properly received it. In the absence of older witnesses to the incident, it was difficult to prove that one had been validly baptized, and it may have been this problem, among others, that brought the church by the fourteenth and fifteenth centuries to attempt the maintenance of formal parish records.

The universalization of the practice of baptizing infants increased the importance of the sacrament of confirmation, for confirmation provided the baptized child with an opportunity to affirm for himself the commitments to the Christian faith that his sponsors had made for him at the font. It was generally agreed that confirmation should be made available to a child when he or she reached the age of reason, but the church councils vacillated in their attempts to determine the exact year after birth in which the appropriate level of maturity officially appeared. There was a tendency to administer the sacrament to younger and younger children, and the conditions of its administration made it difficult to hold to any rigid list of qualifications. Confirmation could be bestowed only by a bishop, and, since many children probably had few chances to make contact with the higher clergy, expediency may have played a greater role than age in determining when the sacrament was received.

At adolescence, most medieval Christians made crucial career decisions, and sacraments were available to bless the commitments they made to either of their two major vocational options. Those who entered the church as clergy received ordination; those who remained among the laity normally married. Ordination was not one rite, but included seven that advanced a man through distinct offices culminating in the priesthood. University students and many church employees took the preliminary steps in the process of ordination in order to place themselves under the jurisdiction of church law. Many remained at this level all their lives. Not everyone who took holy orders exercised a priestly function or possessed the authority to perform sacraments.

Marriage, like ordination, was recognized as a sacrament, although the monastic-ascetic values of the medieval clergy caused them to be somewhat ambivalent toward a ceremony that blessed sexual union. The wedding ritual was often performed outside the entrance to the church, and the party approached the altar for a mass only after the marriage itself had been legally proclaimed. Marriage was nonetheless an honorable estate, and wedding metaphors were extremely popular in the writings of medieval mystics and theologians who attempted to describe the relationship between Christ and the church or God and the human soul.

Ordination could be received in several stages, and later marriages could be contracted if earlier ones were properly dissolved; but baptism, confirmation, marriage, and ordination were ordinarily experienced only once in life. The three remaining sacraments—extreme unction, penance, and the Eucharist—were designed to be used more frequently. Extreme unction was probably employed less often in practice than it could have been in theory. It was a ritual of anointing for the healing of serious illnesses, but in the popular imagination it was associated with the deathbed and was sometimes feared as a sign of the imminent approach of death. In the fortunate event of a recovery, however, it could be applied again as often as needed.

Penance and the Eucharist occupied the bulk of the time that most people spent in the formal practice of their faith. These two rites were designed to work together as a mechanism of correction and encouragement for the perfection of Christian life. Penance involved acts of confessing, repenting, and receiving absolution for sins, and it prepared one for the experience of communion with God in the Eucharist. The early church had practiced the custom of confessing sins publicly in the presence of all the members of a congregation, and it had debated whether or not all sins could be forgiven. Under the influence of Irish monasticism, the early medieval church developed the practice of private confession by an individual to a priest, and, as the church worked out the theory of its role as Christ's representative in history, it came to believe that the merits of Christ and the saints which had been entrusted to the church gave church authorities the power to discharge the penalties for every kind of sin. Certain extremely severe or unusual sins might be reserved to the attention of bishops or popes, but the church believed itself ultimately entitled to grant forgiveness for even the most serious of offenses.

The sacrament of penance gave a sinner forgiveness for his confessed faults. It removed the guilt incurred by sin, but it did nothing to remedy the effect that the absolved sin had already had on the course of human history. It was generally believed, therefore, that a sincere confession ought to be accompanied by a penitential act of apology and symbolic restitution, and it was common practice for a priest to require an absolved sinner to perform a charitable or pious deed before readmitting him to the fellowship of the church. The assigned act, which was called a penance, did not earn forgiveness for the sinner; it merely gave him a vehicle for expressing the sincerity of his repentance and helped him restore the balance of divine justice which his offense had upset. However, the constant association of penances with absolutions made it difficult to remember that the performance of the penance was not somehow a payment for the absolution—particularly when the medieval clergy came to take a more and more legalistic approach to the problem of sin. For the early church father Augustine of Hippo, all sins were indications of the great gulf that divided man from God, and, in light of the radical corruption of human nature that each one of them revealed, the differences among sins seemed almost inconsequential. The clergy of the Dark Ages who struggled to civilize their barbarian converts could not afford, however, to be quite so indifferent to relative degrees of ethical achievement or failure. The pastoral situation they faced caused them to think of sin, not so much as a general condition of estrangement from God, but as various specific actions that were offensive to divine law. Traditions developed that grouped sins in classes and assigned each its price. Books were written to assist priests in their efforts to apply the right degree of discipline to each kind of offense. Some sins were regarded as the unfortunate, but minor, side effects of human frailty; these were called *venial* sins. Others—such as anger, gluttony, sloth, lust, pride, covetousness, and envy—were held to spring from motives of deliberate human perversity. These were called *mortal* sins because of their fatal effect on the soul. As the clergy developed ever more elaborate professional methods for the quantification of sins and penances, it must have been difficult for simple Christians to remember that the forgiveness they sought was freely given them by God through Christ and not purchased at the price of their own penitential labors. The law of man in barbarian societies was a law of compensation and recompense; it was all too easy, therefore, for barbarian Christians to assume that human customs mirrored those of God. It was extraordinarily difficult to maintain the Christian paradoxes of grace in a society based on the simple justice of indemnificatory works.

The legalistic attitudes that colored the medieval Christian understanding of the sacrament of penance also had an effect on the interpretation and use of the Eucharist. The celebration of the Lord's Supper—which got its popular name, Mass, from the words of dismissal that concluded its Latin liturgy (*Ite, missa est*)—was the central rite of the Christian faith. It had clearly been established by the Christ himself, and it was held to communicate in a literal fashion the reality of his miraculous sacrifice on the cross. In the Mass, the actual Body and Blood of Christ were offered for human sins and became physically present in all their power for the benefit of the faithful. Belief in the real presence of the Christ in the consecrated bread and wine led to an elaborate formalization of the ceremony of the Eucharist. The words of the liturgy were precisely fixed by tradition and protected from change to such an extent that the language of the altar ceased to evolve. As a result, the words of the rite were unintelligible to those who knew only the romance or barbarian dialects of the uneducated. Special vessels were developed to contain the bread and wine and to permit the Elements to be administered with honor and security. But opportunities for fearful accidents with the contents of the chalice were too obvious, and the laity generally withdrew from the wine and participated in the Communion only through the more easily transportable bread. The awe inspired by the Elements led in the thirteenth century to the creation of the feast of Corpus Christi which commemorated the institution of the Eucharist. In later years, it became an acceptable practice to display the consecrated Elements as objects of veneration which could be employed like the relics of the saints as a focus for the prayers of the faithful.

The Mass was a realization of the sacrifice of Christ, and, as such, it had inestimable worth as an act for the extirpation of human sin. But the legalistic, quantifying tendencies of medieval pastoral theology led people to feel that the merit that accrued from participation in a single celebration of the Eucharist was a distinctly measurable phenomenon. One Mass was good, but it was not believed to be as effective as multiple Masses devoted to a common objective. There was a tendency, therefore, to multiply celebrations of the Mass and to focus them on the needs of specific persons. Those who could afford it endowed specialized clerics called chantry priests or even whole monastic communities to celebrate Masses on their behalf, and elaborate attempts were made to establish mechanisms that would ensure in perpetuity the regular offering of Masses in memory of certain individuals. Even the poor left small bequests in their wills to finance a few memorial masses or pooled their resources to establish guilds that undertook to procure for their deceased members the benefits of huge numbers of celebrations of the Eucharist.

The clergy's monopoly of literacy during the early medieval period and the distancing of church Latin from the vernacular languages created a situation in which the laity could not take an active part in the recitation of the liturgy of Christian worship. In general, it came to be expected that laymen would attend services, observe attentively, and meditate on the texts of a few previously memorized prayers and creeds. They were present as persons for whom services were being performed, but they had only a minimal part to play in the elaborate rites that unfolded at their altars. A priest was perfectly capable of celebrating a valid Mass without the presence of a congregation, and many priests were routinely employed to conduct services, that had few if any witnesses. The Mass might occasionally have been regarded as a kind of technical service rendered to God by a clerical specialist on behalf of the Christian community. The Sacrament was not so much the celebration of a group of Christians as it was a meritorious act of intercession with God which the clergy performed as their unique professional function.

The professionalization of the practices of the church in its system of sacraments was paralleled in the thirteenth century by a supremely professional statement of the theory of Christian faith. In due time, the clergy thus acquired both a fully developed program for the conduct of their professional services and a thoroughly grounded, rationally defensible articulation of a congruent Christian worldview. The new achievements in Christian philosophy were the result of successful attempts to reconcile the theology of the medieval church with the teachings of the ancient Greeks. The knowledge of ancient Greek science and philosophy had declined drastically in the West during the Dark Ages, but increased commercial and military contacts among the Latin, Greek, and Arabic peoples of the twelfth century led to an exchange of literatures that had a revolutionary impact on European thought. Within a generation, Europe became aware of a wealth of sophisticated scientific thought excelling anything that had been imagined in the medieval West. The great discovery of the early thirteenth century schoolmen was Aristotle. The Aristotelian literature contained the largest and most accurate summation of the fruits of human research and analysis that Western scholars had yet seen. Aristotle had dealt with everything. He had analyzed the mechanisms of sense perception and human thought. He had identified the valid and invalid processes of logic. He had applied his refined tools of observation and inference to the full range of physical and biological phenomena and to the study of the uniquely human concerns of politics, aesthetics, and ethics. He had gone beyond the study of the material world and ventured opinions in metaphysics that touched on the concepts of God and ultimate reality. He seemed to have framed his arguments so carefully and inclusively that it was difficult to fault his conclusions. This was exciting, but somewhat threatening, to the medieval scholar, for Aristotle had not been a Christian. However rationally defensible his opinions seemed to be, they were occasionally in apparent contradiction to the truths of Christian revelation, and so the Aristotelian literature prompted the fear that people might have to choose between the guidances of faith and reason. For a while, the confusion in the medieval schools was so great that some scholars seriously suggested that a rational man might find it necessary to assert two incompatible truths simultaneously—one when he thought as a philosopher and a quite different one when he reasoned as a theologian.

The situation in the early thirteenth century was made all the more difficult by the fact that the first copies of the newly recovered Aristotelian texts were mediated to the Latin West by means of Arabic translations and commentaries. The paganism of the Greeks was filtered through channels of Moslem infidelity, and opportunities for offending Christian sensitivities were doubled. Concern over the potentially misleading nature of the new literature led a provincial synod of 1210 to forbid scholars at the University of Paris to read Aristotle's works on natural philosophy. But the order was virtually impossible to enforce. The medieval scholar was enamored of logic and dialectic, and Aristotle was the undisputed master in these fields. It was impossible simply to study his tools and then to turn one's back on the works in which he himself had applied them to the understanding of man, nature, and the divine. In 1231, the papacy gave in to pressures from the universities and permitted the study of the whole Aristotelian corpus—once accurate versions of the original texts could be established.

By the mid-thirteenth century, Latin translations of Aristotle's works had begun to circulate in the West, and the schoolmen developed a preoccupation with the problem of reconciling Greek philosophy with Christian theology. The most exciting contemporary development in the institutional life of the church was the growth of the mendicant movements, and many of the most famous scholars of the century were attracted to the orders of the Franciscans and Dominicans. The two families of friars evolved distinct schools of thought, and their disputes provided a lively background for the general debate over the meaning of Aristotle for the future of Christian thought.

The Franciscans tended to take a moderate position that attempted to defect as little as possible from the opinions held by the early Western church fathers. Bonaventura (1221-74), the head of the Franciscans, became the leading spokesman for his order at the University of Paris in the thirteenth century. He perpetuated the Franciscans' traditional allegiance to the teachings of Augustine and developed a mystical theology that interpreted all human knowledge as a progress toward an ineffable experience of the reality of God. Bonaventura used Aristotelian logic and ideas where they appeared to him to be applicable, but, like Augustine, he believed the human mind was doomed to fail in its pursuit of truth unless it sought miraculous illumination by divine grace. He believed that truth was perceived, not simply through logic, but by means of the enlightenment of the processes of the human mind by the love of God. Bonaventura held that, without the premises and the inspiration of the practice of faith, philosophy could make little progress toward the apprehension of truth.

The most enthusiastic defenders of Aristotelianism as a basis for Christian philosophy were the Dominicans. The Dominican scholar Albertus Magnus (1200–80) devoted much of his career to the task of interpreting Aristotle's science to the Latin world, and Albert's commentaries constituted major advances in the attempt to recover an accurate understanding of Aristotle's positions. The job of reconciling Aristotelian philosophy with Christian theology was left, however, to Albert's famous pupil, Thomas Aquinas (1226–74). Thomas, the seventh son of the Count of Aquino, was born to wealth and aristocratic privilege. His family held the Neapolitan castle of Roccasecca and enjoyed illustrious connections with the imperial Hohenstaufens. Thomas was the grandnephew of Frederick Barbarossa and the second cousin of one of the most powerful monarchs of the day, Emperor Frederick II. Thomas's family could have eased his path toward almost any career, and, when he early showed a taste for learning and religion, his father arranged for his admission to the prominent motherhouse of the Benedictine order, Monte Cassino. Thomas, however, rejected the lavish arrangements made for his future, and, in 1244, after a period of study at the University of Naples, he vowed himself to mendicancy in the habit of the Dominicans. His family was so chagrined by his repudiation of the privileges of his rank and by his identification of himself with one of the radical fringe groups of the day that they forcibly intervened to prevent him from fulfilling his desire to become a holy beggar. His militaristic brothers imprisoned him in the family castle for a year in a vain attempt to induce him to adopt a more traditional and respectable ecclesiastical vocation. But, in the end, he prevailed against his family's wishes and was sent to study in the Dominican communities at Paris and Cologne.

Thomas's opinions sprang from a profound faith in the unity and accessibility of truth. He believed that the facts of nature, which informed reason, and the facts of faith, which derived from revelation, both sprang from the reality of one God. Since they had a common origin, they could not ultimately be found to contradict one another, and the two avenues of human knowledge—faith and reason—would, therefore, eventually be brought to reveal their essential agreement. He rejected as absurd the position of the Christian students of the Moslem Aristotelian Averroes who argued that there were two standards for judging truth, one for reason and one for faith. He also believed that the Franciscan posture of asserting faith as a restraint on reason could be shown to be excessively timid. Thomas believed that Christian faith and valid natural reason led to the same goal. Since Aristotle was the supreme authority in philosophy—the realm of unaided human reason—Thomas attempted to prove his point by demonstrating the congruity of Aristotelian science and Christian theology. At issue in Thomas's campaign was an understanding of the potential of the human mind. Aristotle's work was premised on the assumption that human reason was an accurate tool that could proceed on its own to analyze human experience and arrive at significant, dependable conclusions. Those who opposed Aristotle feared that his confidence in natural human powers was misplaced and would lead eventually to arrogant errors and a loss of man's proper orientation toward God. They believed with Augustine that human reason had been perverted by sin and was incapable of advancing on its own in the pursuit of truth. Those who declared themselves the champions of Aristotle too often and too readily deified their own incomplete arguments and indicated the worst suspicions of their opponents. It was left to Thomas to see if a path could be charted between the errant rationalism of one camp and the pious obscurantism of the other.

Thomas accepted the premises of Aristotle's epistemology, and he too asserted that all the data contained in the human mind came to it from the senses. Human knowledge was simply an ordering of accurate sense perceptions in valid logical patterns, and all the sublime and ultimate truths apprehended by the human mind could, when analyzed, be demonstrated to be rooted in the lesser realities of mundane experience. Yet Thomas was not an extreme rationalist who sought to deduce the whole content of faith from man's experience of the physical world and the processes of his own mind. Thomas believed human reason to be adequate and trustworthy within its natural limits. What it saw, it saw truly. But some realities transcended the capacity of the mind and were accessible only by faith through revelation. The mind was accurate in what it was able to grasp, but only partially successful in attaining the goal of absolute truth. When properly applied, the rational processes of the philosopher led him to dependable conclusions, but human reason had a natural limit beyond which it could not go. At their outer edges, the conclusions of reason met the assertions of faith, and revelation was discovered not to contradict, but to compliment, the quest of the human sciences.

Thomas described the objects that presented themselves to the senses as entities that were passing from a state of potentiality to one of actuality—that is, sensory objects moved toward the realization of the intelligible essences that defined them as what they were. The healthy mind had the ability to extract from the experience of these objects the common ideas that each object represented in different or partial ways and to form these ideas into generalized concepts. These concepts could then be combined and refined to yield a higher or more comprehensive level of understanding, and eventually it became possible to use information derived from the creation to make certain kinds of inferences concerning the existence of the Creator. At this point, the efforts of the unaided human mind would begin to make contact with the principles of revelation and encounter assertions of faith that might not always be logically demonstrable but that would also not totally oppose opinions supported by valid rational arguments.

Thomas's discussion of the fundamental question of man's knowledge of God gave him an opportunity to illustrate the complementary relationship of faith and reason. Thomas felt that a small portion of man's knowledge of God could be seen to derive from information mediated by the human senses, for, although God was an example of a reality that was not experienced directly in itself in the material world, something could be inferred about him from his effect on the world of the senses. Simply by arriving at an understanding of the logical presuppositions of the concepts of existence and motion, Aristotle had been able to infer the necessity of God's existence as the "prime mover" of the universe. Aristotle's "prime mover" was something less than the full Christian concept of the Creator, for its creative activity was an ongoing eternal process without beginning or end. But Thomas saw no inherent conflict between this idea and the further Christian assumption that God had absolute initiative in inaugurating the creation as well as a continuing function in sustaining it. If the temporal limits of the creation could not be logically demonstrated by philosophy, that was not a denial of either philosophy or faith, but an indication of the inability of the human mind to proceed beyond this point without the assistance of revelation. The fact that the contingency of the creation could not be demonstrated was not a basis for denying Christian beliefs, but simply evidence for the fact that human reason had reached the outer limits of its ability. It was important to demonstrate either the impossibility or the rational necessity of the Christian concept of creation. This impasse served simply to prepare the way for a decision of faith. Thomas believed that those who accepted the benefits of revelation found valuable ideas that completed their natural knowledge and led to true wisdom. Those who chose to reject revelation were left in ignorance and willful error.

Thomas devoted most of his professional life to demonstrating the congruity of faith and reason by integrating the conclusions of the human sciences and the propositions of revelation in one large, self-consistent theological-philosophical system. His work was so well done that, in modern times, his great *Summae* have come to be regarded as history's most complete and accurate statements of the Roman Catholic version of the Christian faith. Thomas's contemporaries, however, had less confidence than subsequent generations in the worth of his achievement. Thomas had a great deal of difficulty with conservative Augustinians who were scandalized by his Aristotelianism. On the other hand, certain extreme Aristotelians were all too willing to associate him with their presumptuous attacks on traditional theological positions. Thomas left Paris in 1272 in the aftermath of a series of strenuous arguments, and he died two years later at the abbey of Fossanuova on his way to yet another debate before a church council at Lyons. Five years before Thomas's death, the bishop of Paris had already proscribed thirteen "Aristotelian" propositions that opponents hoped to trace in part to Thomas's works, and, three years after Thomas's death, some phrases reminiscent of his teachings were finally included in a list of 219 opinions condemned by the church. The Franciscans forbade their students to read his books, but his Dominican brothers defended him and, as early as 1278, came to regard his theology as the official position of their order. Thomas was canonized in 1323, but nothing like a Thomistic consensus developed in the medieval church. In the fourteenth and fifteenth centuries, the universities turned again to the older systems of Augustine and the church fathers, and the interest in philosophy as a basis for a synthesis of theological and natural knowledge declined. Numerous schools of thought developed within the universities; subtle work in epistemology and logic was accomplished; but the goal of a great systematization of all human intellectual endeavors began to seem anachronistic and naive. Thomas's style of thinking proved to be too optimistic for the mood of the waning Middle Ages.

CRISES OF LEADERSHIP

B Y THE LATE THIRTEENTH century, the most expansive period in medieval civilization was over. Europe's population crested and began to decline; economic systems started to show signs of weakness; and antagonisms engendered by growing nationalistic sentiments threatened the political stability of the Continent. The fourteenth century was destined to be a tense period in which old values and institutions were to receive severe testing and new ideas were to challenge traditional beliefs and long-established authorities. It was to be a time when the church had need of the most skillful management in order to maintain its security and develop its potential for international leadership. But it was, unfortunately, to be a century in which ecclesiastical leaders were distracted by a series of crises that narrowed their vision and tarnished the reputation of the institutions entrusted to their care. During the fourteenth century, the church was to become a very efficient, tightly managed organization of professional clergy, but it was to fail to develop the charisma and the universal reputation for spiritual authority necessary to enable it to hold its own in competition with the new centers of national loyalty that were developing at the courts of kings.

At the end of the thirteenth century, however, it must have appeared to those in positions of power that the church was developing adequately toward the goals of independence and influence that Pope Innocent III had set for it. At the time of Innocent's death in 1216, the strongest threat to the freedom of the church was to be expected from the Holy Roman Empire, the only other European institution that could lay claim to universality and divine right. But, by the end of the thirteenth century, the imperial office had been successfully stripped of the powers that had made it a threat to the papacy. Innocent had found it useful in his diplomatic maneuvering to assist the young Hohenstaufen heir, Frederick II, to the throne even though he was well aware of the traditional Hohenstaufen policy of attempting to unite Italy and Germany as a basis for a true revival of the western Roman Empire. The papacy could not risk allowing its Italian territories to be surrounded by the lands of a strong monarch, so Innocent forced Frederick to purchase the support of the papacy by promising never to claim the crowns of both Germany and Sicily. As an added safeguard, Frederick was also obligated to participate in an Eastern crusade that would require him to be absent for a long time from his empire in the West. Frederick proved to be a master of the art of devious politics, and he skillfully managed to fulfill his promises to the papacy without abandoning his family's traditional program of seeking to surround Rome with lands under imperial control. He resigned the double crown of Germany and Sicily for himself, but, following ancient custom, he had his son and heir elected to these honors and continued to wield authority in both nations. The crusade was postponed as long as possible, and it was not until a decade after Innocent's death that Frederick began to make serious preparations for an expedition into the East.

Frederick avoided involvement with the ill-fated Fifth Crusade, which suffered ignominious defeat in Egypt in 1221, and his attempts to solidify his position in northern Italy kept him occupied and the papacy nervous until he finally set out for the East in 1228. His crusade had no sooner departed than it turned around and came home. Frederick claimed that an outbreak of illness among the troops had required a postponement of the project. But the papacy dismissed his explanation as a transparent attempt to avoid fulfilling his vows to the church, and Rome excommunicated him. Undeterred, Frederick departed once again for the Holy Lands and succeeded without the necessity of battle in negotiating a return of Jerusalem to Christian control. The papacy was faced with the embarrassing fact that an excommunicate had succeeded where armies of the faithful had failed, and it refused to recognize Frederick's achievement. As an excommunicate, Frederick could not claim the status of a legitimate crusader, and Pope Gregory IX, seizing the opportunity of Frederick's absence in the Holy Lands, attacked the imperial territories on the frontiers of the papal state. Frederick quickly returned from the East and gave the pope's army a defeat that led to his reconciliation with the church and his release from excommunication in 1230.

Frederick's policies remained unchanged. His vigorously pursued attempts to bring northern Italy under imperial control inspired the papacy to back the Lombard cities against him and to reimpose excommunication on him in 1238. Exasperated by what he considered to be unwarranted secular meddling by a spiritual authority, Frederick launched a propaganda attack on the papacy and invited Europe to rethink the issue of papal claims to political power. The papacy had long used the spurious Donation of Constantine to back up its claim to secular authority. In so doing, Frederick maintained, the papacy clearly confessed that its secular rights did not derive from God but were humanly delegated by the earthly emperor Constantine. As successor to the office of Roman emperor, Frederick considered himself to be Constantine's true heir, and he professed a right to reassume the secular authority that had only been provisionally granted to the church. In a revolutionary move that anticipated developments of the fourteenth and early fifteenth centuries, Frederick appealed to the membership of the church against its leadership and suggested that the people of Europe had the right to do something to curb the excessive ambitions of papal monarchs. Frederick launched a direct attack on the pope's lands in Italy, and Pope Gregory fought back by attempting to rally world opinion against him. A general council was ordered to convene in Rome on Easter, 1241, to consider moves that could be taken against Frederick; but it came to little. Frederick captured a hundred of the clergy who were on their way to attend it and successfully defied church law and public sentiment by imprisoning them as hostages. A few months later Gregory died, and his demise proved to be a serious setback for the church. The college of cardinals had difficulty in agreeing on a successor, and the candidate they finally advanced, Celestine IV, lived to reign only seventeen days. The cardinals failed to reconvene promptly, and political confusion delayed the election of a new pope for a full two years. It was not until June 1243, that the church righted itself and elevated Innocent IV to the papacy. By that time, the situation in Rome had become so insecure that the pope moved his court to Lyons for safety and there finally managed to convene a council that declared Frederick deposed. Militarily the church in exile was unable to do much to defend itself, and it was driven more and more to rely on the support of France—the only nation in the immediate area disposed to assist it.

In 1250, Frederick died of dysentery, and the papacy's fortunes took a turn for the better. Frederick's heir, Conrad IV, survived him by only four years, and the papacy used its French alliance to increase the Hohenstaufens' difficulties. When Frederick's bastard son Manfred attempted to succeed to Conrad's throne in Sicily, the pope invited the French to intervene. Charles, the brother of Louis IX of France, invaded Sicily in 1266, killed Manfred in battle, and executed the last member of the Hohenstaufen line, Frederick's young grandson Conradin. The effect on the empire was disastrous. The German princes had already won considerable independence from their emperor in exchange for support or neutrality during his long struggle with the papacy, and the extinction of his dynasty and his office was little regretted. For almost a quarter of a century, the imperial title lapsed, and Europe lost one of the institutions that might have supported or encouraged its unification. When the tradition of electing emperors was revived in 1272, the office amounted to little more than an empty honor. It had lost its potential for providing Germany and Italy with a basis for the development of strong central governments, and these two nations entered a period of fragmentation and internal disorder that was to complicate their history for the next six hundred years.

The medieval papacy could rejoice in the fact that it had dispelled the threat of a renaissance of the Christian Roman Empire, but Rome's continued independence of secular influences was far from assured. The kind of internationalism that the church and the empire both represented was quickly becoming anachronistic in the late thirteenth century. People now directed their strongest loyalties to the nation states that claimed their political allegiance and to the vernacular cultures that were fast becoming the foundations of distinct, new national identities. The popes no longer had emperors to contend with, but the kings of the emerging European nations, who had no pretentions to claims of universal authority, proved to be stronger threats to the independence and viability of the papacy than had the earlier medieval emperors.

The weakness of the international church in dealing with the new nations of Europe was first revealed during the reign of Boniface VIII (1294–1303). Boniface was heir to a somewhat demoralized papal government. During the forty years that preceded his election, the church had passed through the hands of eleven popes, and the delays between their reigns added up to a total of seven years in which the church had lacked the leadership of a chief executive. Papal political ventures had received rebuffs that would have seemed unthinkable at the beginning of the thirteenth century, and it was clear that some strong stands had soon to be taken if the Roman institution were not permanently to be weakened. It seems to have been Boniface VIII's intention to guard the church's position, not by seeking to exercise new powers, but simply by seriously reaffirming positions his predecessors had taken. There had always been a gap between the rights popes claimed and those they actually attempted to exercise. Most popes realized this, and few of them ever allowed themselves to be trapped between the pretensions of their office and the realities of their power. Boniface, however, misjudged the world with which he had to deal and precipitated disasters that were the source of extreme humiliations for him and his office. His nemesis was none other than the king of France, whose ancestors had been major allies of the papacy during much of the thirteenth century.

As the kings of Europe grew in effective control of their nations, there was an inevitable tendency for them to demand increased jurisdiction over the portion of the church that lay within their territories. Strong pressures therefore strained the ties binding the clergy to the pope and moved Europe toward a system of more or less independent national churches. It was of vital importance for the continued unity of the church that the papacy resist these pressures by opposing royal attempts to interfere with ecclesiastical affairs. The state had a more immediate interest in the wealth of the church than in its theology, and it was on the crucial issue of the right of kings to tax the clergy that Boniface chose to make his stand. He had good reason. The elaborate national bureaucracies that were evolving out of the feudal courts of kings were expensive to maintain even under normal circumstances, and royal requests for financial assistance were becoming increasingly insistent. Boniface's reign happened to coincide with a long and costly military conflict between Philip IV of France and Edward I of England. Both kings needed money for the support of their war and sought to extract funds from the clergy of their respective nations, even though the church had long claimed independence of the state and freedom from the obligation to support secular governments. In 1296, Boniface came to the defense of his clergy by issuing the bull *Clericis laicos,* which reminded the world in no uncertain terms of the church's traditional, if somewhat unrealistic, position on taxation. The two kings who were most directly challenged had little difficulty in demonstrating the necessity for the church to be more cooperative in its dealings with the state. Philip simply halted the export of bullion from France and drastically reduced the flow of money into the papal treasury. Edward announced that persons who did not support the government had no right to its services, and he withdrew the protection of the law from the church and its property. Boniface beat a hasty retreat into a face-saving compromise in which he allowed the clergy, if they so desired, to make voluntary contributions to their kings without the necessity of first seeking papal consent. In reality, the papacy was shown to lack the power needed to guarantee the clergy the freedom from civil authorities that they had long claimed.

Four years later, the question of papal versus royal control of the church came up again. This time, the issue was not money but the personal legal status of the clergy. In 1301, Philip arrested, tried, and convicted the bishop of Pamiers on a charge of treason. The clergy claimed immunity from the jurisdiction of royal courts, and a century earlier a similar dispute between Henry II of England and Archbishop Thomas Becket had ended in defeat for the state. Boniface, therefore, insisted vigorously on the bishop's release from prison, but Philip refused to be intimidated. Instead, he engineered a national consensus supporting a determined policy of opposition to the papacy. A propaganda war was mounted against Boniface, and every group in France was asked to express its willingness to back the king in his defense of the nation against the threat of Roman interference. Boniface fought back by issuing the bull *Unam sanctam*, which iterated in the strongest language the papacy's claim to spiritual authority over every Christian soul in every nation and reminded Philip that the pope, as the absolute ruler of the one true church, had an exclusive monopoly of the means of salvation. In June, 1303, Philip convened the first meeting of the Estates General—a French national representative body created to help him make good his claim to speak, not just for himself as king, but for his people as their staunchly supported leader. Boniface responded by threatening Philip with excommunication and deposition, but before he could act, Philip sent soldiers into Italy who surprised and captured Boniface in his retreat at Anagni. The citizens of Anagni eventually rallied to the defense of the pope and liberated him, but the damage had been done. A king had presumed to order a physical assault on the vicar of Christ, and Europe had failed to come to the pope's aid or even to express its shock at the scandal. It was painfully obvious that the people of Europe were coming to regard the pope, not as a holy agent who always acted with the authority of God, but as a kind of earthly monarch who used the same tools and suffered the same kinds of reverses as the other politicians of Europe.

Boniface died a month after his humiliation at Anagni, and his successors adopted the prudent policy of attempting to molify the French government. Clement V, a former archbishop of Bordeaux who was elected to the papacy in 1305, inaugurated a period of church history in which French influences came to be very strongly felt in papal government. Philip continued to press the advantage that his successful bullying of Boniface had given him, and Clement was forced to purchase a conclusion to the whole affair by consenting to the dissolution of the Order of the Templars and the confiscation of their wealth by the state.

Ill health and the negotiations involved in the destruction of the Templars kept Clement in France for the entire term of his papacy. It was, however, not at all unusual for a pope to travel or reside for long periods of time outside of Rome. The medieval world was accustomed to peripatetic rulers who had no one official capital or seat for their government and who exercised their functions as governors while drifting from place to place throughout their territories. Everyone knew that the popes belonged in Rome, and everyone expected them to return to Rome at their convenience. But, given the chaos that habitually reigned in that city and the turbulence of northern Italian politics, it was not surprising that they delayed their return. The city of Avignon, which lay on a major river system and which was much more central to European affairs than Rome was, proved to be a convenient refuge for the curia. The city was much smaller than Rome and free from the quarrels of the powerful feudal factions that had often made life uncomfortable or even dangerous for the popes who resided in Rome. Avignon was close to such French affairs as the crucial discussions between the warring French and English governments, in which the papacy hoped to play a significant part. But the city was technically not French property; it belonged to the papal vassal who held Sicily. In short, it was a comfortable, convenient, and not entirely inappropriate place for the papacy to establish itself, and over the years the curia drifted into more or less permanent residence at Avignon. Popes occasionally voiced an official intent to return to Rome, but few moves were actually made in that direction. In 1336, Benedict XII began the construction of huge headquarters for the papal government in Avignon, and, in 1348, Clement VI bought title to the city from the heiress of Sicily. It was clear that the popes were in no hurry to expose themselves to the uncertainties of life in Italy.

The prolonged period of residence at Avignon had a noticeable effect on the papal government. Approximately 95 percent of the cardinals appointed during the papacy's seventy years at Avignon were French, and the papal office itself was invariably held by a Frenchman. Modern scholars have suggested that the papacy managed to maintain its independence of the French king, but the sight of a long series of French popes regularly succeeding one another at a residence in a French-speaking area led many nations of Europe to conclude that the leadership of the international church had been nationalized by the French and that other nations would be justified in weakening their ties with an international organization that was no longer truly international. Whatever the actual state of affairs at Avignon, the appearance of the situation had an unfortunate effect on the prestige of the papacy.

The necessity of coping with life at Avignon provided a strong stimulus for the development of the curia. The papal states proved to be impossible to defend from France, and, as they slipped from control, alternative sources of revenue for the support of the papal court had to be found. The pope, like his colleagues the kings, discovered that there was money to be made in providing efficient administrative services, and the Avignonese popes made great strides in the elaboration of systems of papal government. The power of popes in relationship to kings may have declined, but papal control of the clergy and the departments of the church reached a new high. For the first time in its long history, the papacy ceased to be itinerant and settled into permanent headquarters at Avignon, where the church could acquire records, libraries, and an elaborate bureaucracy. The volume of papal correspondence began to grow steadily, and bit by bit the popes developed agencies that pulled much of the church's business into the hands of its central government. By 1350, the pope's right to tax the clergy was firmly established, and a system of papal tax collectors covered Europe. By the 1360's, the pope's claim to control appointments to all ecclesiastical benefices was exploited with such efficiency that Avignon was becoming the central clearinghouse for the placement of clergy throughout Europe. The church courts were expanded to attract as many cases as possible, and extensive disciplinary powers were claimed as the exclusive prerogatives of the pope and his agents. The Avignonese papacy became a model of professional efficiency and administrative thoroughness, and Avignon became the home of one of the most brilliant and bustling courts in Europe. Its virtues did little, however, to build its prestige, for efficiency and thoroughness are not always winning traits in tax collectors. They certainly did nothing to advance respect for the church as a spiritual organization or to increase the moral authority of the popes, whose surroundings and activities seemed to immerse them in worldly concerns.

Inevitably, popular opinion in Europe came to the conclusion that Avignon provided an unhealthy environment for the papacy, and vigorous efforts were made to induce the popes to return to their traditional seat in Rome. Comfortable as they were in Avignon, the popes had a difficult time justifying a permanent transference of the see of Peter to a city Peter had never ruled; so a papal army was finally commissioned to begin the difficult job of regaining control of Rome and the papal states. The political situation in Italy was sufficiently stable by 1367 to enable Urban V to return to Rome, but his stay there proved only to be an extended visit. The administrative bureaucracy of the church had grown too large to move easily. Much of it had remained behind in Avignon, and Urban himself returned to France in 1370 when war broke out once again between France and England. His successor, Gregory XI, was elected in Avignon and spent most of his papacy there. In 1377, he too yielded to the temper of the times and ordered a return to Rome. He survived in Rome for little more than a year, and his death meant that, for the first time in almost eighty years, a papal election was to be held in the Italian city.

The right to participate in the election of a pope was, of course, the major defining characteristic of a cardinal, but the elaboration of papal government at Avignon had increased the duties of the cardinal clergy. They had become leaders of giant departments in the church's vastly expanded administrative system, and the powers of their offices gave them a vision of a new role they might play in the management of Christendom. During a papal interregnum, the college of cardinals assumed special importance as a kind of corporate papal executive for the church, and, since a man acquired the powers of the papacy through the actions of the cardinals, it was only natural that they should eventually come to think of themselves as possessing a permanent right to oversee their appointee in the duties of his office. By the middle of the fourteenth century, they were suggesting that the church's papal monarchy ought to be converted into a system of shared governance in which the pope behaved less like an autocrat and more like an administrative executive for policies and programs designed by the college of cardinals. While they were at Avignon, the cardinals had, in practice if not in theory, some success in bridging the gap between their ambitions and the realities of papal monarchy. At Avignon, the popes were cut off from the economic resources and political privileges of the papal states. In this precarious position, they could not risk a struggle that would disrupt the bureaucracy that kept the church alive.

Gregory XI's death in Rome created a situation in which the pretentions of the cardinals came finally to be challenged. The college of cardinals that met in Rome in 1378 was composed almost entirely of Frenchmen, but it was divided into such jealous factions that it was unable to agree on the elevation of one of its own company to the papacy. The people of Rome, who feared that the election of another Frenchman as pope might lead to a return of the curia to Avignon, rioted in the streets and insisted that the cardinals choose an Italian for the see of Rome. The cardinals deliberated for a month before agreeing on a compromise candidate, a Neapolitan who was archbishop of Bari and vice-chancelor of the curia.

The new pope, who took the name Urban VI, had not been a cardinal and could not draw on the support of a strong party within the college of cardinals. It was probably expected, therefore, that he would be a weak pope who would submit readily to the will of the cardinals. Such did not turn out to be the case. Urban was elected on April 8, 1378, and by the middle of June his autocratic attitudes had so alienated the cardinals that they abandoned him in Rome. All of them— except one who was too old and ill to travel—gathered at Anagni and ordered Urban to join them in a return to Avignon. Urban refused to accompany them to Avignon, where he would have been an Italian without backers in a foreign land. The cardinals then deposed him and elected one of their own number in his place. The new pope, Clement VII, established himself in Avignon, where much of the papal bureaucracy was still ensconced, and revived that city's claim to be the capital of the church. Urban dismissed the behavior of the cardinals as a vain attempt to exercise powers of impeachment they did not have, and he appointed a new college of cardinals that remained with him in Rome.

There had been popes and antipopes before in the history of the church, but none had ever appeared under quite these circumstances. Urban argued that the cardinals could make a pope, but, once they had discharged their electoral function, they had no power to undo their work and depose him. The cardinals agreed that under normal circumstances they could claim no such authority, but they maintained that Urban's election was invalid because it had been conducted under the threat of hostile actions from the Roman mob. The cardinals claimed that they had been prevented from exercising full freedom of choice and that therefore a canonical election had never taken place. In addition, they raised the troublesome constitutional question of what should be done if a pope proved to be incompetent. They charged Urban with numerous crimes and personal insufficiencies and suggested that, in cases—like his—of obvious papal inadequacies, the cardinals had a responsibility to take control of the situation for the good of the church as a whole.

The split in the papacy could have been healed without resort to difficult doctrinal questions had Europe simply decided to ignore one or the other of the two men who claimed the leadership of Christendom. But the political objectives of competing nations made that option unlikely. The French quite naturally preferred a pope who was a Frenchman and who ruled from Avignon, so they pledged support to Clement VII. The English, who were heirs to an ancient tradition of hostility to the French, were inclined to resent the long French monopoly of the papal office and to favor the claims of Urban VI. The allies of these two major powers followed them in bestowing recognition on either Avignon or Rome, and the divisions among nations began to express themselves in a fragmentation of the leadership of the church. From 1378 to 1417, Europe was treated to the unseemly spectacle of the Great Schism, in which opposing lines of popes perpetuated themselves at Rome and Avignon. In 1409, European leaders attempted to heal the schism by appealing to the colleges of cardinals of both popes to depose their pontiffs and unite in the support of a mutually acceptable candidate. But this strategem led only to the establishment of a third line of popes with its seat at Pisa. Each pope claimed to be the one legitimate vicar of Christ, and each proved more than willing to sacrifice the well-being of the church and the peace of mind of Christendom to the maintenance of his own position. For a full generation, the Christians of Europe could not be sure of the validity of the sacraments they received or the legitimacy of the ecclesiastical authorities who ruled over them. They were forced, therefore, to find new ways of satisfying their consciences and to think in terms of effecting significant changes in the functions and structures of their church.

CALLS FOR REFORM

IT WAS UNFORTUNATE FOR the future of the papacy that the Great Schism occurred in the late fourteenth century, for the schism increased the curia's vulnerability to criticism from a society that was becoming increasingly impatient with its own ancient institutions. During most of the twelfth and thirteenth centuries, Europe had enjoyed an expansive period in which its populations had increased and its economy had flourished. Frontiers had been extended, new land had come under cultivation, trade and industry had begun to develop, and standards of living had generally risen. A strong middle class had appeared and had begun to have a liberating effect on the structures of feudal society. The option of town life and the realities of a money economy had weakened the institution of serfdom, and the support of the bourgeoisie had enabled kings to discipline and restrain the nobility. But, by the early fourteenth century, the era of expansion was over, and a series of great plagues and wars accelerated Europe's slide into deep depression. In the changing situation, the infant proletariat class of the cities and the newly liberated farm workers began to discover that the hopes they had developed for their futures were unrealistic. A rigid distinction between labor and capital began to appear in industry, and serfdom returned to the countryside. Disappointed expectations generated a tide of resentment and desperation at the bottom of society which welled up in a series of urban revolutions and peasant rebellions. These spontaneous uprisings were generally unsuccessful, but they were a clear indication of the emergence among the masses of a new mood of aggressiveness and a will for self-determination. People no longer regarded the conditions of their lives as unchangeable; they were no longer reluctant to challenge established authorities and venerable structures that failed to measure up to their expectations and give them the services they needed.

Long before the scandal of the Great Schism, discontent with the leadership of the church had become serious enough to prompt a variety of different kinds of demands for reform. The papacy was quick to tar many of its critics with the brush of heresy, but many of the "heresies" began as sincere reform movements that sought the revitalization of orthodox faith. As early as the twelfth century, Peter Waldo, a merchant from Lyons, had been driven by his concern for the poor and his exasperation with the indifference of the clergy to establish a successful "protestant" movement outside the Roman church. Like many a Christian who had been honored with sainthood, Peter gave himself and his fortune totally to the service of the indigent. The church, however, branded him a heretic, for he challenged the clergy to join him in the radical acts of charity and self-sacrifice that he perceived as necessary emulations of Christ's example. Rather than surrender to the church's demand that he cease his public ministry, he chose to organize his followers into a religious fellowship independent of the authority and sacraments of Rome. A strong Waldensian sect soon established itself in France and Italy and survives into the twentieth century.

Some of the movements opposed by the clergy were highly undesirable expressions of aberrant personalities. There were numerous deluded people who considered themselves to be incarnations of divine principles or persons, and, in the late thirteenth century, there was an outbreak of morbid enthusiasm for a cult of flagellation that promised salvation as a reward for inflicting wounds on the body. During periods of unusual stress—such as the decades of the 1340's and 50's when the Black Death ravaged Europe—these irrational and inhumane phenomena developed a dangerous amount of credibility in the minds of the desperate masses. The church had good reasons for standing firm against them. But some of the persons whom the church ardently opposed were honestly attempting to focus attention on real abuses of ecclesiastical authority or lapses in clerical morality. These spokesmen were witnessing to the fact that something was seriously wrong with the relationship between the church and its people, but their warnings were more often ignored than heeded.

At the center of many of the heretical and orthodox criticisms of the Christian religion lay an indictment of the wealth of the church. In light of the church's inadequate charitable services to society, the frequently immoral or ineffective conduct of its clergy, and the simplicity that the Scriptures described as the characteristic of its leadership during the apostolic generation, it was difficult to find a moral or religious justification for the financial privileges the church claimed. Observers of various degrees of intellectual sophistication were prepared to argue that the corruption of the church resulted from possession of and concern for inordinate wealth.

Contempt for the church's tendency to confuse spiritual and earthly objectives led the Albigensians to revive the ancient heresy of metaphysical dualism as a corrective for the gross materialism of orthodox faith. They came to believe that the spirit could be nourished and protected only by completely denying the flesh and the goodness of the creation. The Waldensians and numerous other less successful groups were driven by their revolt against the worldliness of the church to advance arguments reminiscent of the fourth century Donatist heresy. As these groups found themselves cut off from the fellowship of the Roman church, they came to believe that the sinful or uncharitable state of the orthodox clergy invalidated the sacraments such clergy administered; and the schismatic sects appealed to the purity of their own faith as a basis on which to reestablish true sacraments.

A few particularly robust and aggressive individuals occasionally sought to purify the church by looting her shrines and cloisters and distributing the booty to the poor; but a much more effective witness for reform was made by the organizations of friars who were among the most popular and credible representatives of the church in the thirteenth and fourteenth centuries. Francis of Assisi had begun the friars' movement by vowing himself and his followers to lives of total poverty. Francis believed that the rejection of all possessions enabled him and his followers to live the life Christ had lived and to demonstrate a faith that courageously and literally trusted God's promises to care for those who believe in him. Francis advocated his program of "apostolic" poverty simply as one option among many Christian vocations, and, since he did not insist that the clergy be judged according to his standards, the papacy found a place for his witness within the bounds of orthodoxy. Francis's radical mendicancy worked adequately for a small group of men, but, as the number of his adherents grew, there were increasing pressures urging them to conform to the practices of the more traditional monastic orders. Within its founder's lifetime, the Franciscan movement began to split into two factions over the issue of the proper observance of its vow of poverty. The majority ultimately came to accept a legal fiction whereby they vested title to their property in the papacy and enjoyed the use of possessions without literally owning them. A strict minority, which came to be known as the Spiritual Franciscans, objected to this practice as a betrayal of the principles of their order, and they drifted into the camp of the critics of the papacy. When they began to assert that apostolic poverty was Christ's will for the whole church, they fell afoul of Pope John XXII, and many of them developed openly revolutionary attitudes.

The more radical friars were encouraged in their attempts to reform the church by a wave of apocalyptic fervor that stirred Europe in the thirteenth and fourteenth centuries. A combination of mysterious plagues, cruel wars, and sagging economic systems undercut the self-confidence of the masses and predisposed them to think in terms of cataclysms that would sweep away the hopeless tangles of their lives. The Spiritual Franciscans gave some focus to these feelings by popularizing and perhaps distorting the writings of a visionary Cistercian monk of the twelfth century, Joachim of Flora (ca. 1132–1202). Joachim had theorized that the history of the creation was destined to be played out in three stages: (1) the age of the Father, which corresponded to the revelation of the Old Testament; (2) the age of the Son, which was fast drawing to a close; and (3) an age of the Spirit, which was about to dawn at any moment. The more extreme friars claimed that the Spirit-guided age had begun to appear in the life of Francis of Assisi, who had demonstrated how Christians could render themselves totally dependent on the Spirit of God. The extremists further asserted that the friars were now the true church—or at least the precursors of the form the church was destined to take in the future, when it would be compelled by God to follow their example, divest itself of its property, and become a purely spiritual organization.

The kings of Europe had a certain sympathy for the program of the radical reformers. Such royal support was motivated, not only by sincere concern for the moral and religious condition of the clergy, but also by certain economic and political objectives. As the nations under their direction grew stronger, the kings came more and more to view papal internationalism as a transparent excuse for unwarranted and self-interested interference by a foreign ecclesiastical power in secular affairs that ought not to concern it. Even the great Innocent III had yielded to the temptation to overuse the religious weapons of the church in the pursuit of earthly objectives. He employed or threatened interdicts against nations more than eighty times, and his successors were even more willing than he to risk compromising the spiritual reputation of their office in maneuvering for temporal advantages. It thus became increasingly difficult for popes to convince the people of Europe that the papacy was not confusing the defense of the Christian faith with the promotion of its personal political programs. Kings steadily came to think of popes as political leaders much like themselves, and it galled them that large amounts of revenue flowed from their nations to the support of a rival papal state. Therefore, kings tended to seek ways to limit the effectiveness of papal control over what they were coming to think of as their national churches. The most obvious way to have avoided the royal pressures for the fragmentation and nationalization of the church would have been to "spiritualize" the church by stripping it of its property and its area of overlap with the secular jurisdiction of the state. On the issue of ecclesiastical property, the kings and the radical reformers often found themselves in complete agreement. But a clear and absolute separation of church and state seemed a practical impossibility, and moderate reformers tended instead to think in terms of increasing the royal authority over the church in order to enforce a higher level of discipline than the independent clergy had been able or willing to maintain.

The intellectuals of the fourteenth century were extemely active and inventive in building a case for the right of laymen to reform the clergy. The Franciscan William of Ockham (1280–1349) argued from the presuppositions of nominalistic philosophy that the church was not a kind of metaphysical reality that transcended its individual members and found its head in the pope. The church was simply the name applied to the community of Christian persons, and its beliefs were defined by the Bible and the opinion of the members as a whole, not by the one individual from the fellowship who claimed the title *pope*. In 1318, Dante completed a study of monarchy in which he concluded that world peace should be sought through the establishment of a universal empire under the leadership of a lay lord. The church and the pope were properly to be limited to spiritual functions and not to be allowed to usurp the duties of secular government. In 1324, Marsiglio of Padua published an influential book entitled *Defender of the*

Peace in which he suggested that the church was properly to be understood as a department of the state. According to Marsiglio, the secular affairs of the church should be governed by the state and doctrine should reflect the teachings of the Bible and the common will of all its knowledgeable and prominent members. Marsiglio employed principles derived from Aristotelian philosophy to demonstrate that the pope derived his authority from the consent of the community he governed and was, therefore, subject to regulation and admonition from the church at large.

Similar ideas found expression in England in the work of John Wycliffe (ca. 1320–84). Wycliffe argued that, since the earth was God's by right of creation, possession of its goods was a privilege rightfully enjoyed only by those who stood in a relationship of grace with him. Immoral or uncharitable clergy were in obvious rebellion against the will of God, and the state was, therefore, perfectly justified in depriving them of their wealth. The New Testament provided the standard by which the church and the pope could be judged, and, as Wycliffe read it, it depicted the apostolic church as a commune of spiritually minded individuals who had no need of possessions, temporal power, or the pretentious sacramental privileges that were the hallmarks of the medieval clergy. Wycliffe's opinions helped stimulate the growth of a radical English reform movement known as Lollardy. The Lollards circulated English translations of the Scriptures and urged a democratization of the church in which the individual's study of the Bible might test the authority of ecclesiastical tradition and the validity of priestly sacraments. The royal government was quick to realize, however, that the arguments Wycliffe developed to undercut the claims of the papacy might also be turned against the institution of monarchy, and during the fifteenth century the government conducted an apparently successful campaign for the suppression of Lollardy. Wycliffe's ideas survived, but they had their most revolutionary impact outside England. His books were transmitted through German channels to central Europe, where John Hus (1369–1415) made Wycliffe's thought a catalyst for the creation of an independent Bohemian church that anticipated the Lutheran reformation by a hundred years.

Many of the theories advanced by the intellectual critics of the church had the general effect of diminishing the status of the clergy and increasing the independence and self-sufficiency of the laity. The reformers argued that in certain affairs the church ought to submit to the advice of laymen, and they suggested that the sacramental channels controlled by the priests were not an individual Christian's only avenue of access to God. God was not a prisoner of his church, and when the structures of the church disintegrated, as they did during the Great Schism, it was difficult to believe that relationships with God had become impossible simply because the validity of sacraments could be called into question. It was fortunate for the laity that the period in which the church began to undercut the integrity of its own work as mediator was also a period in which the masses were prepared to claim more responsibility for themselves in the area of religion. The people of the fourteenth century were no longer the illiterate hordes of the Dark Ages. The skills of literacy were spreading to the lower classes of the laity, and, as vernacular translations of the Scriptures came into circulation, it became increasingly reasonable to project a reform for the Christian faith in which acts of personal piety governed by individual Bible study supplemented or replaced the legalistic sacramentalism of the church.

The tendency to think in terms of increased responsibility and freedom for the individual within the church received considerable support from a wave of enthusiasm for mysticism, which swept northern Europe in the fourteenth and fifteenth centuries. The Christian tradition had always acknowledged the legitimacy of the special gifts of the mystic, but mystics often made ecclesiastical officials nervous. A mystic claimed to have a direct personal experience of God that was of a different order from the experiences of grace the church mediated through the sacraments. By entering into an extraordinary individual relationship with divine reality, a mystic inevitably called into question the church's claim to be the only avenue to God, and some mystics yielded to the temptation to appeal to the authority of their personal revelations against the tradition and the Scriptures of the church.

Mystics featured prominently in the history of medieval Christianity. Many of the leading innovators in monastic reform movements were mystics—for example, Bernard of Clairvaux and Francis of Assisi. Scholastic philosophy and theology drew on the inspirations of the mystical experiences of Thomas Aquinas and Bonaventura. And mystical gifts brought a number of women to positions of unusual prominence in the church. Hildegarde of Bingen (1098–1179), Gertrude the Great (ca. 1256–1302), Mechtilde of Hackborn (d. 1310), Bridget of Sweden (ca. 1303–73), Catherine of Siena (1347–80), and Joan of Arc (1412–31) each wielded remarkable amounts of influence on account of her credentials as a mystic. During the fourteenth century, the vocation of the mystic broadened. It was popularized as an ingredient in the religious lives of ordinary Christians and ceased to be regarded simply as the destiny of a few favored individuals. The meditations of John Eckhard (ca. 1260–1327), John Tauler (d. 1361), John Ruysbroeck (1293–1381), Richard Rolle (ca. 1290–1349), Thomas à Kempis (1380–1471), and the anonymous *Theologia Germanica* provided devotional inspiration for countless Christians and helped guide the programs of numerous new religious organizations that were springing up alongside the traditional structures of the church.

The impotence and confusion reflected in many policies of the late medieval church were in no way an indication of a decline in popular enthusiasm for the Christian faith. It is true that the great period of cathedral building and monastic foundation came to an end in the early fourteenth century, but it was succeeded by an era in which faith found expression in larger numbers of less ambitious, but essential, projects. Thousands of parish churches were expensively rebuilt, hospitals and charitable institutions were established, schools were financed, and the vigorous piety of the laity sought expression in new kinds of religious associations. The wealthy cloisters of the traditional orders had by the fourteenth century largely become aristocratic refuges. Most of the cloisters were located in the country far from the cities where important new lifestyles were coming into existence. It was not always easy to gain admission to these retreats, and the ideals of quiet contemplation and flight from the world that they exemplified were somewhat alien to the activist orientation of late medieval religion. It was to be expected, therefore, that the poor and the middle classes would tend to create new forms of religious associations more relevant to their conditions, and, as early as the twelfth century, such religious communities as the Beguines and the Beghards had begun to appear in France, Germany, and the Netherlands. The members of these communities lived semimonastic existences, but they took no permanent vows and, when necessary for reasons of self-support or charity, they maintained close ties with the secular world. Few if any professional clergy belonged to these groups, which therefore had few leaders with enough theological education to provide sound spiritual direction. As a result, the communities were occasionally in danger of straying into heresies. The church remained rather hostile to them until the Franciscans and Dominicans began to assume some responsibility for their conduct. Numerous other associations developed both with and without the favor of the church. There were extreme groups, such as the Brethren of the Free Spirit, that yielded to the pantheistic tendencies in mysticism and earned the enmity of the Inquisition. But there were also respectable societies of clergy and laymen who called themselves the Friends of God and fostered acceptable forms of ascetic discipline and mystical piety. Some very creative and constructive work in education was done by communities that belonged to Gerard Groote's (1340–84) Brethren of the Common Life. The schools of the Brethren contributed to the training of such leaders as the humanist Biblical scholar Desiderius Erasmus (ca. 1466–1536); Thomas à Kempis, the author of the devotional classic *Imitation of Christ;* and Martin Luther, the reformer.

Mystics tended to represent true religion as an inward attitude of personal communion with God, which issued in acts of piety and charity. This point of view, combined with the increasing accessibility of the Scriptures, helped give individual Christians a sense of greater freedom and personal responsibility in the practice of their religion. People were, therefore, somewhat prepared to handle the opportunities for independent action created by the confusion of the Great Schism. The schism prevented the papacy from functioning as a universal monarchy and also called into question the hierarchy's claim to control an exclusive monopoly of the machinery of mediation between man and God. In addition, the schism created an extremely favorable context for reconsidering the arguments of such academic critics of the clergy as Ockham and Marsiglio of Padua, who had argued that the state and the laity had a responsibility to participate in the regulation of the church.

It took a long time for the leaders of Europe to reach a consensus on how the schism should be handled. Despite the suggestions of the more flamboyant theoreticians, the state's legal right to intervene in the affairs of the church was questionable, and several years passed without the formulation of a clear plan of action. Some observers hoped the situation could be settled informally or by the clergy themselves without setting precedents that might compromise the future freedom of the church. Others were eager to use the embarrassment of the schism to transform the papal monarchy into some kind of collegial system of government. Attempts were made to force the deposition or encourage the resignation of some or all of the competing popes. After these efforts proved fruitless, plans were devised to reunite the church through the colleges of cardinals. But the papal courts turned out to be as irreconcilable as the popes themselves, and so the theologians and politicians of Europe were finally forced to consider radical alternatives.

In 1394, the prestigious theological faculty of the University of Paris endorsed the convocation of a universal church council as the most promising approach to a termination of the schism. There were some legal problems with this solution. In the West it had generally been assumed that only a pope could convene a legitimate council, and none of the reigning popes was willing to take that risk. There were those, however, who argued that Constantine's participation in the Council of Nicaea provided a precedent that permitted an emperor to call a council. But even if a legitimate council could be assembled, the law of the church seemed to suggest that it had no authority over a pope. A pope might consult a council and make its pronouncements binding on the church by ratifying them, but a council had no right to legislate in the absence of papal consent or to sit in judgment on a pope. There was, however, a school of scholars called Conciliarists, including Conrad of Gelnhausen, Peter D'Ailley, John Gerson, and Dietrich of Niem, that claimed the schism was an emergency not covered by extant church law. The Conciliarists suggested that, because the leadership of the church had collapsed, the authority of the hierarchy reverted to the church as a whole. They held that it was irrational to allow the goals of the Christian religion to be abandoned simply because the usual means for their pursuit had broken down. When the authorities who had been entrusted with responsibility for the good of the Christian community could no longer fulfill their duties, the community had an obvious natural right to convene in a universal council and reconstitute its leadership.

In the absence of other promising and more traditional suggestions, the arguments of the Conciliarists gradually gained support throughout Europe. There were practical difficulties in arranging a meeting on the scale required, but, in 1414, the Pisan pope, John XXIII, was finally brought to cooperate with the Emperor Sigismund in calling for a gathering of clergy and the representatives of kings at the Swiss city of Constance. The council remained in session from 1414 to 1418, and it proved to be one of the largest and most colorful international congresses of the Middle Ages. The delegates to the council intended not simply to find a way to end the schism, but also to establish the council as a permanent church governing body that could implement ecclesiastical reform. The nations of Europe were waning in enthusiasm for the support of the competing lines of papal claimants, and the schism proved relatively easy to end. John XXIII of Pisa was captured in an attempt to flee the council and was forced to abdicate. Gregory XII of Rome agreed to resign once the council recognized the legitimacy of his reign. The line of popes at Avignon refused to yield to the council, but, without the continued recognition of major European nations, its claims became absurd. The cardinals at the council then proceeded to elect one of their number to the papacy, and, with the ascension of Martin V on November 11, 1417, the Great Schism came to an end.

The Council of Constance was less successful in dealing with the problem of reforming the church. It tried, condemned, and executed a number of heretics—including John Hus, who had come to the council under the protection of the emperor's guarantee of safety. But once the schism had been terminated, the most pressing and exciting business of the meeting was concluded, and the enthusiasm of the delegates began to wane. The new pope was eager to prevent the council from enacting too much legislation and usurping too many of the traditional prerogatives of his office, so he encouraged an early adjournment by dealing with issues on his own in separate, private conversations with the representatives of each nation. Few reforms were enacted, but, before the council dissolved, it passed decrees that proclaimed the supremacy of councils in the church and ordered popes henceforth to convene councils at regularly scheduled intervals.

Pope Martin V obeyed the directives of Constance and arranged for a council to meet at Pavia in 1423. There was little pressing business, and the council dissolved in a few months. Martin died early in 1431, and his successor, Eugene IV, inherited the council scheduled to meet in Basel later that year. The Council of Basel got off to a slow start, but it soon discovered an issue that generated controversy. The council entered into negotiations with representatives of the schismatic Bohemian Hussite movement and assumed jurisdiction over matters of doctrine and heresy, which the pope felt belonged exclusively to his domain. The situation became even more strained when the beleaguered emperor of Constantinople sought Western aid against the Turks by suggesting that it might be possible to arrange a reunion of the Greek and Latin churches. When Pope Eugene insisted upon ignoring Basel and conducting the conference with the Greeks at a council of his own in Italy, Basel made an ill-advised move that brought the whole Conciliarist movement into disrepute. The council rashly deposed Eugene and, on November 5, 1439, chose an elderly layman, the Count of Savoy, to take his place on the papal throne. Europe was shocked to realize that the threat of papal schism was abroad again. This time, however, the split was being inaugurated, not by a corrupt papal court, but by the very institution that had been invented to reform and preserve the integrity of the church. Basel was unable to generate much popular support for a move that seemed to threaten the stability of Europe for no good reason. The council's radicalism had an effect opposite from its intent, for it now appeared to many that a powerful papal monarchy was a better guardian of the integrity of the church than a fractious and undisciplined council. The council at Basel died a slow death by attrition, and, in the absence of any strong protests from kings or clergy, the popes neglected to convene the other councils that the decrees of Constance had ordered. Disillusionment with the conciliar movement was general enough by 1460 to enable Pope Pius II formally to repudiate the opinion that a church council has power over a pope. The initiative that had been seized by the Council of Constance in 1414 came to nothing. By the end of the fifteenth century, the church was, in theory at least, an unquestioned papal monarchy. Although the conciliarist position again found advocates in the eighteenth century, the Roman Catholic church conclusively rejected it in 1870, when the First Vatican Council received Pope Pius XII's proclamation of the dogma of papal infallibility.

Even though the medieval popes succeeded in winning recognition for their autocracy, they lacked the power to reform the church in ways that would have avoided the Protestant schisms of the sixteenth century. The kings of Europe were becoming powerful enough to force the papacy to grant extensive degrees of autonomy to what were in effect national churches. As early as 1438, the French defined a very spacious position for themselves within the papal monarchy. In the Pragmatic Sanction of Bourges, the French insisted upon a curtailment of the pope's right to intervene in the appointment of French clergy, the abolition of certain kinds of papal taxes, and the limitation of the right of the papal court to hear appeals from the jurisdiction of the French clergy. Similar agreements were ratified in 1448 for the Hapsburg Empire and in 1482 for Spain.

There was little that a pope could do to counter the divisive forces of nationalism, and many of the fifteenth and early sixteenth century popes seem to have yielded to the dominant mood of their day and behaved as if they were little more than leaders of a papal state. They immersed themselves in the complicated politics of Italy and dealt with other politicians in an unscrupulous, if realistic, style that did nothing to advance their reputations as spiritual leaders. Their personal behavior was often a source of public scandal. Reports of corruption at the papal court reached legendary proportions during the reign of the Borgia pope Alexander VI (1492–1503). The spiritual motivation and the international perspective that had characterized the highest medieval hopes for the papacy proved to be untenable. But the institution of the papacy was not a total failure. It had led the church in a remarkably successful campaign to pioneer efficient forms of government and defend ideals of clerical independence, and there were many achievements to which it could point with pride. The church had forged admirable administrative tools for itself and for the secular governments it nurtured. It had fostered education and the recivilization of Europe. It had greatly advanced mankind's understanding of Christian doctrine, and it had inspired a vital new age of artistic imagination and achievement. But the society that the medieval church had been organized to lead was different from the society that was now coming into existence in Europe. The paternalistic, authoritarian procedures that had enabled the clergy to subdue and elevate the rude populace of the Dark Ages generated more resistance than loyalty when applied to the sophisticated citizenry of the late medieval period. Humanism was abroad, spreading belief in the individual and his birthrights of independence, self-determination, and reason. Fervor for the Christian faith was intense, but, by the end of the Middle Ages, it was finding expression in forms that the leaders of the church were unprepared by their traditions to accept or direct.

Chapter Five

—◄●●►—

The Triumph of Pluralism

LUTHER AND THE SPARK OF REFORMATION

DESPITE THE VARIED PRESSURES applied by saints, scholars, heretics, and the conciliarist movement, medieval ecclesiastical institutions successfully resisted change into the early sixteenth century. But in the wake of the excommunication in 1521 of an obscure Augustinian monk and university professor, Martin Luther, a massive revolt against the authority of the church finally swept across Europe. The European branch of the Christian movement was permanently split into two channels, and two contrasting views of the essential Christian mysteries of grace and salvation successfully established themselves in the Western church. The "Catholic," or "Roman," element continued the traditional medieval emphasis on a person's responsibility to work toward his salvation. The Protestant groups revived the ancient Pauline proclamation of salvation as a gift of God freely bestowed on people without reference to their individual merits. The Protestant organizations tended to stress the omnipotence of God and his totally free initiative in awarding the grace of salvation; the Catholic establishment emphasized the reasonableness of God and his just insistence upon human accountability. Both camps possessed themes that were genuine parts of Christian tradition, and both points of view had advantages to offer in the struggle to comprehend the paradoxes that lie at the root of Christian faith. Without "Protestant" concern for God's freedom, Christianity might degenerate into a shallow, legalistic system of rewards and punishments. Without "Catholic" concern for human responsibility, the Christian faith could succumb to quietism, licentiousness, or antinomianism. There were, therefore, valuable perspectives enshrined in the programs of both parties, but conditions in the sixteenth century were such that the two differing views could no longer be developed under the aegis of one universal Christian institution.

The momentous division of the church that occurred in the sixteenth century is everywhere associated with the name of Martin Luther (1483–1546), but it was neither entirely his responsibility nor solely his achievement. There were few things in Luther's message that the church had not heard before. His enemies dismissed him as a resuscitator of the Hussite heresy, and his friends defended him as one in a line of true interpreters of the Pauline Epistles. But it was Luther's destiny to be situated at a time and place that gave his voicing of the old call for ecclesiastical reform unique catalytic power. For reasons often beyond his control, he became the symbolic center of a coalition of parties that were independently pressing for social, political, economic, and ideological changes. The result of his pursuit of his personal objectives was a chain reaction of mutually supportive events that brought secular governments to the assistance of theological reformers and inspired the masses of Europe to exert their influence on delicate balances of power. A demand for reform thus finally issued in a Reformation that marked the dawning of a new epoch in European history and the opening of the modern phase in the Christian movement.

Martin Luther was not born a rebel against the church, and it was only slowly and with some reluctance that he allowed himself to be pushed into such a position. For thirty-eight of the sixty-three years of his life, he sought his personal religious assurances in strictly traditional ways. His father, Hans Luther, a self-made man of moderate property, destined him for a career as a lawyer, and he pursued his education at schools at Mansfeld, Magdeburg, Eisenach and at the University of Erfurt. At the age of twenty-two, Luther underwent a struggle of conscience that drove him, against his father's will, to terminate preparations for a secular vocation and to enter the cloister of the Augustinian Eremites at Erfurt. He professed his monastic vows in September, 1506, received ordination to the priesthood, and celebrated his first mass on May 2, 1507. In 1508, his order assigned him responsibility for teaching at its center at the University of Wittenberg. There, in 1512, he earned the title of Doctor of Theology. Luther's behavior as a monk was sufficiently orthodox to merit his promotion to positions of responsibility in his order. In 1510, he visited Rome on business relevant to a proposed reorganization of the Augustinian Eremites, and, in 1515, he became vicar for a district containing eleven of their houses. In addition to his university lectures, he accepted an invitation in 1515 to be a regular preacher in the churches of Wittenberg. It was this pastoral experience that finally helped to bring into focus the lessons of his personal spiritual odyssey, his academic studies of the Scriptures, and his sense of responsibility as a Christian.

As a young monk, Luther had been thoroughly traditional in his understanding of Christian theology. His order inclined to the nominalist position of William of Ockham and taught a system of thought that exalted faith over reason. But when it came to the practical concerns of seeking personal assurances of salvation, the order recommended a firm adherence to the sacramental system of the church. Luther believed the church's claim to be able to forgive all the sins confessed to its priests, and he utilized the sacrament of penance to a degree that might have struck some of his contemporaries as morbid. Luther's sense of sin and his consciousness of the depth of his rebellion against God proved to be stronger than the comfort the sacraments offered. Luther was deeply concerned about the fact that the total confession of all sins seemed a practical human impossibility. Some sins were inevitably forgotten, others were committed so casually as not to be recognized for what they were, and new sins flooded the soul so rapidly that confession could hardly keep up with them. Yet all sins that were not confessed were inexorably imputed to the debt of their author and placed him in peril of damnation. The standard of perfection that God represented and that he demanded of his creatures was in reality beyond a reasonable hope of achievement, and the demands of God's justice seemed to Luther to compel God to adopt a merciless attitude toward the impotence of human sinners. It was not that Luther was a greater sinner than other men or that he had some particularly onerous burden on his conscience. But, like Augustine, he was acutely aware of the significance of apparently petty sins. The more he strove to confess and mend his faults, the more clearly aware he became of their extent and of the gulf of alienation that they revealed to exist between the human and the divine. The more he came to understand the persistence of his rebellious inclinations, the less confident he became in his ability to subdue his sinful nature and become a creature who could merit the approval of the perfect God.

Luther's struggles with his soul plunged him into a depression that began to lift only after he devoted himself to the study of the Scriptures. From 1513 to 1519, he lectured at Wittenberg on the Psalms and the Pauline Epistles, and his meditation on these texts gradually brought him to a new understanding of the sinner's position before God. In retrospect, a passage from Romans (1:17) was seen to have had pivotal significance: "For in it [i.e., the Gospel] the right-eousness of God is revealed through faith for faith; as it is written, 'He who through faith is righteous shall live.'" Luther's biblical research convinced him that the righteousness God demanded of his creatures was not their own achievement, but a righteousness that God imputed to them by grace. The "good news" of the Gospel was not that people could earn salvation by obeying a new Christian law enshrined in the sacramental disciplines of the church. The good news was that, in Christ, God offered free salvation to sinners while they were still sinners. Nothing a person was or did or ever could do would merit the gift God offered. God in his mercy freely granted undeserved worth to sinners and enabled them at his own expense to satisfy the requirements of divine justice. The reconciliation of the dictates of divine love and justice was a miracle that took place inside the mystery of God and not in his external relations with his creatures. Luther's iteration of the Pauline-Augustinian doctrine of salvation by grace alone was to become the cornerstone of a new Protestant theology, but Luther was slow to realize its potential as a basis for criticizing the practices of the medieval church. He was aware not of having invented a new idea, but simply of having restated a fundamental old one. It was only when he began to act on his new insights in response to specific abuses of ec-clesiastical authority that the radical implications of his position began to be revealed.

The issue that brought Luther's ideas to the attention of Europe and precipitated the opening phase of the Reformation was a dispute over an indulgence that Pope Leo X in 1514 authorized for sale in Germany. An indulgence was simply a remission of the penance due for a confessed sin, and, when properly used, it was an instrument of mercy and charity. It gave the clergy a justification for removing a penance that proved too onerous for the sinner on whom it had been imposed. An indulgence also provided a method of offering the assurance of salvation to those who were cut off from the regular ministry of the sacraments. The church believed that its power to grant indulgences derived from the fact that it was the trustee of a great treasury of spiritual merit that accrued from the labors of Christ and the saints. The church further believed itself free to apply this merit for the benefit of persons who were unable to discharge their own penitential obligations. At first, indulgences seem generally to have been limited to the remission of specific penances for past sins, but, during the First Crusade, the papacy began to offer plenary indulgences covering past and future penances to those who undertook to fight the infidel in lands where the normal Christian channels of grace were difficult or impossible to maintain. In this light, the promise of an indulgence came to be seen as an inducement to perform a service for the church, and the church increasingly yielded to the temptation to expand the range of services for which it considered indulgences to be appropriate rewards. When expressions of loyalty took the form of monetary contributions to the church and received recognition in the granting of indulgences, it was difficult to avoid creating the impression that the church was selling remission of the penalties of sin.

This was certainly the conclusion Luther's parishioners were drawing in 1517 when the archbishop of Mainz's agent, a Dominican friar named John Tetzel, began to merchandize indulgences in the neighborhood of Wittenberg. Tetzel hawked his spiritual wares shamelessly and under what Luther considered to be false pretenses. Luther was troubled by the effect of Tetzel's sales campaign on the discipline of the people and determined to try to correct some of the popular misapprehensions concerning indulgences. On October 31, 1517, in compliance with common medieval university traditions, he invited the community to discuss the subject of indulgences by posting a list of ninety-five theses which he was willing to defend in public debate. Luther seems to have assumed that the practices and attitudes to which he objected were simply local abuses and that his theses would find general support in Rome. He was wrong. His theses implied a criticism of the universal practices of the papacy and denied the basis of the absolute spiritual power that Rome claimed to be able to exercise.

Men had already been condemned to death as heretics for making statements similar to Luther's, and the church moved quickly to discipline him. In April, 1518, he was called to a meeting of the leaders of his order in Heidelberg to explain his behavior, and by summer he received a summons to appear in Rome. Luther appealed to the elector of Saxony, Frederick the Wise, for help, and Frederick arranged for him to be interrogated under potentially more favorable circumstances. In October, 1518, Luther met the papal legate, Cardinal Cajetan—who was also the leader of the Dominican order to which Tetzel belonged—at a German imperial diet in Augsburg. Since Cajetan believed firmly in the absolute spiritual authority of the papacy, he was unimpressed by Luther's attempts to use the Scriptures as a basis for judging the practices of the pope. After two weeks in Augsburg, Luther abandoned his attempt to interpret his position to Cajetan and returned to Wittenberg to await excommunication. There were many at Augsburg who resented the papacy's German policies and who were attracted to Luther's cause. The elector Frederick was particularly energetic in the effort to see to it that Luther received a hearing.

Luther's opinions received both clarification and wider circulation in the wake of a debate held in Leipzig the following summer (1519). Under pressure from his opponent, John von Eck of the University of Ingolstadt, Luther found himself ever more frequently opposing the authority of the Scriptures to later church traditions. He upheld his firm conviction that salvation came through faith alone and not from the merit of good works. In addition, Luther now approached the second fundamental principle of Protestant theology—the belief that the Scriptures are the church's sole authority for determining questions of faith. He came to believe that the papacy, the hierarchy, and the councils of the church were, when regarded from the standpoint of the history of their evolution, simply human institutions which had no more than human authority. The Bible alone constituted a record of God's revelation that could provide an unchanging norm for criticizing and directing the development of Christian practice. If it were objected that the Bible was simply a record of the earliest phase in the development of the tradition of the church, it could at least be argued that Scripture was the only record of the phase closest to the origin of the Christian revelation in the lives and the experiences of the companions of the Christ. Historically speaking, all later generations were dependent upon it for their knowledge of the supremely authoritative words and deeds of the founder of their faith, and anyone who wished to make departures from the biblical description of Christian life had to justify the innovations.

The more Luther thought about the authority of the Bible and his conviction that salvation came by faith alone and not by works, the more he questioned the established structures and practices of the medieval church. Like many who had preceded him in the fourteenth and fifteenth centuries, he could see no support in the Scriptures for the papacy, the hierarchy, and the sacramental system that had come to dominate the exercise of the Christian religion in Europe. Since Luther rejected all attempts to earn salvation by means of human deeds, he understood the sacraments, not as mechanisms for obtaining spiritual merit, but as opportunities for God to manifest promises of grace. Sacraments functioned because God freely willed to use them from time to time to reveal his grace to those to whom he accorded salvation. The power of the sacraments derived from the faith that accompanied them, not from any mysterious spiritual privileges accorded the clergy who performed them. The clergy could not, therefore, use their privilege of administering sacraments as a basis for claiming unique spiritual status or power within the church. Luther believed that each person stood in direct relationship to God through his own faith. Since questions of merit were irrelevant in determining matters of salvation, no one needed a mediator—such as the church and its clergy—to do anything for him. Everything that needed to be done for a sinner's salvation had already been done by God himself in Christ; no further works by priests or laymen were required. Since everyone who was saved was saved by faith, no one possessed merits that caused him to be highly regarded by God and that conferred the ability to influence God on behalf of others. Every individual was on the same footing in his relationship with God, and, therefore, every person was his own priest. By the miracle of faith, he stood directly in the divine presence without the need of an intercessor other than Christ himself. The church assisted each Christian simply as the community of others like himself, and its priesthood was a function equally shared by all its members.

By 1520, Luther's ideas were clear enough to form the beginning of an identifiably Protestant theology, and Luther had become a symbol around which a number of different kinds of dissidents had rallied. Since the possibility of an accommodation with the papacy seemed increasingly remote, Luther called for the convocation of a church council and in 1520 published a series of three pamphlets designed to take his quarrel with Rome directly to the people. The pamphlets (*An Address to the Christian Nobility of the German Nation, The Babylonian Captivity of the Church,* and *The Freedom of a Christian*) were noteworthy in that some of them were addressed to the laity and all of them circulated among lay people. As a result, Luther's struggle became something more than a dispute among academic theologians. Luther was fortunate in that the advances in the technology of printing made by John Gutenberg (ca. 1400-68) provided the means to reach and exploit the potential of the growing literacy of the masses. Without the publicity that printing made possible, it is doubtful that Luther could have rallied enough popular support to resist the governmental and ecclesiastical forces that lined up against him. His opinions and arguments were probably understood and debated by a larger segment of society than those of any of the medieval critics of the church who had preceded him. His ideas circulated throughout Europe and encouraged numerous other aspirant reformers to make their opinions known. And, as a result, something much like a popular movement for the reform of the church finally began to take shape.

The papacy was alert to what was happening, and, on June 15,

1520, the bull *Exsurge domine* officially condemned the Lutheran heresy and gave Luther two months in which to retract and make his peace with the church. Luther refused, and, on January 3, 1521, he was excommunicated. Frederick the Wise remained firm in his support of Luther and induced the new emperor, Charles V, to give Luther a hearing before the imperial diet that was to convene in Worms on January 6. Luther attended the diet under the protection of the emperor's safe-conduct, but the diet failed to reconcile him with the papacy. Luther refused to accept the authority of arguments based on ecclesiastical tradition and made his appeal directly to Scripture and reason. The fundamental presuppositions of Lutheranism were thus clearly contrasted with those of Catholicism, but no method was found to resolve the basic disagreement over the locus of authority in the church. Catholicism perpetuated the absolutist claims of the medieval papal monarchy, and Luther insisted that the Scriptures and reason provided a basis for criticism and regulation of the papacy.

Luther left Worms on April 26, 1521, and went into retreat at the castle of the Wartburg. There he spent a year in prudent seclusion working on a German translation of the Scriptures and watching the development of events that were beyond his control. Emperor Charles V joined the pope in the condemnation of Luther, and Luther's rebellion against the church acquired important political associations. Luther emerged as the champion, not only of those who were exasperated by the behavior of unworthy clergy, but also of those who had grievances against secular leaders.

The spread of the Lutheran Reformation was greatly assisted by the political fragmentation of Germany that had resulted from the medieval church's successful attempts to weaken the Holy Roman Empire. The title of emperor was still current and was borne by the Hapsburg king, Charles V. But the title carried with it little real authority over the German nobility, and Charles's responsibilities for family properties in ·the Netherlands, Austria, and Spain kept him from becoming too deeply involved in German affairs. In the west, he was faced with the machinations of an ambitious French monarchy which was determined to halt the expansion of Hapsburg power in the Netherlands and Italy. In the east, he confronted a powerful Turkish threat to his family's Austrian territories. Constantinople had fallen to the Turks in 1453, and, in 1520, Sultan Suleiman the Magnificent began a sweep up the Danube which brought him by 1529 within reach of the walls of Vienna. The situation in the east remained precarious until Suleiman's death in 1556.

In the absence of any effective central authority in Germany, the nobility were free to follow their whims in responding to the options of the Lutheran Reformation. The elector of Saxony permitted Wittenberg to restructure its churches and schools along lines suggested by Luther, and, by 1528, many of the major northern feudatories and free cities had declared for the reform. The Lutheran party developed great skill in communicating its program to the people by means of inexpensive pamphlets ornamented with woodcut illustrations and cartoons. Luther himself developed books of simple sermons for use by the clergy who were faced with the problem of making his ideas intelligible to the masses, and he contributed greatly to the evolution of German culture by encouraging the use of music and hymns in Protestant worship.

Luther's interests and skills were theological, not political, and his opinions on church-state relations won him powerful friends among the lay lords who favored the development of independent national churches. In the absence of a strong organization of his own, Luther was forced to rely on the assistance of the secular government in promoting his reforms. In 1528, he endorsed a program for the guidance of the state's ecclesiastical inspectors and thus gave a kind of official recognition to the state's right to administer the church. As the Reformation progressed, Luther felt compelled to identify himself with the established governmental authorities, for reformation threatened to lead to a degree of revolution and chaos that alarmed him. Luther had established a dangerous precedent by appealing to the authority of his own reading of the Scriptures against the traditions of the church, but he seems to have been slow to realize that others might adopt his method and arrive at different conclusions. During his stay at the Wartburg, his followers in Wittenberg had disagreed among themselves and had damaged the reputation of their cause by perpetrating a number of excesses in their attempts to reform the city. Strange enthusiasts with bizarre opinions, who had always existed on the periphery of the medieval church, now began to identify themselves with the Lutheran movement and to challenge the right of any authority to interfere with what they perceived to be God's guidance of their consciences. Such persons remained a relatively harmless nuisance until 1524. In the spring of that year, a series of unorganized, spontaneous peasant revolts broke out in southwestern Germany. Similar responses to desperate economic and political conditions had occurred in England in 1381 and in France during the fifteenth century. The English revolt had brought the Wycliffite reform into disrepute, and the French uprising had undercut the development of parliamentary institutions. The German peasants' wars were in no way a part of the program of the Lutheran reform, but the peasants felt with some reason that their fight against oppressive medieval structures was simply an extension of Luther's cause. Luther was vocal in his support of political and economic reform, but the extremes of revolution repelled him. In 1525, he published a violent attack on the peasants and threw in his lot with the nobles who were fighting to restore order and maintain their ancient privileges. The peasants were brutally subdued, and in triumph Luther denied his opponents' charges that the Reformation necessarily entailed a total upheaval of society. By allying itself with the propertied classes, however, Lutheranism lost some of its appeal for the masses and opened the way for other reform movements to seize valuable initiatives.

Early in the 1520's, another strong center of reform had begun to develop in the Swiss city of Zurich. The Swiss movement owed its existence to Luther's inspiration, but it soon demonstrated that Luther would find it difficult or impossible to establish a common front with all who honored him. The Zurich reform was the work of Ulrich Zwingli (1484-1531), a humanist priest who was almost exactly the same age as Luther. Early in his career, Zwingli emerged as an outspoken critic of political and religious abuses of many kinds, and, in 1519, in the wake of a personal crisis, he determined to identify himself with the Lutheran ideas that were beginning to circulate in Switzerland. In 1521, he boldly began to use his position on the staff of the leading church in Zurich to oppose his bishop and call for reforms that would bring the life of the church into conformity with his reading of the New Testament. Zwingli concurred with Luther in the belief that salvation came by faith, not works; but the conclusions the Swiss priest drew from this conviction were more extreme than Luther's. Zwingli advocated stripping the churches of all ornaments and symbols that recalled the works righteousness of Catholicism, and he redesigned patterns of worship to focus on preaching and Bible study. Since he believed with Luther that the sacraments derived their power to save from the faith with which they were received, he regarded them simply as symbols of the presence of faith. In this he was more radical than Luther, and Luther found it impossible to reach agreement with the Zwinglians on the definition of sacraments. Luther's insistence upon confessing a real presence of Christ in the sacrament of the Lord's Supper was an indication of the conciliatory approach to reform he favored, and Zwingli and others were unhappy with what they perceived to be Luther's needless conservatism.

By 1524, the people of Zurich had decided to take Zwingli's suggestions, to seize control of their church, and to make changes in the practice of their religion that would put them at odds with Rome and the government of the Swiss Confederation. It was not long before Bern, Basel, and other centers followed their example and a Zwinglian movement began to penetrate Germany from the south. Since a strong Catholic reaction to the Reformation was anticipated as soon as the emperor concluded his struggles with the French and the Turks, a unification of the Lutheran and Zwinglian parties seemed to be in their mutual best interests. Luther and Zwingli met in Marburg in the fall of 1529, but they were unable to agree on a common interpretation of the reformed faith. Protestant Christianity was destined by its commitment to the inviolability of individual consciences to evolve as a pluralistic phenomenon. Zwingli returned to Zurich and promoted an aggressive program of reform which soon embroiled the cantons of Switzerland in civil war and which brought him to his death on the battlefield in 1531. Zurich declined in importance as a center for reform, and the Swiss Protestant movement took quite a different direction in the next generation under the leadership of Geneva.

The Lutherans were left alone to pursue the imperial government's recognition of their right to exist. The rulers of their potentially hostile neighbors, the Catholic districts of Germany, had no sympathy with Protestantism as a religion, but they also had no interest in strengthening the emperor's hand in what they felt were their internal affairs. Consequently, a diet that met in Speyer in 1526 induced the emperor to agree provisionally that each German state should be allowed to follow its own religious preference. Charles V attempted on later occasions to terminate this arrangement and force a return of the Lutherans to papal supervision, but he was unsuccessful. At Augsburg in 1530, the Lutherans presented him with a confession of faith that symbolized their maturation as an independent church with a program that was more than a collection of objections to assorted Roman customs. In 1535, Luther assumed the authority to ordain Protestant clergy. The Lutheran princes organized themselves into a defensive league which enabled them to survive a long period of conflict with the emperor, and, although Luther did not live long enough to see it, they ultimately succeeded in obtaining the emperor's consent to a division of Germany into Lutheran and Catholic districts. Religious liberty was not established, and the right of the state to direct the religious practices of its people was not challenged. But thereafter, various parts of Europe offered people different options in the practice of the Christian faith. The religious monopoly of the medieval church was finally broken.

THE PROTESTANT OFFENSIVE

LUTHER'S CONCEPT OF SALVATION by faith alone, his reliance on the sole authority of the Scriptures in determining the content of doctrine, and his advocacy of the priestly rights of each individual believer created a distinctively Protestant point of view. But it quickly became apparent that one could hold these principles and still maintain opinions quite different from Luther's own. Although the word *protestant* came into use about the year 1529 to refer to Luther's followers in the German diet who protested the emperor's attempts to curtail their religious liberties, Lutheranism and Protestantism were not to evolve as synonymous terms. Luther's experience with Zwingli was an early indication of the fact that not all Protestant consciences would respond to the authority of the Bible in the same way. The Protestants would, therefore, not be able to follow the example of Rome and establish a "universal" (i.e., "catholic") ecclesiastical organization. Instead, the Protestant "church" was to develop as an amorphous group of autonomous—and often antagonistic—sects and denominations. Even the Lutheran branch of the movement was to fragment and to be exceeded in influence by currents for reform that were developing outside Germany.

From Germany, Lutheranism had some success in spreading into Scandinavia and central Europe. As early as 1526, King Frederick I of Denmark, a former duke of Schleswig-Holstein, moved in the direction of establishing a state church with Lutheran sympathies. He hoped to strengthen his throne by gaining control of the clergy, but Danish Lutheranism was not firmly established until the reign of his successor, Christian III (1536-59). Christian conquered Norway and Iceland and imposed the Lutheran reform on them. Sweden joined the movement under the leadership of its king Gustavus Vasa (1523-60), who personally espoused Lutheran doctrines and also hoped to use the resources of a nationalized church for the support of a more effective central government.

In central Europe, Lutheranism spread in the wake of German economic and cultural influences, but the absence of strong monarchies made it difficult for whole nations effectively to be re-formed. Catholicism was able in the long run to regain much of the in-fluence it initially lost, but Lutherans did succeed in putting down per-manent roots in Poland, Lithuania, Hungary, and Transylvania. Bohemia and Moravia were already under the influence of the cen-tury-old Hussite movement, and, although the Bohemian Brethren sects sympathized with many of Luther's ideas, they were slow to iden-tify themselves with the Lutheran movement.

There were numerous other groups that might have associated themselves with the parties led by Luther and Zwingli, but that were insistently repudiated by the two leading reformers. These groups con-stituted a kind of left wing of the Reformation, but they were united more by their dislikes than by their affirmations. Since many of them were extreme biblicists, they often expressed a common antipathy to infant baptism on the basis that the custom lacked Scriptural precedent. Their tendency to require adult converts who had been bap-tized as children to be baptized again caused their enemies to lump them all together as Anabaptists, but many quite different opinions were represented among them.

Some radicals developed among Luther's followers, but the most famous of the early Anabaptist leaders were associated with Zwingli's reform. In 1522, a young humanist named Conrad Grebel (1498–1526) became one of Zwingli's converts and devoted himself to the study of the New Testament. Grebel and his friends soon found that their read-ing of the Scriptures led them to an understanding of the church that differed significantly from Zwingli's. For them, the church was a com-munity of converts who were gathered out of secular society and com-mitted to a code of ethics that made no compromises with the realities of a sinful world. For them, there could be no alliance between the church and the state, for membership in the church was a privilege of grace, not a birthright like citizenship.

It was perhaps their insistent criticism of church-state alliances, which were major strategies of the Lutheran and Zwinglian reforms, that caused their Protestant brethren to oppose them so vehemently. Luther and Zwingli were all too aware of the anarchy that might de-velop within the reform without the restraining authority of the state. Protestantism was a mode of Christian faith that emphasized the autonomy of individual consciences, and such commitment to princi-ples of self-determination made the movement uniquely vulnerable to schisms. Luther and Zwingli objected to the corrupt and inflexible au-thorities enshrined in the Roman church, but the reformers had no illusions about the necessity of maintaining some kind of control over the wills and inclinations of individual Christians. To them, the Anabaptists seemed to be irresponsible enthusiasts who pushed the Protestant principles to absurd extremes and who exposed society to the threat of chaos. Such fears were not entirely groundless. Some Anabaptists drew a sharp line between the community of the saved in the church and the crowd of the damned outside it, and they refused any longer to discharge their responsibilities to the state. Others sought to act literally on certain words of Christ, and they became pacifists or advocates of the abolition of private property. Through their Bible studies, some of them became so steeped in the apocalyptic mood of the early church that they proclaimed an imminent end to the world and threw off the normal restraints of decent human conduct. Others were so moved by the experience of grace that they rejected the authority of law and Scripture and claimed to be able to live beyond the distinction between good and evil. A notorious group came to power in 1534 in the Westphalian community of Münster and used their opportunities to turn the city into a scandalous mockery of the Christian concept of the kingdom of God on earth.

Zwingli and Luther both advocated harsh measures against the Anabaptists, and tens of thousands of them were martyred. Persecution served only to strengthen and diffuse the movement, and the Anabaptists established permanent footholds in Germany, the Netherlands, and eastern Europe. Attempts made to unite them under one creed or church order failed, and they persisted as a number of distinct, colorful sects. The largest of these was formed in response to the work of Menno Simons (1496–1561), a Catholic priest who joined the Reformation as a result of Luther's teachings. The Mennonites thought of themselves as a community of individually called Christians who were dedicated to living lives that would reflect the grace that had saved them. Their total loyalty to what they perceived to be the will of God occasionally brought them into conflict with the state, but their sincerity and their peaceful conduct ultimately won them a degree of respectability and influence. Through them, the tradition of extreme reliance on the individual's perception of God's grace, which was the hallmark of the radical branch of the Reformation, lived on to inspire later Baptist and Quaker sects.

The Reformation won its smallest successes in the lands that bordered the Mediterranean. Humanist circles in Italy and Spain took an intellectual interest in the movement, and some universities and trading centers with strong ties to Germany developed small Protestant communities. In general, however, the importance of the papacy to Italy and the extensive control that the Catholic kings of Spain and France had already acquired over their national churches hindered the spread of the Reformation to these countries. France was, of course, close to strong Protestant centers in Switzerland, Germany, and the Netherlands, and for a while it looked as if Francis I might favor the Protestant cause. A vigorous Reformation party thus had an opportunity to establish itself in France, but, by 1540, the government's vacillating attitudes had forced many of the party's most determined members to flee. Switzerland provided a haven for some of them, and it was at Geneva that a young French exile named John Calvin (1509-64) led the Reformation into the second phase of its development.

Calvin, like Luther, was the son of an ambitious and successful middle class family. He was born in the city of Noyons and prepared for a career in the church by studying theology at Paris and law at Orleans and Bourges. His humanistic studies exposed him to the literature of the Reformation, but he seems to have shown little interest in Protestantism until 1533, when he came under the influence of Gerard Roussel and Nicholas Cop, a reform-minded rector of the University of Paris. After Cop was charged with heresy in 1534, Calvin left Paris for a period of retreat at Saintonge. It was there that he seems to have decided to surrender his ecclesiastical benefices and decline the ordination for which he had been preparing. A royal edict against Protestants issued in autumn, 1534, pressured him into leaving France, and he fled to Basel where in 1536 he published the first edition of his *Institutes of the Christian Religion.* The *Institutes* was intended as an introduction to Christian theology and as an apology for Protestantism, but, as Calvin expanded and revised the book in numerous later editions, it became much more than that. The *Institutes* provided Protestantism with its first comprehensive, systematic theology and established Calvin as the leader of a new era in the history of the Reformation. Luther had successfully challenged the medieval Roman church's exclusive hold on the European mind, but Lutheranism developed as a relatively conservative, largely German phenomenon. The theology of the *Institutes,* which became known as Calvinism, formed a new, aggressive Protestantism that was destined to have an incalculable influence on the evolution of European and American culture.

Calvin shared Luther's allegiance to the three Protestant principles of salvation by faith alone, the priesthood of all believers, and the sole authority of Scripture in determining questions of doctrine and discipline. But Calvin was in some ways more extreme and consistent in his understanding of the implications of these ideas than Luther was. For Luther, the concept of salvation by faith was an extrapolation from his personal struggle for assurance and his study of the Scriptures. For Calvin, the belief was also a logical implication of the Judao-Christian concept of God, and he drew from it an unflinchingly strict doctrine of predestination. Calvin had a strong sense of the majesty of the God of the Old Testament who was the omnipotent Creator and the omniscient Judge of all mankind. He believed that a correct understanding of God's absolute self-sufficiency required one to postulate that God was not dependent on the contingent events of human history for his knowledge of the ultimate end of creation. God must have known in his act of creation what the course and outcome of his deed would be. There were no other centers of power with which he had to compromise and no unexpected events on whose outcome he had to wait. From the beginning of time, therefore, the destiny of every created being was predetermined in the knowledge of God. Human deeds and actions within history were totally without significance in determining questions of salvation or damnation. The decision about a person's end was taken by God before the individual's beginning, and if one enjoyed the blessings of salvation, he possessed them only because of God's grace and not as a result of human merit.

The doctrine of predestination was beautifully congruent with the Judao-Christian concept of the Creator and provided the clearest possible context for understanding the Protestant assessment of the significance of faith and works in the event of salvation; but there were some problems with the doctrine. Luther favored it only as a description of a Christian's retrospective view on his personal experience of faith in God's promises. To assert predestination as a universal philosophic principle seemed to him to imply that God predestined people to both salvation and damnation; if this were the case, it seemed logical to question the justice of God's actions and the reality of human responsibility for sin. Calvin, however, boldly asserted a doctrine of double predestination and insisted that the concept should in no way be construed to imply that the damned did not truly merit their fate or that God was the author of their sin.

The doctrine of predestination inspired a great deal of controversy among Calvin's followers, who busied themselves for years in suggesting numerous refinements in its interpretation or qualifications of its implications. Some took a hard line and insisted that God had predestined the course of history prior to the creation. Others suggested that God's predestination applied to the world only after it had been freely corrupted by Adam. Some felt that their confidence in God's merciful nature and in his powers of predestination justified the assertion that he would ultimately effect the salvation of all his creatures.

Many Christians were concerned that Calvin's theory of predestination, or election as it was sometimes called, made a mockery of human freedom and encouraged moral quietism. Toward the end of the sixteenth century, a Dutch theologian, Jacob Arminius (1560–1609), gave his name to a movement that advocated a kind of conditional predestination. The Arminian party argued that man was not totally depraved by his inheritance of Adam's sin and that human beings retained a responsibility to participate in their own salvation. God's grace was freely offered to all, but it was not irresistibly imposed on those who received it. It had to be apprehended by those for whom it became a means for salvation, and the doctrine of election was simply a reference to God's foreknowledge of the identity of the persons who would use their freedom to accept the gift that God freely offered them. Strict Calvinists objected, however, that the postulation of a need for a person to cooperate with the grace of salvation was simply a reassertion of the righteousness of human works, and they condemned Arminianism as a heretical corruption of the Protestant proclamation of salvation by grace. But the Arminian solution to the puzzles of predestination appealed to many, and Arminian ideas have featured in the theologies of several very successful Protestant denominations.

The impetus toward quietism that one might fear to find lurking in Calvin's doctrine of predestination was effectively countered by his interpretation of the concept of the priesthood of all believers. Calvin went beyond the basic Protestant conviction that there were no uniquely priestly vocations that earned their practitioners spiritual merit. He asserted that every respectable human calling ought to be an arena for glorifying God. Human actions were impotent as instruments for obtaining salvation, but they were not without significance as indicators of the presence or absence of grace in a particular individual's life. Calvin believed that grace naturally issued in good works and inspired a life lived in obedience to God's law. Good deeds did not earn salvation, but they might reveal the nature of the decision God had already made concerning the salvation of their author. Persons who were flagrantly sinful were obviously not recipients of grace and were justly subject to eviction from Christian communities. Only those who demonstrated the fruits of righteousness had a reasonable hope of being discovered to be among the elect. Only they, therefore, could lay claim to positions of respect, security, and privilege in a Christian society. Their virtues were not the source of the grace they manifested, but their good deeds were a sign of the salvation that had already freely been accorded them and the faith that was at work in them. Works did not make a person a Christian, but they were the basis of his claim to be treated as one. Calvinism thus had the seemingly paradoxical effect of denying the spiritual significance of human achievements while inspiring an extremely active pursuit of the tangible evidence of virtue.

Calvin joined Luther in acknowledging the Bible as the sole authority for the definition of doctrine and virtue, but the Genevan theologian attempted to be more literal and direct than Luther in applying Scripture to public life. Calvin's confidence in the sufficiency of the Scriptures for all spiritual needs caused many of his followers to conceive a contempt for nonbiblical traditions and rituals. An iconoclastic stripping of their churches resulted. Many beautiful objects, harmless customs, and cherished festivals were discarded simply because their use could not be supported from the Scriptures. The tendency to seek justification from the Bible for all human actions also exposed Calvinists to the temptations of an uncharitable legalism, and it is all too easy to fault them in retrospect for acts of arrogance and presumption.

Calvin set high goals for his people and laid tremendous responsibilities on their leaders. He understood the Bible to be the complete and only record of God's will for his creatures. Calvin assumed, therefore, that biblical precepts of revelation contained all the laws necessary for the governance of human communities and that the Creator called every society of the elect to become an example of the kingdom of God on earth. Calvin viewed the church and the state, not as loci of separate sacred and secular authorities, but as two dimensions of the administration of the same divine law. The church was the state in pursuit of knowledge of God, and the state was the church in manifestation of the will of God. Since the true church was the community of the elect, only those persons who could give evidence—by means of histories of virtuous conduct—of their probable election could claim membership in it and exercise rights in the state. The elect ought not to resent or resist attempts on the part of their colleagues to inspect their behavior, and true Christians also should not shy away from the responsibility of judging the witness of others. If people were truly called, they were called to be the kingdom of God. Bold decisions frequently had to be made, but they were made in a humble trust in the validity of one's election—which was maintained only by a continuous process of agonizing self-scrutiny and submission to criticism. Calvin had ample opportunities to illustrate his theories of social responsibility, for he spent much of his life in intimate involvement with the government of the city of Geneva. Geneva began to drift toward Protestantism in the early 1530's as a part of its general program to rid itself of the domination of its bishop and the dukes of Savoy. In 1536, William Farel, a French Protestant who was working in Geneva as a result of its alliance with the Protestant city of Bern, induced Calvin to abandon his intent to live in Strasbourg and help with the reorganization of the newly reformed city. Power struggles within the community forced both men to leave Geneva in 1538, but, after an absence of three years in Strasbourg, Calvin was invited to return and spent the rest of his life dominating the development of the city and making it the capital of the Reformation. Geneva was organized as one ecclesiastical community under the direction of a coalition of clergy and laity who had extensive powers to enforce conformity to the strict moral codes and religious disciplines that Calvin understood to be the law of God. The government did not hesitate liberally to apply punishments of exile or execution to those who were convicted of crimes against the faith or serious breaches of morality. In 1553, Calvin boldly defended Geneva's burning of Michael Servetus for his heretical denial of the doctrine of the Trinity. But Geneva became a secure refuge for large numbers of Protestant fugitives, and the scholars among them made it a major center for education, the production of propaganda, and the management of mission projects. From Geneva, a new and invigorated form of Protestantism thrust out into Europe and extended the horizons of the Reformation.

Unlike Luther, Calvin was successful in coming to an understanding with the Zwinglian churches. By 1552, he and the Zwinglians had reached an accord on the sacraments and other fundamental points of doctrine, and, two years after Calvin's death, the publication of the Second Helvetic Confession provided a basis for the union of the two traditions in what came to be known as the Reformed branch of Protestantism. From Switzerland, Reformed doctrines spread into southern Germany and received the support of the elector of the Palatinate, Frederick III. There at the University of Heidelberg in 1563, a catechism was composed that established a moderate Calvinism as a basis for a successful German Reform movement.

Religious developments in Switzerland and Germany naturally tended to spread along the banks of the Rhine and to make their influence felt in the Netherlands. At the beginning of the Reformation period, the Netherlands were part of Charles V's Hapsburg Empire, and, although Lutherans and Anabaptists established themselves there, he successfully contained their influence. But his Spanish-born heir, Philip II (1555-98), had trouble commanding the allegiance of the people. During his reign, a popular movement for national independence began to develop. The movement drew on Protestant ideals—such as autonomy of conscience and Biblical law—which radiated from Geneva. By 1566, there was a Belgic Confession that provided a program for a Dutch Calvinism. A war broke out shortly after that and led in 1581 to the establishment of the northern provinces as an independent nation that became known as Holland. The success of the popular revolution made the nation one of the most open societies in Europe, and the Dutch developed a laudable tradition of offering asylum to refugees from all kinds of religious persecution.

France, which was Calvin's homeland, also developed a strong Protestant party, the Huguenots, which associated itself with the Swiss Reformation. The Huguenots seem to have originated as a kind of underground church that derived its clergy and its inspiration from Geneva. The French government was sporadically harsh in its treatment of Protestants, but there were some converts to the reform even in the circle of the royal family itself. France was a large nation whose management was made difficult by the existence of vigorous noble factions and strong traditions of autonomy in local affairs. Some districts came to identify their personal interests with the ideals of the Reformation, and these areas offered strenuous resistance to the policies of the monarchy. Wars of religion flared up during the regency of Henry II's wife, Catherine de Medici (1519–89). A truce concluded in 1570 was abruptly shattered in 1572 by Catherine's surprise massacre of Protestants on St. Bartholomew's Day. The struggles continued until Henry of Navarre, an erstwhile Protestant, ascended the throne in 1593. Henry officially returned to Catholicism, but, in 1598, he published the Edict of Nantes which established a policy of religious toleration for France. A century later, however, the growing power of the absolute monarchy tipped the balance against the Protestants, and they were suppressed.

Calvinism's influence on the unique reform movements that developed in the British Isles had a much more lasting and far reaching effect on the evolution of European culture. The English Reformation owed its origin more to a nationalistic revolution against papal authority than to a ground swell of discontent with the medieval Catholic practice of the Christian faith. The English were more interested in making their church English than in becoming Protestant, and the antipapal parties who favored the reform were a long time in deciding how far they would go in the direction of the theologies and church polities of Luther and Calvin.

Although King John (1190–1216) had once sought certain diplomatic advantages by an elaborate act of deference to the pope, England had a long history of resistance to papal authority. John Wycliffe and William of Ockham, two of the most famous critics of the late medieval papacy, worked in England. The Lollard movement constituted one of Europe's oldest popularly sustained agitations for reform. And the English parliament had on several occasions taken bold actions in curtailing the freedom of the clergy. In the mid-fourteenth century, Parliament invalidated King John's submission of England as a fief to the papacy, and the body passed the portentous Statutes of Provisors and Praemunire, which forbade appeals to Roman courts and limited England's financial obligations to the papacy.

Despite this strong tradition of ecclesiastical independence, the English people and their government do not seem to have been attracted to earlier phases of the Continental Reformation. The large English merchant class was in close contact with events in the Netherlands and northern Germany, and Luther's writings were available for discussion in England before 1520. But England produced no major Protestant theologians and few persons who were eager to identify themselves with the German reform movement. The humanists of Oxford and Cambridge were energetic students of the literature that the Reformation produced, but their studies seem to have had little effect on official policies. The most famous of them, William Tyndale (ca. 1492–1536), found it necessary to complete and publish his English translation of the Scriptures in Germany. Henry VIII had a refutation of Luther's heresies published under his name in 1521—for which he was rewarded by the pope with the title Defender of the Faith. In the 1520's, there were burnings of both books and heretics in England. Even after these events had reversed themselves and the Reformation was proclaimed in England, no figure emerged who merited comparison with Luther or Calvin. The leading intellectual of Henry VIII's reign was Thomas More—who was not a Protestant, but a Catholic martyr who chose to die rather than deny his allegiance to the papacy. There were, therefore, few inspired theologians to assist the politicians who engineered the English Reformation, and England was a long time in reaching an understanding of the content of its Protestantism.

The English Reformation developed under the direction of the monarchs of the Tudor dynasty and had its origin in the diplomatic and domestic difficulties of the second of the Tudor kings, Henry VIII (1509–47). The Tudors had become kings as leaders of a revolutionary faction of the nobility that triumphed over and exterminated the ancient Plantagenet royal line during the War of the Roses. As heir to a man whom some regarded as a usurper, Henry had reason to be concerned about the solidification of his family's position. He spent lavishly on a brilliant court designed to build among his own people his reputation as a king, and he sought international recognition by rushing to the defense of the papacy against Luther and by intervening in the struggles of the French monarchy and the Hapsburg Empire. His military ventures produced few results, however, and his expensive foreign entanglements exposed him to critics in the English Parliament. It was with some justification, therefore, that, as he grew older, he developed a preoccupation with the problems of siring a son who could assist him in stabilizing the throne by guaranteeing its undisputed succession. By 1527, Henry had been married for eighteen years to Catherine of Aragon, but, of the six children their union had produced, only one, a daughter named Mary, had survived infancy. Henry was acutely aware of the fact that a woman had never ruled England in her own name. Only a male heir could secure the dynasty, and, to produce one, Henry was convinced that he needed a new wife. His candidate was Anne Boleyn, one of Catherine's ladies-in-waiting.

In 1527, Henry requested permission from Pope Clement VII to separate from Catherine. He had reasonable legal grounds in that Catherine was the widow of his brother and their marriage had originally required a papal dispensation from the Biblical prohibition against such unions (LEVITICUS 20:21). There was also the practical problem of Catherine's fertility: such problems had carried some weight with the papacy in making decisions in similar cases in the past. But Clement was not free to give Henry the verdict the English king wanted, for the pope was at the time a virtual prisoner of Catherine's nephew, the emperor Charles V. Faced with the necessity of antagonizing one of the two kings, Clement made the safest choice and refused Henry the right to remarry. Henry attempted to put pressure on the papacy by progressively increasing his claims to royal control of the church in England. The pope, however, remained unmoved, and, in 1533, Anne Boleyn's pregnancy required Henry to abandon his hopes through her or to take decisive action. Parliament severed ties with the papacy, and Henry appointed a new archbishop of Canterbury, Thomas Cranmer, as the highest ranking ecclesiastical authority recognized by England. The archbishop then granted Henry his divorce and recognized Anne as queen. The pope responded by excommunicating Henry, but the English Parliament remained loyal to its king, who in 1534 officially became the head of the Church of England.

Henry was content to have the Reformation halt at that point. He moved closer to Continental Protestant policies in 1539 when he completed the dissolution of England's monasteries, but his motives were more financial than theological. Archbishop Cranmer favored a more radical Lutheran reform of the church, but, at the time of Henry's death in 1547, England's ties with her Catholic past were still quite strong. Edward VI (1547–53), Henry's only son and the child of his third wife, Jane Seymour, was a sickly ten-year-old youth at the time of his succession. During his brief reign, his advisors accelerated England's drift toward Protestantism; but his death brought to the throne Henry's eldest child, Mary, the daughter of Catherine of Aragon. Mary was, of course, an ardent Catholic who deeply resented her father's reform program, and she vowed to return England to Rome. She martyred a large number of Protestant sympathizers and forced others to flee England. Many of them took refuge in the Netherlands or in Switzerland, where they acquired a taste for Calvin's radical Protestantism. After Mary died in 1558, her halfsister, Henry's daughter by Anne Boleyn, ascended the throne as Elizabeth I. Elizabeth's claim to the monarchy depended upon the validity of Henry's marriage to Anne, so there was little question of the sincerity of her Protestant loyalties. But, throughout her reign, she pursued a moderate policy that attempted to make the Church of England a Protestant institution that would be minimally offensive to Catholic feelings. She insisted upon being recognized as the head of the church, but beyond that she placed few demands on her subjects. The English church retained its episcopal structure and much of its ancient liturgy and pomp. Elizabeth's attempts at compromise failed to please everyone, for a militantly Protestant party was steadily developing among the middle classes. The democratic implications of Calvin's theology appealed to them, and they favored his thorough purging of the symbols of medieval Catholic faith and clerical privilege. The English institution of Parliament gave the militant Protestants a means of making their opinions known, and, in the generation that followed Elizabeth's, they drew together into a Puritan political party that became powerful enough to challenge the continued existence of the monarchy.

The strongest center of Calvinism in the British Isles was not England but Scotland, where the politics of nationalism early encouraged the growth of a native church. In order to counter attempts by England to expand northward, the Scottish monarchy had in the late thirteenth century inaugurated a policy of allying itself with France, England's perennial enemy. The alliance worked as a defense against English ambitions, but it created at the Scottish court a strong French presence which was much resented by the masses and some of the nobility. As the French government steadily increased its opposition to the Reformation, the Protestant cause acquired a new appeal in Scotland as a means for developing and demonstrating the nation's determination to defend its autonomy.

Luther's ideas had begun to circulate in Scotland in the early 1520's. Some French Protestants seem to have been active in publishing them, but their strongest channel of mediation seems to have been through Scottish students who studied at German universities. It was not, however, until 1544 and the conversion of a Catholic priest named John Knox (1505–72) that Scotland found its national religious leader. In 1546, Knox took part in the assassination of a Catholic cardinal and found himself condemned to a period of service at the oars of a French galley. He regained his freedom in time to win a reputation as a preacher in England during Edward VI's reign. When Mary came to power, he joined the flight of English Protestants to the Continent and eventually settled in Geneva, where he became a strict Calvinist. In 1557, the Protestant nobles of Scotland—fearing that their queen's marriage to the king of France might lead to a diminution of national independence—launched a revolt in defense of their homeland. Knox returned to Scotland in 1559 to advise the rebels, and, in 1560, the Scottish Parliament weakened its ties with France, terminated its relationship with the papacy, and established a new national church. The Church of Scotland adopted a Presbyterian constitution in which the office of bishop was abolished and responsibility for the management of the church was lodged in committees of elders—clergy and laymen elected to represent the interests of local congregations. Calvin's theology and the somewhat austere liturgical customs of the Genevan church gave the Scots materials for the development of a distinct form of Protestantism which, together with the democratic implications of Presbyterian church polity, had a considerable influence on the evolution of the English Puritan movement.

THE REORGANIZATION OF CHRISTIAN EUROPE

THE SUCCESS OF THE Protestant revolution created an environment in which the Roman church finally came to terms with calls for reform. The medieval conciliarists had failed to create an international movement for the renewal of the church, and the papacy had generally triumphed over immoderate critics—such as the Dominican friar Savonarola, who from 1491 to 1498 led the city of Florence in a localized experiment in radical ecclesiastical reform. But there were powerful persons and groups who succeeded in maintaining allegiance to Rome while voicing effective objections to abuses of spiritual authority, and they came to have increased significance in the church's struggle with the Protestant challenge. The vigorous reform programs and harsh repressive measures of Cardinal Ximenes de Cisneros (1436–1517) did much to undercut sympathy for the Protestant cause in Spain. Elsewhere, highly motivated persons publicized and partially met the need for renewal by organizing themselves into voluntary associations that encouraged frequent use of private devotions, the sacraments, and attendance at sermons as means for spiritual development. Groups like the Oratory of Divine Love, which functioned in Rome from 1517 to 1527, had a profound influence on the future of the church through the effect they had on leaders of the stature of Pope Paul IV and Cardinal Cajetan, Luther's scholarly opponent.

Throughout the sixteenth century, currents of orthodox piety continued to run strong in the traditional channels of mysticism and monasticism. The monks and mystics did not always think of themselves as reformers, but the spiritual and charitable services they rendered the people did much to foster the loyalty of the masses to the Roman church. Teresa of Ávila (1515–82). John of the Cross (1542–91), and Frances de Sales (1567–1622) composed devotional literature of permanent significance, and the image of fervent piety they fostered helped to stimulate a recommitment to religion and a rebirth of interest in monastic vocations. Much of the mystical thought of the period focused on the struggle of the individual soul to purify itself and ascend to an ecstatic union with God, and such personalized religion served as a kind of response to the concepts of grace and works that lay at the root of Protestant doctrine. Teresa of Ávila inspired her order, the Carmelites, with an intense interest in ascetic practices. Even the radical, or "spiritual," branch of the Franciscans gave birth to a reform group, the Capuchins, who criticized their brethren for failing to emulate the poverty and the faith of Francis. The impulse toward ascetic self-sacrifice that motivated the mystics encouraged some of them to give themselves totally to the needs of others, and numerous service orders—such as the Theatines, the Clerks Regular of St. Paul, and the Ursulines—appeared during the first half of the sixteenth century. Their ministries of charity not only strengthened the church's contribution to society, but also provided models and increased pressures for the reform of the other clergy.

No group was as significant as the Jesuits, however, in helping the Roman church form a constructive response to the challenge of Protestantism and the expanding horizons of Europe. The Society of Jesus was the creation of Ignatius Loyola (ca. 1491–1556), a Spanish soldier who in 1521 laid down his weapons and devoted himself to the service of the church. It was his original intent to serve as a missionary in the Holy Lands, but, when he discovered that his education was inadequate to that task, he threw himself into a course of study that by 1528 had brought him to the University of Paris. There a small group of like-minded individuals gathered around him and in 1534 joined him in pledging themselves to the mission field. The political situation in the East made it impossible for them to reach Jerusalem, so they turned instead to Rome and placed themselves at the disposal of the papacy. In 1540, Pope Paul III recognized them as an official order of the church and endorsed their adoption of a unique constitution. The Jesuits evolved as an elite society of carefully chosen, thoroughly trained, ruthlessly disciplined men who thought of themselves as warriors commissioned to defend and advance the autocratic powers of the papacy. They were burdened with few of the liturgical duties, routines, or physical limitations that characterized other orders, but they practiced a quasi-military discipline that preserved their integrity and enabled them to use their freedom to take on difficult and unusual tasks. To combat heresy—the most immediate and obvious challenge to papal authority—they became involved in education and in the supervision of the pious practices of the laity. Such Jesuits as Peter Canisius (1521–97) were instrumental in helping the papacy curb Protestant advances in southern Germany and regain territories in central Europe. Others, including Francis Xavier (1506–52), accompanied the explorers who were beginning to build the great European colonial empires. The Jesuits dealt with people as diverse as the barbarous Indians of South America and the sophisticated Chinese, and the order's work gave real substance to papal claims of universal dominion. The Jesuits became deeply involved in the politics of Europe, and their total commitment to the cause of papal absolutism sometimes exposed them to suspicions of utilizing questionable means for the attainment of what they so obviously held to be divinely ordained ends.

Many of the popes of the sixteenth century were sympathetic toward the cause of reform and attempted within the practical limitations of their political situations to make changes in the life of the church. Luther's antagonist Leo X (1513-21) did not live long enough to grasp the full significance of Luther's actions; his successor, Hadrian VI (1522-23), lacked support in the curia for any effective rectification of abuses; and Clement VII (1523-34) was too beset by the problems of the wars of Charles V and Francis I to accomplish much in the way of a reorganization of the church. It was not until the papacy of Paul III (1534-49) that the first real steps toward reform were taken. Paul appointed excellent men to the college of cardinals, and, in 1537, he received a report from them detailing the ecclesiastical abuses that required immediate attention. The report, which was hailed by Protestants as a vindication of their cause, certainly indicated that a major effort would be needed to purify the church. In 1540, Paul established the Jesuit order, and, in 1542, he centralized the work of the Inquisition in Rome, but much more had to be done. Early in his career, Luther had appealed to a church council to deal with the problem of reform, and, as the Reformation progressed, many of the clergy and laity involved in its turmoils came to favor Luther's solution. Mindful that the medieval conciliarist movement had generated attacks on papal authority, the popes were slow to comply. But, as the Protestants moved apart from the Catholics in doctrine and resolve, there was progressively less danger that Protestants might gain control of a council and use it against the papacy. By 1545, therefore, Paul was ready to respond positively to requests for a council, and delegates were invited to assemble in the Tirolean community of Trent.

The great Council of Trent met intermittently from 1545 to 1563, and it succeeded in equipping the Roman church to deal with the realities of the Protestant revolution. The council was not so much an instrument of reform as an occasion for the redefinition of doctrine in opposition to Protestant attacks. It performed this function so well that it laid the foundation for the evolution of the modern Catholic church. Luther and other Protestant leaders declined to attend a council that refused at the outset to recognize the Protestant appeal to Scripture against ecclesiastical tradition; so Trent was a meeting of Christians who were still nominally loyal to Rome. And Rome used the council so cleverly that it became an instrument for strengthening papal claims to supremacy over the church. By the time the council had finished its work, it had endorsed an ultramontane, or Italian, program of papal absolutism as the constitution of the church, and it had reaffirmed medieval opinions concerning Scripture, the authority of tradition, the efficacy of the seven sacraments, and the nature of clerical privileges. Some of the points of doctrine or practice that most offended Protestants were now affirmed as essential elements of Catholic faith. The pope's unique authority to define doctrine was implied. The Vulgate translation of the Scriptures was imposed on the church even though Catholic humanist scholars had already demonstrated a need for correcting it. The necessity of good works as supplements to faith in the pursuit of salvation was affirmed. The doctrine of transubstantiation and the understanding of the Mass as a meritorious sacrifice was reasserted—along with the belief that masses were meritorious deeds that could be applied to the benefit of souls in purgatory. The use of relics and the invocation of saints were defended. The validity of indulgences was accepted. And the council affirmed that virginity and the celibate vocation were spiritually superior to the married state. Few reforms were actually endorsed by the council, but its general recognition of papal authority and the validity of traditional doctrines strengthened the hand of the papacy in dealing with abuses.

The last half of the sixteenth century saw a series of popes who were able to use their office for the effective reorganization of the church. Paul IV (1555–59), a former member of the Oratory of Divine Love and a leader of the Inquisition, curbed financial abuses of spiritual functions in the curia and made numerous worthy appointments. He urged a vigilant policing of the morals of the clergy and their people, and he began the practice of compiling an Index of dangerous books whose possession and study were to be forbidden to Catholics. Under Pius IV (1559–65) and Pius V (1566–72), improved instruments for the practice of Catholic piety began to be prepared. A revised breviary, or book of prayers for private devotions, came out in 1566; a new missal containing the rites for public worship was published in 1570; catechisms that served as guides for meditation and instruction were circulated; and, toward the end of the century, a purified version of the Vulgate received official recognition. Under Sixtus V (1585–90), the papacy began to rebuild the city of Rome in a style suitable for the seat of a leader who had in no way relinquished his claims to spiritual supremacy over the world; during the reign of his successor, Paul V (1605–21), the great Vatican church of St. Peter was finally brought to completion. The emergency of the Reformation had passed. The papacy had at last put its house in order, mastered its indecisiveness, and prepared itself to join Catholic monarchs in wars for the extirpation of Protestantism.

There had been military conflicts between Protestants and Catholics almost from the beginning of the Reformation. Charles V had fought the Lutheran princes of the Schmalkaldic League in 1546. His son, Philip II (1556–98), sustained a long war with the Calvinists of Holland and sent a famous, but abortive, armada against the Protestant queen of England in 1588. France endured a generation of religious hostility before proclaiming a truce in the Edict of Nantes of 1598. But the wars of religion of the seventeenth century were in some ways phenomena quite different from these initial clashes. They were frequently longer and bloodier, for they were fought by parties that had had time to organize and equip themselves for serious struggles. And they were somewhat ambiguous in the motives which inspired them, for they contributed more to the establishment of absolutist governments than to triumphs of religion.

In every instance, the wars of the seventeenth century brought control of religious affairs more firmly into the hands of secular governments and increased tendencies to identify specific religious orientations with patriotic loyalties. In Germany, where a profusion of independent sovereignties made the political situation extremely unstable, disputes over religion enflamed a shockingly destructive war. The Reformation had had great initial success in sweeping much of Germany into the Protestant camp. The early solidarity of the youthful reform movement and the temporary disorientation of the Catholic church created a situation in which Germany enjoyed a generation of relative peace and quiet following the agreements at Augsburg in 1555. But, by the turn of the century, potentially hostile parties had had opportunities to catch their breaths, reassess their situations, and prepare to reopen the war for dominance of the German people. In the interim, the Council of Trent, the reformed papacy, and the Jesuit order had done much to strengthen Catholic bases in Germany. Bavaria and Austria were again Catholic, and Bohemia, Poland, and Hungary were showing signs of returning to full papal allegiance. On the other hand, the Protestant movement had begun to yield to internal pressures that threatened to tear it apart. Luther's death in 1546 left German Protestantism without a strong leader or a symbolic figure who could keep the forces of Protestant individualism under control. Luther's most obvious successor would have been his younger colleague, Philip Melanchthon (1497–1560), but many of Melanchthon's contemporaries found him too moderate in his humanistic interpretation of Luther's ideas. Different systems of Lutheran theology were developed at the universities of Wittenberg, Jena, Königsberg, Marburg, Tübingen, and Leipzig, and, although the disagreements among them often seem petty in retrospect, their controversies provided justifications for political disputes among the governments they served. By 1580, a kind of Lutheran consensus began to emerge in favor of the opinions of ecclesiastical leaders from Swabia and Saxony; but the spread of Calvinism into Germany tended to fuel new arguments and excuse additional political divisions among Protestants.

The worst potential of this unhealthy situation was finally realized in 1618 in the outbreak of the Thirty Years War. The war was inaugurated by the heir to the Hapsburg empire, Ferdinand of Styria, who in 1618 claimed the Bohemian throne and moved to curtail the liberties of his Protestant subjects. A popular revolution broke out, and the Protestants offered their support to Frederick V, the elector of the Palatinate, in his bid for the Bohemian crown. Ferdinand, however, soon succeeded to the imperial title and organized a Catholic alliance with the duke of Bavaria and the king of Spain against Frederick. By 1622, the Catholic armies had triumphed in Bohemia and overrun the Palatinate, and they seemed to be on their way to winning control of Germany. The Lutheran kings of Scandinavia were threatened, however, by the resurgence of a militant Catholicism in Germany; so they came to the support of the Protestant cause. Christian IV of Denmark failed in 1625 to halt the Catholic advance, but, in 1630, King Gustavus Adolphus of Sweden staged a spectacular invasion of Germany which by 1632 had knifed through the Catholic heartland of Bavaria. Although they were Catholics, the French were eager to block the expansion of Hapsburg power, so they joined the Swedes in support of the German Protestants. The result was the reduction of the war to a stalemate in which neither side could make significant progress against the other. All parties gradually came to realize that their resources were being seriously sapped by their uselessly destructive confrontation, and, by 1648, they were willing to call an end to it. The Peace of Westphalia left Germany's political and religious situation much as it had been prior to the war. The Hapsburg attempt to establish a German Catholic empire had been blocked, but no Protestant prince had appeared with the power to unite Germany. Germany remained what the medieval struggle between church and state had made it, a collection of hundreds of mutually antagonistic principalities. If anything, Germany's situation was worse than before, for its tiny states were seriously reduced in population, retarded in social development, and confirmed in religious hostilities by the ravages of the war.

France, like Germany, was at the beginning of the seventeenth century a society that tolerated different religious loyalties among its peoples. And in France, as in Germany, this produced an unstable situation that proved to be intolerable to the government. The Edict of Nantes (1598) had recognized Protestant control of a number of important cities in France and had come close to creating a Protestant state within what was officially a Catholic nation. But the Catholic monarchs Louis XIII (1610–43) and Louis XIV (1643–1715) and their brilliant advisors, the cardinals Richelieu (1585–1642) and Mazarin (1602–61), soon faced the task of protecting France from encirclement by a Hapsburg empire that had already established itself in Spain, Italy, the Netherlands, and portions of Germany. As a result, they were in no mood to tolerate potential rebels at their backs. It was their intent to strengthen France and make it the arbiter of Europe by concentrating all the nation's resources in the hands of an absolute monarchy. They had had many opportunities to observe situations in which religious quarrels had become bases for challenging political allegiances, and they had good reason to doubt the loyalty and to fear the ambitions of the French Huguenots. The Protestant nobility and bourgeoisie derived inspiration for resistance to the government from Calvin's theology and Reformed church polity, and there was no question of the fact that the hierarchical traditions of Catholicism were more compatible with monarchy than was the Protestant ideal of the autonomy of the individual conscience. The French kings decided, therefore, that the development of a system of royal absolutism in France required a correlative enforcement of universal allegiance to one royally sanctioned church. Nothing much could be done about the Protestants, however, until the Peace of Westphalia gave France a respite from the Hapsburg threat.

In 1648, a Protestant party led a protest against taxes and foreign policies which disrupted the government and increased the young Louis XIV's desire to suppress the Huguenots. By means of a series of acts stretching over twenty years, Louis steadily withdrew rights from Protestants and made it increasingly difficult for them to remain in France. Finally, in 1685, he revoked the Edict of Nantes, enforced conformity to the Catholic faith, and compelled the remnants of the Huguenot party to flee. France was again a Catholic nation, but it was in no way a state that tolerated a significant degree of papal interference in the affairs of what it had come to regard as its national church. Ever since the fifteenth century, the French kings had claimed extensive rights of self-determination for the French clergy, and Louis continued this tradition in 1682 by issuing the Four Articles of Gallicanism, which deprived the pope of all real power over the French Catholic church. The papacy objected strenuously and refused to appoint new bishops to vacated French sees. Louis decided not to force the issue to the point of schism with Rome and agreed to a compromise that saved face for the pope but left the French church virtually under the control of the state.

The restoration of the Catholic unity of France failed to free the nation from the threat of doctrinal controversy and religious factionalism. In place of the old quarrel between Protestantism and Catholicism, seventeenth century France developed a dispute between two parties of Catholics, the Jansenists and the Jesuits. The Jansenist group took its name from a bishop of Ypres, Cornelius Jansen (1585–1638), who taught a form of Catholicism that was sympathetic with "Protestant" concerns for the power of God in grace and the role of faith in the salvation of individuals. They revived the study of the theology of Augustine of Hippo, an indisputably orthodox father of the church in whose works they found ideas not incompatible with aspects of Calvinism. Jansenist attitudes were totally unacceptable to the Jesuits, who were the avowed enemies of heresy and Protestantism in any form and who favored the more church-centered, hierarchical theology of Thomas Aquinas. In 1653, the Jesuits brought the pope to condemn a series of Jansenist propositions, and they encouraged Louis to persecute the sect. The Jansenist monastery at Port Royal was destroyed in 1709, but the Jansenists survived deep into the eighteenth century as an underground movement with a grudge against the monarchy.

The triumph of Catholicism in France was to a certain extent balanced by the emergence of England as a strong Protestant nation. The ambiguous nature of the motives that had led the English monarchy to endorse the Reformation created some confusion in attempts to understand the theological orientation of the Church of England. In origin, English Protestantism was neither Lutheran nor Reform, and there were many who hoped to see it remain a kind of Anglo-Catholicism—a national church that was Catholic in all its doctrine and practice except its attitude toward the pope. Much of the seventeenth century was given over to the struggle to define the nature of English Protestantism and to discover the implications of the new faith for the partnership of church and state.

Queen Elizabeth I (1558–1603) did a superb job of charting a path between the radical Protestant and conservative Catholic positions, but, by the dawn of the seventeenth century, the active hostility of

Catholic Spain and the growing importance of the English commercial classes were moving England into a more overtly Protestant position. When Elizabeth died in 1603 and the throne passed to her distant cousin James I (1603–25), the English Parliament included a strong Puritan party that hoped the new king would agree to a more radical reform of the national church. James, however, had been king of Scotland since 1568, and in Scotland he had dealt with an aggressive Calvinism that nourished his suspicions of the antimonarchical tendencies of Protestantism. James was an advocate of royal absolutism, and he was convinced that a hierarchically organized state church was the best religious system for a thriving monarchy. He approved a new English translation of the Bible, the King James Version, which came to have an incalculable influence on the evolution of English literature. But he refused to heed Puritan requests for purges of liturgies and creeds and the abolition of the episcopacy. Puritan clergy who were too outspoken in their advice to the king found themselves deprived of their pulpits, and it was during James's reign that the stream of Puritan emigration from England really began. Many of the early expatriates went to Holland, where congenial Calvinism and an atmosphere of toleration enabled them freely to develop their religious preferences into distinctive practices. Some of these emigrants then moved on to permanent homes in the English colonies in North America. But others returned to England confirmed in their commitment to radical Protestantism. Anabaptist scruples about the validity of infant baptism led to the establishment of an English Baptist sect in Holland in 1609 and in England in 1612. Presbyterian and Congregationalist convictions concerning the locus of authority in the church spawned the appearance of other separatist groups that opposed royal control of the church. Pressures from radical Protestant groups disturbed the king but did not have the effect of driving him back to Catholicism. James found the English Catholics as disruptive as the Protestants, and, after Guy Fawkes led a group of Catholics in an abortive attempt to assassinate the king and the Parliament in 1605, James persecuted the Catholic faith.

The existence of the Parliament gave the English people an instrument for use in blocking the attempts of their monarchs to acquire the absolute powers that the French kings were successfully cultivating. The English king lacked the authority to tax enjoyed by French monarchs, and his dependence on Parliament for financial assistance enabled that body to influence royal policies. There was, therefore, an obvious conflict between the theories of monarchy advanced by the

English kings and the practical realities of politics that their parliaments jealously guarded. Since the membership of Parliament drew heavily on the Puritan middle classes, the legislative body also tended to represent religious opinions more radical than those of the king. The potential for disagreement between these two centers of power finally erupted in a bloody confrontation during the reign of James's son Charles I (1625–49).

Charles objected in principle to Parliament's tradition of limiting the monarchy by threatening its financial stability; so he attempted to devise extraparliamentary methods of taxation. His fiscal policies stirred up a great deal of resentment which tended only to be increased by his ecclesiastical program. Charles hoped to strengthen the English monarchy by enforcing universal acceptance of the doctrines and practices of the royal church. In 1633, he appointed William Laud to the office of archbishop of Canterbury, and Laud ruthlessly set about policing the conduct of the clergy. The Puritans were outraged, and the Scots chose to rebel against the king rather than accept Laud's edicts. In 1640, the Scots gave the Puritans an opportunity to organize their resistance to the king. The Scots invaded northern England, and Charles was forced to convene a parliament to raise funds for the defense of the realm. When this body, which became known as the Long Parliament, began to make inroads on Charles's royal prerogatives, he attempted to intimidate it with a show of force. He succeeded only in precipitating a civil war. Parliament allied itself with the Scots and fielded an army that in 1646 captured the king.

The Protestants of England proved to be too divided in their opinions to form a lasting coalition for the government of England. Conferences at Westminster drew up confessions and catechisms that now form authoritative statements of Presbyterian doctrine, but that failed at the time to unite England's Protestants. Parliament managed, however, under the forceful leadership of Oliver Cromwell (1599–1658) to administer England. In 1646, it executed the king and abolished the monarchy. But Parliament failed to establish a true popular government. Cromwell held England together with the powers of a military dictator, but, at his death in 1658, no one capable of taking his place could be found. Fearing chaos, Parliament hastened to restore the monarchy, and Charles I's son Charles II (1660–85) returned to England from his refuge in France. The radical Puritans were discredited by their conduct during the interregnum, and the new king's personal religious preferences were Catholic. But the English Parliament was not so completely cowed as to surrender its traditional political functions or abandon its Protestantism. When Charles died in 1685 and his avowedly Catholic brother James II (1685–88) ascended the throne, Parliament began to fear a royal attempt to subvert the Reformation. James's pro-Catholic policies were so offensive to his subjects that, in 1688, Parliament switched its allegiance to his daughter Mary and assisted her and her husband, William of Orange, in evicting James from England. Under William and Mary, England finally reached an understanding of its religious identity. Anglicanism, a moderate form of Puritanism with Arminian tendencies, received recognition as the official state church; but the various separatist Protestant groups were allowed to continue functioning. Catholicism was, however, actively discouraged, and it was not until the nineteenth century that religious liberty was extended to English Catholics.

The general trend toward the establishment, of state churches in Europe continued into the eighteenth century and affected both Protestant and Catholic nations. In Spain, the monarchy's early strength, its control of the machinery of the Inquisition, and its history of occasional dominance of the papacy permitted the nation to evolve a distinctive form of Catholicism that was rigidly orthodox and fervently loyal to a pope who had virtually no control over it. The Hapsburg rulers of Austria and Tuscany—Maria Theresa (1740–80), Joseph II (1780–90), and Leopold II (1790–92)—disposed freely of the Catholic churches in their territories. And in Prussia, Frederick I (1713–40) and Frederick II, "the Great" (1740–86), administered the religious affairs of their subjects through a department of state.

The radical accommodation of the church to the state was also an ingredient in the experience of the Christian communities of the East, which developed independent of, or on the periphery of, European influence. Many of the ancient Christian heretical sects managed to perpetuate themselves through the Middle Ages and to find a way to exist as minority subcultures in alien religious environments. Nestorians survived in Persia and India and thrived for a while in China. Monophysites and Monothelites were represented in Armenia and Syria and among the Copts of Egypt and Ethiopia. The Orthodox congregations of the Byzantine Empire shared the fate of these heterodox groups when the Christians lost political control of the eastern Mediterranean. The Moslem governments tolerated the presence of nonconforming religions but generally organized them as distinct and politically circumscribed communities within the state. Moslem officials dealt with Christians, not as individuals, but as members of a church, and the Christian clergy were often given the burdensome duty of collecting taxes and policing the services demanded by the state. Christians were seriously disadvantaged, but, even under these circumstances, the ancient sects found it difficult to overcome their traditional antagonisms. In 1672, a council met in Jerusalem and endorsed a creed that has often been cited as a general definition of Eastern Orthodoxy, but no serious move was made to unite the Christians of the East. By the seventeenth century, authority over the churches of the East was being claimed by a nation that had no association with their origins.

Russia had acquired its Christian religion and much of its civilization through contact with the Byzantine Empire, but the nation's great size and the diversity of its people retarded its political and cultural development. After Constantinople fell to the Turks in 1453, the prince of Moscow—as the ruler of the only major Christian city of the East still in Christian hands and as a relative by marriage of the Byzantine imperial family—proclaimed Moscow the "third Rome" and himself a *czar*, or "caesar." But pagan traditions lived on in Russia for a very long time and had a strong influence on the evolution of Russian Christianity. The Russian church tended to develop its faith through practice rather than doctrine, and it grew to place great emphasis on the perpetuation of rituals and liturgies. Russian Christians understood these practices, not as symbolic expressions of intellectual convictions or theologies, but as direct historical links with divine powers. Any change in them was seen as an unjustifiable challenge to the authority of the past and an invalidation of their power. Despite this interest in the precise execution of ritual, by the seventeenth century there was in reality no conformity in traditions of worship throughout Russia. The vast expanse of the nation, the strength of local pagan customs, and the near barbarity of the people had permitted the development of peculiar, idiosyncratic rites that their adherents took to be the essence of the Christian faith.

In 1666, the patriarch of Moscow, Nikon, undertook, with the support of the czar, to reform Russian Orthodoxy and bring it in line with the historical liturgies of the ancient Eastern Orthodox tradition. His program met with strong resistance and culminated in the schism of the Old Believers. The Old Believers became an apocalyptic cult that denounced the government as an instrument of Satan and proclaimed an imminent second coming of the Christ. They developed revolutionary tendencies and survived into the eighteenth century as a serious threat to royal authority and the personal security of government officials. Peter the Great (1682–1725) pressed ahead with additional reforms as part of his policy of strengthening European influences in Russian culture. He put the church under the direct control of a minister of state, disposed freely of its property, dominated its councils, and employed the clergy as agents in the secular affairs of the civil administration. The impoverishment of the lower clergy and their humiliation in the service of the state—which increased during the reign of Catherine the Great (1762–96)—seriously hindered their ability to serve their people. Russian religion consequently became a very complex phenomenon in which monasteries assumed unusual significance as oases of orthodox faith, sects proliferated among the masses, and the upper classes followed western Europe's shifting currents of theological opinion.

THE PATHS OF PLURALISM

DESPITE THE NUMBER OF sects and denominations that proliferated in Europe in the wake of the Reformation, a certain logic can be seen in the movement of their theological interests. The originality of Luther's and Calvin's presentations of the faith challenged medieval academic conventions and opened a whole range of new possibilities for the explication of the Christian message. There was a period of initial excitement and confusion while attempts were made simply to understand what was being said by the reformers. Catholic theologians had insufficient time in which to formulate their best responses, and Protestants were still uncertain of the full implications of the positions they were taking.

As the Reformation moved into its second generation, efforts were made to stabilize its development. The Catholic church was able to define its dogma at Trent by drawing on a wealth of seasoned medieval theology. But Protestants were acutely aware of their lack of grounding in medieval tradition and increasingly annoyed by the fact that their appeals directly to Scripture often involved them in serious disputes of interpretation with one another as well as with their common Catholic opponents. Some of the furor that Protestants vented on heretics was doubtless an expression of anxiety over the search for a defensible basis for Protestant doctrine.

During the late sixteenth century and much of the seventeenth, Lutheran and Reformed scholars indulged a preoccupation with the problem of defining the meaning of orthodoxy in their respective traditions, and they began to refine the rather imprecise imagery of the early reformers into a technical vocabulary for a science of Protestant theology. In the absence of any other authority, they tended to use the Bible as a collection of propositions from which systems of doctrine could be inferred. Their method for dealing with contradictions and differences of opinion was to appeal to reason and engage in subtle analyses of terms and critiques of complex arguments. As a result, their writings often resembled the works of their medieval predecessors, the Catholic Scholastic philosophers. The Lutheran Scholastics spent a great deal of time analyzing the meaning of Luther's proclamation of the doctrine of salvation by faith and its implications for an understanding of human responsibility under God's law. Calvinists focused their attentions on the related question of predestination and its effect on concepts of human freedom and determinism. In both traditions, the most conservative thinkers tended to triumph. Their theologies succeeded in preventing compromises of the ideas that were central to the messages of the reformers, but they did so at the cost of making these ideas rigid doctrinal positions. In the hands of the Scholastics, Protestant thought tended to become a complex system of deductions from inherited intellectual premises. Such theology had little relationship to an individual's actual experience of grace, faith, and salvation.

Not all Protestants were content with the official Scholastic representations of their faiths, and the seventeenth century brought the establishment of groups that argued for a renewed experience and practice of religion rather than for the continued refinement of theology. The focus of their interests was not the development of doctrine, but the encounter with God that made religion a living reality in the lives of individuals. Their view of religion as a radical experience of personal salvation rather than a voluntary intellectual assent to the truth of doctrine caused them to be known as pietists, for they insisted that the practice of piety was the heart of true religion.

Pietists appeared at about the same time in both the English and Continental Reformations, but they developed their missions in a variety of ways. They were all, in part, a reaction to the rise of state churches and an official Protestantism that routinely confused questions of citizenship with those of religious loyalty. The pietists all tended to see themselves as a "church" within the Church—called into existence by God to remind others of the power of authentic religious commitment. Some of them remained within their denominations as leavening agents; others drifted off to found new sects; and a few came to question the validity of attempts to express the true church of faith in the form of visible human communities.

In England, the pietist movement manifested itself powerfully in a sect that acquired the name Quaker from the tendencies of its members to give physical expression to the intensity of their religious emotions. The Quakers sprang up in response to the life of George Fox (1624–91), a son of an English weaver, who in 1647, on the authority of his own religious experiences, took the doctrine of the priesthood of all believers seriously and began to preach the Gospel. Fox was not a trained, licensed clergyman. He believed that true religion was not taught to people from books, but was revealed to them in their hearts. He felt that God did not confine his truth to philosophical systems or even to the words of Scripture, but that he freely expressed it directly in the internal life of each Christian. The Quakers asserted that every human being was endowed with an "inner light" that was a witness to the reality of God. They believed that this personal inspiration was the seat of the only religious authority a responsible Christian could recognize. Fox saw no need for a professionally trained and licensed ministry equipped with creeds and sacraments. For him, the church was simply a gathering of similarly motivated individuals who followed in each moment of their lives the dictates of their consciences. Fox's opponents believed his theories were a parody of Protestant confidence in individuals and formed an open invitation to anarchy, and he and his sect were vigorously persecuted.

In Germany, the Lutherans found an early pietist spokesman in an orthodox clergyman named Philip Spener (1635–1705). Spener undertook to revive the state church he served by stimulating the organization of prayer and study groups that met in the homes of laymen and fostered personal religious development. He was opposed by some clergy who feared that groups of enthusiastic, but ill-informed, laymen might develop schismatic tendencies, but his call for a revival of a religion of personal commitment did not go unheeded. He and his pupil, August Hermann Francke (1663–1727) had a strong influence on the program of a university founded at Halle in 1694. Halle became a center for training pietist clergy, but the imperatives of the pietist conscience made the place much more than that. The town became the home of charity schools, orphanages, and publishing houses that served as models for similar institutions elsewhere, and Halle served as a force for the development of Protestant missionary movements.

One of the most influential persons to be touched by the mood of Halle was Nicholas Zinzendorf (1700–60), a Saxon nobleman who used his estates to provide asylum for Protestants who were forced by the revival of Catholicism to flee their homeland in Moravia. Under

Zinzendorf's guidance, the Moravian Brethren attempted to build a community that would exemplify pietism's ideal of charity, sincere devotion, and Christian moral concern. Zinzendorf hoped that this community might become a catalyst for the revival of the Lutheran church, and it did undertake important missionary responsibilities. But the state churches of Germany failed to respond to Zinzendorf's program, and, by 1745, the Moravians had organized as a distinct Protestant denomination. They had a unique triumph, however, in that it was through them that German pietism made a contribution to the development of an important religious movement in England.

John Wesley (1703–91) was an Anglican clergyman who had been trained in a somewhat legalistic, High Church tradition. During his career as a student at Oxford, he participated in a prayer and Bible study group much like the societies favored by Spener and other pietists. There, in 1735, he made the acquaintance of George Whitefield, a flamboyant pulpit orator of pietist leanings; but Wesley's early conduct as a churchman was thoroughly conventional. In 1735, he undertook to become a missionary in the new American colony of Georgia, and during his voyage to this post he first made the acquaintance of the Moravians. He was impressed by their unswerving confidence in God's promises and by the obvious joy they derived from the practice of their religion. Wesley was a failure as a missionary, and, when he returned to England in 1738, he was more conscious than ever of the contrast between his personal doubts and the evidences of assurance manifested in the conduct of the Moravians. In London, Wesley renewed his contacts with the Moravians, and there, on the evening of May 21, 1738, he finally had a personal experience of the divine reality of which they spoke. While attending an Anglican meeting at which Luther's *Commentary on Romans* was read, Wesley was overcome by a sudden feeling of love and trust, and the course of his life was changed. He immediately departed for Germany for a firsthand look at Zinzendorf's Moravian community and then returned to England to preach wherever he could find a pulpit. In the spring of 1739, he followed Whitefield's example and began to address crowds in the fields and on the streets in order to seek out the people who rarely ventured into churches. The response to this work was gratifying, and he soon had enough followers to begin to organize a network of prayer and study groups among those who were touched by his message. These Methodist societies—whose name originally was a term that ridiculed their systematic approach to the cultivation of faith—sprang up everywhere in Britain and in the English colonies. The groups were intensely popular and obviously met a need not satisfied by the regular services of the Anglican church. But Wesley opposed a Methodist schism from the Anglican communion, and it was not until after his death that the English Methodists separated themselves from the Anglican establishment and became an independent denomination.

The pietist sects were assisted in their work by periodic waves of religious enthusiasm that swept Europe and America during the eighteenth century, but the dominant intellectual tendency of the period was rationalistic. Protestant Scholasticism had continued to thrive at universities and in state churches, and, at the end of the seventeenth century, it received new stimuli from the appearance of the philosophies and sciences that were to make the ensuing era an Age of Reason, or a period of Enlightenment.

The rationalistic attitudes that prevailed in Europe during the eighteenth century had their origin in the theories of René Descartes (1596–1650). Descartes, who was a brilliant mathematician, was fascinated by the phenomenon of human thought, and he devised procedures of logical analysis that challenged Europe's traditional assumptions concerning the nature of authority. For him, authority was not a quality added to an idea by the power or divinity of those who asserted it or by the antiquity of its development. Authority was simply a potency that was innate in ideas that were true, and, if it existed, its presence could be demonstrated by careful rational analysis. Descartes believed he could prove that human thought was self-validating and that absolute skepticism was a logical impossibility. He invited his students to reject all assumptions and all attitudes taken on faith and to attempt to doubt everything. He assured them that when they did, they would not fall into a void of ignorance, but they would discover that they could not rationally doubt one thing: the fact of their own doubting. This fact established a self-authenticating base, which was dependent on no theological or philosophical assumptions. Descartes felt that, from this point of departure, it would eventually be possible to employ reason to construct a complete system of human knowledge that was self-evident and, therefore, indisputably true. Descarte's suggestions were enthusiastically received, for they offered hope of an escape from the doctrinal controversies and clashes of authorities that had made a shambles of much Catholic and Protestant thought. Descartes's hope for a universal science and his confidence in reason as a tool adequate for its discovery heralded the emergence of a new age in Western intellectual history.

The achievements of Isaac Newton (1642–1727) in using reason to explain the structures of nature and developments in the experimental sciences seemed to many to confirm Descarte's prognostications. Human reason was an instrument capable of unlocking the mysteries of nature. It was not long, therefore, before attempts were made to see if religious knowledge could be acquired in the same way that the knowledge of natural objects was obtained. The doctrines of the major world religions were compared, their similarities and differences were noted, and some scholars believed that they could perceive a common system of ideas that they all affirmed. Belief in the existence of this common ground among religions encouraged speculations that fundamental religious truths were not dependent on historical revelations, but were facts of nature. If they were facts of nature, it was assumed that they ought to be amenable to rational demonstration. The attempt to create a religion of reason that deduced its precepts, not from authority or Scripture, but from a logical analysis of human experience gave birth to the philosophy of Deism.

Deism found an early champion in Matthew Tindal (1657-1733), who argued that rational human beings could discover for themselves all the religious knowledge they needed without resort to the Bible or to ecclesiastical traditions. Tindal believed the Bible to be a rude approximation of the true religion of nature, and he saw no justification for accepting those portions of scripture that were objectionable to reason. Tindal assumed that a rational God would not command his creatures to tolerate ignorance or superstition out of a sense of loyalty to him. Instead, God would bid people to use the reason that was their noblest faculty to obtain the knowledge they needed in order to fulfill their functions as human beings. The Deist movement flourished as part of the general euphoric confidence in reason that characterized European intellectual circles during the first half of the eighteenth century. But enthusiasm for Deism declined after such philosophers as Joseph Butler (1692-1752), David Hume (1711-76), and Immanuel Kant (1724-1804) began to demonstrate the naiveté of the Enlightenment's understanding of reason. The validity of Descartes's arguments was challenged, and the rational "certainties" of scientific observation were shown in fact to be probabilities that depended for their effectiveness on the willingness of the human mind to trust them. Long before the century drew to its close, the cult of reason had become an anachronism, and the broader dimensions of human personality—which related to concepts of inspiration, mystery, and revelation—had begun again to be appreciated.

Deist attitudes had a curious effect on the relation between religion and politics in Europe. They provided a context of freedom but removed the motivation to use the opportunities of liberty. If one accepted the Deist argument that all religions were fundamentally the same, it seemed absurd to continue to take the trouble to enforce conformity to one religious tradition or another. Tolerance of religious differences therefore became fashionable in important circles, and religious pluralism became politically acceptable to governments that previously had rejected it. But the spread of Deist attitudes also created a situation that was not conducive to the prosperity of free religious organizations. Deism reduced religion to a few simple propositions about God and ethics and nourished the feeling that religious commitments were inconsequential. Throughout Europe, the established churches existed in a rather easy relationship with the states that supported them, and neither their clergy nor their laity were, on the whole, noteworthy for the evidences they gave of deep personal commitment to specifically Christian ideals.

In an age dominated by absolute kings, strong nation-states, and Deist attitudes, the pope had the problem of finding himself ignored in the consultations that determined the course of European politics. The extensive controls that kings established over national Catholic churches curtailed Rome's influence over its people and dried up its sources of financial support. The narrowly partisan, ardently papal attitudes of the Jesuits were out of keeping with the moods of religious tolerance and indifference that characterized the age, and, in 1773, Pope Clement XIV yielded to political pressures and dissolved the order. The suppression of the Jesuits proved to be temporary, for they were reestablished in 1814. But the humiliation of the Jesuits, who had traditionally been among the strongest advocates of papal absolutism, was an indication of the desperate weakness of the papal monarchy. The pope proved to be totally unable to defend the church against the forces of the French Revolution or himself against the predatory policies of Napoleon. Pius VI's death in 1799 in a French prison was a fitting symbolic conclusion to a century that had been replete with frustrations for the papacy.

The nineteenth century enjoyed an atmosphere quite different from that of the eighteenth. Some of the Enlightenment's confidence in reason survived in the form of an enthusiasm for scientific and technological research, and the fruits of this labor were magnificent. But the nineteenth century also spawned a romantic movement that thought itself the antithesis of the arid rationalism of the Enlightenment and took as its program the exploration of the extrarational faculties of the human spirit. This change in perspective had a profound influence on Christian theology. Enlightenment theologians had often represented Christianity as a kind of philosophy or system of ideas that stood in need of rational explanation; but, when they approached Christianity in this manner, they found it difficult to do justice to the vital dimensions of faith that inspire the irrational, but crucial, responses of love, loyalty, and hope. The nineteenth century theologians who were influenced by the emotionalism of the romantic movement sought to replace the Enlightenment stress on religion as knowledge with an emphasis on religion as feeling. The finest example of romantic Protestant theology is probably to be found in the work of Friedrich Schleiermacher (1768–1834), a Berlin University professor who had received part of his education in Moravian schools. Schleiermacher suggested that the source of the phenomenon of religion was to be found, not in reason, but in feeling. He argued that the beginning point for religion was not an idea, but a feeling of unconditional dependence. This feeling was a creature's unavoidable confrontation with the reality of its contingent, created being. As such, it pointed beyond itself to God and could become an avenue for contact with him. Reflection on the feeling of dependence and the implications of its existence could give rise to concepts and doctrines, but these intellectualizations could never acquire the authority to compromise the feeling that inspired them.

Schleiermacher's approach to Christianity through an analysis of a general human consciousness of religion helped to nurture the development of a liberal tradition in European theology. Schleiermacher thought of Christianity simply as one form of expression for a universal feeling of absolute dependence, which could and did express itself in a wide variety of faiths. As the historians and scientists of the nineteenth century acquired more information about non-Christian religions and a clearer understanding of the evolution of Christian traditions, they were favorably impressed by the potential utility of the inclusiveness and flexibility of Schleiermacher's definition of religion. Schleiermacher explained a religion as a result of an individual's reflection on his own consciousness. If one accepted Schleiermacher's point of view, one would naturally expect to discover what the scholars of the period were finding: that there was a multitude of functionally valid religions in the record of human experience, and that these religions were, not systems of eternal verities, but historical phenomena that evolved and changed with the situations of their adherents. The authority of these faiths derived, not from any external power of divine endorsement, but from the internal feelings of the persons who professed them.

The nineteenth century was a period of rapid expansion of the frontiers of human knowledge as well as a time in which vast amounts of information were acquired and assembled into monuments of scholarship. Much of the new information threatened to unsettle ancient certainties and to pit faith against reason with a brutality unprecedented in the history of the Christian movement. Particularly disturbing was the emergence in German universities of a school of "higher criticism" which applied scientific techniques of textual analysis to the Scriptures themselves. The work of F. C. Bauer (1792–1860) on the New Testament and Julius Wellhausen (1844–1918) on the Pentateuch began to hint at the complex process of evolution that had brought the Bible into existence. As a result, theology required a new understanding of how these historically contingent, occasionally contradictory texts could still be accepted as the word of the eternal God.

Increased knowledge of the history of religions and a clearer understanding of the process by which the Bible came into being combined with theories that the natural sciences advanced concerning the evolutionary connection between the human and animal worlds to constitute a challenge of stupendous proportions to continued acceptance of what had formerly been assumed to be basic Christian truth. The new discoveries and ideas appeared to some to threaten the uniqueness of Christianity, to undermine the authority of its Bible, and to deny the moral and spiritual capacities of human beings. Such liberal theologians as Albrecht Ritschl (1822–89) and Adolf Harnack (1851–1930) drew on Schleiermacher's confidence in religion as a natural dimension of human self-consciousness to assert a faith in a Christian God who adjusted his revelation to the growing capacities of his creatures. Liberals were not disturbed by discoveries about Christianity's past, for they believed that religions were evolutionary systems. It was to be expected that religions would show a history of change and progress that paralleled the development of the human mind, for they sprang from the feelings analyzed by the mind. The trustworthiness of a religion derived, not from its ability to represent an absolute, unchanging authority, but from the power of its ideas to become relevant to contemporary human needs by promoting morality, justice, and hope.

Some Christian or secular scholars were not as optimistic as the liberals. Arthur Schopenhauer (1788–1860), Ludwig Feuerbach (1804–72), and Friedrick Nietzsche (1844–1900) each predicted with a degree of regret or enthusiasm the passing of the Christian faith. And Søren Kierkegaard (1813–55) boldly proclaimed the necessity for Christians to abandon the security of reason if they wished to practice their faith. The liberal position and the whole theological tradition that derived from Schleiermacher was vigorously opposed in the early twentieth century by a school of neoorthodox theologians who took their cue from Karl Barth. Barth argued that Christianity derived, not from human experience, but from the objective revelation of God contained in the Scriptures. Barth's concept of a dialectical relationship between God and the world protected the ancient Judao-Christian perception of God's radical transcendence.

The liberal intellectual strain in the Christian movement of the nineteenth century was both challenged and complemented by the growth of a large evangelical party. Evangelicalism, which was nourished by some of the same impulses as pietism, was a form of Christian faith that emphasized personal religious experiences and the obligations of Christians to demonstrate their convictions in deeds that served others. The evangelicals sometimes tended to be antagonistic to academic theology, but they actively promoted the life of the church—and they were largely responsible for the tremendous effect of Christianity on the social concerns of their day. Evangelicals financed missionaries, schools, hospitals, orphanages, and publishing houses. They backed crusades for prison reform, temperance, and the abolition of slavery. And, despite occasional lapses into obscurantism, the evangelical movement did much to ease the uncertainties of life in the nineteenth century and to make Christianity a force for the pursuit of justice and morality in human communities.

Evangelical denominations were not the only Christian organizations that showed signs of strength in the nineteenth century. The papacy made a remarkable recovery from the debacle of the Napoleonic era and emerged once again as a major influence in world affairs. The revival of the papacy took the form of a successful attempt to gain recognition of the absolute monarchical powers accorded popes by the Council of Trent. The triumphant papal policy of the nineteenth century was an ultramontanism that bluntly opposed medieval Catholic doctrine to the scientific, liberal, or modernist intellectual movements of the period. Romanticism assisted the papal cause by promoting a fascination with medieval culture and a renewed appreciation of the emotional power of Roman sacramental religion. And a century of experience with state domination revived an appreciation among the higher clergy of the advantages of a strong papacy that could assist them in maintaining a degree of independence from secular control. Several of the popes of the nineteenth century proved to be vigorous men who were willing to push their advantages and take strong positions. In 1854, Pius IX set a valuable precedent for the establishment of papal absolutism by defining the dogma of the immaculate conception without consulting a council of the church; and, in 1864, in the *Syllabus of Errors,* he made sweeping claims for the church's right to supremacy over the state. In 1878, Leo XIII ascended the papal throne and used the twenty-five years of his reign to enforce conformity within the church to the Thomistic doctrines that he declared to be tradition's best statements of orthodoxy. By the dawn of the twentieth century, the papacy had returned to a position of power in the Catholic church and in world affairs, but it had clearly committed itself to an authoritarian program that put it at odds with the dominant democratic values of the modern era.

Chapter Six

A New Environment

THE TRANSMISSION OF
CHRISTIANITY TO THE NEW WORLD

CHRISTOPHER COLUMBUS'S VOYAGE OF 1492 was an event destined to have profound influence on the evolution of European civilization and the history of the Christian church, for the New World opened by Columbus was in many ways a stimulus urgently needed for the rejuvenation of Western values and institutions. Europe was in trouble. As early as the fourteenth century, it had begun to struggle with conditions of economic and political adversity that had shrunk its populations, reduced its productivity, shaken its traditions, and challenged its self-confidence. By the time the medieval period had drawn to its symbolic close with the discoveries of the Iberian explorers, it had become very difficult for the people of Europe to retain their former senses of identity. The dominant forces of the day must have appeared to those who witnessed them as pressures pushing toward a progressive fragmentation of the West. Numerous international struggles among powerful monarchs—complicated by the maneuvers of the middle classes at their backs—kept the geographical and political systems of Europe in a state of flux. The new scientific theories and artistic perceptions of the Renaissance tore at long-established values. And the Reformation of the church once and for all laid to rest the myth of Europe as a "Christendom" united in one universal religious faith.

The undeveloped territories of the Western Hemisphere were a potential answer to many of Europe's problems. These lands provided immense stores of mineral wealth and unlimited agricultural opportunities. In addition, their empty spaces were a new frontier for masses of people who either could not be cared for by the European social systems or could not be content within the confines of conduct and belief tolerated by established authorities. Awakened by novel reports of bizarre people and places, stimulated by an influx of new wealth, and stabilized by the export of dissidents and nonconformists, the Old World recovered its balance, its self-confidence, and its imagination. A new era in Western civilization dawned as Europe expanded its continental institutions into bases for global empires.

The New World was exploited for the sake of a richer life in Europe, but Europe paid for its expanded resources by exporting to its colonies some of its most energetic citizens and freshest ideas. It was not long, therefore, before the new lands had evolved distinct identities of their own and were able to interact creatively with their mother countries. The political and economic influence of the New World on the Old has long been apparent to the most casual observer, but it has taken more time to acquire recognition for the fact that the Americas have also had a profound cultural influence on Europe. Nowhere is the vitality of the new civilization of the Americas more visible than in the vigor it has given to the Christian movement. In the New World, religion took on original forms and churches acquired unique functions. These developments enabled Christian traditions to once again make significant contributions to the continuing development of Western civilization.

It would be surprising indeed if religion had not emerged as a major concern in the New World, for the European explorer and the immigrant accepted as self-evident a belief that civilization and the Christian religion were one and the same thing. One could not be fully extended without the other, and the political conquest of a new land was almost always accompanied by the area's spiritual conversion. A few individuals, such as Bernardino de Sahagún, recognized that native, non-Christian religions deserved study and scholarly description. But the vast majority assumed the inferiority of pagan traditions and moved immediately to replace them with the religions of Europe.

The missionary fervor of the first explorers of the New World found frequent expression in their literature, and the names they gave to their discoveries often made their Christian intentions clear. Columbus, who sailed in a ship dedicated to the Virgin, named the first land he spotted in the New World *San Salvador,* "Holy Savior," and as a matter of course he made reports to his king on the spiritual as well as the secular condition of the natives. Those who followed in Columbus's wake continued to plant their crosses beside their flags and to claim lands in the names of both their nations and their God.

The desire to spread the Christian Gospel was at one and the same time an honest motivation and a sly rationalization for the acquisition of empires.

The Western Hemisphere was in the beginning almost exclusively at the disposal of the Spanish. Other nations sent out explorers, such as France's Jacques Cartier and England's John Cabot, to establish bases for future claims; but, for almost a century, Spain alone was in a position to attempt to take possession of the new lands. Tremendous efforts were put forth. In the first half of the sixteenth century, the South American coast was charted, and Spaniards wandered as far north as Nova Scotia. Between 1513 and 1542, Balboa crossed Panama to discover the Pacific Ocean, Hernando Cortez subdued the Aztecs of Mexico, Francisco Pizarro destroyed the Inca empire in Peru, Ponce de Léon explored Florida, De Soto discovered the Mississippi River, Francisco de Coronado penetrated what is now the southwestern United States, and the coast of California was investigated.

The vigorous exploratory activity of the Spanish gave the Roman Catholic church the first opportunity to establish the Christian faith in America. Franciscan and Jesuit priests accompanied the explorers and faced great hardships in their efforts to convert the American Indian and accustom him to Catholic disciplines. They had virtually universal success in South America in establishing rich new varieties of Catholic culture which helped create strong identities for the nations that eventually emerged there. They also made major efforts to claim the North American continent, but here they met with almost total defeat.

Spanish Catholics moved into North America in three widely separated areas. A number of attempts were made to plant colonies as far north on the Atlantic coast as Virginia, but a permanent settlement was not achieved until 1565, when St. Augustine was founded in Florida. In St. Augustine, the Franciscans established a base for a mission to the Indians of what is now the southeastern United States, and, by the early seventeenth century, they were claiming tens of thousands of converts. Ultimately their efforts came to nothing, for the eastern seaboard was colonized in the same century by English Protestants, who routed the Indians and destroyed their sympathy for the white man's religions.

In the Southwest, the activities of the Franciscans met with moderate success. By 1610, they had claimed a large area around San Juan, New Mexico, and created a system of missions, or plantations, managed by the friars and staffed by Indian converts. In the course of two decades, twenty-five missions and sixty thousand Indians came under the control of the Franciscans, but the situation proved to be unstable. In 1680, an Indian revolt pushed the white man back into Texas, and the Franciscans never again recovered the full extent of their former territories. By the middle of the nineteenth century, when these lands came under the jurisdiction of the United States, there were few priests and missions remaining to witness to the effort the Spanish had made for the Christianization of the Southwest.

The most successful Spanish Catholic mission in North America was the system of Franciscan plantations that grew out of the work of Junipero Serra in California. California had been casually explored in the seventeenth century, but no serious attempt was made to establish permanent settlements there until the middle of the eighteenth. The Franciscans set up a mission at San Diego in 1769, at Monterey in 1770, and at San Francisco in 1776. By 1780, there were churches at Santa Barbara, San Jose, and Los Angeles as well. The mission system seems to have worked well in California. Tension between the Indian and the white man was less there than in other areas, and the climate did not strain relationships by requiring unusually arduous labor from the converts who resided on the church plantations. By the middle of the nineteenth century, the Franciscans were claiming to have converted one hundred thousand Indians in California, but the unique Catholic culture that had begun to evolve there was nearly obliterated in 1849, when the great gold rush inundated California with Protestant fortune hunters who had little sympathy either for the Indian or for the Catholic religion. When all was said and done, the years of attention that the Spanish had given to planting their faith in North America bore little fruit.

Spain was not the only nation that attempted to establish the Roman Catholic faith on the North American continent. Early in the seventeenth century, the French began to develop their claims in the area. The city of Quebec was established in 1608, and from there fur traders, explorers, and missionaries spread out into the American wilderness. Louis Joliet and his priest companion, Jacques Marquette, investigated the Great Lakes and upper Mississippi from 1670 to 1675. René Robert Cavelier de La Salle explored the mouth of the Mississippi in 1682, and, with the foundation of New Orleans in 1718 and Fort Duquesne (now Pittsburgh) in 1753, the French drew together a network of forts that cut directly through the center of the continent. Jesuit missionaries did courageous work among the Indians in these territories, but the French government failed to maintain a firm hold on the lands it had explored. Louisiana was ceded to Spain in 1762 and Canada to Britain in 1763 as a result of a complicated series of wars fought both in Europe and America, and French Catholic culture remained alive in America only at the extremes of the French Empire in Quebec and New Orleans and in a few Mississippi River villages.

By the end of the eighteenth century, it was clear that both the French and the Spaniards had failed to make their religions and cultures dominant in North America. An occasional citizen of the infant United States would still speak of the dangers of Catholic encirclement of the new nation, but the strongest and most expansive forces in North America were those of the Protestant populations of the eastern seaboard, who were already on their way toward control of the continent and intimidation of the hemisphere.

There are many theories concerning the reasons for the Protestant triumph in the competition for North America, but one explanation seems beyond dispute. The Spanish and French Catholics sent armies, explorers, and missionaries, but they sent relatively few immigrants who would commit themselves to permanent residence in the territories their nations opened up. An attempt was made to plant a Catholic tradition among native Indian peoples, but, without the support of a strong core of resident European families, it was difficult to educate the aborigines and put down strong roots for alien European traditions. Relatively few Catholics wished to leave Europe for the New World, for in few parts of Europe were they seriously inconvenienced. The situation was quite different for Protestants. They were expelled from Catholic France from time to time and found life difficult in many sections of Germany. It was frequently the case, as in England, that Protestants could get along with Protestants no more easily than they could with Catholics; and, from the sixteenth century on, each generation of Protestants produced its share of reformers and radicals who yearned for a free environment in which to follow their unique perceptions of the imperatives of God. Sooner or later, their attention was bound to turn to the open spaces of the New World, and, when it did, they were disposed to immigrate, not as soldiers and missionaries, but as families who desired to leave Europe behind and build a new identity for themselves in the American wilderness. They came in large numbers, and they came to stay; the Indians fell back before their attack, and the continent of North America became host to a strong, self-perpetuating Protestant culture.

It is certainly not the case that all the seventeenth and eighteenth century immigrants to North America came in flight from religious persecution or in pursuit of religious objectives. But, in addition to other motives, most of the immigrants had strong, exclusively Protestant religious convictions. Much of the impetus for the development of America came from financial entrepreneurs, but a desire for wealth did not imply an indifference to religion. The first successful English colony in North America was planted on the James River in Virginia in 1607, not by religious refugees, but by a company of London businessmen. Their plan was, however, not simply to rape the American environment and return to England, but to remain permanently, develop resources, and create a profitable, continuing relationship between colony and mother country. The men and women who were to develop the new land were to have families, and they were certainly to continue to live as English people. That meant that they would as a matter of course require English law, English houses, English furniture, and the ministrations of the English church. An Anglican priest accompanied the first settlers and established at Jamestown the first Protestant church in North America.

The next major wave of English immigration began in 1620 with the appearance of the Pilgrims in Plymouth and swelled after the Boston-based Massachusetts Bay Company began to attract large numbers of Puritan settlers in 1630. The Pilgrims were clearly religious dissenters who fled Europe in pursuit of a place to practice the religion of their conscience, but the later Puritan immigrants, while often equally disillusioned with Europe, were not unaware of the economic and political opportunities the New World offered.

Mixed as the motives of the immigrants may have been, most of the early colonies took immediate and strong positions on the question of religion, and their legislation seldom reflected the attitudes of religious liberty and the custom of separation of church and state that were later to become a hallmark of the American way of life. Most of the groups that settled here so as to practice their own religions came in pursuit of freedom for themselves, but not of religious liberty as a general principle. Many were convinced that they were in possession of the true version of the Christian faith, and they saw no reason to tolerate inferior forms of religion. The need for freedom to practice the one true faith did not imply a commitment to a position of toleration for all religious beliefs, and an attitude of toleration could, indeed, be interpreted as a sign of inadequate religious conviction that was an opportunity for sin. In 1645, Nathaniel Ward, an influential New England clergyman, learned with horror that the residents of a Caribbean island had adopted a charter that granted "free stableroom and litter for all kind of consciences, be they never so dirty or jadish, making it actionable—yea, treasonable—to disturb any man in his religion or to discommend it, whatever it be;" and he admonished them, "If the devil might have his free option, I believe he would ask nothing else but liberty to enfranchise all false religions and to embondage the truth; nor should he need" *(The Simple Cobler of Aggawam in America).*

Most early colonists seem to have assumed that the churches of America would be organized along traditional European lines as establishments endorsed and supported by the state. There was no general agreement as to which churches ought to be established in America, but there was a firm conviction current in many of the colonies that a viable state required a clear legal commitment to one form or another of the Christian religion. There is much to be said for such an idea, for no society can survive unless there is a widespread consensus among its citizens concerning values and objectives. Religion and the church have traditionally been means whereby the moral agreement essential to peaceful communal life is reached and policed; and, in the eyes of many early Americans, religious freedom implied social anarchy. Few colonies were inclined to experiment with religious liberty unless pressured to do so by the pursuit of other objectives.

In Virginia, the Anglican church became the legal establishment. Taxes were collected for its support, its clergy were regulated by the state, and an attempt was made to enforce attendance at its services. But the Virginia establishment was not notably successful. The Anglican church attempted to organize itself in America, as in England, in systems of territorial parishes designed to be administered by bishops. But no Anglican bishop was ever appointed for America, and the vastness of the American landscape defeated the concept of parishes. There were too few Americans too thinly distributed over too much land for parishes to function as well in the colonies as they did in England. It was often necessary for people to commute considerable distances to attend services, and it was virtually impossible for a priest to keep track of his widely scattered flock. The Anglican establishment in Virginia played a rather weak role in the evolution of the colony, and it was in Virginia in 1776 that the first move was made by the members of an American church to disestablish their formerly state-supported institution.

Elsewhere in the South, Anglican establishments were attempted with a similar lack of success. In 1669, the constitution of the Carolinas made a formal commitment to Anglicanism, but the provision proved impossible to implement after the colony began to attract large numbers of non-Anglican immigrants. Georgia established Anglicanism in 1755 but did little to interfere with the free practice of other Protestant faiths—although the threat of the Spanish in nearby Florida did cause Catholicism to be suppressed as a religion subversive to the best interests of the colony.

The most successful of the early religious establishments were those of Puritan New England. Defeated in their attempts to persuade England to adopt their religious views, the Puritans had come to New England convinced that God had created the New World as a refuge in which his kingdom on earth was finally to be established. Europe had, in their opinion, failed to follow the Reformation to its conclusion and had thus fallen short of the will of God as expressed in the Scriptures. Hence, God had opened virgin territories to a remnant of the faithful, who, like the Jews before them, now went out to the wilderness a chosen people with a commission to build a perfect society centered on the service of God.

For people who held convictions like these there could be no question of endorsing religious liberty, for the practice of any but the true religion was the practice of a life leading to damnation. Freedom to pursue false religions was nothing more than license to continue in sin, and one did a person no favor by allowing him a freedom of conscience that led him to perdition. The Puritans intended to set up a perfect society patterned after the laws of God as revealed in their reading of the Scriptures and organized for the suppression of sinful impulses. The Massachusetts colonists saw the church and the state simply as two inseparable sides of one human community that served one God under one system of moral law. The only freedom of religion such a society could admit would be the freedom to stay away from its community if one could not accept its disciplines. It was self-evident to the Puritans that a person could not be a responsible citizen unless he were also a true and devout Christian; for the state, like the church, was simply a realization of God's law. It was perfectly reasonable, therefore, to grant political rights only to those who were members in good standing of the one true church.

The New England Puritans acquired a colonial charter that gave them a remarkable degree of independence of the English king and Parliament. As a result, they could govern themselves much as they saw fit and draw the bonds of conformity as tight as they wanted. In

1646, the colony drew up an act against heresy that decreed banishment for holders of a wide variety of religious opinions and death to those who returned to Massachusetts obdurate in condemned beliefs. The laws were taken quite seriously, and the vigor with which they were enforced at the expense of common liberties occasioned something of a scandal in England. The Puritan leadership found Quaker attitudes particularly offensive, and two Quakers, Mary Fisher and Ann Austin, who attempted to enter the Port of Boston in 1656 were jailed, treated with indignity, and deported after a confinement of five weeks. Others received similarly harsh treatment, and, between 1659 and 1661, four persons were hanged in Boston as punishment for their religious opinions.

Certain colonies in seventeenth and eighteenth century America did conduct experiments in religious toleration. Some were simply opportunistic. For example, the proprietors of New Jersey, George Carteret and John Berkeley, offered freedom of religion as a means of attracting settlers to their undeveloped lands. After the English acquired New York from the Dutch in 1664, the new rulers made their peace with the native population by stating that there was to be no interference with the religions already being practiced. Maryland was originally chartered as a colony without an established church, but this arrangement was a matter of necessity rather than principle. The only colony designed as a refuge for Roman Catholics, Maryland owed its existence to George Calvert, An English convert to Catholicism who acquired land from Charles I in 1632 for Catholics who wished to escape Protestant domination in England. Calvert could hardly have expected a Protestant king and Parliament to charter a Roman Catholic establishment in the midst of England's colonial empire, so Maryland obtained a constitution that guaranteed freedom of religion to Catholics and to all others who might wish to reside there. The experiment was not a success. As it turned out, there were few English Catholics who wished to emigrate, and Maryland soon had more Protestant citizens than Catholic ones. An act concerning religion passed by the colonial government in 1649 defined toleration as applying only to Christian beliefs and made it a capital offense to deny the divinity of Jesus or the doctrine of the Trinity. When the English civil war broke out, revolts against the Catholic Calverts occurred in Maryland. By 1691, the Calverts had lost control of their colony and seen the Anglican church established there. Catholics continued to live in Maryland, but they were forbidden the public practice of their religion and disenfranchised.

Much more impressive experiments with freedom of conscience— not as a means to an end, but as a positive value in and of itself—were conducted in the colonies of Rhode Island and Pennsylvania. Rhode Island was the brainchild of a renegade Boston clergyman named Roger Williams (1603?–83). Williams, a Cambridge-educated Anglican priest, arrived in Boston in 1631 and found that he did not fit into the church-state system the Puritans had imposed on the colony. He objected to what he felt were the oppressive, elitist policies of the Massachusetts government and emerged as a champion of the rights of the Indians who were being summarily dispossessed by royal land grants. In 1635, the authorities in Boston judged him incorrigible and decreed his deportation to England. He fled into the wilderness before the sentence could be carried out and survived the winter with the assistance of friendly Indians. The following year, he purchased land from the Indians and announced the establishment of a settlement called Providence, which he intended as a refuge for persons persecuted for religious beliefs. Ultimately, Williams and the colony came under Baptist influence, but, although Williams seems never to have been very sympathetic toward the Quakers, Rhode Island remained true to its commitment to freedom of conscience.

Equally successful and on a much grander scale was the "Holy Experiment" that William Penn (1644–1718) conducted in his colony of Pennsylvania. Penn, the son of a wealthy English admiral, as a young man abandoned the established church of England and embraced the doctrines of the Quaker sect. The Quakers, who were officially named the Society of Friends, were then a new movement initiated by the preaching of George Fox, and they drew most of their membership from the lower classes. They aroused considerable opposition in both England and the colonies, for they seemed to push Protestant individualism to an extreme that threatened anarchy. For them, the Reformation doctrines of free grace, the sufficiency of Scripture for the knowledge of God, and the priesthood of all believers, implied that God dealt in his acts of salvation directly with each individual. No clergy and no church organizations were necessary. Each person could come into immediate contact with God, and no a priori forms, customs, or standards could set limits to the freedom of such interaction. Total reliance upon the guidance of the Holy Spirit tended to lay the Quakers open to charges of excessive emotionalism and anti-intellectualism and to raise the specter of uncontrollable heterodoxy. But the Quakers were people who had great confidence in God and man, and they had no doubt that orderly human life would be possible even in a society of totally autonomous individuals if they each stood in a sincere relationship with God.

It was this conviction that William Penn determined to put to the test in 1681 when he induced Charles II to pay off a debt owed the Penn family by granting them ownership of a huge tract of undeveloped land in America. Penn's colony was conceived as a refuge for Quakers, who were often not welcome elsewhere, but Pennsylvania was to be much more than that. It was to be an attempt at the establishment of a just society in which people of many beliefs and backgrounds could freely participate. The land originally acquired from the king was repurchased from the Indians, and Pennsylvania was spared the worst of the endemic conflicts between red and white men. Since the Quakers had no fixed ecclesiastical system of their own and since they held the autonomy of the individual to be a supreme value, very few institutions were imposed on immigrants to Pennsylvania. From the beginning, the colony had extensive powers of self-government, an abundance of cheap or free land for the industrious poor, and total freedom of religion. Penn had little apparent desire for homogeneity in his colony and actively recruited, not only Quakers, but also religious dissenters from the Continent. The Anabaptists of Germany sent numerous sects as did the more orthodox branches of the German Reform and Lutheran traditions. Pennsylvania provided a home for Quakers, Anglicans, Lutherans, Moravians, Dunkers, Schwenckfelders, Mennonites, Amish, and even Roman Catholics; and the colony thus became the first major example of the religiously pluralistic society that was eventually to become the norm for the American way of life.

THE REBIRTH OF CHRISTIANITY IN THE AMERICAN ENVIRONMENT

THE REVOLUTION OF 1776 was in religion, as in other aspects of American life, a crucial turning point. The English colonies entered into the war holding a wide variety of conflicting religious opinions and emerged from the upheaval with a workable consensus on an ecclesiastical policy for their new nation. The consensus was as daring as it was expeditious: total separation of church and state, total freedom of conscience, universal toleration for all religions. No government in history had ever made such a complete renunciation of the right to oversee the beliefs of its people; no nation had ever before dared to risk the moral chaos and disruptive conflicts of values and goals that such a policy might seem to entail.

It must be admitted that a policy of separation of church and state was the easiest way out of serious political difficulties that might have prevented the degree of intercolonial cooperation needed for the revolution. Beyond a general commitment to Protestant ideals, there was no agreement among the colonists regarding denominational or ecclesiastical structures. The delegates to the Continental Congress from New England would never have accepted the establishment of an Anglican, episcopally governed church; and Virginia would have resisted a Puritan congregationalist institution with equal vigor. If the question of a national commitment to a particular kind of religion had come up, it would have vastly complicated the discussion of the urgent political concerns that lay at the heart of the desire for revolution. The founding fathers might have agreed that America was and should remain a Protestant country, but such feelings could not have been given public expression. The alliance between the colonies and Catholic France was crucial to the success of the revolution, and serious diplomatic problems would have resulted had the colonists made their Protestantism a goal of the revolution. Even a commitment to exclusively Christian principles would have complicated the efforts that a small, but helpful, minority of American Jews were making on behalf of the war. Thus, the Declaration of Independence said nothing whatsoever about religion beyond an assertion that the revolution was morally justifiable by an appeal to natural law and therefore congruent with God's will. When the Constitution was finally ratified in 1789, it contained only a prohibition as a guide for the future religious development of the nation: "no religious test shall ever be required as a qualification to any office of public trust under the United States" (Article VI). The Constitution's hands-off approach to religion was given some expansion almost immediately in the first of the series of amendments to the Constitution commonly known as the Bill of Rights: "Congress shall make no law respecting an establishment of religion, or prohibiting the free exercise thereof. . . ." But nothing positive was said on the crucial question of how the new nation was to define its values and support a workable moral order for its society.

Political expediency was not the only force that moved the United States in the direction of the radical disestablishment of religion and minimized discussion of the topic in the documents of the revolution. A policy of separation of church and state would not have long survived the revolution had it not been congruent with the religious convictions of the vast majority of the American people. The closing decades of the eighteenth century were, when judged from estimates of church attendance and support, among the most religiously lukewarm in American history. The churches had not yet learned to cope with the challenges of the American environment. People lived too thinly dispersed across the country to be gathered easily into traditional parishes, and the materialistic advantages of the frontier and the political activism of the revolutionary period provided potent distractions from religious concerns. It might be argued that a large number of Americans were relatively indifferent to religion and therefore felt no need for the state to endorse a relationship with a church. But the American commitment to separation of church and state was much more than a casual expression of mass indifference to religion, for the eighteenth century had seen the emergence of two movements that had helped prepare the country for the adoption of a policy of total freedom of conscience almost as a matter of course. The "Great Awakening" of the 1740's, which had a brief but strong effect on the religion of the masses, and the philosophy of Deism, the dominant ideology among the intellectuals of the revolution, both helped inspire the belief that it would be unnecessary, and unwarranted, for the new nation to regulate the ecclesiastical institutions of its people.

The Great Awakening, which was simply a sudden and widespread eruption of popular enthusiasm for religion, formed the first of a series of four similar phenomena that occurred at more or less regular intervals in the course of American history. Early in the 1720's, clergy working in many different parts of the country began to notice heightened interest in their preaching. Church attendance in some parishes began to grow astronomically, and reports of emotionally charged conversion experiences became commonplace. Jonathan Edwards in New England, Gilbert Tennent and Theodore Frelinghuysen in the middle colonies, and Samuel Davies in the South each remarked, with a mixture of gratitude and incredulity, that he perceived on every side an unexpected, intense recommitment of America to the Christian faith. The taste for religious discourse became so great that it could not be satisfied by the normal cycle of local church services, but spilled over into mass meetings convened to hear the oratory of traveling evangelists. The most famous of these speakers was George Whitefield, an English associate of John Wesley's, who toured America in 1738 and 1739 with unprecedented success. Even the sophisticated Ben Franklin confessed in his *Autobiography* that, whenever he heard Whitefield's preaching, he was so moved that he emptied his pockets in contributions to worthy causes in spite of himself.

Religion was in vogue in the colonies by the 1740's, but it took a form different from the disciplined, intellectual rigor of traditional American Calvinism. The faith of the Great Awakening tended to emphasize feelings rather than creeds, and it often showed a cavalier indifference to denominational lines. Anyone who could testify to having had a strong emotional experience of God was acceptable as a Christian, and the strength of a believer's commitment was more important than the catalogue of his beliefs. Similar religious experiences were reported by members of every denomination, and, since these experiences were seen as the heart of true religion, the sense of the importance of the traditional differences among the denominations began to fade. The emotional similarities among communions became more apparent than their points of intellectual or creedal distinction. It seemed that everyone was experiencing faith in the same way; hence it seemed logical to conclude that the separate denominations were simply expressions of one religion. The experiences of Baptists, Anglicans, and Congregationalists were identical; the messages from their pulpits seemed similar, focusing as they did more on feelings than on ideas. Hence, many Americans began to believe that there really were no important differences among Christian denominations or even among major religions. It was felt that, for a variety of historical reasons, people might prefer to apply different religious labels to themselves, but the reality that believers celebrated was one and the same in every church. Finite human minds might disagree on points of doctrine, but the essential fact in religion was a universal consensus of the heart. The majority of Americans experienced religion similarly and therefore felt secure in ignoring doctrinal conflicts. In any event, most people regarded such conflicts as primarily the concern of an intellectual elite for whom they had little sympathy. Because the common man felt in his heart that his fellows agreed with him on the essentials of faith, he believed it was completely unnecessary for the state to endorse any particular type of religion, especially if such advocacy would endanger important political objectives. The Great Awakening did not succeed in bringing America permanently back into her churches, but it did establish a mood of confidence that enabled many to contemplate a future of religious pluralism without alarm.

By a quite different process, the leaders of the American revolutionary government reached almost identical opinions. Not all Americans were Calvinists or pietists. The Unitarian movement was formally established at King's Chapel, Boston, in 1787, and there were numerous liberals and rationalists in the colonies. The eighteenth century was the age of the Enlightenment, an era intoxicated by the ability of the human mind to analyze and explain the workings of the natural world in terms of rational models. American philosophers, like European intellectuals of the period, believed that their new systems of rational scientific inquiry literally provided the key to the comprehension of final, universal truth. Their success in uncovering scientific information about the natural world inspired them unwarrantedly to assume that the principles of the rational mind were identical to the laws of nature and the structures of God's own being. All things suddenly seemed to stand open to human investigation and human understanding; all beliefs needed to be reexamined and justified by rational demonstration. Even the concept of God and the values of the Christian religion were to be accepted, not on faith, but as the conclusions of rational arguments based on clear and certain human experiences. The attempt to clarify the rational, essential core of man's religious consciousness led to the creation of the Deist philosophy. The Deists argued that in religion, as in all other areas of human activity, no beliefs need be accepted except those that could rationally be demonstrated as true.

There was no difficulty in proving the existence of God: Aristotle, Anselm, and Aquinas had marshaled numerous solid arguments. But adjustments had to be made in other, specifically Christian, beliefs. It was offensive to one's reason, for instance, to assume that the omnipotent, omniscient Creator would bring into being anything but a perfectly functioning universe. After a perfect act of creation, divine intervention in the created realm for purposes of improvement and regulation would be unnecessary. Hence, God was rightly to be seen as the architect of the universe, but not as a force that continued to live in and tinker with it. Man was completely on his own within the creation, and it was irrational to expect God to interfere with the processes of nature on human behalf. God equipped man at the time of birth with all the powers of mind and body needed in order to cope with the world, and a person's primary religious duty was simply to use and develop his innate powers and become a fully rational being.

The Deists further observed that the development of a human individual naturally required a degree of assistance from others, and so they argued that man had a rational commitment to the moral codes that are necessary for the functioning of human communities. The individual was designed to find fulfillment as a social, and, consequently, moral being; but morality itself could be a rational concept only if good were rewarded and evil punished. Unfortunately, human beings had long known that such did not invariably appear to be the case in this life. It was therefore logical to assume the existence of a future life in which justice was invariably done and the rational moral balances were struck.

These and similar lines of thought brought the Deists to a rational reconstruction of the Judao-Christian heritage. The Deist point of view preserved the figure of God, a sense of human moral obligation, and a confidence in the immortality of the soul. These religious doctrines were based, not simply on tradition or blind faith, but on defensible rational arguments. Since the Deist statement of religious belief was logically demonstrable, its adherents held it to be indisputably true and necessarily destined for universal acceptance. Inferior intellects might fail to grasp immediately the inevitability of Deist conclusions in religion and might cling for a while to the superstitions of the past, which promoted the illusion that there were real differences among true systems of religious belief. But sooner or later, when education had perfected the rational abilities of the masses, all people would naturally come to conclude that the Deist philosophy was the one clear and defensible statement of the themes inaccurately preached by the traditional religions. Since mankind was by nature rational and a rational person could no more deny the tenets of Deist philosophy than he could the principles of logical argumentation, it was as completely unnecessary for a government to take a position in defense of a specific religion as in support of the law of gravity. True religion, like any other fact of nature, would in time establish itself beyond question. Therefore, a commitment to freedom of conscience was ultimately, not an endorsement of a perpetual, chaotic state of religious pluralism, but an expression of confidence in the belief that religious pluralism was destined to fade with all other irrational notions that owed their existence to the temporarily underdeveloped intellect of the common man.

Washington, Franklin, Jefferson, Adams, and many of the other leaders of the new republic's institutions joined with the masses in a general willingness to ignore the ancient problem of the need to enforce religious conformity in order to create a viable political community. Few people doubted the necessity for a degree of agreement within a state on religious and moral issues, but, because they were influenced by either the emotionalism of the Awakening or the rationalism of the Enlightenment, most people believed it unnecessary to set up legal institutions to enforce a national consensus on values. The state could safely grant total freedom of conscience, for it had reasons to believe that a unanimity of religious opinion among its citizens was inevitable.

The endorsement of a principle of separation of church and state for the federal government contributed to a rapid decline of support for the traditional state ecclesiastical establishments, which gradually disappeared from American life. Virginia led the way by disestablishing its Anglican institutions in 1776, and, by the time Massachusetts followed suit in 1833, there were no formal alliances remaining between church and state anywhere in the country. Not all the American clergy were happy about this development. Although he later changed his mind after some experience with the success of voluntary organizations in American society, Lyman Beecher (1775-1863) admitted that, when Connecticut voted to disestablish its churches, "It was as dark a day as ever I saw. The odium thrown upon the ministry was inconceivable. The injury done to the cause of Christ, as we then supposed, was irreparable" (*Autobiography* 1. 344). Many doubted that religion could survive in the intensely secular American environment without the full support of the law and the public treasury.

The clergy had good reason to despair over the inability of the Christian churches to establish themselves in the United States, for, by the time the Revolution had been won and the country reorganized, interest in religious institutions had sunk to shockingly low levels. In 1800, less than 10 percent of the population was affiliated with a church, and there were numerous reports of widespread ignorance of the most basic points of Christian doctrine. A noted traveling preacher, Freeborn Garrettson, recorded in his diary accounts of meetings with people who were ignorant of the names of key figures from the Old Testament and of the very existence of Jesus and the major denominations of the Protestant religion.

If the Christian faith were to have any hope of survival as a part of the life of the new nation, America stood in desperate need of reconversion. But the groups on which the responsibility for domestic missionizing fell were not in a very strong position to discharge it. The Revolution had left many of the American denominations in organizational disarray. The Anglicans had been seriously hurt by their close association with and dependence on England. A large number of Anglican laymen and clergy had returned to England in opposition to the revolution, and the success of the war cut off the English monetary support and episcopal supervision that had been essential to Anglican church life. There were no Anglican bishops in America, and so rites of confirmation and ordination could not be celebrated here. There was no more tax money to support clergy or mission projects. Still, the Anglican movement managed to survive. The church adopted a less nationalistic name—Episcopalian, after its form of polity—and in 1784, thanks to the initiative of Samuel Seabury, it acquired its first bishop and began to evolve an independent American organization.

The discomfiture of the Anglicans in the postrevolutionary period occasioned the birth of a denomination that was destined to play a major role in American religious history. The Methodist movement had begun in eighteenth century England as a means of bridging the gap between the aristocratic leadership of the Anglican church and the lives of the poor. The founder of the movement, an Oxford-educated Anglican priest named John Wesley, had begun by preaching to the unchurched masses and ended by organizing them into religious societies designed to supplement the sacramental ministrations of the Anglican church. Wesley adopted unusual methods in reaching his people, and both he and his followers were often regarded with distrust by the Anglican establishment. As a result, the Methodists were forced to maintain a rather strong organization, but it was not until 1784 that Wesley sanctioned the radical step of breaking with the Anglican institution in America and setting up an independent Methodist denomination there. He had little choice. The serious weakening of the Anglican church in America left too few ordained clergy to care for the Methodists. They had to either commission their own religious leaders and perform their own sacraments or lose the fruits of their work in America. Wesley appointed Francis Asbury and Thomas Coke superintendents (a title that was soon dropped for the more traditional *bishop*) for the American Methodist movement, and, in December 1784, a conference of clergy in Baltimore officially organized the new denomination.

Most of the other American churches had less difficulty adjusting to the responsibilities of freedom, but all of them went through some period of confusion. The Puritan churches of New England had no ties with England and lost nothing from that quarter in the Revolution, but they faced the challenge of the loss of state support and establishment status. The necessity of living as voluntary organizations presented the Presbyterian, Baptist, and Congregationalist churches with dangerous temptations. These groups had always granted an extensive degree of independence to their local congregations, and, in the radical freedom of the American environment, they were in danger of a frag-

mentation that could cost them all meaningful denominational identity. Throughout the early nineteenth century, these groups suffered
numerous splits and factions that seriously hampered their efforts to
cope with the religious situation in the new nation.

In the end, the groups that best adapted to the American environment were the Methodists, who had an episcopal tradition, and the
Baptists, who represented opposing, congregationalist, views on
church organization. Indeed, these two groups were destined to become the largest Protestant denominations in the United States and to
come closest to evolving an original American version of Christian
piety. The secret of their success probably lay in their total willingness
to adapt to the realities of American life during the crucial early national period. America was at that time a large country with few centers of population. It was an expanding frontier of rugged individ-
ualists struggling to dominate a potentially rich, but difficult, land. It
was a nation in a hurry with little time for education or the niceties of
ritual and doctrine. It was a society with an enthusiasm for the future
and little interest in or knowledge of the past. The Methodists and
Baptists accepted the country on those terms and produced a version
of Christianity that was suited to the fluid, vigorous frontier. Taking
their cue from the European pietist movement, which had sent many a
successful sect to America, and from the experience of the Great
Awakening, the Methodists and Baptists tended to interpret Christianity as a religion of personal feelings and moral commitments, not
as a system of metaphysical doctrines or liturgical traditions. When
conducted on this level, the church could be relevant to the underedu-
cated, highly active American frontiersman, and the Methodists and
Baptists were not slow in developing unique institutions that could
reach the scattered American population. Both denominations minimized requirements for the intellectual training of their clergy and
stressed demonstrable effectiveness as a preacher and a "call" from
God over any system of human credentials. The Baptists created a
weakly centered denomination led by associations of virtually independent farmer-preachers—local men who were self-supporting and
often without formal education, but whose potential for religious
leadership was recognized and encouraged. Such men might not have
been able to lead sophisticated church organizations, but they were
available on the frontier to provide occasional religious services whenever the opportunity arose, and they shared the language and the concerns of their people in a direct and intimate way. The Methodists approached the problem of maintaining a religious presence among the

people somewhat differently: they attempted to support a clergy of full-time itinerant preachers who rode regular circuits through the countryside and held services wherever people could be found. There were no parishes and few church buildings, but the Methodists organized their routes so carefully that they touched even the most remote portions of the expanding country. The circuit riders were not always around when people needed them, nor could they provide weekly services, but they circulated frequently enough to keep the memory of Christian worship alive on the frontier.

In addition to these institutions of the Methodists and Baptists, the American frontier produced a unique substitute for traditional forms of the church, an occasional interdenominational religious conference known as the camp meeting. The camp meeting emerged quite naturally from the realities of frontier religion and did much to increase the impact of Christianity on the evolution of American society. Life on the frontier was lonely, tense, and hard; opportunities for association with other people were rare and often difficult to organize. One of the strongest emotional needs the frontiersmen must have had, despite their frequent assertions of total self-sufficiency, was an opportunity to gather into groups and enjoy the fulfillment of human contact. It was fortunate for the future of the churches that religion proved to be a remarkably acceptable vehicle for drawing people together. News of the approach of an itinerant minister might prompt the scattered residents of an area to gather together to meet him, and the temporary population density produced by such an event could provide an opportunity for rare social, as well as religious, functions. It was not long before the frontier preacher learned to exploit and organize this phenomenon for the best advantage of his ministry. By coordinating his itinerary with those of other clergy, he could occasionally team up with them in the leadership of meetings that promised to be so spectacular that people would travel for days in order to camp at the rendezvous points and enjoy a week or two of continuous religious services. A Presbyterian clergyman by the name of James McGready is traditionally credited with having inaugurated in 1800 the first true camp meeting, on the Gasper River in Kentucky. But no matter who invented it, the camp meeting was an idea whose time had come. By the early 1800's, it had become a standard feature of life everywhere on the frontier, and it has continued in modified forms into the present generation as a popular and uniquely American religious institution.

The tactics of the frontier churches met with phenomenal success, and their influence was felt even in the cities of the eastern seaboard. Americans began to flood back into their churches, and the country experienced its second "Great Awakening." During the first half of the nineteenth century, membership in the Methodist denomination increased seventeenfold; the Baptists were poorly organized and kept few records, but their growth seems to have been equally impressive; the Presbyterians, during the same period, averaged about ten thousand converts a year. By the 1830's, America was clearly on her way back into the mainstream of the Christian movement—so much so that Alexis de Tocqueville, a sympathetic foreign observer of antebellum America, wrote that, in his opinion, there was "no country in the world where the Christian religion retains a greater influence over the souls of men than in America" (*Democracy in America,* p. 303).

The church returned to the center of American life partly because Americans of the early nineteenth century generally favored organizations and societies of all kinds. There was in the country great enthusiasm for the liberties guaranteed by the new Constitution and a great determination to show the world that free men cooperating in associations of their own choosing could build a society more perfect than any that had yet appeared in human history. The old Puritan conviction that America was the chosen land in which God's kingdom was finally to be established reasserted itself in a new form, and the citizens of the infant nation began to organize to combat every known social evil. The principle of voluntarism worked so magnificently that it sometimes seemed as if a problem had only to be identified for a group to spring up and assume responsibility for it. Workers and money were found for a long list of worthy causes, and many of these campaigns seem to have been considered aspects of Christian moral concern. But the form of Christianity that eventually came to dominate American life often focused more on the needs of the autonomous individual than on his obligations to his fellowmen. Such an emphasis could be justified by the belief that the best way to reform a society was to reform each of its members individually; but there were also strong historical reasons for America's preference for the cult of the individual.

The churches of nineteenth century America that achieved the greatest growth rate were those that embraced the form of the Christian faith developed on the frontier. A denomination that hoped to survive there had to be able to accomplish much in relatively brief periods of time. Most frontier Americans had no permanent parish organization to foster and discipline a life of continuous Christian activity. The church appeared only in the bursts and flashes of the occasional meetings in which it attempted to recall its people from the errors into which they had wandered during its absence. The urgency of the situation required the church to jettison concern for "frills" and "nonessentials" and telescope the full range of religious life into an occasional, powerful experience of conversion and regeneration. Therefore, many people came of necessity to consider religion, not as a daily regimen, but as an occasional corrective applied for the salvation of recurrently lost souls. The practice of religion became for many the pursuit of revival—an activity centered on the experience of a series of conversions and reconversions to the Christian faith.

During the period of the second "Great Awakening," Americans developed a taste for revivalism that set the tone for their future religious evolution. The original Great Awakening took place within the confines of established denominational and parish structures and maintained contact with the historic theologies of the Christian movement. The second "Great Awakening," because of its frontier origin, often served as an emotional substitute for the steady discipline of regular life within a Christian community. The religion of the second Awakening thus had weaker roots in Christian traditions than did the first and, for all its emotional fervor, had less intellectual content.

The combination of a lack of contact with the theologies of the past and a lack of support from well-rooted local Christian communities opened the religious enthusiasm of the second "Great Awakening" to a number of temptations. First, it was all too easy to assume that true religion was an affair of the heart, not a conviction of the mind—that faith was a species of feeling, not of knowing, and that there was virtue, therefore, in a priggish antiintellectualism. Second, without the nurture of an established church to direct inspired Christians into lives of service to others, conversions often led nowhere or became ends in themselves. Experiences of conversion were frequently quite dramatic and as entertaining for those who observed them as elevating for those who underwent them. But unless such experiences were carefully handled, they could become an invitation to a peculiar kind of idolatry that reduced religion to a personal experience of emotional gratification. In unscrupulous or inept hands, a religious revival could seem more like a circus than like a traditional Christian gathering. Despite such problems and dangers, revivalism achieved a popularity that enabled it to set the tone for the development of much of American Christianity.

Even though America does not have a religious establishment, it has rarely been without a popularly recognized national religious spokesman. Since the period of the second "Great Awakening," most such spokesmen have been, not pastors of important parishes, but self-made revivalists who claim to work on behalf of no particular denomination but for the general advancement of the Christian religion itself. The spokesman is in effect a clergyman without a church and without denominational support. He differs from the frontier circuit rider in that he serves, not as a substitute for traditional forms of the church, but as a supplement to their ministries. He is a clerical specialist—a professional revivalist whose job it is to produce revivals of religious enthusiasm that will return converts to the traditional churches of their choice. He concerns himself primarily with the initiation of Christian faith in individuals, not with the long-term development of faith in communities or the specific application of Christianity to social problems.

The first of the great national evangelists was Charles Grandison Finney (1792–1875), an upstate New York lawyer who turned to professional religious activities after his conversion in 1821. At the time of his conversion, Finney had long been an active member of the Presbyterian church, but he had manifested no very remarkable piety and had sought no theological education. His conversion experience was of such significance to him, however, that he became convinced that he had been singled out for a special religious vocation despite his lack of preparation. Fifty years later, he was still able to describe with vivid intensity the experiences of October 10, 1821, when the direction of his life had changed. He wrote that he had felt it was high time he settled the issue of his soul's salvation, so he had cleared time in his work schedule and given himself over to meditation. After a few days of anxiety over his sins, he had been granted an extraordinary vision:

> As I went in [to the back room of his law office] and shut the door after me; it seemed as if I met the Lord Jesus Christ face to face. It did not occur to me then, nor did it for some time afterward, that it was wholly a mental state. On the contrary it seemed to me that I saw him as I would see any other man. He said nothing, but looked at me in such a manner as to break me right down at his feet.
> . . . I must have continued in this state for a good while. . . . But I know as soon as my mind became calm enough to break off from the interview, I returned to the front office. . . . But as I turned and was about to take a seat by the fire, I received a mighty baptism of the Holy Ghost. . . . the Holy Spirit descended upon me in a manner that seemed to go through me, body and soul. I could feel the impression, like a wave of electricity, going through and through me. Indeed it seemed to come in waves and

waves of liquid love; for I could not express it in any other way. It seemed like the very breath of God. I can recollect distinctly that it seemed to fan me, like immense wings.

No words can express the wonderful love that was shed abroad in my heart. I wept aloud with joy and love; and I do not know but I should say, I literally bellowed out the unutterable gushings of my heart. These waves came over me, and over me, and over me, one after the other, until I recollect I cried out, "I shall die if these waves continue to pass over me." I said, "Lord, I cannot bear any more;" yet I had no fear of death.

How long I continued in this state, with this baptism continuing to roll over me and go through me, I do not know. (*Memoirs,* pp 19-21)

Finney submitted to a brief apprenticeship under his local pastor before receiving from the St. Lawrence Presbytery a license to preach, but he rejected the suggestion that he enter a university for regular theological training. He believed his own reading of the Bible and his conversion experience had given him all the theology he needed, and he distrusted the "wonderful theological fiction" taught in traditional divinity curricula. He had reasons for his caution. Finney did not feel called to settle down and assume pastoral duties as leader of a congregation. There were men enough for that job. Finney's commission was to travel among the established Christian communities and breathe into them a desperately needed new life, for he saw himself as a specialist in the recruitment of nominal Christians to real Christianity. Finney's experience with his task gradually caused him to develop a theology seriously at odds with the doctrines of grace and salvation that had long formed an important part of the messages of major branches of American Protestantism.

Luther and Calvin had taught that people were saved by the free gift of God's grace. Salvation was not earned by anything a person did or by any innate virtues he or she might have. God gave this gift to those to whom he willed to give it, and his reasons were not open to human scrutiny. Such Reformation theologies protected the majesty of God and did justice to the concept of his omnipotence, but they were open to the charge that they encouraged quietistic behavior. If a person could do nothing to earn salvation, then why should one strive to be good or accept the discipline of a religious life? And if God alone were responsible for the salvation of mankind and experiences of conversion, what possible justification could there be for a professional evangelist? How could a revivalist presume to offer an experience of salvation that could only be delivered if his timing happened to be congruent with the inscrutable will of God?

Finney answered all these questions simply by dismissing many of the Calvinist ideas that had long been the basis of his denomination's teaching and by substituting for them a theology that must have struck many in his day as nothing more than good solid American common sense. America was not a land of passive, meditative people accustomed to wait on the will and the initiative of God. America was a nation of activists, of persons who had been taught to value independence and self-sufficiency. If an American wished salvation, it was reasonable to assume that he would go after it in the same way he went after anything else he wanted in life—in a head-on frontal attack. This, indeed, was the approach to the Christian faith that Finney advocated. He claimed to have willed himself into his own conversion, and he saw no reason why others could not do what he had done. He stated quite bluntly that, if a person had not yet felt the power of grace in conversion, it was not God's fault. One could not hide behind some mysterious doctrine of divine election. If a person was not saved, the blame lay in that person's own inadequate pursuit of salvation. It was certainly true that a Christian did not earn his salvation; that was a free gift earned for him by Christ's sacrifice. But a would-be Christian did need to appropriate the gift of salvation by an act of his own will, and, if he really wanted to be saved, he could be, simply by resolving to abandon his sins and to accept Christ. Finney saw the revivalist as a specialist in techniques that could quicken the human will for repentance, awaken the desire for salvation, and trigger the experience of this desire's fulfillment.

Finney's inventiveness in devising means for bringing people to a crisis of anxiety for the state of their souls served his critics as a source of excellent ammunition. He departed from contemporary standards of taste by praying for people by name in public, by inviting women to testify at his meetings, by scheduling protracted meetings that ran on for several evenings in a row, and by the invention of the "anxious bench," a seat at the front of his meetings where sinners on the brink of conversion might sit and receive the full effect of his personal exhortation and the attentions of the crowd. When it was pointed out to Finney that his "science" of evangelism was simply a system for the psychological manipulation of people, he was not offended. He argued that his techniques were justified because they served to activate the human will to appropriate the promises of salvation. Conversion experiences did result from the application of Finney's methods, and the fact that the conversions were induced by conscious human action in no way implied that the salvation they indicated was inauthentic. The revivalist was in Finney's eyes a more responsible guardian of souls than the Calvinist clergyman whose belief in divine predestination reduced him to a state of pastoral impotence.

In Finney's revivalism, America found a variant of the Christian tradition that perfectly mirrored the activist values of the American way of life. And in the revivalist himself, America found the chief spokesman for her emerging national consensus on religious beliefs. The heads of the major denominations and the regularly appointed occupants of church pulpits were not to be the stars of American religion. That honor was reserved for the minister without a church, the spokesman for religion in general who voiced the faith of the people. That minister, through the example of his power and demonstrable success, provided the regular clergy with a model that was hard to resist.

THE MATURATION OF AMERICAN CHRISTIANITY

REVIVALISM, IN A WAY, vindicated the confidence that the authors of the Constitution had placed in the future of religion in America. The movement helped the nation work toward agreement on religious issues without the application of governmental pressures. By the mid-nineteenth century, America had found her religious identity and embraced it enthusiastically. She had clearly begun to think of herself as a Christian nation, and, even more explicitly, as a Protestant one. Social forces and patterns of immigration had done what the government had refused to do: they had established a body of similar Protestant denominations as the generally accepted expressions of an authentically American religion. In part, Protestantism triumphed because of the rarity of non-Protestant immigration to America prior to 1800. The census of 1790 placed the total population of the nation at about four million persons, of whom a mere twenty-five thousand had Roman Catholic backgrounds and two thousand were Jews. Almost everyone in America had a Protestant heritage, so it was not difficult to agree on Protestant ideas as a basis for the life of the nation. At no point had Protestant domination been written into the law of the land, but, legal promises of religious freedom to the contrary, groups of later non-Protestant immigrants found themselves faced with a de facto Protestant religious establishment. They had to either challenge this establishment or conform to it.

The first group to acquire sufficient numbers to contest the Protestant domination of America were the Roman Catholics. Their experiences proved to be similar to those of the Jews and other later immigrants. America in the colonial period had never been hospitable to

Catholics. Many of the colonies, strong in their memories of European antagonisms, had prohibited all Catholic immigration or permitted Catholics only on the condition that they not practice their religion or claim civil rights. Even Maryland, which had been founded as a Catholic colony, had finally adopted an oppressive anti-Catholic policy.

The Revolution changed all this. The patriots gained a new perspective on the Catholic religion because of their enthusiasm for their French allies. Such Catholics as John and Charles Carrol of Maryland, the Marquis de Lafayette, and Count Pulaski made highly visible contributions to the success of the Revolution, and there were even Catholic contingents in the Continental Army. It was certainly the case that Catholics had no reason to desire a continued relationship with Protestant England and would, on that issue at least, be above suspicion in their patriotism.

There also did not appear to be much risk in according Catholics political and religious freedoms, for there were few Catholics in the nation and their church was a weak and pitiful thing. The administration of the American Catholic church was the responsibility of the English Catholic missionary society based in London, but that relationship had, of course, been made impossible by the Revolution. No one had ever dared suggest sending a Catholic bishop to establish hierarchy in America, for fear of extreme Protestant reactions. Therefore, most of the American Catholic clergy were members of religious orders, particularly the Jesuit order, who had volunteered to try to do what they could in a difficult mission field. In 1773, however, the Jesuits themselves had come under strong criticism from the pope, and for several years their order was thrown into chaos. Without support from either Rome or England, circumstances became very bad indeed for the American Catholic clergy, and there may have been only twenty or twenty-five of them still active in America in the years following the Revolution.

Despite the difficulty of the situation, France took a strong interest in seeing that an American Catholic church was organized. The key to the establishment of a viable church was the appointment of an American bishop, for without a bishop the sacramental and disciplinary life of a Catholic community simply could not function. Fortunately, victorious America was in a sufficiently mellow mood to tolerate such an appointment if a candidate of unquestionable patriotic credentials could be found. Benjamin Franklin suggested that an obvious choice was a Jesuit priest named John Carrol (1735–1815), who had worked for the Revolution as an ambassador in Canada, and who was a cousin of the Charles Carrol who had signed the Declaration of Independence. The pope was not accustomed to having nations thrust candidates for episcopal office on him, but, through the mediation of the French, an exception was made in this case, and John Carrol was consecrated in 1790.

The Catholic church was now to be allowed to function openly and equally among the other national religious institutions, but its long history of oppression had left it in a highly demoralized state. Carrol centered his administration in Baltimore, for he estimated that the majority of American Catholics lived in Maryland and southern Pennsylvania. He then set about organizing parishes, identifying Catholic laymen and gathering them for worship, and finding priests to care for them. The shortage of priests willing to work in America gave Carrol severe staffing problems until July 14, 1790, when the French church became more helpful to her American protégé than she had intended. The French Revolution broke out, and, among its wilder excesses, it decreed a national repudiation of the Catholic religion. The French clergy suddenly became refugees, and a number of them sought employment in America.

The influx of French clergy set the stage for the first major conflict between Catholic customs and the American environment. There had been good reasons in the past for the Protestants of America to be suspicious of attempts to plant the Catholic church in the midst of their democracy, for the Protestant values of the American way of life were at odds with traditional Catholic belief and practice at several crucial points. None was more troublesome than the patently undemocratic structure of the church itself. Catholics believed that God himself delegated his absolute authority to the pope, who in turn mediated it to the bishops and the lower clergy. The people stood at the bottom of a hierarchy of divine authority, and they had no control over their church. American Protestants found this monarchical pattern extremely distasteful and even threatening if it implied a tacit advocacy of similar political institutions. There was something un-American and unwelcome about the traditional structure of the Catholic church, and this was apparent not only to American Protestants, but even to the American Catholics, who had long been under the influence of Protestant, democratic customs.

The flood of French priests into the American Catholic church brought the issue of church democratization to a head. From 1790 to 1810, the church tripled in size—thanks to the leadership of Bishop Carrol and the inauguration of the first of the great waves of Irish im-

migration. The new Irish-American Catholics were English speaking
and fervently democratic, and they had serious problems in relating to
the French priests whom their bishop assigned to their parishes and
who were establishing themselves in the administration of the church.
Bishop Carrol had little choice in making his appointments, for there
were few American priests available and many French ones. His administration was, however, accused of insensitivity to the needs of the
laity, and sentiment developed among the trustees of the Catholic parishes for resisting the authority of their bishop. From Buffalo, New
York, to Charleston, South Carolina, groups of trustees organized to
demand a democratic reform of the church and to insist that parishes
be given a voice in the selection of their priests. In true American fashion, the Catholic laymen argued that the people who paid the bills had
a right to select the man they employed. Such an opinion was, of
course, a repudiation of traditional Catholic structures of authority
and a distinct embarrassment to Bishop Carrol. The trustees could,
after all, point to the fact that their bishop had been chosen for consecration because of his acceptability to his constituency, not simply by
the fiat of the pope. It was one thing, however, for the church to make
an occasional compromise and another for it to permit a basic change
in its constitution. Bishop Carrol repudiated the arguments of the
trustees, but the conflict continued to disrupt the life of the church for
a generation after his death in 1815. In practice, the Catholic hierarchy attempted compromises with the people whenever possible, but,
in theory, the proposal for a democratic reform of the church had been
rejected outright. Protestant observers took alarm at this state of affairs and began to express concern that the Catholic church was not
going to accept integration into American society as a democratic institution.

As the nineteenth century unfolded, Protestants became more and
more anxious about the Catholic presence in America. Not only was
the church resisting assimilation, but it was growing uncomfortably
large. The Catholic church of the revolutionary period had been a tiny
institution, but, thanks to floods of Irish immigration, it had become
by mid-century the largest single religious organization in the country.
It was strikingly visible and was developing considerable political
strength in certain cities. Few Irish immigrants settled in the countryside to resume the agrarian lifestyle that had brought them to the
brink of starvation in their homeland. Large numbers of them stayed
in the ports of entry, found employment in industry, and accumulated
in urban ghettos. Social conditions in these ghettos were often ap-

palling, and America's first experience with the slums of the industrial revolution was associated with the Irish Catholics who peopled them. To decent, middle class Protestant Americans, the newcomers seemed to be corrupting what previously had been a neat and orderly society. The fact that the Irish were more victim than cause of the situation in which they found themselves did little to ease the distress with which they were viewed. Concentrated as they were in cities, speaking English, and enfranchised as soon as they stepped off the boat, Irish factions soon became factors to be reckoned with in the political affairs of important cities.

To many in early nineteenth century America, the country seemed to be coming under attack by infiltration: the United States was being flooded by persons who were both foreign and Catholic. Some commentators even thought they could see a plot in the pattern of Catholic immigration. In 1835, two books appeared: Lyman Beecher's *Plea for the West,* and Samuel F. B. Morse's *Foreign Conspiracy against the Liberties of the United States.* Both books claimed that the Catholic kings of Europe and the pope were fostering Catholic immigration in a move to undercut American democracy. These and similar ideas seemed sufficiently reasonable to enough Americans to inspire the beginning of a program of public resistance to Catholic influences.

A so-called Nativist Movement had been slowly building in intensity since the 1820's, when the appearance of a number of anti-Catholic journals, such as *The Protestant Vindicator,* provided a vehicle for those who wished to argue that the Catholic faith and American democracy were incompatible. The Catholics organized journals to argue the case in their own defense, but, by the 1830's, the debate had degenerated to the level of slander. A year after the books by Morse and Beecher were published, a curious volume appeared bearing the name of a certain Rebecca Reed and entitled *Six Months in a Convent.* It purported to be a disclosure of the secret immorality of priests and nuns, and it was followed in 1836 by a similar work, Maria Monk's *Awful Disclosures . . . in the Hotel Dieu of Montreal.* Monk's book was so popularly received that she followed it in 1837 with a sequel, and it inspired imitation in a volume entitled *Rosamond, or a Narrative of the Captivity and Sufferings of an American Female Under the Popish Priests in the Island of Cuba.* Under the influence of literature of this kind, the Nativist movement took a turn toward violence. In 1834, the Ursuline Convent in Boston was burned by a mob, and, in 1842, Philadelphia endured three days of rioting in which thirteen persons were killed and churches and homes destroyed. There were uprisings of a similar, but less destructive nature, in New York City as well.

By the late 1840's, Nativist sentiment was strong enough to support the emergence of a Nativist political party officially known as the Order of the Star Spangled Banner. Its platform was the restriction of election to public office in the United States to native-born Protestants. The secretive nature of the party earned it the nickname the "Know-Nothing Party," and as such it became a major factor in the national elections of 1852. The party dominated a number of state legislatures and sent sizable contingents to Congress. In 1856, it ran Millard Fillmore for the presidency. The Civil War and the slavery issue distracted the nation from the immigrant problem, and the "Know-Nothings" faded from politics. Sentiment against Catholics remained strong enough, however, to spawn new nativist organizations—such as the American Protective Association of 1884—and to complicate the presidential campaigns of Al Smith in 1928 and John Kennedy in 1960.

The leaders of the Catholic church in America were well aware of the antagonism surrounding them and, in the latter half of the nineteenth century, moved to demonstrate that their church could make a positive contribution to the development of American society. Catholic scholars wrote articles citing precedents for democratic ideals in classic works of Catholic philosophy and theology. The church also attempted to deal constructively with the social problems of American cities—problems that posed as great a threat to the intimate welfare of the Catholic masses as to their image in middle class Protestant circles. The church supported the movement to outlaw child labor at the risk of antagonizing the industrial establishment and also placed itself in the forefront of numerous other reform programs. By working effectively for the betterment of American society, the church hoped to establish its credentials as a loyal American institution.

The plan exposed the church to attack from a new quarter: it generated in papal circles serious suspicions that American Catholics were accommodating too much to American Protestant ideologies. Indeed, American bishops had done their best to urge the papacy to moderate its monarchical claims. The bishops had even suggested that the church be democratized to the extent of increasing the role of the council of bishops in determining doctrine and policy. But the papacy moved instead in the direction of the doctrine of papal infallibility, which was promulgated at the First Vatican Council of 1869, and began to clamp down on the American reformers. It was not until the 1890's and the reign of Leo XIII, however, that the American Catholic church came under severe disciplinary pressure from Rome. In the bull *Longinqua Oceani,* Leo rebuked certain American bishops who had spoken out in favor of the separation of church and state and also cautioned American Catholics against assimilation by Protestant society. This warning was followed in 1899 by the bull *Testem Benevolentiae,* which raised the question of the existence of a distinctly American heresy. In the bull, the pope identified a number of opinions that could not be held by orthodox Catholics, and several of his admonitions hit at common assumptions of the American way of life. The pope resisted all suggestions that the church should conform to society. Holding to the belief that the church was an unchanging standard to which society must adapt, he cautioned against the devaluation of the passive virtues of prayer and meditation in the activist American environment, and he repudiated once and for all any attempt to extend democratic principles to the church.

The effect of this Americanist Controversy was to move the American Catholic church into a more cautious program. As the twentieth century dawned and the flood of Catholic immigration continued, the church turned its attention inward. It accepted a degree of second-class citizenship in America, and worked, through a system of schools, colleges, and parish social organizations, to develop a Catholic minority society within the framework of Protestant America. The church remained content with a kind of semiforeign status until the 1950's, when the liberal atmosphere of the Second Vatican Council and the religious enthusiasm of the period again raised the question of a closer integration of Catholic practice and American institutions.

Catholics were not the only Americans who struggled with problems of religious adjustment and development in the Protestant shadow. Jews had major difficulties in finding acceptable identities for themselves in America, and their efforts in this direction split their communities into the three major "denominations" of American Judaism: Reform, Orthodox, and Conservative.

The American Protestant majority was not immune to pressures for change and development during the nineteenth century. Protestants were particularly active in the evolution of movements and societies related to evangelizing or to Christian social concerns. The fervor for missionary activities struck America at about the same time as proselytizing societies were being organized in Britain. By the 1820's, there were numerous American organizations for the support of mission work on the frontier and in foreign fields. The concern for missions gave birth to tract and Bible societies, which devoted themselves to increasing the supply of religious literature and to promoting educational opportunities. In a similar vein, the American Sunday School Union was set up in 1824 to assist the rapidly expanding Sunday school movement. Other Christians gave their attentions to a wide variety of societies organized to combat social problems. The slavery question gave rise to a number of groups with programs ranging from simple emancipation to deportation of blacks. Prison reform was a vital issue in which America took an international lead, and notable work was done likewise in establishing insane asylums and schools for the deaf and dumb. The temperance movement was inaugurated in Connecticut in 1813, and this movement in turn strengthened organizations active in pursuit of women's rights.

Protestant exuberance and imagination in nineteenth century America were too strong to be contained within the limits of these societies and the traditional denominations that had been imported from Europe. The nineteenth century was an era of great inventiveness in the sphere of religion, and the period saw the emergence of dozens of sects and cults, some of which were destined to survive as significant new denominations.

One of the most successful religious innovators of the period was Joseph Smith (1805–44), whose work resulted in the establishment of the Church of Jesus Christ of Latter-Day Saints, popularly known as the Mormons. Smith was born in Vermont in 1805 and spent his youth in an area near Palmyra, New York. He was a man of little education but powerful imagination and charismatic qualities. In 1830, Smith began his career as a religious leader by raising money for the publication of a book that he claimed was his translation of an ancient text whose hiding place had recently been revealed to him. The original manuscript had been written on golden plates and concealed by a being named Mormon, the last member of a race of early Americans that finally became extinct. This race had had a connection with the Jews of the Old Testament. The *Book of Mormon* and Smith's subsequent revelations became the basis for a new scripture and a new variant of the Christian movement. Smith and his family moved to Kirtland, Ohio, in 1831 and there organized the first Mormon church. The Kirtland experiment failed during the financial panic of 1837, and Smith and his followers moved farther west to Missouri and finally to Nauvoo, Illinois. There, Smith reached the peak of his career. He induced the Illinois authorities to grant the new community at Nauvoo a charter that virtually guaranteed it freedom from outside influences, and he set about constructing a theocracy in which he was free to experiment with new religious institutions. His independence of American laws and his challenge to accepted moral precepts created significant tensions between him and the non-Mormon residents of Illinois.

In 1844, the Nauvoo community began to divide into conflicting factions, and news of Smith's advocacy of polygamy began to reach the outside world. Reaction was so violent that the Mormons were forced out of Nauvoo and Smith was lynched from the Carthage, Illinois, jail on the night of June 27, 1844. The Mormons split into two groups following his death, and the larger segment accepted the leadership of Brigham Young, a convert from Methodism who had helped organize the moves the community had had to make in the past. Young led them deep into the wilderness to the Great Salt Lake of Utah. He hoped that isolation from the outside world would enable them to develop their unique institutions without interference.

By the 1850's, the frontier had advanced as far as Utah, and the conflicts between Mormon and non-Mormon broke out again. The end of the nineteenth century found Utah surrounded by U.S. states and territories, and the Mormons were required to make their peace with the Union. The major block to according Utah statehood was the Mormon religious practice of polygamy. In 1879, the Supreme Court decreed that polygamy could not be tolerated in American society and that the Mormons would have to alter their religion in order to receive their political rights. The court justified its decision by explaining that religious freedom did not imply freedom to undercut institutions, such as marriage, that were fundamental to the American way of life. The court's action seemed to imply that, when basic values were in dispute, Constitution or no Constitution, the government would interfere with the free practice of religion. The Mormons eventually gave in to overwhelming societal pressures, the revelation concerning polygamy was placed in abeyance, and in 1896 Utah received statehood. The Latter-Day Saints have grown to become a large and respectable movement which in the minds of many is associated with the Protestant tradition, but Mormon doctrines involving belief in various levels of spiritual preexistence, unusual modes of revelation, and restrictive racial attitudes tend to significantly distance the group from orthodox Christianity.

Mormonism was not the only new addition to the American religious scene in the nineteenth century. Other groups of note derived their inspiration from the preaching of a Vermont farmer and Baptist layman named William Miller (1782–1849). Miller became convinced by his study of the Bible that it was possible to predict a date for the end of the world, and, after some equivocation, he decided that the Scriptures pointed to 1844 as the last year of man's temporal existence. When his prophecies failed, he lost the major part of his fol-

lowing, but his project continued to inspire interest among groups of
Christians who came to be known as Adventists because of their concern with the second coming of Christ. Adventist groups have formed a
number of sects that have found a permanent place for themselves in
American society. The Seventh Day Adventists came into existence in
1862 under the leadership of Ellen G. Harman (1827–1915), who had
been a follower of Miller's and who was a recipient of many visions
that became a basis for a new Adventist theology. In 1872, a Philadelphia tailor named Charles Taze Russell (1852–1916) inaugurated a
group that developed adventist concerns in a more radical direction.
They have prospered significantly in the twentieth century under the
name "Jehovah's Witnesses," and their theology has carried them far
afield from the mainstream of the Christian tradition.

The last half of the nineteenth century also saw the appearance of
another notably successful cult: Christian Science. Christian Science
was in theory and in organization the work of Mary Baker Eddy
(1821–1910), a chronic invalid who mastered her illnesses in 1862 as a
result of the attainment of new levels of religious understanding. Eddy
taught that illness and death were illusions that had no power over a
properly enlightened person, and she stressed the importance of maintaining a sense of oneself as a part of nature. In her emphasis on the
oneness and perfection of nature, she denied the reality of evil and
showed a sympathy for the philosophy of the New England transcen-
dentalists. Eddy's church survived her to become a prosperous and virtually ubiquitous national institution.

The combination of religious freedom and cheap land tended to
make nineteenth century America an arena for the development of numerous less successful and occasionally bizarre religious experiments.
Throughout the whole period of the eighteenth and nineteenth centuries, there was considerable American interest in the establishment of
religious communes that could test out in practice a wide variety of
lifestyles. As early as the period of the first Great Awakening, a Protestant monastic community modeled loosely after European examples
had appeared at Ephrata, Pennsylvania, and it managed to perpetuate
itself into the twentieth century. Similar groups, including the Dorri-
lites, Winchelites, the Bullard's Pilgrims, the Society of the Universal Friend, and the Rappites, appeared and prospered for various periods of time.

None of them was more creative in dealing with the American environment than the group known as the Shakers. The Shakers were a
sect founded by an Englishwoman of radical Quaker background, Ann

Lee Stanley (1736–84), who emigrated to America in 1774. By 1776, she and a few followers had acquired land near Albany, New York, and had organized an agrarian commune that aimed to provide its members with a spiritual, but humane, context in which to live. The objectives and style of the community captured the imagination of the day, and the second "Great Awakening" flooded the Shaker organization with converts. By the 1850's, there were nineteen Shaker settlements scattered about the country, and the movement had a total membership of about six thousand. The Shakers were notable not so much for their theology, which was peculiar primarily in the veneration it accorded Ann Lee Stanley as a revelation of the feminine aspect of God, as for their contributions to American culture. The Shakers believed in lives of total simplicity, and they designed buildings and furniture that minimized ornament and took form from function. In so doing, they created a powerful school of American folk art that has been widely praised in the twentieth century. They had no respect for meaningless work, and they took an interest in the invention of gadgets and laborsaving devices which they were not loath to share with the outside world. They maintained a strict rule of celibacy, but they acknowledged a complete equality between the sexes in managing their communal affairs and maintained a semblance of normal family life in their relations with each other and in the attention they showered on orphaned children. In general, they seem to have lived productive, quiet lives that met their religious objectives without denying too many aspects of their humanity. The sect is still in existence, but it is quite small and no longer accepts new members.

America also provided a home for groups like the Amish and the Hutterites, which are examples of archaic European societies that have translated themselves to the New World and preserved themselves intact into the modern era by rigorously avoiding all communication with those outside their own community. Many other American communes, however, have thought of themselves, not as retreats for their members, but as models for the reform of society at large. New England produced in 'Hopedale' and 'Brook Farm' communal experiments that sought to put into practice the harmless, if impractically romantic, dream of a return to nature. Robert Owen's socialist community at New Harmony, Indiana, and John Humphrey Noyes's group marriage society at Oneida, New York, were conducted as radical, but scientific, experiments with alternatives to accepted American institutions of private property and family life. All were a testimony to the vitality of the Christian tradition which had rooted itself in the American environment and begun once again its fertile stimulation of the human conscience and imagination.

THE FRUITION OF AMERICAN CHRISTIANITY

AMERICAN SOCIETY WAS CONFRONTED with many challenges during the nineteenth century. Challenges to political unity expressed themselves most violently in the Civil War. Challenges to traditional moral and social values came to light in the struggle with the urban and industrial revolutions. Challenges to accepted religious beliefs emerged from the attempt to deal with new information developed by the natural sciences. To most of these challenges, the majority of American religious groups responded in a reactionary fashion, and rarely did a new or creative approach emerge from the mainline churches. The nation's political and social problems simply became an excuse for a further fragmentation of the Christian movement in the United States.

Disputes over the validity of revivalism divided and subdivided a number of major denominations during the early decades of the century, but it was not until midcentury that the major splits occurred. The churches of the Civil War period preferred to imitate the political disunity of the nation rather than stand against the forces that tore the country apart, and the great nationwide denominations divided before the Union did. Only the northern-based Congregationalists, Unitarians, and Quakers were able to agree on a condemnation of slavery. The Methodists, Presbyterians, and Baptists, who represented a cross section of the country, debated the issue on numerous occasions but were incapable of resolving their disagreements. In 1844, the Methodists led the way into schism. The Baptists separated in 1845, and the Presbyterians followed suit on the eve of the war.

The success of the North in the war and the liberation of the slaves provided even more impetus for ecclesiastical fragmentation. Robbed of a political vehicle for the expression of regional identities, large numbers of Americans elected to preserve the regional divisions of their churches as expressions of their unresolved hostilities. For example, it was not until 1939 that the Methodists were able to overcome the emotions of the Reconstruction era and convene a nationally united church. The liberation of the slaves added racist motives to political ones and occasioned even more denominational subdivisions. The racist fragmentation of the Christian movement in America had begun as early as 1794, when a confrontation over segregation in Philadelphia's St. George's Methodist Church led to the secession of the black members of the congregation and the founding of America's first black denomination, the African Methodist Episcopal Church. In the South, the whites of the antebellum period seem to have preferred to keep their slaves within the white churches rather than give the blacks an organization of their own. On many plantations, an "invisible institution" gave expression to a unique black version of the Christian faith, but black Christianity was not encouraged to make itself public until the postwar period. At that time, a few courageous voices spoke out against racism, but the majority opinion carried the nation into an era of segregation, and the blacks found themselves pressured out of the white churches in which they had long participated. Religion was the only personal cultural heritage of which many former slaves were conscious, and it was, therefore, not too surprising to find them turning to new church groups as a means of organizing their separated existence within American society. For many years, the lives of the American blacks focused on their churches, which in addition to spiritual services gave them bases for establishing desperately needed educational, economic, and political agencies. Within their churches, blacks experienced more freedom of self-determination than they could find in the wider arena of American secular life. Consequently, blacks with talent for leadership have most often developed it through ecclesiastical structures, and they have been understandably lukewarm to recent overtures for reunion with predominantly white denominations. Ecumenical invitations have, however, been infrequent and the church remains, despite the contributions of numerous Christians to the civil rights movement of the 1950's, one of the most segregated institutions in American society.

Nineteenth-century American churches dealt with the social problems resulting from the unregulated capitalistic economy of the "Gilded Age" in as ambiguous a manner as they met the political and racial challenges of the period. America continued to play host to millions of immigrants, who crowded into the industrial labor force of the nation and created urban growth without precedent in history. Many of the immigrants were minimally skilled, illiterate in English, and at the mercy of the industries that gave them their only hope of employment and survival. Builders could not keep up with demand for space in the exploding cities, and slum conditions proliferated. The Protestant Christian majority in America reacted inadequately to the moral challenge of the situation and began its flight to safer communities. Most of the new immigrants were not Protestant and did not seek or find a welcome in the Protestant churches. Even the Catholic church, which did recognize a degree of responsibility for the newcomers, tended to divide parishes along ethnic lines. Such parish organization preserved memories of the nationalistic antagonisms the immigrants had brought with them from Europe and supported snobbish distinctions between early and later waves of immigration. The common impulse of the more established Christian communities was to look on the plight of the newcomers with a degree of horror, disgust, and self-righteousness.

The leading revivalist of the period, Dwight L. Moody (1837–99), expressed the simplistic convictions that many middle class Americans held concerning the problems of the cities. Moody believed these problems could be solved by converting individuals to the Christian religion and the work ethic. He preached that there was nothing basically wrong with American political or economic institutions. If people suffered deprivation in America, their problems resulted from their individual failures and did not indicate any inadequacy in the structure of American society. Moody exhorted his congregations to look to their personal relationships with God; if those were brought into good order, then all the blessings of prosperity and success would inevitably follow. Henry Ward Beecher (1813–87) was equally blunt in his assertion that poverty was simply a result of sin, and he encouraged the more privileged classes to feel secure in their wealth, which he interpreted as a clear testimony to their virtue and industriousness.

America came to accept the idea that, if all people became good, then a good society would automatically appear. As a result, the attention of late nineteenth century reformers turned to the battle against the sins of the underprivileged classes. One of the most visible and, therefore, most easily combatable of sins was the abuse of alcohol by the poor. The turn-of-the-century evangelist "Billy" Sunday (1863–1935), whom opinion polls of the period listed as one of the ten greatest men in America, asserted simply that drunkenness was the root of all sin and all social evil. He argued that, if drink were banned, then money would be more wisely spent, the economy would be stimulated, the standard of living would rise, labor agitators would lose their power over the masses, and family life would stabilize. There had long been a temperance movement in America. As early as 1865, there were thirteen "dry" states in the Union; but the crusade against liquor did not hit its stride until the end of the nineteenth century, when religious America threw the full weight of its social concern into combating this one evil. Moral reform societies metamorphosized themselves into political parties, and, as a result of their work and an expenditure of millions of dollars, the Constitution was amended in 1920 to prohibit the drinking of alcoholic beverages in America. The laws proved impossible to enforce and, in 1933, they were repealed—although some local governments still decree prohibition in one form or another in the areas under their jurisdiction. The reform did not work; it was a clear example of a trivialization of the Christian concept of sin and did little to increase respect for Christian leadership in American society.

Some Christian groups in America did attempt to deal at close quarters with the problems of the poor. The Young Men's Christian Association, which was pioneered in England in the 1840's, appeared in America in Boston in 1851 and proved to be a practical means of alleviating some of the difficulties of city dwellers. The associations were convenient halfway houses for young men moving into the cities and provided recreational and educational opportunities that were desperately needed. By the end of the century, the YMCA movement had become a universal feature of American urban life and had attained such popularity that it narrowly avoided the temptation of assuming ecclesiastical functions and emerging as a new and independent Protestant denomination.

The Christian movement spoke to the plight of the poor more often through the generation of new denominations than by the regeneration of old ones. The most successful new Christian groups to rise out of the social concerns of the period were those which, like the Salvation Army, broke with past traditions and adopted structures dictated by the work they felt called to do. The founder of the Salvation Army, William Booth (1829–1912), had been associated with the Methodist movement in England but found that the Methodists of his day had become too middle class to be relevant to the problems of the truly poor. In 1864, Booth began establishing in the slums of London preaching and social service centers in which he attempted to deal directly with the spiritual and physical needs of the destitute. His enthusiasm communicated itself to his followers, who accepted a strict discipline and developed a quasi-military model for their assault on sin and suffering. The first members of the Army arrived in America in the 1880's and were greeted with distrust and overt persecution, but they endured to become an accepted part of the national religious scene and to establish centers in virtually every American city. Groups like the Army have done much to ease the symptoms of poverty for people with whom they manage to come in contact. But the work of these groups has had little effect on the causes of economic exploitation and the abuses that create the misery of the poor.

Many Christians of the late nineteenth century were as inadequate in their attempts to cope with the intellectual challenges of their day as they were in their moves to discharge their social responsibilities. The church's major intellectual problem was the assimilation of the new worldview of the natural sciences. Geology had made great progress during the century in providing a new scheme for dating the epochs of creation. Biologists had devised a new understanding of the origin of man and his intimate integration into his natural environment, and this formulation seemed, on the surface at least, to be incongruent with traditional understandings of biblical teachings. In addition to scientific assaults on former certainties, Americans in the last half of the century began to hear of German scholarly work in historical and textual criticism of the Scriptures. This research seemed to some to call into question the possibility of the Bible's divine inspiration and to represent Scripture as simply a fallible human document.

The necessity of coping with this new information and with the acute social problems of the day split the American Christian movement into two major camps: the liberals and the conservatives. Both positions were somewhat less than true to the full range of traditional Christian values. The liberals erred in the direction of uncritically accepting the opinions and prejudices of their age. They turned to the future with an unwarranted degree of confidence and underestimated the problems of society; and they so willingly reinterpreted the Christian faith in terms congruent with the tastes of their generation that they robbed the faith of the independence it needed in order to provide a balanced perspective on their programs. The liberals often seemed to accept as a scientific norm anything that emerged from the application of new modes of thought, and to believe that such new concepts inevitably expressed in clear, modern terms the truths veiled in the traditional mythical vocabulary of religion.

The conservatives were hardly more helpful in their attempts to deal with the tremendous advances of Western science. They seem to have begun with the assumptions that whatever was new was suspect simply because of its newness and that, when new ideas came into conflict with old ones, the new ideas could generally be assumed to be incorrect. The conservatives advocated a blind trust in the ability of past values to meet modern challenges. Their approach was almost a mirror image of the confidence with which the liberals dismissed the past as a locus of ideas relevant to the present. The conservative position, because it most often clung to familiar ideas and rejected new concepts out of hand, was the easier stance for most people to adopt. It satisfied a common human desire to avoid facing the threats of a rapidly changing environment by retreating to a past made secure by the selective processes of memory. The conservatives produced an appealing program that lay within the intellectual reach of most people; so it is not surprising to find that a number of strong new Protestant denominations began to appear in America expressly to give voice to conservative principles.

The new churches were sometimes referred to as Fundamentalist organizations because of their allegiance to a platform of five ideas that turn-of-the-century conservatives held to be essential for traditional Christian faith. The conservatives were unwilling to maintain communion with anyone who would not assent to belief in the inerrant truth of a literal interpretation of the Scriptures, the virgin birth of Jesus, the "satisfaction" theory of Christ's death, the resurrection of the physical body, and the second coming of Christ. In defense of these principles, numerous groups seceded from the older denominations, and the "holiness" movement of the late nineteenth century began a process that created the Churches of the Nazarene, the Assemblies of God, the Free Methodists, and the scores of pentecostal denominations and sects that still continue to appear.

Much of the antipathy of the conservative wing of American Christianity to modern modes of thought came to be focused on the theory of biological evolution. Many conservatives felt that this theory posed the strongest challenge of the new sciences to their understanding of the dignity of man and the reliability of the Scriptures, and they often elected to take strong stands on this controversy. In disregard of American traditions of open discussion and free speech, conservative pressures moved eleven state legislatures to prohibit the teaching of the theory of evolution in public schools. The debate between science and religion in the political arena became an issue of national concern in 1925, when William Jennings Bryan and Clarence Darrow met to argue against each other in the trial of a Tennessee teacher, John Scopes, who was accused of having violated his state's exclusion of evolutionary theories from its schools' curricula. The case was decided against Scopes and the theory of evolution, and, as late as the 1960's, similar disputes were still seeking adjudication in the nation's courts.

The split between conservative and liberal separated two poles of the Christian movement that had in the past often served to maintain healthy tensions within denominations. But with the Christian religion represented in early twentieth century America by extremists of either accommodation or reaction, the ancient traditions of the church were not often in a position to afford the country useful advice or criticism. Americans supported their churches with unprecedented gener-osity and enthusiasm, but the churches' influence on American society often seemed not to warrant the backing they received. It has become commonplace for scholars to accuse American Christianity of having developed into a culture religion, a secret establishment, that serves only to ratify, not to challenge, the values of modern American life. This is a harsh judgment, but one that is not completely unwarranted. In the 1870's, for instance, when America headed into the third "Great Awakening," the Christian religion once again became the recipient of mass popular support. But, during the same period, the country strug-gled reluctantly with the abuses of its capitalistic economic system and moved into its first foreign wars. The major churches chose in most cases simply to ratify the programs adopted by the nation's busi-ness and political leaders. A totally unregulated economy was en-dorsed despite the manifest social evils of the "Gilded Age," and the chauvinistic pronouncements of leading pulpiteers during the Span-ish-American War and First World War can only serve to embarrass those who read them now from a more balanced perspective on the Christian tradition's hope for love and justice for all people.

The third "Great Awakening" faded out in the debacle of prohibi-tion and the worldly orientation generated by the economic boom of the 1920's. The subsequent depression of the 1930's was not enough to reverse the trend toward religious indifference. To those who experi-enced the disillusionment of the depression, it seemed as if the values of the American way of life had been shown to be false, and these values were by that time so closely identified in the popular mind with the teachings of the Christian faith that religion was discredited and the churches were confronted by an attitude of cynicism and disbelief. The churches seem to have had little to say to the nation's leaders in the 1930's—save to encourage them to stay with the traditional Amer-ican virtues of rugged individualism and avoid a move in the direction of a socialist system. More and more, the Christian church in America was willing to identify itself with the peculiar political institutions of American democracy and to assert that any defection from them was a defection from the will of God. Even Roosevelt's New Deal legislation was suspect and met with little clerical support.

The emergencies of the great war of the 1940's pushed America out of its economic and spiritual depression, and the legacy of the war for the 1950's was an era of unprecedented national prosperity. Amer-ica emerged from the war on the winning side, and it was the only na-tion of the West whose industrial systems had not been damaged by the conflict. Temporarily, the world was to be an American market, and the nation prospered as never before. The revived economy seemed to be a vindication of the American way of life, and with this reaffirmation of faith in America came a renewed confidence in the Christian religion, with which American success had long been associated.

The 1950's saw the appearance of the nation's fourth "Great Awakening," and once again religion became a national preoccupation. Major denominations reported increases in membership of up to 75 percent; millions of dollars were spent on construction of churches to handle the flood of worshipers. Even the new mass medium of television devoted valuable prime time hours each week to religious spokesmen like the Roman Catholic Bishop Fulton Sheen. The religion of the "Awakening" was clearly a religion that affirmed American prosperity and power. In some hands, the Christian faith was presented as a self-serving religion that said much about the benefits people could derive from God and little about human charity and responsibility. Certain fabulously popular books, such as Norman Vincent Peale's *The Power of Positive Thinking,* could be read as apologies for Christianity which endorsed the faith because of its usefulness in promoting success in secular endeavors. The prophetic tradition, which in Biblical times had strongly criticized nations that gave in to the temptations of their prosperity, was not the dominant Christian tradition of the fourth "Great Awakening."

Nor was there the least hesitancy in the 1950's in equating American interests and institutions with the will of God as expressed in the Christian faith. The leading national spokesman for American religion during the decade was the Baptist evangelist "Billy" Graham (b. 1918). Graham began to emerge as a major evangelist in 1950 by utilizing radio and television in combination with the mass meetings that had long been a part of the American revivalist tradition. The acclaim and support he received from the American people and their political leaders suggest that he came as close as anyone in the period to verbalizing the common understanding of the Christian religion. For Graham, the success of Christianity was simply to be equated with the success of America, and he preached Christianity as the religion of the cold war. The triumph of democracy was at one and the same time the triumph of the Christian God. America's enemies, the communist states, could safely and self-righteously be opposed, not simply as alternative human political systems, but as literal agents of Satan. A religion that is willing to damn the enemy unconditionally and to assert that the will of the nation is the will of God is a religion destined to be welcomed in the seats of power.

The euphoria of the fourth "Great Awakening" faded in the disil-lusionment with power engendered by the war in Viet Nam and the sense of insecurity that began to invade American economic life in the 1970's. Culture religion ceased to be quite as popular as it had been, and some churches began to report a decline in support. But the situa-tion was not entirely negative: some welcomed it as an opportunity for a return to a more authentic Christian witness to American society. There had always been voices of protest raised against the corruptions of mass religion in America. The early twentieth century was note-worthy for the theological activities of Walter Rauschenbusch (1861–1918), who attempted to remind the churches of the social re-sponsibilities inherent in the Christian way of life. Reinhold Niebuhr's (1892–70) lucid restatements of the paradoxes of Christian faith trans-lated the ancient traditions into modern symbols that had remarkable relevance for an understanding of the societies involved in the Second World War. The European neoorthodox movement, which violently opposed the accommodation of religion to cultural objectives and which stressed a strict interpretation of the realities of human sin and the miracle of divine forgiveness, found a sympathetic hearing among a vocal minority of American religious leaders. Reports circulated concerning numerous "underground" churches that attempted to keep alive a prophetic Christian witness to the injustices and hypocrisies they perceived in American life. The new procedures endorsed by the Second Vatican Council were welcomed by many members of the American Catholic community. Proposals for the reunification of some Protestant denominations were seriously pursued. Civil rights and peace movements found willing sponsors in the churches, and Christian symbols once again helped people compel their social and political institutions to be true to their own highest goals. Other groups of Christians were moved once again to emphasize the individ-ual emotional fulfillments of the Christian faith, and a charismatic movement enlivened Protestant and Catholic communities alike. For a time, an image of Jesus Christ became a symbol of aspiration for a party of youthful Americans who promoted religion as a means for surviving the tensions of adolescence and the threat of drugs. On the fringes of the youth movement, attempts were made to relate the Christian tradition to the very different religions of the East and to a wide variety of popular psychotherapeutic techniques. The sheer num-ber of these different responses seems to indicate that America's in-volvement with the Christian movement is as intense today as at any other time in history.

Postscript

THE TWENTIETH CENTURY HAS not, in many respects, been
a period filled with notable triumphs for the Christian movement.
In the United States, the custom of identifying theism and patriotism
has led to periods of enthusiasm for religion, and, although attendance
figures fluctuate, support for churches remains strong. But there are
those who argue that American religion has little content and that it
serves more often to ratify national self-interest than to challenge consciences with the imperatives of Scripture. In recent years, Europe has
produced notable scholars who have made exciting contributions to
the development of Christian theology. But European state churches
often lack vitality. The people of Europe have been preoccupied with
the problems of surviving two major wars, and the church won few
adherents by its conduct during the great global conflicts. The papacy
has often been criticized for its accommodation to fascism in Italy and
Spain and its silence before Nazi atrocities. And the Protestant
churches of Germany, with the exception of small but important
minorities, acquiesced to Hitler's corruption of their people. In addition, the rise of atheistic communism has caused Christianity a serious
loss of ground. Christian missionary achievements in China have been
virtually obliterated, and, although the Bolshevik Revolution failed in
its stated intent to wipe out the Orthodox church, religious activities
have been drastically curtailed in Russia and Eastern Europe.

The self-serving arrogance of culture religions, the willful blind-
ness of Christian conservatives, the vacuousness of liberals, the forth-
right denial of the continued relevance of basic Christian symbols by
"death of God" theologians, the failure of Christian organizations to
surmount their divisions, and the victories of secular states over the
power of religion might suggest that the Christian movement is coming

to its end. But apostasy is not a new phenomenon. There have been times when Christian institutions enjoyed more popularity than they do today, but the religion practiced in them has almost always fallen short of its own standards. The history of Christianity has been a history of the avoidance, as well as the pursuit, of virtue and responsibility.

Perhaps the strength of the Christian movement should be measured, not by the number of people who at any particular time are willing to identify themselves with the church, but by the movement's ability in each generation to shake off persistent corruptions and renew itself in the lives of a few. So long as these few persist, the witness of the tradition lives in a form that can provide help for societies that are brought by events to confess their need for regeneration. Profound paradoxes lie at the root of Christian faith, and they elude definitive explication. But for two millenia they have fascinated minds and prodded people to liberate themselves from securities that leave the full extent of human potential unexplored. So long as Western civilization maintains the will to live, there will be a need for the puzzles of faith, which have been major stimuli for the development of Western consciousness.

A SELECTED BIBLIOGRAPHY OF SUPPLEMENTARY READINGS

Chapter One
A NEW COVENANT

Aron, Robert. *Jesus of Nazareth: The Hidden Years.* New York: Morrow, 1961.

Barrett, Charles. *Jesus and the Gospel Tradition.* London: Society for Promoting Christian Knowledge, 1967.

——————, ed. *The New Testament Background: Selected Documents.* New York: Macmillan, 1957.

Baum, Gregory. *The Jews and the Gospel.* Westminster, Md.: Newman Press, 1961.

Bauman, Edward. *The Life and Teaching of Jesus.* Philadelphia: Westminster Press, 1960.

Beare, F. W. *The Earliest Records of Jesus.* New York: Abingdon Press, 1962.

Beck, D. M. *Through the Gospels to Jesus.* New York: Harper and Row, 1954.

Bonsirven, Joseph. *Palestinian Judaism in the Time of Jesus Christ.* New York: Holt, Rinehart and Winston, 1964.

Bornkamm, Günter. *Jesus of Nazareth.* New York: Harper & Row, 1960.

Bowman, John. *Jesus' Teaching in Its Environment.* Richmond, Va.: John Knox Press, 1963.

Bruckberger, Raymond. *The History of Jesus Christ.* New York: Viking Press, 1965.

Bultmann, Rudolf. *The History of the Synoptic Tradition.* Oxford: B. Blackwell, 1963.

——————. *Jesus and the Word.* New York: Charles Scribner's Sons, 1934.

Bundy, W. E. *Jesus and the First Three Gospels.* Cambridge, Mass.: Harvard University Press, 1955.

Burkitt, Frances. *Jesus Christ: An Historical Outline.* London: Blackie and Son, 1932.

——————. *The Earliest Sources for the Life of Jesus.* New York: Constable and Co., 1910.

Canon of Muratori. In: Hennecke, Edgar. *New Testament Apocrypha.* Edited by Wilhelm Schneemelcher. Translated by R. Wilson. Philadelphia: Westminster Press, 1959.

Carmichael, Joel. *The Death of Jesus.* New York: Macmillan, 1963.

Clement. *The Letter to the Corinthians, I Clement.* Translated by F. X. Glimm. In: *The Apostolic Fathers.* The Fathers of the Church, edited by Ludwig Schopp, vol. 1. New York: Christian Heritage, 1947.

Connick, C. Milo. *Jesus: The Man, the Mission and the Message.* Englewood Cliffs, N.J.: Prentice-Hall, 1974.

Conzelmann, Hans. *A History of Primitive Christianity.* Nashville: Abingdon, 1973.

_____ *The Theology of St. Luke.* New York: Harper & Row, 1960.

Cullman, Oscar. *The Christology of the New Testament.* London: SCM Press, 1959.

Danielou, Jean. *The Theology of Jewish Christianity.* Chicago: H. Regnery Co., 1964.

Daniel-Rops, Henry. *Jesus and His Times.* New York: Dutton, 1954.

Davies, William. *Christian Origins and Judaism.* Philadelphia: Westminster Press, 1962.

Deane, Anthony. *The World Christ Knew.* London: Eyre and Spottiswoode, 1944.

Dibelius, Martin. *Jesus.* Philadelphia: Westminster Press, 1946.

_____ *From Tradition to Gospel.* New York: Charles Scribner's Sons, 1935.

Dix, Gregory. *Jew and Greek: A Study in the Primitive Church.* Philadelphia: Westminster Press, 1953.

Dodd, Charles. *The Founder of Christianity.* New York: Macmillan, 1970.

Elliott-Binns, Leonard. *Galilean Christianity.* London: SCM Press, 1956.

Eusebius. *Ecclesiastical History,* 2 vols. Vol. 1 translated by Kirsopp Lake, New York: G. P. Putnam's Sons, 1926. Vol. 2 translated by J. E. L. Oulton, Cambridge, Mass.: Harvard University Press, 1942.

Finkelstein, Louis. *The Pharisees.* Philadelphia: The Jewish Pulication Society of America, 1962.

Fuller, R. H. *The Foundations of New Testament Christology.* New York: Charles Scribner's Sons, 1965.

Garrard, Lancelot. *The Historical Jesus: Schweitzer's Quest and Ours after Fifty Years.* London: Lindsey Press, 1956.

Goppelt, Leonard. *Apostolic and Post-Apostolic Times.* London: Black, 1970.

Grant, Frederick. *The Growth of the Gospels.* New York: Abingdon Press, 1933.

_____ *The Life and Times of Jesus.* New York: Abingdon Press, 1921.

Grant, R. Michael. *The Jews in the Roman World.* New York: Charles Scribner's Sons, 1973.

_____ *Miracle and Natural Law in Graeco-Roman and Early Christian Thought.* Amsterdam: N. Holland Publishing Co., 1952.

Hunter, Archibald. *Paul and His Predecessors.* Philadelphia: Westminster Press, 1961.

James, M. R. *The Apocryphal New Testament.* Oxford: Clarendon Press, 1953.

Jaubert, Annie. *The Date of the Last Supper.* Staten Island, N.Y.: Alba House, 1965.

Jeremias, Joachim. *The Problem of the Historical Jesus.* Philadelphia: Fortress Press, 1964.

——————. *The Parables of Jesus.* London: SCM Press, 1963.

Johnson, S. E. *Jesus in His Homeland.* New York: Charles Scribner's Sons, 1957.

Josephus. *Against Apion.* Translated by H. St. J. Thackeray. New York: G. P. Putnam's Sons, 1926.

——————. *The Jewish Wars,* 2 vols. Translated by H. St. J. Thackeray. New York: G. P. Putnam's Sons, 1927-28.

——————. *Antiquities,* 6 vols. Translated by H. St. J. Thackeray, Ralph Marcus, Allen Wikgren, and L. H. Feldman. Vol. 1, New York: G. P. Putnam's Sons, 1930; vols. 2-6, Cambridge, Mass.: Harvard University Press, 1934-65.

Justin Martyr. *I Apology.* Translated by Thomas B. Falls. In: *The Writings of St. Justin Martyr.* The Fathers of the Church, edited by Ludwig Schopp, vol. 6. New York: Christian Heritage, 1948.

Kee, Howard, and Young, Franklin. *Understanding the New Testament.* Englewood Cliffs, N.J.: Prentice-Hall, 1957.

Kilpatrick, G. D. *The Origin of the Gospel according to St. Matthew.* Oxford: Clarendon Press, 1946.

Kirschbaum, Engelbert. *The Tombs of St. Peter and St. Paul.* New York: St. Martin's Press, 1959.

Lieberman, Saul. *Hellenism in Jewish Palestine.* New York: Jewish Theological Seminary of America, 1950.

Lightley, John. *Jewish Sects and Parties in the Time of Jesus.* London: J. A. Sharp. 1925.

Loos, H. van der. *The Miracles of Jesus.* Leiden: E. J. Brill, 1965.

McKnight, E. V. *What is Form Criticism?* Philadelphia: Fortress Press, 1969.

Martyn, J. L. *History and Theology in the Fourth Gospel.* New York: Harper & Row, 1968.

Marxsen, Willi. *Mark the Evangelist.* New York: Abingdon Press, 1969.

Moule, Charles. *The Birth of the New Testament.* New York: Harper & Row, 1962.

Mowry, Lucetta. *The Dead Sea Scrolls and the Early Church.* Chicago: University of Chicago Press, 1962.

Neil, William. *The Life and Teaching of Jesus.* Philadelphia: Lippincott, 1965.

Niebuhr, H. Richard. *Resurrection and Historical Reason.* New York: Charles Scribner's Sons, 1957.

Nineham, D. E., ed. *Historicity and Chronology in the New Testament.* London: Society for Promoting Christian Knowledge, 1965.

Pannenberg, Wolfhart. *Jesus—God and Man.* Philadelphia: Westminster Press, 1968.

Perry, M. C. *The Easter Enigma.* London: Faber and Faber, 1959.

Pliny the Younger. *Letters and Panegyricus,* 2 vols. Translated by Betty Radice. Cambridge, Mass.: Harvard University Press, 1969.

Ramsay, William. *The Christ of the Earliest Christians.* Richmond, Va.: John Knox Press, 1959.

Reumann, John. *Jesus in the Church's Gospels.* Philadelphia: Fortress Press, 1968.

Ringgren, Helmer. *The Faith of Qumran.* Philadelphia: Fortress Press, 1961.

Rowley, Harold. *Jewish Apocalyptic and the Dead Sea Scrolls.* London: University of London, Athlone Press, 1957.

Sabourin, Leopold. *The Names and Titles of Jesus.* New York: Macmillan, 1967.

Saunders, E. W. *Jesus in the Gospels.* Englewood Cliffs, N.J.: Prentice-Hall, 1967.

Schonfield, Hugh. *A History of Biblical Literature.* New York: New American Library, 1962.

Schürer, Emil. *History of the Jewish People in the Time of Jesus.* Edinburgh: T. and T. Clark, 1890.

Streeter, B. H. *The Four Gospels: A Study of Origin.* 4th ed. London: Macmillan and Co., 1930.

Suetonius. "Claudius." In: *The Twelve Ceasars.* Translated by Robert Graves. Harmondsworth, England: Penguin Books, 1957.

Tacitus. *Annals,* 3 vols. Translated by J. Jackson. Cambridge, Mass.: Harvard University Press; vols. 1 & 2, 1937; vol. 3, 1943.

Toombs, L. E. *The Threshold of Christianity.* Philadelphia: Westminster Press, 1960.

Vermes, Geza. *Jesus the Jew: An Historian's Reading of the Gospels.* London: Collins, 1973.

Winter, Paul. *On the Trial of Jesus.* Berlin: Walter de Gruyter and Co., 1961.

Chapter Two
THE SEARCH FOR DEFINITION

Altaner, Berthold. *Patrology.* New York: Herder and Herder, 1960.

Bainton, Roland. *Early Christianity.* Princeton, N.J.: J. P. Van Nostrand, 1960.

Baker, George. *Constantine the Great and the Christian Revolution.* New York: Barnes and Noble, 1967.

Bauer, Walter. *Orthodoxy and Heresy in Earliest Christianity.* Philadelphia: Fortress Press, 1971.

Bouyer, Louis. *The Spirituality of the New Testament and the Fathers.* New York: Desclée Co., 1963.

Brandon, Samuel. *The Fall of Jerusalem and the Christian Church.* London: Society for Promoting Christian Knowledge, 1951.

Bultmann, Rudolph. *Primitive Christianity.* New York: World Publishing Co., 1956.

Campenhausen, Hans. *Ecclesiastical Authority and Spiritual Power in the Church of the First Three Centuries.* London: Black, 1969.

Carrington, Phillip. *The Early Christian Church.* Cambridge: University Press, 1957.

Chadwick, Henry. *The Early Church.* Harmondsworth, England: Penguin Books, 1967.

Clement. *The Letter to the Corinthians, I Clement.* Translated by F. X. Glimm. In: *The Apostolic Fathers.* The Fathers of the Church, edited by Ludwig Schopp, vol. 1. New York: Christian Heritage, 1947

Cochrane, Charles. *Christianity and Classical Culture.* New York: Oxford University Press, 1957.

Copleston, Frederick. *A History of Philosophy,* Vol. 2, no. 1. Garden City, N.Y.: Doubleday and Co., 1962.

Cullmann, Oscar. *The State in the New Testament.* New York: Charles Scribner's Sons, 1956.

Danielou, Jean. *A History of Early Christian Doctrine.* Philadelphia: Westminster Press, 1973.

Daniel-Rops, Henry. *The Church of Apostles and Martyrs.* New York, E. P. Dutton and Co., 1960.

Davies, William. *Christian Origins and Judaism.* Philadelphia: Westminster Press, 1962.

Elliott-Binns, Leonard. *The Rise of the Christian Church.* Cambridge: University Press, 1929.

Epistle to Diognetus. In: *The Ante-Nicene Fathers.* Edited by Alexander Roberts and James Donaldson. Rev. ed. edited by A. Cleveland Coxe. 1884. Reprint. Grand Rapids, Mich.: William B. Eerdmans, 1973.

Eusebius. *Ecclesiastical History,* 2 vols. Vol. 1 translated by Kirsopp Lake, New York: G. P. Putnam's Sons, 1926. Vol. 2 translated by J. E. L. Oulton, Cambridge, Mass.: Harvard University Press, 1942.

Foster, John. *After the Apostles: Missionary Preaching of the First Three Centuries.* London: SCM Press, 1951.

Fousek, Marianka. *The Church in a Changing World: Events and Trends from 250 to 600.* St. Louis: Concordia Publishing House, 1971.

Frend, W. H. C. *The Rise of the Monophysite Movement: Chapters in the History of the Church in the Fifth and Sixth Centuries.* Cambridge: University Press, 1972.

Glover, T. R. *The Conflict of Religions in the Early Roman Empire.* Boston: Beacon Press, 1960.

Goodenough, Erwin. *The Church in the Roman Empire.* New York: H. Holt, 1931.

Grant, Frederick. *Roman Hellenism and the New Testament.* New York: Charles Scribner's Sons, 1962.

Grant, Robert. *Augustus to Constantine: The Thrust of the Christian Movement into the Roman World.* New York: Harper & Row, 1970.

_____. *The Apostolic Fathers.* New York: Thomas Nelson and Sons, 1964.

Green, Edward. *Evangelism in the Early Church.* London: Hodder and Stoughton, 1970.

Greenslade, Stanley. *Church and State from Constantine to Theodosius.* London: SCM Press, 1954.

_____. *Schism in the Early Church.* New York: Harper & Row, 1953.

Guignebert, Charles. *The Early History of Christianity, Covering the Period from 300 B.C. to the Origin of the Papacy.* New York: Twayne, 1962.

Guitton, Jean. *Great Heresies and Church Councils.* New York: Harper & Row, 1965.

Halliday, W. R. *The Pagan Background of Early Christianity.* New York: Cooper Square Publishers, 1970.

Hewitt, Frederick. *The Genesis of the Christian Church: A Study of Acts and the Epistles.* London: E. Arnold, 1964.

Horace. *Satires, Epistles, and 'Ars Poetica.'* Translated by H. R. Fairclough. New York: G. P. Putnam's Sons, 1961.

Ignatius. *Letter to the Magnesians.* Translated by G. G. Walsh. In: *The Apostolic Fathers.* The Fathers of the Church, edited by Ludwig Schopp, vol. 1. New York: Christian Heritage, 1947.

_____. "Ephesians." Translated by Gerald G. Walsh. In: *The Apostolic Fathers.* The Fathers of the Church, edited by Ludwig Schopp, vol. 1. New York: Christian Heritage, 1947.

Jedin, Hubert. *Handbook of Church History.* New York: Herder and Herder, 1965.

Jones, Arnold. *Constantine and the Conversion of Europe.* London: Hodder and Stoughton, 1948.

Juvenal. *Satires.* Translated by G. G. Ramsay. New York: G. P. Putnam's Sons, 1918.

King, Noel. *The Emperor Theodosius and the Establishment of Christianity.* London: SCM Press, 1961.

Kleist, James A., trans. *Didache.* Westminster, Md.: Newman Press, 1948.

Laistner, Max. *Christianity and Pagan Culture in the Later Roman Empire.* Ithaca, N.Y.: Cornell University Press, 1967.

Lietzmann, Hans. *A History of the Early Church,* vols. 1–4. New York: World Publishing Co., 1949-53.

Livy, *History of Rome,* 13 vols. Vols. 1-3 translated by B. O. Foster, Cambridge, Mass.: Harvard University Press, 1939-40. Vols. 4 & 5 translated by B. O. Foster, New York: G. P. Putnam's Sons, 1926 & 1929. Vols. 6-8 translated by E. G. Moore, Cambridge, Mass.: Harvard University Press, 1940, 1943, & 1949. Vols. 9-11 translated by E. T. Sage, Cambridge, Mass.: Harvard University Press, 1935-36. Vol. 12 translated by E. T. Sage & A. C. Schlesinger, Cambridge, Mass.: Harvard University Press, 1938. Vol. 13 translated by A. C. Schlesinger, Cambridge, Mass.: Harvard University Press. 1951.

Meinardus, Otto. *Christian Egypt, Ancient and Modern.* Cairo: Cahiers d'histoire egyptienne, 1965.

Minear, Paul. *Images of the Church in the New Testament.* Philadelphia: Westminster Press, 1960.

Momigliano, Arnaldo, ed. *The Conflict between Paganism and Christianity in the Fourth Century.* Oxford: Clarendon Press, 1963.

Moule, Charles. *The Birth of the New Testament.* London: Black, 1966.

Mowry, Lucetta. *The Dead Sea Scrolls and the Early Church.* Chicago: University of Chicago Press, 1962.

Musurillo, Herbert. *The Acts of the Christian Martyrs.* Oxford: Clarendon Press, 1972.

_____. *The Fathers of the Primitive Church.* New York: New American Library, 1966.

Nock, Arthur. *Early Gentile Christianity and its Hellenistic Background.* New York: Harper & Row, 1964.

Oulton, John, and Chadwick, Henry. *Alexandrian Christianity.* Philadelphia: Westminster Press, 1954.

Pickman, Edward. *The Mind of Latin Christendom.* London: Oxford University Press, 1937.

Pliny the Younger. *Letters and Panegyricus,* 2 vols. Translated by Betty Radice. Cambridge, Mass.: Harvard University Press, 1969.

Purinton, Carl. *Christianity and Its Judaic Heritage.* New York: Ronald Press Co., 1961.

Ricciotti, Giuseppe. *The Age of Martyrs: Christianity from Diocletian to Constantine.* Milwaukee, Wis.: Bruce Publishing Co., 1959.

Richardson, Cyril; Fairweather, Eugene R.; Hardy, Edward R.; and Shepherd, Massey H., Jr. *Early Christian Fathers.* Philadelphia: Westminster Press, 1953.

Saint Leo the Great. *Letters.* Translated by Brother Edmund Hunt. New York: Fathers of the Church, 1957.

Sandmel, Samuel. *The First Christian Century in Judaism and Christianity.* New York and Oxford: Oxford University Press, 1969.

Schlatter, Adolf. *The Church in the New Testament Period.* London: Society for Promoting Christian Knowledge, 1955.

Schnackenburg, Rudolf. *The Church in the New Testament.* Freiburg, West Germany: Herder and Herder, 1965.

Schweizer, Eduard. *Church Order in the New Testament.* Naperville, Ill.: A. R. Allenson, 1961.

Shepherd of Hermas. Translated by J. Marique. In: *The Apostolic Fathers.* The Fathers of the Church, edited by Ludwig Schopp, vol. 1. New York: Christian Heritage, 1947.

Stevenson, James, ed. *Creeds, Councils, and Controversies: Documents Illustrative of the History of the Church, A.D. 337-461.* New York: Seabury Press, 1966.

Suetonius. "Claudius." In: *The Twelve Caesars.* Translated by Robert Graves. Harmondsworth, England: Penguin Books, 1957.

Tacitus. *Histories,* 2 vols. Translated by Clifford H. Moore. Cambridge, Mass.: Harvard University Press, 1937 & 1943.

Tertullian. *Apology.* Translated by E. J. Daly. In: *Tertullian.* The Fathers of the Church, edited by R. J. Deferrari, vol. 10. New York: Fathers of the Church, 1950.

Tyson, Joseph. *A Study of Early Christianity.* New York: Macmillan Co., 1973.

Weiss, Johannes. *Earliest Christianity.* New York; Harper & Row, 1937.

Weltin, Edward. *The Ancient Popes.* Westminster, Md.: Newman Press, 1964.

Wiles, Maurice. *The Christian Fathers.* Philadelphia: J. B. Lippincott Co., 1966.

Zeiller, Jacques. *Christian Beginnings.* New York: Hawthorn Books, 1960.

Chapter Three
THE GREAT SYNTHESIS

Abelard, Peter. *Sic et Non* [Yes and No]. In: *Patrologia Latina.* Edited by Jacques Paul Migne. Paris, 1855.

Adams, Henry. *Mont-Saint-Michel and Chartres.* New York: Collier Books, 1963.

Anselm. *Cur Deus Homo*. Translated by Joseph M. Colleran. Albany, N.Y.: Magi, 1969.

——————. *Monologium and Proslogium*. Translated by Sidney N. Deane. Chicago: Open Court, 1903.

Athanasius. *Life of St. Anthony*. Translated by H. Ellershaw. In: *Nicene and Post-Nicene Fathers*. Edited by Philip Schaff and Henry Wace. New York: Christian Literature Co., 1892.

Augustine. *The City of God*. Translated by Henry Bettenson. Harmondsworth, England: Penguin Books, 1972.

——————. *Confessions*. Translated by Vernon J. Bourke. New York: Fathers of the Church, 1953.

Bainton, Roland. *The Medieval Church*. Princeton, N.J.: Beacon Press, 1962.

Baldwin, Marshall. *Christianity through the Thirteenth Century*. New York: Harper & Row, 1970.

——————. *The Medieval Church*. Ithaca, N.Y.: Cornell University Press, 1953.

——————. *The Medieval Papacy in Action*. New York: Macmillan Co., 1940.

Baldwin, Summerfield. *The Organization of Medieval Christianity*. New York: H. Holt and Co., 1929.

Barraclough, Geoffrey. *The Origins of Modern Germany*. New York: Capricorn, 1963.

Bonner, Gerald. *St. Augustine of Hippo: Life and Controversies*. Philadelphia: Westminster Press, 1963.

Brezzi, Paolo. *The Papacy: Its Origins and Historical Evolution*. Westminster, Md.: Newman Press, 1958.

Brooke, Christopher. *Medieval Church and Society: Collected Essays*. London: Sidgwick and Jackson, 1971.

Brooke, Zachary. *The English Church and the Papacy, From the Conquest to the Reign of John*. Cambridge: University Press, 1931.

Brown, Peter. *Religion and Society in the Age of St. Augustine*. London: Faber and Faber, 1972.

Burghardt, Walter. *Saints and Sanctity*. Englewood Cliffs, N.J.: Prentice-Hall, 1965.

Chitty, Derwas. *The Desert a City: An Introduction to the Study of Egyptian and Palestinian Monasticism under the Christian Empire*. Oxford: B. Blackwell, 1966.

Chodorow, Stanley. *Christian Political Theory and Church Politics in the Mid-Twelfth Century: The Ecclesiology of Gratian's Decretum*. Berkeley and Los Angeles: University of California Press, 1972.

Corbett, James. *The Papacy: A Brief History*. Princeton, N.J.: J. P. Van Rostrand, 1956.

Daly, Lowrie. *Benedictine Monasticism: Its Formation and Development through the Twelfth Century*. New York: Sheed and Ward, 1965.

Daniel-Rops, Henry, *The Church in the Dark Ages*. New York: Dutton, 1959.

——————. *Cathedral and Crusade: Studies of the Medieval Church, 1050–1350*. New York: Dutton, 1957.

Dawson, Christopher. *The Making of Europe: An Introduction to the History of European Unity*. New York: Meridian Books, 1956.

Deanesly, Margaret. *A History of the Medieval Church, 590-1500.* London: Methuen and Co., 1925.

Duckett, Eleanor. *The Wandering Saints.* London: Collins, 1959.

Evans, Robert. *One and Holy: The Church in Latin Patristic Thought.* London: Society for Promoting Christian Knowledge, 1972.

Flick, Alexander. *The Rise of the Mediaeval Church.* New York: G. P. Putnam's Sons, 1909.

Geanakoplos, Deno. *Byzantine East and Latin West: Two Worlds of Christendom in Middle Ages and Renaissance: Studies in Ecclesiastical and Cultural History.* New York: Barnes and Noble, 1966.

Gilchrist, John. *The Church and Economic Activity in the Middle Ages.* New York: St. Martin's Press, 1969.

Gimpel, Jean. *The Cathedral Builders.* New York: Grove Press, 1961.

Godfrey, John. *The Church in Anglo-Saxon England.* Cambridge: University Press, 1962.

Grabowski, Stanislaus. *The Church: An Introduction to the Theology of St. Augustine.* St. Louis: Herder, 1957.

Gratian. *Decretum* [Concordance of Discordant Canons]. In: *Patrologia Latina.* Vol. 187. Edited by Jacques Paul Migne. Paris. 1891.

Guignebert, Charles. *The Early History of Christianity, Covering the Period from 300 B.C. to the Origin of the Papacy.* New York: Twayne, 1962.

Guillemain, Bernard. *The Early Middle Ages.* New York: Hawthorn Books, 1960.

Hertling, Ludwig. *Communio: Church and Papacy in Early Christianity.* Chicago: Loyola University Press, 1972.

Hill, Bennett, ed. *Church and State in the Middle Ages.* New York: John Wiley and Sons, 1970.

Hillgarth, J. N., ed. *The Conversion of Western Europe, 350-750.* Englewood Cliffs, N.J.: Prentice-Hall, 1969.

Hunt, Noreen, ed. *Cluniac Monasticism in the Central Middle Ages.* London: Macmillan Co., 1971.

Hussey, Joan. *Church and Learning in the Byzantine Empire, 867-1185.* London: Oxford University Press, 1937.

Knowles, David. *Christian Monasticism.* New York: McGraw-Hill Book Co., 1969.

Kuntz, Benjamin. *From St. Anthony to St. Guthlac: A Study in Biography.* Berkeley and Los Angeles: University of California Press, 1926.

Lacarriére, Jacques. *Men Possessed by God: The Story of the Desert Monks of Ancient Christendom.* Garden City, N.Y.: Doubleday and Co., 1964.

Leclercq, Jean. *The Spirituality of the Middle Ages.* New York: Desclée Co., 1968.

Lombard, Peter. *Sentenciae.* In: *Patrologia Latina.* Vol. 192, 522-962. Edited by Jacques Paul Migne. Paris, 1855.

Mayer, Hans. *The Crusades.* London: Oxford University Press, 1972.

Morrison, Karl. *Tradition and Authority in the Western Church, 300-1140.* Princeton, N.J.: Princeton University Press, 1969.

Mourant, John. *Introduction to the Philosophy of St. Augustine.* University Park, Pa.: Pennsylvania State University Press, 1964.

Neill, Thomas, and Schmandt, Raymond. *History of the Catholic Church.* Milwaukee, Wis.: Bruce Publishing Co., 1965.

Nicol, Donald. *The Last Centuries of Byzantium, 1261-1453.* London: Hart-Davis, 1972.

O'Brien, John. *The Medieval Church.* Totowa, N.J.: Littlefield, Adams, and Co., 1968.

O'Leary, De Lacy. *The Saints of Egypt.* New York: Macmillan Co., 1937.

Jones, Arnold. *The Decline of the Ancient World.* London: Longmans, Green and Co., 1966.

Palanque, Jean. *The Church and the Dark Ages.* London: Burns and Oates, 1960.

Panofsky, Erwin. *Gothic Architecture and Scholasticism.* New York: Viking Press, 1957.

Payne, Pierre. *The Fathers of the Western Church.* New York: Viking Press, 1951.

Runciman, Steven. *A History of the Crusades,* 3 vols. Cambridge: University Press, 1951-54.

Russell, Jeffrey. *A History of Medieval Christianity: Prophesy and Order.* New York: Crowell, 1968.

Schnurer, Gustav. *Church and Culture in the Middle Ages.* Paterson, N.J.: St. Anthony Guild, 1956.

Simson, Otto von. *The Gothic Cathedral.* New York: Pantheon Books, 1956.

Southern, Richard. *Western Society and the Church in the Middle Ages.* Harmondsworth, England: Penguin Books, 1970.

Tellenbach, Gerd. *Church, State and Christian Society at the Time of the Investiture Contest.* Oxford: B. Blackwell, 1966.

Tierney, Brian. *The Crisis of Church and State, 1050-1300.* Englewood Cliffs, N.J.: Prentice-Hall, 1964.

Tout, Thomas. *The Empire and the Papacy, 918-1273.* London: Rivingtons, 1958.

Trevor-Roper, Hugh. *The Rise of Christian Europe.* London: Thomas and Hudson, 1966.

Ullmann, Walter. *A Short History of the Papacy in the Middle Ages.* London: Methuen, 1972.

_____.*The Growth of Papal Government in the Middle Ages.* London: Methuen, 1970.

Van Zeller, Hubert. *The Benedictine Idea.* London: Burns and Oates, 1959.

Volz, Carl. *The Church of the Middle Ages: Growth and Change from 600 to 1400.* St. Louis: Concordia Publishing House, 1970.

Vryonis, Speros. *Byzantine and Europe.* London: Thomas and Hudson, 1967.

Williams, Schafer, ed. *The Gregorian Epoch: Reformation, Revolution, Reaction?* Boston: D. C. Heath, 1964.

Zarnecki, Jerzy. *The Monastic Achievement.* London: Thomas and Hudson, 1972.

Chapter Four
An Age of Crises

Artz, Frederick. *The Mind of the Middle Ages.* New York: Knopf, 1953.

Bachrach, Bernard, ed. *The Medieval Church: Success or Failure?* New York: Holt, Rinehart and Winston, 1972.

Barraclough, Geoffrey. *Papal Provisions: Aspects of Church History, Constitutional, Legal and Administrative, in the Later Middle Ages.* Oxford: Blackwell, 1935.

Binns, L. E. *Innocent III.* London: Methuen and Co., 1931.

Bowsky, William, ed. *The Black Death: A Turning Point in History?* New York: Holt, Rinehart and Winston, 1971.

Brooke, Christopher. *Medieval Church and Society.* New York: New York University Press, 1972.

Chenu, Marie. *Toward Understanding Saint Thomas.* Chicago: H. Regnery Co., 1964.

Clark, James. *The Great German Mystics.* Oxford: B. Blackwell, 1949.

Cohn, Norman. *The Pursuit of the Millenium: Revolutionary Millenarians and Mystical Anarchists of the Middle Ages.* New York: Oxford University Press, 1970.

Copleston, Frederick. *Aquinas.* Baltimore: Penquin Books, 1967.

Dante. *On World-Government (De Monarchia).* Translated by Herbert W. Schneider. 2nd rev. ed. New York: Bobbs-Merrill Co., 1957.

Flick, Alexander. *The Decline of the Medieval Church.* London: K. Paul, Trench, Trubner and Co., 1930.

Gilchrist, J. T. *The Church and Economic Activity in the Middle Ages.* New York: St. Martin's Press, 1969.

Gill, Joseph. *The Council of Florence.* Cambridge: University Press, 1959.

Gilmore, Myron. *The World of Humanism.* New York: Harper, 1952.

Gilson, Etienne. *The Spirit of Medieval Philosophy.* New York: Sheed and Ward, 1936.

Huizinga, Johan. *The Waning of the Middle Ages.* Harmondsworth, England: Penguin Books, 1955.

Hyma, Albert. *The Brethren of the Common Life.* Grand Rapids, Mich.: Wm. B. Eerdmans Publishing Co., 1950.

Jacob, Ernest. *Essays in the Conciliar Epoch.* Manchester, England: Manchester University Press, 1953.

_____. comp. *Essays in Later Medieval History.* New York: Barnes and Noble, 1968.

Knowles, David. *The Evolution of Medieval Thought.* Baltimore: Helicon Press, 1962.

Lea, H. C. *A History of the Inquisition in the Middle Ages.* New York: Harbor Press, 1955.

Leff, Gordon. *Heresy in the Late Middle Ages: The Relation of Heterodoxy to Dissent.* Manchester: Manchester University Press, 1967.

Lerner, Robert. *The Heresy of the Free Spirit in the Later Middle Ages.* Berkeley and Los Angeles: University of California Press, 1972.

Loomis, L. R. *The Council of Constance.* New York: Columbia University Press, 1962.

McFarlane, Kenneth. *John Wycliffe and the Beginnings of English Nonconformity.* London: English Universities Press, 1952.

Manning, Bernard. *The People's Faith in the Time of Wycliffe.* Cambridge: University Press, 1919.

Margull, Hans. *The Councils of the Church.* Philadelphia: Fortress Press, 1966.

Marsiglio of Padua. *Defensor Pacis [Defender of the Peace]*. Translated by Alan Gewirth. New York: Columbia University Press, 1956.

Mollat, Guillaume. *The Popes at Avignon, 1305–1378*. London: T. Nelson and Sons, 1963.

Moorman, John. *A History of the Franciscan Order*. Oxford: Clarendon Press, 1968.

Morrall, John. *Political Thought in Medieval Times*. London: Hutchinson, 1958.

Morris, Colin. *The Discovery of the Individual, 1050–1200*. London: Society for Promoting Christian Knowledge, 1972.

Nicol, Donald. *The Last Centuries of Byzantium, 1261–1453*. London: Hart-Davis, 1972.

Packard, S. R. *Europe and the Church under Innocent III*. London: G. Bell and Sons, 1927.

Parker, G. H. W. *The Morning Star: Wycliffe and the Dawn of the Reformation*. Exeter, England: Paternoster Press, 1965.

Peter Lombard. *Sententiarum libri quatuor* [Sentences]. In: *Patrologia Latina*, (192): 519–963. Edited by Jacques Paul Migne. Paris, 1855.

Petry, Ray, ed. *Late Medieval Mysticism*. Philadelphia: Westminster Press, 1957.

Pirenne, Henri. *Economic and Social History of Medieval Europe*. London: Kegan Paul and Co., 1936.

————————. *Medieval Cities*. Princeton, N.J.: Princeton University Press, 1925.

Powell, J. M. *Innocent III*. Lexington, Mass.: D. C. Heath, 1963.

Rashdall, Hastings. *Universities in the Middle Ages*. London: Oxford University Press, 1942.

Rogers, Francis. *The Quest for Eastern Christians: Travels and Rumor in the Age of Discovery*. Minneapolis: University of Minnesota Press, 1962.

Russell, Jeffrey. *A History of Medieval Christianity: Prophesy and Order*. New York: Crowell, 1968.

Shannon, Albert. *The Popes and Heresy in the Thirteenth Century*. Villanova, Pa.: Augustinian Press, 1949.

Smalley, Beryl. *The Study of the Bible in the Middle Ages*. Oxford: B. Blackwell, 1951.

Smith, John. *The Great Schism*. New York: Weybright and Talley, 1970.

Southern, R. W. *Western Society and the Church in the Middle Ages*. Harmondsworth, England: Penguin Books, 1970.

Spinka, Matthew. *Advocates of Reform from Wycliffe to Erasmus*. Philadelphia: Westminster Press, 1953.

————————. *John Hus and the Czech Reform*. Hamden, Conn.: Archon, 1966.

Taylor, H. O. *The Medieval Mind*. Cambridge, Mass.: Harvard University Press, 1959.

Thomas á Kempis. *Of the Imitation of Christ*. Translated by Justin McCann. Westminster, Md.: Newman Press, 1954.

Thomas Aquinas. *Summa contra gentiles*. Translated by English Dominican Fathers. London: Burns, Oates & Washburn, 1923.

————————. *Summa Theologica*. Translated by English Dominican Fathers. New York: Benziger Bros., 1948.

Tierney, Brian. *Foundations of Conciliar Thought.* Cambridge: University Press, 1965.

——————. *The Crisis of Church and State, 1050-1300.* Englewood Cliffs, N.J.: Prentice-Hall, 1964.

Tipton, Leon, ed. *Nationalism in the Middle Ages.* New York: Holt, Rinehart and Winston, 1972.

Turberville, A. S. *Medieval Heresy and the Inquisition.* London: Hamdem, 1964.

Ullmann, Walter. *Origins of the Great Schism.* London: Burns and Gates, 1948.

Volz, C. A. *The Church of the Middle Ages.* St. Louis: Concordia Publishing House, 1970.

Winkworth, Susanna, trans. *Theologica Germanica.* Rev. ed. edited by J. Bernhart. New York: Pantheon, 1949.

Chapter Five
THE TRIUMPH OF PLURALISM

Alexander, H. G. *Religion in England, 1558-1662.* London: University of London Press, 1968.

Althaus, Paul. *The Theology of Martin Luther.* Philadelphia: Fortress Press, 1966.

Altholz, Josef: *The Churches in the Nineteenth Century.* Indianapolis: Bobbs-Merrill, 1967.

Bainton, Roland. *Women of the Reformation.* Minneapolis: Augsburg Publishing House, 1971.

——————. *The Age of The Reformation.* Princeton, N.J.: Van Nostrand, 1956.

——————. *Here I Stand: A Life of Martin Luther.* New York: Abingdon-Cokesbury, 1950.

Baker, Frank. *John Wesley and the Church of England.* Nashville: Abingdon Press, 1970.

Bangert, William. *A History of the Society of Jesus.* St. Louis: Institute of Jesuit Sources, 1972.

Beck, G. A. *The English Catholics, 1850-1950.* London: Burns, Oates and Washbourne, 1950.

Binchy, Daniel. *Church and State in Fascist Italy.* London: Oxford University Press, 1970.

Blayney, Ida. *The Age of Luther: The Spirit of Renaissance Humanism and the Reformation.* New York: Vantage Press, 1957.

Bolshakov, Serge. *Russian Nonconformity.* Philadelphia: Westminster Press, 1950.

Bourdeaux, Michael. *Opium of the People: The Christian Religion in the U.S.S.R.* London: Faber and Faber, 1965.

Bowen, Desmond. *The Idea of the Victorian Church: A Study of the Church of England, 1833-1889.* Montreal: McGill University Press, 1968.

Brinton, Henry. *The Context of the Reformation.* London: Hutchinson, 1968.

Burghardt, Walter, ed. *The Idea of Catholicism: An Introduction to the Thought and Worship of the Church.* Cleveland: Meridian Books, 1964.

Burns, Edward. *The Counter Reformation*. Princeton, N.J.: Van Nostrand, 1964.

Burrell, Sidney, ed. *The Role of Religion in Modern European History*. New York: Macmillan Co., 1964.

Bury, John. *History of the Papacy in the Nineteenth Century, 1864-1878*. London: Macmillan Co., 1930.

Calvin, John. *Institutes of the Christian Religion*. Edited by John T. McNeill. Translated by Ford Lewis Battles. Philadelphia: Westminster Press, 1960.

Casserly, Julian. *The Retreat from Christianity in the Modern World*. New York: Longmans, Green, 1952.

Chadwick, Owen. *The Reformation*. Harmondsworth, England: Penguin Books, 1972.

Clebsch, William. *England's Earliest Protestants, 1520-1535*. New Haven, Conn.: Yale University Press, 1964.

Cochrane, Arthur. *The Church's Confession under Hitler*. Philadelphia: Westminster Press, 1962.

Collins, Ross. *Calvin and the Libertines of Geneva*. Toronto: Clarke, Irwin, 1968.

The Confession of Faith, the Larger Catechism, the Smaller Catechism, the Directory for Public Worship, the Form of Presbyterian Church Government. London: W. Blackwood and Sons, 1913.

Considine, John, ed. *The Church in the New Latin America*. Notre Dame, Ind.: Fides Publishers, 1964.

Cracraft, James. *The Church Reform of Peter the Great*. Stanford, Calif.: Stanford University Press, 1971.

Cragg, Gerald. *The Church and the Age of Reason, 1648-1789*. Harmondsworth, England: Penguin Books, 1960.

_____. *From Puritanism to the Age of Reason: A Study of Changes in Religious Thought within the Church of England, 1660-1700*. Cambridge: University Press, 1950.

Curtiss, John. *Church and State in Russia: The Last Years of the Empire, 1900-1917*. New York: Columbia University Press, 1940.

Daniel-Rops, Henry. *The Church in the Eighteenth Century*. London: Dutton, 1964.

_____. *The Church in the Seventeenth Century*. London: Dutton, 1963.

Dawson, Christopher. *The Dividing of Christendom*. New York: Sheed and Ward, 1965.

Dickens, Arthur. *The German Nation and Martin Luther*. London: Edward Arnold, 1974.

_____. *The English Reformation*. London: Collins, 1967.

_____. *Thomas Cromwell and the English Reformation*. New York: Macmillan Co., 1960.

Dillenberger, John, and Welch, Claude. *Protestant Christianity Interpreted through Its Development*. New York: Charles Scribner's Sons, 1954.

Donaldson, Gordon. *The Scottish Reformation*. Cambridge: University Press, 1960.

Dru, Alexander. *The Church in the Nineteenth Century; Germany, 1800-1918*. London: Burns and Oates, 1963.

Drummond, Andrew. *German Protestantism since Luther*. London: Epworth Press, 1951.

Elton, Geoffrey. *Reformation Europe, 1517-1559.* New York: Harper & Row, 1963.

Erikson, Erik. *Young Man Luther: A Study in Psychoanalysis and History.* New York: Norton, 1958.

Ferris, Paul. *The Church of England.* Harmondsworth, England: Penguin Books, 1964.

Fireside, Harvey. *Icon and Swastika: The Russian Orthodox Church under Nazi and Soviet Control.* Cambridge, Mass.: Harvard University Press, 1971.

Foss, Michael. *The Founding of the Jesuits, 1540.* New York: Weybright and Ealley, 1969.

Galton, Arthur. *Church and State in France, 1300-1907.* New York: B. Franklin, 1972.

Grimm, Harold. *The Reformation Era, 1500-1650.* New York, Macmillan Co., 1973.

—————. *The Reformation in Recent Historical Thought.* New York: Macmillan Co., 1964.

Gurian, Waldeman, and Fitzsimons, M. A. *The Catholic Church in World Affairs.* Notre Dame, Ind.: University of Notre Dame Press, 1954.

Hales, Edward. *The Catholic Church in the Modern World: A Survey from the French Revolution to the Present.* Garden City, N.Y.: Hanover House, 1958.

Haugaard, William. *Elizabeth and the English Reformation.* London: Cambridge University Press, 1968.

Henry VIII. *Assertio septem Sacramentorum.* Translated by Thomas Webster. Rev. ed. edited by L. O'Donovan. New York: Benziger Brothers, 1908.

Hughey, John. *Religious Freedom in Spain: Its Ebb and Flow.* London: Carey Kingsgate Press, 1955.

Hutchinson, Francis. *Cranmer and the English Reformation.* London: English Universities Press, 1951.

Jones, Francis. *The Church in Communist China: A Protestant Appraisal.* New York: Friendship Press, 1962.

Knox, Ronald. *Enthusiasm: A Chapter in the History of Religion, with Special Reference to the Seventeenth and Eighteenth Centuries.* Oxford: Clarendon Press, 1950.

Kooiman, Willem. *Luther and the Bible.* Philadelphia: Muhlenberg Press, 1961.

Kung, Hans. *Structures of the Church.* New York: T. Nelson and Sons, 1964.

Latourette, Kenneth S. *Christianity in a Revolutionary Age: A History of Christianity in the Nineteenth and Twentieth Centuries.* New York: Harper, 1958.

Leonard, Emile. *A History of Protestantism.* London: T. Nelson and Sons, 1965.

Leslie, Shane. *The Oxford Movement, 1833-1933.* Milwaukee, Wis.: Bruce Publishing Co., 1933.

Littell, Franklin. *The Anabaptist View of the Church: An Introduction to Sectarian Protestantism.* Hartford, Conn.: American Society of Church History, 1952.

Lochman, Jan. *Church in a Marxist Society: A Czechoslovak View.* New York: Harper & Row, 19ʼ౹ʋ.

Lortz, Joseph. *The Reformation in Germany.* New York: Herder and Herder, 1968.

Luther, Martin. *An Address to the Christian Nobility of the German Nation.* Translated by Charles M. Jacobs. Rev. ed. edited by James Atkinson. In: *The Christian in Society.* Vol. 1. Luther's Works, edited by Helmut T. Lehmann, vol. 44. Philadelphia: Fortress Press, 1966.

——————— *Against the Robbing and Murdering Hordes of Peasants.* Translated by Charles M. Jacobs. Rev. ed. edited by Robert C. Schultz. In: *The Christian in Society.* Vol. 3. Luther's Works, edited by Helmut T. Lehmann, vol. 46. Philadelphia: Fortress Press, 1967.

——————— *The Babylonian Captivity of the Church.* Translated and edited by Bertram Lee Woolf. In: *The Basis of the Protestant Reformation.* The Reformation Writings of Martin Luther, vol. 1. London: Lutterworth Press, 1953.

——————— *The Freedom of a Christian.* Translated by W. A. Lambert. Revised edition edited by Harold J. Grimm. In: *Career of the Reformer.* Vol. 1. Luther's Works, edited by Helmut T. Lehmann, vol. 31. Philadelphia: Fortress Press, 1957.

NcNeill, J. T. *History and Character of Calvinism.* New York: Oxford University Press, 1954.

——————— *Modern Christian Movements.* Philadelphia: Westminster Press, 1954.

Maier, Hans. *Revolution and the Church: The Early History of Christian Democracy, 1789-1901.* Notre Dame, Ind.: University of Notre Dame Press, 1969.

Marlowe, John. *The Puritan Tradition in English Life.* London: Cresset, 1956.

Moeller, Bernd. *Imperial Cities and the Reformation.* Philadelphia: Fortress Press, 1972.

Neill, Stephen, ed. *Twentieth Century Christianity: A Survey of Modern Religious Trends by Leading Churchmen.* London: Wm. Collins Sons and Co., 1961.

Nichols, James. *History of Christianity, 1650-1950: The Secularization of the West.* New York: Ronald Press Co., 1956.

Niesel, Wilhelm. *The Theology of Calvin.* Philadelphia: Westminster Press, 1956.

Norwood, Frederick. *The Development of Modern Christianity since 1500.* New York: Abingdon Press, 1956.

O'Connell, Marvin. *The Counter Reformation, 1559-1610.* New York: Harper & Row, 1974.

O'Dea, Thomas. *The Catholic Crisis.* Boston: Beacon Press, 1968.

Orr, James. *The Light of the Nations: Evangelical Renewal and Advance in the Nineteenth Century.* Grand Rapids, Mich.: Wm. B. Eerdmans Publishing Co., 1966.

Ozment, Steven. *The Reformation in Medieval Perspective.* Chicago: Quadrangle Books, 1971.

Pelikan, Jeroslav. *Spirit versus Structure: Luther and the Institutions of the Church.* New York: Harper & Row, 1968.

Perry, Elisabeth. *From Theology to History: French Religious Controversy and the Revocation of the Edict of Nantes.* The Hague: M. Nijhoff, 1973.

Philips, Charles. *The Church in France, 1789-1848.* New York: Russell and Russell, 1966.

Poland, Burdette. *French Protestantism and the French Revolution: A Study in Church and State, Thought and Religion, 1685-1815.* Princeton, N.J.: Princeton University Press, 1957.

Powicke, Frederick. *The Reformation in England.* New York: Oxford University Press, 1941.

Quinlan, David. *Roman Catholicism.* London: English Universities Press, 1966.

Ravitch, Norman. *Sword and Mitre: Government and Episcopate in France and England in the Age of Aristocracy.* The Hague: Mouton, 1966.

Reyburn, Hugh. *The Story of the Russian Church.* New York: A. Melrose, 1924.

Rhodes, Anthony. *The Vatican in the Age of the Dictators, 1922-45.* London: Hodder and Stoughton, 1973.

Rouse, Ruth, ed. *A History of the Ecumenical Movement, 1517-1948.* Philadelphia: Westminster Press, 1954.

Rupp, Ernest. *Luther's Progress to the Diet of Worms.* New York: Harper & Row, 1964.

Schmidt, Albert. *John Calvin and the Calvinistic Tradition.* New York: Harper, 1960.

Searle, Graham. *The Counter Reformation.* London: University of London Press, 1974.

Shuster, George. *Religion behind the Iron Curtain.* New York: Macmillan Co., 1954.

Smith, Herbert. *Henry VIII and the Reformation.* New York: Russell and Russell, 1962.

Spinka, Matthew. *The Church in Soviet Russia.* New York: Oxford University Press, 1956.

Spinks, G. S. *Religion in Britain since 1900.* London: Dakers, 1952.

Spitz, Lewis. *The Reformation: Basic Interpretations.* Lexington, Mass.: D. C. Heath, 1972.

Tawney, R. H. *Religion and the Rise of Capitalism.* London: John Murray, 1926.

Thomas, Winburn. *The Church in Southeast Asia.* New York: Friendship Press, 1956.

Walton, Robert. *Zwingli's Theocracy.* Toronto: University of Toronto Press, 1967.

Wand, John. *A History of the Modern Church from 1500 to the Present Day.* London: Methuen, 1955.

Williams, George. *The Radical Reformation.* Philadelphia: Westminster Press, 1962.

Wood, Arthur. *The Inextinguishable Blaze: Spiritual Renewal and Advance in the Eighteenth Century.* Grand Rapids, Mich.: Wm. B. Eerdmans Publishing Co., 1960.

Zahn, Gordon. *German Catholics and Hitler's Wars: A Study in Social Control.* New York: Sheed and Ward, 1962.

Chapter Six
A NEW ENVIRONMENT

Ahlstrom, Sydney. *A Religious History of the American People.* New Haven, Conn.: Yale University Press, 1972.

Andrews, Edward. *The People Called Shakers*. New York: Oxford University Press, 1953.

Bailey, Kenneth. *Southern White Protestantism in the Twentieth Century*. New York: Harper & Row, 1964.

Beecher, Lyman. *Plea for the West*. New York: Leavitt, Lord, and Co., 1835.

──────. *Autobiography*. Edited by Charles Beecher. New York: Harper and Bros., 1864.

Berger, Peter. *The Noise of Solemn Assemblies: Christian Commitment and the Religious Establishment in America*. Garden City, N.Y.: Doubleday and Co., 1961.

Blanshard, Paul. *American Freedom and Catholic Power*. Boston: Beacon Press, 1949.

Bloch-Hoell, Nils Egede. *The Pentecostal Movement*. Oslo: Universitetforlaget, 1964.

Brauer, Jerald. *Protestantism in America*. Philadelphia: Westminster Press, 1965.

Brodie, Fawn. *No Man Knows My History: The Life of Joseph Smith, the Mormon Prophet*. New York: Alfred A. Knopf, 1945.

Bucke, Emory, ed. *The History of American Methodism*. Nashville: Abingdon Press, 1964.

Carroll, Peter. *Religion and the Coming of the American Revolution*. Waltham, Mass.: Ginn-Blaisdell, 1970.

Carter, Paul. *The Spiritual Crisis of the Gilded Age*. DeKalb, Ill.: Northern Illinois University Press, 1972.

Cauthen, Kenneth. *The Impact of American Religious Liberalism*. New York: Harper & Row, 1962.

Cherry, Conrad. *God's New Israel: Religious Interpretations of American Destiny*. Englewood Cliffs, N.J.: Prentice-Hall, 1971.

Clark, Elmer. *The Small Sects in America*. New York: Abingdon-Cokesbury, 1949.

Clebsch, William. *From Sacred to Profane America: The Role of Religion in American History*. New York: Harper & Row, 1968.

Cousins, Norman, ed. *"In God We Trust:" The Religious Beliefs and Ideas of the American Founding Fathers*. New York: Harper, 1958.

Cross, Robert. *The Church and the City, 1865–1910*. Indianapolis: Bobbs-Merrill Co., 1967.

Cross, Whitney. *The Burned-Over District: The Social and Intellectual History of Enthusiastic Religion in Western New York, 1800–1850*. New York: Harper & Row, 1965.

de Tocqueville, Alexis. *Democracy in America*. Translated by Henry Reeve. Rev. ed. edited by Francis Bowen and Philips Bradley. New York: Alfred A. Knopf, 1953.

Douglas, William. *The Bible and the Schools*. Boston: Little, Brown, 1966.

Ellis, John. *American Catholicism*. Chicago: University of Chicago Press, 1969.

Fauset, Arthur. *Black Gods of the Metropolis: Negro Cults in the Urban North*. Philadelphia: University of Pennsylvania Press, 1944.

Fellman, David. *Religion in American Public Law*. Boston: Boston University Press, 1965.

Ferm, Vergilius. *The American Church of the Protestant Heritage.* New York: Philosophical Library, 1953.

Filler, Louis. *The Crusade against Slavery, 1830–1860.* New York: Harper & Row, 1960.

Finney, Charles G. *Memoirs.* New York: A. S. Barnes and Co., 1876.

Franklin, Benjamin. *Autobiography.* Edited by Henry Steele Commager. New York: A. S. Barnes and Co., 1944.

Frazier, E. Franklin. *The Negro Church in America.* New York: Shocken Books, 1964.

Furniss, Norman. *The Fundamentalist Controversy, 1918–1931.* New Haven, Conn.: Yale University Press, 1954.

Garrettson, Freeborn. *The Experience and Travels of Mr. Freeborn Garrettson.* Philadelphia: J. Crukshank, 1791.

Gasper, Louis. *The Fundamentalist Movement.* The Hague: Moulton and Co., 1963.

Gleason, Philip, ed. *The Catholic Church in America.* New York: Harper & Row, 1970.

Greeley, Andrew. *Religion in the Year 2000.* New York: Sheed and Ward, 1969.

Handlin, Oscar. *The Uprooted: The Epic Story of the Great Migrations That Made the American People.* New York: Little, Brown, 1951.

Handy, Robert. *The American Religious Depression, 1925–1935.* Philadelphia: Fortress Press, 1968.

Heimert, Alan. *Religion and the American Mind from the Great Awakening to the Revolution.* Cambridge, Mass.: Harvard University Press, 1966.

Herberg, Will. *Protestant-Catholic-Jew.* Garden City, N.Y.: Doubleday and Co., 1960.

Higham, John. *Strangers in the Land: Patterns of American Nativism, 1860–1925.* New Brunswick, N.J.: Rutgers University Press, 1955.

Hinman, George W. *The American Indians and Christian Missions.* New York: Fleming H. Revell Co., 1933.

Holloway, Mark. *Heavens on Earth: Utopian Communities in America, 1680–1880.* New York: Dover Publications, 1966.

Hudson, Winthrop. *Religion in America.* New York: Charles Scribner's Sons, 1965.

—————. *American Protestantism.* Chicago: University of Chicago Press, 1961.

Kauper, Paul. *Religion and the Constitution.* Baton Rouge: Louisiana State University Press, 1964.

Koch, Gustav. *Republican Religion: The American Revolution and the Cult of Reason.* New York: Henry Holt and Co., 1933.

McAvoy, Thomas. *The Great Crisis in American Catholic History, 1895–1900.* Chicago: Henry Regnery Co., 1957.

—————, ed. *Roman Catholicism and the American Way of Life.* Notre Dame, Ind.: University of Notre Dame Press, 1960.

McLoughlin, William. *Modern Revivalism: Charles Grandison Finney to Billy Graham.* New York: Ronald Press Co., 1959.

—————, and Bellah, Robert, eds. *Religion in America.* Boston: Houghton-Mifflin, 1968.

Marty, Martin E. *Righteous Empire: The Protestant Experience in America.* New York: Dial Press, 1970.

_____. *The New Shape of American Religion.* New York: Doubleday and Co., Harper, 1959.

Maynard, Theodore. *The Catholic Church and the American Idea.* New York: Appleton-Century-Crofts, 1953.

Mead, Sidney. *The Lively Experiment: The Shaping of Christianity in America.* New York: Harper & Row, 1963.

Meyer, Donald. *The Positive Thinkers: A Study of the Quest for Health, Wealth, and Personal Power from Mary Baker Eddy to Norman Vincent Peale.* Garden City, N.Y.: Doubleday and Co., 1965.

Miller, Perry. *The American Puritans.* Garden City, N.Y.: Doubleday and Co., 1956.

_____. *Errand into the Wilderness.* Cambridge, Mass.: Harvard University Press, 1956.

Moberg, David. *The Church as a Social Institution.* Englewood Cliffs, N.J.: Prentice-Hall, 1962.

Monk, Maria. *Awful Disclosures . . . in the Hotel Dieu of Montreal.* New York: 1836.

_____. *Further Disclosures . . . concerning the Hotel Dieu of Montreal.* New York: Leavitt, Lord, and Co., 1837.

Morais, Herbert. *Deism in Eighteenth Century America.* New York: Columbia University Press, 1934.

Morgan, Richard. *The Politics of Religious Conflict: Church and State in America.* New York: Pegasus, 1968.

Morse, Samuel F. B. *Foreign Conspiracy against the Liberties of the United States.* New York: Leavitt, Lord, and Co., 1835.

Mullen, Robert. *The Latter-Day Saints: The Mormons Yesterday and Today.* Garden City, N.Y.: Doubleday and Co., 1966.

Needleman, Jacob. *The New Religions.* New York: Doubleday and Co., 1972.

Niebuhr, H. Richard. *The Kingdom of God in America.* New York: Harper, 1937.

The Social Sources of Denominationalism. New York: Henry Holt and Co., 1929.

Olmstead, Clifton. *Religion in America, Past and Present.* Englewood Cliffs, N.J.: Prentice-Hall, 1961.

Peale, Norman Vincent. *The Power of Positive Thinking.* Englewood Cliffs, N.J.: Prentice-Hall, 1952.

Pfeffer, Leo. *Church, State, and Freedom.* Boston: Beacon Press, 1953.

Reed, Rebecca. *Six Months in a Convent.* New York: Leavitt, Lord, and Co., 1835.

Rosamond, or a Narrative of the Captivity and Sufferings of an American Female under the Popish Priests in the Island of Cuba. Philadelphia: Samuel B. Smith, 1836.

Rowley, Peter. *New Gods in America.* New York: D. McKay Co., 1971.

Roy, Ralph. *Apostles of Discord: A Study of Organized Bigotry and Disruption on the Fringes of Protestantism.* Boston: Beacon Press, 1953.

Sandeen, Ernest. *The Roots of Fundamentalism, British and American.* Chicago: University of Chicago Press, 1970.

Schneider, Herbert. *Religion in Twentieth Century America.* New York: Atheneum, 1964.

Schneider, Louis, and Dornbusch, Sanford. *Popular Religion: Inspirational Books in America.* Chicago: University of Chicago Press, 1958.

Shields, Currin. *Democracy and Catholicism in America.* New York: McGraw-Hill Book Co., 1958.

Sinclair, Andrew. *Prohibition: The Era of Excess.* Boston: Little, Brown and Co., 1962.

Smith, Timothy. *Revivalism and Social Reform in Mid-Nineteenth Century America.* Nashville: Abingdon Press, 1957.

Sweet, William. *The Story of Religion in America.* New York: Harper, 1950.

—————. *Revivalism in America.* New York: Charles Scribner's Sons, 1944.

Torbet, Robert. *A History of the Baptists.* Philadelphia: Judson Press, 1950.

Tyler, Alice. *Freedom's Ferment.* Minneapolis: University of Minnesota Press, 1944.

Ward, Nathaniel. *The Simple Cobler of Aggawam in America.* London, 1647. Quoted in: *The American Puritans: Their Prose and Poetry.* Edited by Perry Miller. Garden City, N.Y.: Doubleday and Co., 1956.

Washington, Joseph R., Jr. *Black Religion: The Negro and Christianity in the United States.* Boston: Beacon Press, 1964.

Weber, Max. *The Protestant Ethic and the Spirit of Capitalism.* New York: Charles Scribner's Sons, 1958.

Weisberger, Bernard A. *They Gathered at the River: The Story of the Great Revivalists and Their Impact upon Religion in America.* Boston: Little, Brown, 1958.

White, Edward. *Science and Religion in American Thought.* Stanford, Calif.: Stanford University Press, 1952.

Wright, Louis. *Religion and Empire: The Alliance between Piety and Commerce in English Expansion, 1558–1625.* Chapel Hill: University of North Carolina Press, 1943.

General Index

Biblical Reference Index

319

A. Daniel Frankforter is a history professor at Pennsylvania State University. He has studied at the Drew University Theological School, Columbia University's Philosophy Department, the Georg-August-Universitat in Germany, Penn State, Cornell, and Union Theological Seminary, and held pastoral positions at Williams College and with the United Methodist Church. Dr. Frankforter's teaching specialties include ancient and medieval history and religious studies.